CULTURE A   IS

ONE WEEK LOAN

Culture and
tional—thr
three them
globally; an
ling discuss
affected pu
the "corpor
studies on t

With co
collection o
important i
scholars, res
the business
into their pr

Krishnamu
of Business, Massey University, in Wellington, New Zealand. He taught previously at Purdue University, the University of Florida, and Nanyang Technological
University, and has served as visiting professor at universities in three continents.
In 2004, he was awarded the prestigious Pathfinder Award from the Institute for
Public Relations (USA) for original scholarly research contributing to the public
relations body of knowledge.

Dejan Verčič, PhD, FCIPR, is founder of Pristop Agency and Professor of Public
Relations and Communication Management at the University of Ljubljana,
Slovenia. Among his clients are governments, domestic and international corpora-
tions, and associations. He organizes the Lake Bled International Public Relations
Research Symposia, held annually in Bled, Slovenia.

Routledge Communication Series
Jennings Bryant/Dolf Zillmann, Series Editors

Selected titles in Public Relations (advisory editor James E. Grunig) include:

CULTURE AND PUBLIC RELATIONS

Links and Implications

Edited by
Krishnamurthy Sriramesh
and Dejan Verčič

NEW YORK AND LONDON

First published 2012
by Routledge
711 Third Avenue, New York, NY 10017

Simultaneously published in the UK
by Routledge
2 Park Square, Milton Park, Abingdon, Oxon OX14 4RN

Routledge is an imprint of the Taylor & Francis Group, an informa business

© 2012 Taylor & Francis

The right of Krishnamurthy Sriramesh and Dejan Verčič to be identified as the authors of the editorial material, and of the authors for their individual chapters, has been asserted in accordance with sections 77 and 78 of the Copyright, Designs and Patents Act 1988.

Trademark notice: Product or corporate names may be trademarks or registered trademarks, and are used only for identification and explanation without intent to infringe.

Library of Congress Cataloging in Publication Data
Culture and public relations : links and implications / edited by Krishnamurthy Sriramesh and Dejan Vercic.
p. cm. – (Routledge communication series)
Includes bibliographical references and index.
1. Public relations—Cross-cultural studies. 2. Intercultural communication. I. Sriramesh, Krishnamurthy. II. Verčič, Dejan.
HM1221.C85 2012
303.48′2–dc23
2011043935

ISBN: 978–0–415–88726–7 (hbk)
ISBN: 978–0–415–88727–4 (pbk)
ISBN: 978–0–203–14923–2 (ebk)

Typeset in Bembo by Prepress Projects Ltd, Perth, UK

SUSTAINABLE
FORESTRY
INITIATIVE
Certified Sourcing
www.sfiprogram.org
SFI-00555
The SFI label applies to the text stock.

Printed and bound in the United States of America by Walsworth Publishing Company, Marceline, MO.

CONTENTS

INTRODUCTION

Krishnamurthy Sriramesh and Dejan Verčič

Public relations is an occupation. It can also be viewed as a practice that has aspirations of becoming a profession. One can say it is a social science, and a social technology. We are convinced that it is also a cultural practice and therefore this book is long overdue.

Under its current English name, which is also widely used in many other languages, *public relations* is an artifact of American culture but also largely influences and shapes it. Viewed from this perspective, public relations operates as a specific form of management of *communication* and *relationships*. It is strategic in its intent and focused on the production of envisioned changes among groups of people, organizations, or the society at large.

Whereas by its managerial logic public relations embodies the engineering spirit of machines, culture embodies spontaneity. To talk about societal, organizational, or occupational culture is to imply that not everything can (or should) be managed. Bringing culture and public relations into the same context or title implies that we recognize the interplay of conscious and unconscious forces in organizational contexts. As discussed at length in Chapter 1, public relations as a managerial (engineering) practice has antecedents in societal cultures in which it is practiced, is itself a cultural practice governed not exclusively by conscious forces, and has consequences for the cultural environments in which it thrives.

Given the important relationship between the two concepts, the interplay between culture and public relations deserves to be analyzed but it has long been sidelined by the body of knowledge of public relations. At least three forces have forced both academics and practitioners to now begin to pay closer attention to the nexus between culture and public relations. The first and most significant is globalization in all its forms, the second involves changes in public relations practice and pedagogy, and the third is the growing influence and realization of the importance of public relations to contemporary societies. For these very good reasons, in 2009 we decided to set "Culture and Public Relations" as the theme of the sixteenth International Public Relations Symposium (popularly known as BledCom: www.bledcom.com). Some of the essays contained here are based on the presentations delivered at that conference.

Globalization and the Twenty-First Century

Globalization is not new to human civilization and therefore the global interdependence that we currently see cannot just be described as a twenty-first-century phenomenon (Sriramesh, 2010). The twenty-first century started as a unipolar world, with the U.S. liberal democracy and market economy representing the final stage of human development or, as Francis Fukuyama called it, the end of history. It is now clear that in just a decade we have entered a multipolar world in which different countries and different cultures have begun to compete more or less peacefully on the global stage. In addition to the US there still exist the traditional powers of Europe (as the European Union) and Russia (being both "old," as the core of the former Soviet Union, and "new," as a constitutive member of emerging markets and powers). Newly emerging economies have received global attention and their own acronym BRIC: Brazil, Russia, India, and China. These four will soon be complemented by South Africa and the likes of Indonesia and Nigeria and probably a few other countries. This emergence of new forces also means that these countries will bring their cultural idiosyncrasies to the dialogue, making this an ever more diverse conversation caused by an increasingly interdependent world. Managerial practices and public relations among them are shaped by the myriad worldviews and habits of all these different cultures. Today, an increasing number of academics and practitioners have recognized their erstwhile blindness to the opportunities that different cultural perspectives offer and the challenges they pose for communication managers. Globalization is teaching us that the way we have lived, worked, and communicated, is not the only, or even the best, way.

Changing Public Relations Practices and Teaching

In its modern incarnation, public relations has its origins in Germany (late nineteenth century) and the US (early twentieth century) and began as a publicity practice, a way to appear in mass media in a favorable light or disappear from an unfavorable editorial portrayal. Since then it has traversed a long path and become a consulting practice responsible for pro- or anti-social behavior of powerful actors, governments, corporations, non-profits, and other actors capable of enlisting public relations practitioners beyond developed Western democracies. What public relations practitioners do, how and why they do it, can vary from one organization to the next so much that it is hard to fathom why all those varied activities still exist under the single label *public relations*. Professional associations have been trying to give coherence to this multitude of practices, but with limited success. Occupational differences within public relations are not of a quantitative nature that can be measured as more or less knowledge, practice, or resources but are of a qualitative nature that can best be described by different occupational cultures.

Growing Influence and Importance of Public Relations

Regardless of the "identity crisis" that one may discern in the public relations field, among the many consequences of globalization is also an increased inter-dependence among people and organizations within the same national borders as also between countries. This increased interdependence has made manage-ment of relationships, and therefore communication, ever more important. As actors on both the national and global stages, we are increasingly being made aware of that need and the truth that our future depends on our ability to com-municate and relate well. This makes public relations a reflexive practice in that it shapes our lives by its very availability. Major economic, political, and social actors plan with an eye on public relations needs and the consequences of their actions; so much so that in the English language some actions that are performed only because of their communicative potential are known as "pure PR."

Given all of these intricacies, we felt a book that discusses the various ways in which culture intersects with communication in general, and public rela-tions in particular, was long overdue. When we envisaged this volume, we had intended it to contain three distinct sections that addressed the three ways in which the relationship between culture and public relations can be addressed: culture as an "environment" that influences public relations; public relations as itself a culture; and public relations' impact on culture (organizational and societal). However, when the manuscripts were finalized, our earlier assump-tions (as discussed in Chapter 1) were confirmed: conceptualization and the nascent body of literature in public relations is limited mostly to the first rela-tionship, culture as an environment for public relations practice; the other two relationships are yet to be studied in depth. There is a dire need for studies that address the other two aspects as well if the body of knowledge is to become holistic and thereby keep pace with the demands resulting from globalization.

Overview of the Chapters

Chapter 1 addresses the importance of studying the nexus between culture and public relations, highlighting ethnocentricity in the current body of knowledge.

Globalization, a phenomenon that is not new to the twenty-first century, has made it imperative that we pay attention to culture. Offering a definition of culture, the chapter identifies three levels at which the relationship between culture and public relations is apparent: culture as an environment for public relations practice, public relations as a culture in itself, and the impact of public relations practice on the cultures of organizations and societies. It stresses that only the first of these three linkages has been explored empirically thus far, albeit by a small number of studies, and calls for future studies to also explore the other two aspects of this important relationship.

Public relations continues to be perceived as a Western concept; the next two chapters address the intersection between Western thought, culture, and public relations. In Chapter 2, Bob Heath offers an interesting juxtaposition between *Classical Western* rhetorical tradition and *modern* public relations (the term *modern* is important because one cannot discount the truth that public relations is probably as old as human civilization). In presenting this perspective of the ancient and the modern, he discusses how public discourse, as a culture of democratic deliberation, serves as the voice of competing interests. We should note the emphasis on "Western" rhetoric because one of the significant lacunae in the body of knowledge is the over-reliance on Greek rhetoric—mainly because scholars from the East have not ventured to bring the wisdom from their traditions into the public relations body of knowledge. The field would benefit immensely by increased attention to filling this gap in the literature. In Chapter 3, Aleš Debeljak critically examines the processes that led to the rise of the modern Western paradigm—"a package of Western ideas and technologies" as he calls it. He argues that this "package" represents the backbone of the globalized capital order. Contending that "local elites" adopt these tools according to specific needs, he says the varieties of these responses to a global challenge make it possible to reject the division of the world into "the West and the rest."

Chapter 4 addresses an important, yet highly neglected, topic: the interplay between indigenous cultures and public relations. For almost a decade now, ethnocentricity in public relations scholarship and education has been discussed (e.g. Sriramesh, 2002). Judy Motion and her co-authors discuss how public relations professionals can develop meaningful relationships with indigenous populations—a significant stakeholder—so that power sharing, equitable participation, and mutually beneficial outcomes are achieved. They emphasize the importance of cultural contexts and traditional and contemporary principles, protocols, and practices that influence indigenous engagement processes. Just as culture and communication are interdependent, so are culture and identity. In Chapter 5, Bey-Ling Sha and her co-authors address the intersection between culture and identity. Defining identity in relation to culture, the authors present the ways in which the notions of identity may be relevant for public relations practice and scholarship including organizational identity, reputation and coalition-building, message development and branding, organizational identity development, and social responsibility and ethics.

The next six chapters address culture as an "environment" for public relations practice with examples from Asia, Africa, Europe, and North America. In Chapter 6, Yi-Hui Christine Huang presents a theoretical framework that, she contends, should advance public relations research in regions where Chinese culture dominates. The hope is that such a conceptual framework will foster reliable and valid comparisons of public relations practices in China and other countries and regions. In Chapter 7, Julia Jahansoozi and her co-authors discuss the approaches of the petroleum industry to build community relationships among the diverse cultures in Nigeria. It is a well-known fact that the relationship between the petroleum industry and communities such as the Ogoni is severely strained. They contend that culture has a significant influence on how the petroleum industry engages with the local communities, which bear the brunt of the impact of this polluting enterprise. In Chapter 8, Jens Seiffert and Guenter Bentele chart the history of the interplay between public relations and culture in Germany since the nineteenth century, when modern public relations began to be practiced in the country. They submit that public relations in Germany evolved between two antipodal concepts of political culture: Max Weber's idea of the "iron cage" and Jürgen Habermas's work on deliberative democracy and communicative action.

In Chapter 9, Lee Edwards addresses the notion of public relations as *culture* and "a site for cultural practices." In doing so, she reviews professionalization literature to discuss whether public relations is a profession. She explores the interconnectedness between structural artifacts (education, professional qualifications, and formal training) and cultural professional norms conceptually, and then offers empirical data from the UK to discuss the implications of these theoretical constructs on public relations practice. In Chapter 10, Maria Antonieta and her co-authors discuss the evolution of the public relations industry in Mexico vis-à-vis the country's economic, political, and social development. The authors conclude that, in the Mexican context (as in most other parts of the world—see Sriramesh and Verčič, 2009), public relations practice is sought in regions where economic, political, and cultural activities are most evolved: urban areas and tourist locations. However, there is hope because public relations is slowly beginning to expand beyond the corporate sector to public and social sectors as well. In Chapter 11, Mathew Allen and David Dozier discuss theoretical issues relevant to global public relations and explicate the relationship between culture and public relations using a case study of the interactions between U.S. military public affairs officers (PAOs) and Arab journalists. The authors explore the "collision" of two cultures that are distinct in many aspects. Public affairs officers are trained to standards dictated by Western culture, emphasizing individualism and professional, business-like approaches to the practice. Arab journalists live and work in a collectivist culture and react from those perspectives when confronted by U.S. Military PAOs. The authors use the cultural differences highlighted in this case study to frame different worldviews of the nature of relationships between organizations and the public.

The next two chapters take a critical perspective on public relations and culture in the backdrop of globalization. In Chapter 12, Mohan Dutta explores the public relations function of knowledge production within the political and economic agendas of neoliberal governance. In particular, he addresses how marginalization and oppression are often reinforced through what he calls "circuits of knowledge." The chapter advocates participatory collaboration among subaltern sectors of the globe so as to challenge and change unequal social structures. In Chapter 13, Jacquie L'Etang addresses the intersection between two disciplines: anthropology and public relations. Contending that ethnographic work within the public relations context has been limited, the author advocates greater use of ethnography in order to conduct basic research about public relations practice as *culture(s)* and practitioners as *culture workers*. The chapter defines key aspects of anthropology and ethnography and their relationship with social theory and reviews literature in organizational behavior and management, marketing, and media studies to contend for a specialized field within the public relations discipline called "public relations anthropology."

The final two chapters address different aspects of public relations *as culture*. In Chapter 14, Dejan Verčič and Jon White write that business and public relations cultures are different because of different traditions. This is so because of the different educational training that practitioners of the two disciplines receive, the differences in the personality of practitioners of the two disciplines, and the significant differences in the remuneration for practitioners. These differences have important consequences in shaping the values of the members of these two disciplines and therefore the differences in their cultures as well. The authors see both positive and negative aspects in this cultural divide.

The final chapter of the book addresses the culture of public relations agencies. Chapter 15 describes three types of public relations firms—depicting, one could argue, three cultures as well. The first is the public relations agency that has a publicist or journalistic culture. The second is an agency that has a business culture and thereby is predominantly commercial, with the intention of buying cheap and selling dear. The third type of public relations agency is the public relations consultancy that has a professional culture. His chapter also articulates how public relations firms exhibit multiple cultures.

Acknowledgements

We hope readers will find these essays informative, illuminating, and helpful in advancing the body of knowledge to make it more holistic. This project would not have been possible without cooperation from many people. First of all, we would like to thank our students around the world who have contributed mightily to our cultural education. Without them, we would not have been where we are. We also wish to thank practitioners around the world—some of whom also participated at BledCom 2009 and discussed culture and public relations as a vital issue—who have contributed to our education. We wish to thank our friends and colleagues who have contributed thought-provoking essays to make this book a reality. Publishing this volume has not been without its challenges—attributable also to the very topic itself. We wish to thank the Pristop staff who, year after year, make it possible for us to host BledCom symposia. Finally, we wish to thank our families for being patient while we travel the world learning new cultural norms and relating them to public relations. The efforts of scores of people will have been worthwhile if this book is useful to its readers and ultimately spawns research that expands our cultural horizons.

References

Sriramesh, K. (2002). The dire need for multiculturalism in public relations education: An Asian perspective. *Journal of Communication Management*, 7(1), 54–77.

Sriramesh, K. (2010). Globalization and public relations: Opportunities for growth and reformulation. In Heath, R. E. (Ed.), *Encyclopedia of public relations*. Thousand Oaks, CA: Sage, pp. 691–707.

Sriramesh, K. and Verčič, D. (2009). *The handbook of global public relations: Theory, research, and practice* (revised and expanded edition). New York: Routledge.

1

CULTURE AND PUBLIC RELATIONS

Formulating the Relationship and Its Relevance to the Practice

Krishnamurthy Sriramesh

Introduction and Rationale

Although communication has been innate to humans since the origin of the species, one can reasonably conclude that communication scholarship is a twentieth-century phenomenon. It was in 1914 that perhaps the first national association of communication scholars was formed in the United States as the National Association of Academic Teachers of Public Speaking. Over nearly a century, that association has undergone changes in nomenclature reflecting the widening interests of its members extending beyond speech communication. Today the same association is known by the more generic name of National Communication Association, showcasing a wider array of communication disciplines. Public relations scholarship, whose primary focus is the use of communication to build relationships, has also come of age only since the mid 1970s even though the practice itself can be dated back to pre-biblical times in many parts of the world (Sriramesh, 2004).

Culture, a phenomenon that is innate to human beings, has a relatively longer history of scholarship than communication or public relations. However, attempts to link culture with public relations began only in the 1990s. Although the twenty-first century is not the first time the world has witnessed globalization (see Sriramesh, 2010, for a review of globalization in previous centuries), one might make a reasonable assertion that the onset of globalization in the final decade of the twentieth century and into the new millennium has put culture at the forefront of organizational studies and of communication. Three decades ago, the organizational communication scholar Smircich (1983) noted that "culture is an idea whose time has come." In 1992, Sriramesh and White (1992) contended that culture's impact on public relations could not be discounted any longer and had hoped that the

1990s and the twenty-first century would bring increased focus and research on the key relationship between culture and public relations. Even though the Maastricht Treaty and the North American Free Trade Agreement (NAFTA) had yet to be signed and globalization had not yet become the buzzword it is today, we contended then that "to communicate to [with] their publics in a global marketplace, public relations practitioners will have to sensitize themselves to the cultural heterogeneity of their audiences . . . The result will be the growth of a culturally richer profession" (p. 611). However, as will be reviewed in this chapter, attempts at studying the key linkage between culture and public relations in the two decades since we wrote that have been few and far between. As a result, the public relations body of knowledge has developed, and continues to develop, ethnocentrically. There is a dire need for studies that will strive to make the body of knowledge more holistic.

A few examples help illustrate the presence of ethnocentricity in practice and scholarship providing the rationale for this book—the first dedicated to assessing the nexus between culture and public relations. First, one sees the wide practice of the adoption, or translation, of American or British public relations textbooks by educators and universities in distant cultures with negligible or no attention given to "localizing" the contents, concepts, and examples (see Sriramesh, 2002, for a longer critique). A second example is the practice in public relations scholarship of discussing values with little or no reference to culture. The *Journal of Public Relations Research*, a leading public relations scholarly journal, heralded the new millennium with the publication of a special issue on the *values* (emphasis added) needed for effective public relations practice in the twenty-first century. The thoughtful essays in the special issue discussed, among other things, professional values, activist values, feminist values, and postmodern values, but the term *culture* appeared only once in the entire issue. Another example is the essay assessing the "state of the field" in one of the premier communication journals (Botan and Taylor, 2004) that did not make a single mention of the relevance of culture to public relations. Further, Botan and Taylor were silent about any developments in the field of global public relations research, which includes the work of at least three or four dozen scholars from Asia, Africa, Latin America, and Europe (and some from the US as well). That is a genre of research that has been developed since 1990 and it is surprising that even the peer reviewers of this prestigious journal did not point out this gap to the authors during the review process.

A similar ethnocentricity can be noted in public relations education as well. As a prelude to the dawn of the new millennium, the Public Relations Society of America (PRSA) tasked the Commission on Public Relations Education (CPRE) in the United States to "determine the knowledge and skills needed by practitioners in a technological, *multicultural, and global society* [emphasis added] and then recommend learning outcomes." After due deliberations, the Commission offered its recommendations in its *Port of Entry* report published in October 1999. These recommendations fell far short of what is required for a robust curriculum that prepares students for operating with the holistic perspective that our globalizing world demands. For example, of the 10 "necessary knowledge" factors that the Commission recommended for PR graduates, only one related to globalism—"multicultural and global issues"— and it was listed tenth. In the list of 20 "necessary skills" that PR graduates ought to possess, only three can be subsumed to contribute to multicultural public relations education: "sensitive interpersonal communication" (13), fluency in a foreign language (14), and applying cross-cultural and cross-gender sensitivity (20) (see Sriramesh, 2002, for a longer critique). The CPRE revised its recommendations in 2006 but the changes vis-à-vis the relevance of culture are minimal and tell us we have a long way to go in making public relations scholarship relevant to a globalizing world.

The above examples also alert us to the fact that "ghettoizing" discussions of "culture" in public relations scholarship, limiting them only to studies related to "international public relations" or "global public relations," would be a serious disservice both to practitioners and to students. A review of recently published scholarly volumes in public relations reveals the pattern whereby public relations concepts and theories are discussed in almost total isolation from culture, and only as an afterthought one sees brief descriptions of culture, or "global issues" at the end of the volume. A discussion of culture is vital to every public relations concept, strategy, and skill—the central theme of this book. What is culture and how should the public relations body of knowledge view this concept?

Definition and Scope of Culture

The term *culture* has been variously defined by anthropologists and ethnographers. Kroeber and Kluckhohn (1952) listed over 164 accepted definitions and about 300 more variations of these definitions. The first comprehensive definition can be attributed to Tyler (1871), who saw culture as "that complex whole which includes knowledge, belief, art, morals, custom, and any other capabilities and habits acquired by man as a member of society" (p. 1). The expansive nature of the term, and thereby its malleability, was also highlighted by Kroeber and Kluckhohn, who defined culture as a "set of attributes and products of human societies, and therewith of mankind, which are extra-somatic and transmissible by mechanisms other than biological heredity" (p. 145). Culture is so all-encompassing that it is hard to define/describe it, and often one is not aware of one's own cultural traits and idiosyncrasies. This makes culture hard to measure, a key requirement for scholars and researchers. Hofstede (1984) posited that the presence of culture can be seen at three levels: the *universal* level (at which as human beings we all share certain characteristics), the *collective* level (at which only those belonging to a certain collectivity share some common characteristics, mainly as a result of acculturation), and the *individual* level (at which our cultural traits are molded in unique ways by the individual experiences that each of us has).

Acculturation contributes to the sharing of cultural traits. But which factors help determine the culture of a collectivity? Kaplan and Manners (1972) identified four *determinants* of culture. The first, *technoeconomics*, is indicative of the impact that technology and economics have on the development of cultural characteristics in a society. At no time in history is this link more evident than in the twenty-first century with the onset of new/social media as a direct result of an increasingly global economy. The second, *social structure*, refers to the impact of the institutions of a society on the culture of its peoples. As we shall presently see, political and economic institutions, among other things, have a direct impact on culture and also public relations. The third, *ideology*, is indicative of the values, norms, worldviews, knowledge, philosophies, and so on espoused by the members of a society. Finally, *personality* refers to the adoption of individual personalities by members of a society based on acculturation that happens at home, at school, and in the workplace. One can see parallels between the collective and individual levels identified by Hofstede and these four cultural determinants.

The culture of a society influences, but can often be different from, the culture of organizations in that society, which requires us to assess the relationship between societal culture and organizational culture separately (Sriramesh and White, 1992; Sriramesh et al., 1992). Especially beginning in the early 1980s, there were many studies on organizational culture, which added many new dimensions to the discussion such as the interplay of cultures, subcultures, and countercultures within organizations. Hofstede's (1984) studies of culture in the organizational context led to the identification of first four and then five dimensions of culture, and his work dominates discussion of culture within organizations. Almost 30 years on from his seminal study in which he sought to assess the cultural idiosyncrasies among managers of an organization hailing from 39 countries, his five dimensions of culture continue to be used by scholars in public relations. After a review of the studies linking culture with public relations (see Sriramesh, 2006), I critiqued the almost sole reliance on Hofstede's dimensions of culture in public relations scholarship and contended that the field needed studies that would not only look at cultural characteristics that were common across a number of societies (as the dimensions Hofstede identified were) but equally importantly look also at cultural traits unique to a society. Lewis (2006) built on the work of Hofstede and Stuart Hall and offered new perspectives on cross-cultural differences. One such addition is his discussion of what he calls "cultural types." Rather than pigeonholing cultures as Hofstede did with his cultural dimensions, Lewis offered a continuum on which he placed different countries based on three dimensions: linear-active (cool, factual, decisive planners), multi-active (warm, emotional, loquacious, impulsive), and reactive (courteous, amiable, accommodating, compromisers, good listeners) (Figure 1.1).

Expanding the Scope of "Culture"

In order to link the term *culture* effectively with public relations, we need to expand the scope of the term beyond societal culture. Because of the interdisciplinary nature of public relations practice, and thereby scholarship, we would have to examine the political culture, economic culture, societal and organizational culture, media culture, and activist culture of a society, as mentioned by Sriramesh and Verčič (2009a). Currently, we have at best a few conceptual linkages between public relations and these five cultures, suggesting that the opportunities for research and knowledge building in this field are plentiful.

In identifying the link between political economy (a combination of political and economic cultures) and public relations, Duhe and Sriramesh (2009) observed that "a political economy approach to public relations examines the interplay between organizations and publics with particular attention paid to the conflicts, expectations, and constraints imparted upon relevant parties by a powerful *combination* of social, economic, and political forces" (p. 25). We further contended that "the collaborative, democratic, and relationship-building functions of public relations" had the potential to help not only developed

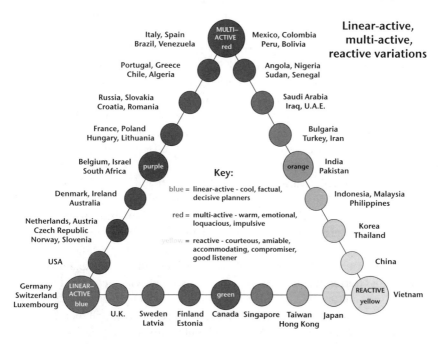

FIGURE 1.1   Cultural Types: The Lewis Model. *Source*: Lewis (2006) with permission from Richard Lewis Communications (2006).

economies but also economies that are in the ascendancy, such as the BRIC countries. We (Sriramesh and Duhe, 2009) also offered several avenues for future research linking political economy and public relations under three broad categories: the primary purposes of a nation's economic activity, the role of the state in the economy, and the structure of the corporate sector and civil society. Several factors are important in determining the relationship between public relation and the political economy of a society, such as the predominant objective that drives a nation's economy, the roles of liberty, equality, harmony, and community in the economy, the extent to which the economy is open to the outside world, the extent to which the economy is in transition, and the extent to which "winners" and "losers" exist in the economy and the dynamics of the relationship between these groups. One can say with a great deal of confidence that currently the public relations body of knowledge has few studies that have provided empirical evidence linking political economy with public relations—a gap that needs to be addressed in the second decade of the new millennium.

Although public relations scholars have recognized the innate relationship between mass media and public relations, much of that conceptualization has been one-dimensional, as if there were a single media culture in all regions of the world. Mass communication scholars have studied differences among the mass media in different parts of the world since the mid 1950s, when Siebert, Peterson, and Schramm (1956) offered four normative theories of mass media. Over the next few decades, several other scholars expanded the discussion of the different media cultures in different societies (e.g. Merrill and Lowenstein, 1971, 1979; Merrill, 1974; Hachten, 1981, 1993; Martin and Choudhury, 1983). The normative theories of the mass media offer a useful guide to the differences in media cultures around the world that should be of great use to public relations practitioners. However, with the passage of time and changes in the political (ideological) landscape around the world, these normative theories do not offer the same level of utility as they once did. For our purposes, it would be helpful to reduce the differences inherent in different media systems to three principal factors: media control, media diffusion (outreach), and media access (Sriramesh and Verčič, 2009b). Media control is often confused with media ownership but should be seen as beyond ownership, assessing who has the *de facto* power to influence media content in a society. This is often a direct manifestation of the political and economic culture of that society. *Media diffusion* refers to the extent to which the mass media consumed by the members of a society. This can also be explained as the amount of "outreach" of the mass media of a society, which can also be linked to economic culture. Media access is the extent to which the media of a society are open to providing an avenue for the content generated by all members of a society without undue discrimination. A combination of these factors provides us with insights into not only the media culture of a society, but also the other cultures outlined in this section as well. The significant factor to be noted is the interdependence among these cultures—reflecting the interdisciplinary nature of public relations itself.

Activist culture also has a direct impact on the nature of public relations in a society. Addressing the interplay between activists and organizations, Kim and Sriramesh (2009) have offered a model that describes the interplay between activism and the four other cultures discussed here. Based on that analysis one of the postulates we offered was that "societies that have pluralistic political systems, free or at least partly free media systems, and greater individualism among the populace, are more likely to foster higher levels of activism requiring more symmetrical or strategic approaches to public relations practice" (p. 92). We concluded that organizations "that are not sensitive to the dynamism in their socio-cultural environments will pay the price by losing public trust and relationships with key stakeholders" (p. 92) that often results in a loss of reputation as well. Recognizing the paucity of empirical studies linking public relations with activism, we offered a set of research questions and propositions that, we hoped, would spawn further empirical research on the relationship between activist culture and public relations.

The Public Relations–Culture Nexus

Examining the term *culture* based on the work of anthropologists and extending its scope to include political economy as culture, media culture, and activist culture enriches the assessment of the relationship between public relations and culture. The relationship between culture (thus broadly defined) and public relations, is discernible in three principal ways. Discussing each of these not only provides us with a history of the body of knowledge linking public relations with culture but also helps us reflect how much farther we need to go in our efforts to build a holistic body of knowledge of public relations—one that accounts for the public relations–culture nexus.

Culture as an Antecedent for Public Relations Practice

The first, and perhaps most obvious, genre of relationship between culture and public relations is evident in the complex ways culture becomes the "environment" in which public relations is practiced and therefore culture deeply impacts such practice. Every human being is influenced by culture while also contributing to the constant shaping and reshaping of culture, be it the culture of a society or of an organization. Whether one is conscious of it or not, culture has a deep impact on the way every human behaves, and that includes the way we communicate with fellow human beings in both interpersonal and organizational settings. Because public relations is fundamentally a communication activity that seeks to foster relationships, the culture–public relations link is best conceptualized by viewing the culture–communication relationship, which has a longer history and thus a more expansive and established body of knowledge. Culture influences every aspect of human communication: verbal, non-verbal, and symbolic. Acculturation, occurring principally at home, at school, and in the workplace, is how each human gets oriented to the ways of the culture of a collectivity, including organizations. For centuries, scholars of rhetorical communication have proposed the use of *ethos, pathos*, and *logos* for effective communication (Heath, 2000; also Chapter 2 in this book). One can discern how peoples of different societies use ethos, pathos, and logos differently in their communication, which provides us with an insight into one of the ways cultural diversity is manifested in the way individuals communicate (e.g. Yoshikawa, 1993).

Empirically linking culture with public relations requires the researcher to operationalize culture. Culture is hard to define but even harder to measure because its malleable nature is evident in the subconscious level of humans. This often makes it difficult for individuals to discern their own cultural idiosyncrasies. Despite the inherent challenges of empirically studying culture, Hofstede was among the first to identify first four, and then five, dimensions of culture; he admitted that those were not comprehensive and more work needs to be done to identify other dimensions. The current body of knowledge of public relations consists almost exclusively of studies belonging to this first genre: analyzing culture as an "environment" for public relations practice. Most of the studies in this genre also have predominantly used the dimensions of culture proposed by Hofstede (1984, 2003). The first attempts to assess culture as an "environment" for public relations practice began in the late 1980s with a preliminary analysis of south Indian organizations using personal interviews (Sriramesh and Grunig, 1988). Prior to that there was no mention of culture as a variable that affects public relations in public relations literature including the PRSA's body of knowledge of project of 1988. As a follow-up to the analysis of south Indian organization, an ethnographic analysis of 18 southern Indian organizations (Sriramesh, 1992) was perhaps the first study to link societal culture empirically with public relations. It used only one of the dimensions of culture that Hofstede had identified—*power distance*—and linked it to the stratification evident in Indian society. The study also highlighted the fact that power distance and deference to authority are two sides of the same coin, as illustrated by the experiences of a chief executive who wanted to bring a more egalitarian culture into his organization but faced resistance from subordinate staff members who felt uncomfortable; likewise more than half the public relations managers agreed that a consultative manager loses the respect of subordinates or is perceived as being weak (Sriramesh, 1996, pp. 188–189).

A more expansive conceptual and empirical attempt followed for the study popularly known as the *Excellence Project* (Grunig, 1992). We began by conceptually distinguishing the relationship between public relations and *societal* culture (Sriramesh and White, 1992) and between it and *organizational* culture (Sriramesh et al., 1992), positing that the culture of a society and the culture within organizations play key roles in the way communication is practiced by organizations both internally and with external publics. Subsequently, the Excellence Project gathered empirical evidence linking organizational culture with public relations (Sriramesh et al., 1996). The project did not linking societal culture for several reasons, including the fact that the study focused only on public relations in three English-speaking cultures (the US, the UK, and Canada).

Kim (2003) studied the impact of Hofstede's fifth dimension—Confucian Dynamism—on public relations by analyzing the public relations strategies and activities of a multinational corporation. The author found that the corporation predominantly used the personal influence model to communicate with domestic publics while preferring the two-way models to relate to its publics abroad. Further, Kim found, the corporation predominantly used Confucian thought to relate to domestic publics whereas its global public relations was to be "as rational as possible" (p. 90). There was evidence in her study that the corporation's domestic public relations was driven to suit the values of the local culture whereas its global public relations tended to be more culturally relativistic to suit the local cultures.

Rhee (1999) is probably the only scholar to have attempted to empirically link public relations with all five dimensions of culture posited by Hofstede. Rhee concludes, among other things, that "[A]lthough conceptually affiliated with high power distance . . . Confucianism may not be detrimental to achieving excellence in public relations" (p. 185). Most of the research on the culture–public relations relationship has been conducted in a few countries of Asia. In one of the few non-Asian studies, Verčič, Grunig, and Grunig (1996) linked public relations with the first four dimensions that Hofstede identified. The authors found, not surprisingly, that their three interviewees often could not agree on whether a certain cultural idiosyncrasy was really Slovenian.

The over-reliance on Hofstede's (1984, 1991) dimensions to link culture with public relations is a notable failing in the body of public relations knowledge. Whereas Hofstede's dimensions have certainly proved useful for the early studies that linked culture with public relations, the second generation of studies must now identify idiosyncrasies specific to a culture and link them with public relations. Some of this work has begun but much more needs to be done. *Guanxi*—a cultural dimension specific to Chinese culture—is perhaps the only unique cultural dimension that has garnered attention from public relations scholars (e.g. Kipnis, 1997; Huang, 2000; Aw, Tan, and Tan, 2002; Hung, 2003). The relationship between public relations and the concepts of *wa, amae, tatamae*, and *honne*—specific to Japanese culture—have been explored by Sriramesh and Takasaki (2000). Several other concepts unique to Japanese culture such as *katachi de hairu* (entering self-fulfillment through the rules) or the importance of the business card (*meishi*) to bring credibility to inter-personal communication have not been explored at all. There is a dire need for studies that identify dimensions of culture unique not only to Asia but to societies in other regions of the world and link them with public relations. In sum, culture as an antecedent for public relations has been the most popular genre of research in the culture–public relations linkage but even that relation-ship has not been studied in adequate breadth or depth.

The Impact of Public Relations on Society/Organizational Environments

Its overuse does not reduce the truth of the clichéd adage: information is power. As purveyors of information, surely public relations practitioners have the opportunity to wield power, which is often manifested in both positive and negative ways. The second way of discerning the culture–public relations nexus is in the ways public relations affects a society, given the enormous potential to influence that is inherent in the field. Scant research currently exists on "public relations effects"—the ways in which public relations affects a society and its culture. By contrast, in the field of mass media, a discipline closely related to public relations, scholars have studied media effects on soci-ety since the middle of the twentieth century, offering various theories such as *uses and gratification* (Katz et al., 1974), *diffusion of news* (Jeffords and Rabinovitz, 1994; Englehardt, 1994), *agenda setting* (Dearing, 1996), *spiral of silence* (Noelle-Neumann, 1993), and *cultivation theory* (Thussu, 2000).

Similar theorizing is lacking, and needed, in public relations. Perhaps the only direct reference to the "social role" of public relations was offered by Grunig (1992) when he briefly described five social roles for public relations as a corollary to his longer elucidation of symmetrical and asymmetrical world views (which are no doubt influenced by culture). Apart from that, much of what has been written about the impact of public relations on society has been offered by external observers who critique public relations from the outside, most often highlighting its role as a "hired gun" by corporations with selfish motives—as typified in the book *Toxic Sludge Is Good for You: Lies, Damn Lies, and the Public Relations Industry* by Stauber and Rampton (1995). One may point to many case studies in which public relations has been caught with its hand in the cookie jar—whether it is the involvement of a leading public relations agency in orchestrating a young girl's lies to a nation and thereby to the world, resulting in a war that still reverberates around the world, or the more recent revelations of an influential public relations operative in India engaging in questionable influence peddling. Wikileaks, no matter one's perspective on it, provides at least partial insights into the "behind the scenes" world of public relations. The infamous "Radia tape episode" in late 2010 in India is another example that revealed ante-room dealings undertaken by a well-heeled public relations consultant with personal ties to politicians, corporate leaders, and journalists.

In almost every instance, such cases that portray public relations in a negative light have been provided by investigative journalists and those outside the public relations field who typically offer the negative picture of the field. As we go to press, the UK is dealing with a scandal of massive hacking of citizens' telephones by the media and at least one well-known public relations practitioner is in the middle of it all. The one lesson that one can derive from all of these negative portrayals of the public relations industry is that linking public relations almost exclusively with corporations contributes to the poor reputation of the field by portraying public relations practitioners as agents of selfish corporate interests. *Publisher's Weekly* described *Toxic Sludge Is Good for You* as "a chilling analysis of the PR business . . . a cautionary reminder that much of the consumer and political world is created by for-hire mouthpieces in expensive neckties" (*Publishers Weekly*, n.d.)

For their part, those within public relations also deserve to be criticized for not focusing attention on the broader social roles of the practice. A review of the content of public relations textbooks, discussions at conferences, professional seminars organized by public relations associations and institutes, and the like reveals the predominant attention that is paid to corporations by those within the field to the exclusion of governments and non-governmental organizations (NGOs), which arguably have more public relations activities— much of it altruistic. Highlighting these more positive social roles will provide a truer picture of public relations, helping repair at least some of the poor reputation of the field.

Communication for Development (C4D) is a field in which public relations has played a significant role, but that role has not been studied with much depth and included in the body of knowledge. Information campaigns have been a mainstay of work by international agencies in the developing world at least since the middle of the twentieth century with the establishment of the United Nations and its agencies such as the FAO, WHO, UNICEF, and UNESCO. Apart from NGOs, governments also have invested significant resources in nation building and national development around the world. They also use public relations strategies and techniques for these purposes even if they do not use the term *public relations*, instead using the more generic term *public communication* or *public information* to describe their activities.

Public Relations as Culture

The third aspect of the public relations–culture relationship focuses on public relations as *a culture*. Viewing public relations as a culture is a reflective activity with great returns that provides the field with a distinct identity. Who is a public relations person? What makes a good public relations practitioner?

Are public relations people born or made? Although these questions have been addressed in the past, the discussions have been disjointed and the field continues to struggle when answering the question "Who are we and what is our purpose?" Because public relations is quite malleable and interdisciplinary, both in practice and in scholarship, its place in society and the body of knowledge continue to be a focus of debate and disagreement among those within, and outside, public relations. One example would be the low numbers of public relations-oriented articles that are published in more generic scholarly journals. The recent editor of a leading journal in the communication field had this to say about public relations scholarship: "I am engaged in *peripheral scholarship* [emphasis added] when I address issues about political advertising, media uses in political campaigns, or public relations tactics" (Phau, 2008, p. 600).

The debate continues on whether public relations is a communication discipline or a management discipline and whether it is a practice or a profession, as evidenced by this remark by Cheney and Christensen (2001), who viewed public relations as a "contested disciplinary and interdisciplinary terrain" (p. 167). Similarly, McKie (2001) advocated a broadening of the body of knowledge by infusing "new science." The situation is not much different vis-à-vis public relations practice, which continues to be perceived as a supporting or peripheral activity by fields such as marketing and advertising (Grunig et al., 2002). Several scholars (Kotler and Mindak, 1978; Hallahan, 1992; Lauzen, 1992) have offered different combinations of the interplay between marketing and public relations. White and Mazur (1995) suggested that public relations could become either a "technical practice using communication techniques to support marketing activities" or a "social practice helping organizations to fit into their social environments" (p. 266). They observed that "[T]o progress, it will need to mark out its agenda, and invest in a programme of research and development to do this" (p. 266). There is overwhelming sentiment that the social role of public relations—and thereby its identity—is a work in progress.

Addressing public relations as "a" culture, thus provides us with a tool to address the identity issue thereby helping us position public relations in the broader communication context.

Conclusion and the Future

The theme of this chapter is that, despite recent strides, ethnocentricity abounds in the practice of public relations scholarship. As a field, we will be neglecting culture at our own peril. Globalization requires public relations practitioners to be holistic and thus nimble in communication and relationship building. The future is very bright for the field because of the importance of communication to all types of organizations that are expanding into new markets and cultures, and organizations will look to public relations to build those cultural bridges. However, public relations scholarship is steeped in ethnocentricity by such things as largely relying on Western models of practice, knowledge derived mostly from Western experiences, and focusing almost exclusively on the communication activities of corporations. Practitioners have relied for far too long on trial and error or anecdotal evidence to communicate with cross-cultural and global audiences. Scholars would do well to advance the body of knowledge by addressing the ethnocentricity that is holding the field back by embarking on research programs that broaden the horizons of the field. Culture could be one of the "new sciences" that McKie (2001) advocated in order to help increase the relevance of public relations scholarship to practice and ultimately to society. The most urgent task for scholars is to build a database of empirical evidence that practitioners (representing corporations, governments, and non-profits) can use to reach out to their relevant publics. Such a database which will expand the body of knowledge and increase the relevance of scholarship to the practice and to society. It is hoped that the chapters in this book will help those who wish to embark on research programs that address the vital link between culture and public relations.

References

Aw, A., Tan, S. K., and Tan, R. (2002). *Guanxi and public relations: An exploratory qualitative study of the public relations–guanxi phenomenon in Singapore firms*. Paper presented to the Public Relations Division of the International Communication Association, Seoul, South Korea, July 15–19.

Botan, C. H. and Taylor, M. (2004). Public relations: State of the field. *Journal of Communication*, 54(4), 645–661.

Cheney, G. and Christensen, L. T. (2001). Public relations as contested terrain: A critical response. In Heath, R. L. (Ed.), *Handbook of public relations*. Thousand Oaks, CA: Sage, pp. 167–203.

Dearing, J. W. (1996). *Agenda-setting*. Thousand Oaks, CA: Sage.

Duhe, S. and Sriramesh, K. (2009). Political economy and global public relations research and practice. In Sriramesh, K. and Verčič, D. (Eds.), *The global public relations handbook* (revised edition). New York: Routledge, pp. 22–46.

Englehardt, T. (1994). The Gulf War as total television. In Jeffords, S. J. and Rabinovitz, L. (Eds.), *Seeing through the media: The Persian Gulf War*. New Brunswick, NJ: Rutgers University Press, pp. 81–95.

Grunig, J. E. (1992). *Excellence in public relations and communication management: Contributions to effective organizations*. Hillsdale, NJ: Lawrence Erlbaum Associates.

Grunig, L. A., Grunig, J. E., and Dozier, D. M. (2002). *Excellent public relations and effective organizations*. Mahwah, NJ: Lawrence Erlbaum Associates.

Hachten, W. A. (1981). *The world news prism: Changing media, clashing ideologies*. Ames: Iowa State University Press.

Hachten, W. A. (1993). *The growth of media in the Third World: African failures, Asian successes*. Ames: Iowa State University Press.

Hallahan, K. (1992, August). *A typology of organizational relationships between public relations and marketing*. Paper presented at the annual conference of the Association for Education in Journalism and Mass Communication, Montreal.

Heath, R. L. (2000). A rhetorical perspective on the values of public relations: Crossroads and pathways toward concurrence. *Journal of Public Relations Research*, 12(1), 69–92.

Hofstede, G. (1984). *Culture's consequences*. Beverly Hills, CA: Sage.

Hofstede, G. (1991). *Culture and organization: Software of the mind*. London: McGraw-Hill.

Hofstede, G. (2003). *Culture's consequences, comparing values, behaviors, institutions, and organizations across nations* (2nd edn.). Newbury Park, CA: Sage.

Huang, Y. H. (2000). The personal influence model and *gao guanxi* in Taiwan Chinese public relations. *Public Relations Review*, 26, 216–239.

Hung, C. J. F. (2003, May). *Culture, relationship cultivation, and relationship outcomes: A qualitative evaluation on multinational companies' relationship management in China.* Paper presented at the Public Relations Division in the 53rd annual conference of International Communication Association, San Diego.

Jeffords, S. J. and Rabinovitz, L. (1994). *Seeing through the media: The Persian Gulf War.* New Brunswick, NJ: Rutgers University Press.

Kaplan, D. and Manners, R. A. (1972). *Culture theory*. Englewood Cliffs, NJ: Prentice-Hall.

Katz, E., Blumler, J. G., and Gurevitch, M. (1974). Utilization of mass communication by the individual. In Blumler, J. G. and Katz, E. (Eds.), *The uses of mass communications: Current perspectives on gratifications research*. Beverly Hills, CA: Sage, pp. 19–32.

Kim, H. S. (2003). Exploring global public relations in a Korean multinational organization in the context of Confucian culture. *Asian Journal of Communication*, 13(2), 65–95.

Kim, J.-N. and Sriramesh, K. (2009). A descriptive model of activism in global public relations research and practice. In Sriramesh, K. and Verčič, D. (Eds.), *The global public relations handbook* (revised edition). New York: Routledge, pp. 79–97.

Kipnis, A. (1997). *Producing guanxi: Sentiment, self, and subculture in a north China village.* Durham, NC: Duke University Press.

Kotler, P. and Mindak, W. (1978). Marketing and public relations: Should they be partners or rivals? *Journal of Marketing*, 42(10), 13–20.

Kroeber, A. L. and Kluckhohn, C. (1952). *Culture: A critical review of concepts and definitions*. Papers of the Peabody Museum of American Archeology and Ethnology, 47. Cambridge: Harvard University.

Lauzen, M. M. (1992). Public relations roles, intraorganizational power, and encroachment. *Journal of Public Relations Research*, 4, 61–80.

Lewis, R. (2006). *When cultures collide: Leading across cultures* (third edition). Boston, MA: Nicholas Brealey International.

McKie, D. (2001). Updating public relations: "New Science," research paradigms, and uneven development. In Heath, R. L. (Ed.), *Handbook of public relations*. Thousand Oaks, CA: Sage, pp. 75–91.

Martin, L. J. and Chaudhury, A. G. (1983). *Comparative mass media systems*. White Plains, NY: Longman.

Merrill, J. C. (1974). *The dialectic in journalism: Toward a responsible use of press freedom.* Baton Rouge: Louisiana State University Press.

Merrill, J. C. and Lowenstein, R. L. (1971). *Media, messages, and men*. New York: Longman.

Merrill, J. C. and Lowenstein, R. L. (1979). *Media, messages, and men*. New York: Longman.

Noelle-Neumann, E. (1993). *The spiral of silence: Public opinion – our social skin*. Chicago: University of Chicago Press.

Phau, M. (2008). Epistemological and disciplinary intersections. *Journal of Communication*, 58, 597–602.

Publishers Weekly. (n.d.). Review of "Toxic sludge is good for you." Retrieved from http://www.prwatch.org/tsigfy.html.

Rhee, Y. (1999). Confucian culture and excellent public relations: A study of generic principles and specific applications in South Korean public relations practice. Unpublished Master's thesis, University of Maryland at College Park, Maryland, USA.

Siebert, F. S., Peterson, T., and Schramm, W. (1956). *Four theories of the press*. Urbana: University of Illinois Press.

Smircich (1983). Concepts of culture and organizational analysis. *Administrative Science Quarterly*, 28, 339–358.

Sriramesh, K. (1992). The impact of societal culture on public relations: Ethnographic evidence from India. *Public Relations Review*, 18(2), 201–211.

Sriramesh, K. (1996). Power distance and public relations: An ethnographic study of southern Indian organizations. In Culbertson, H. and Chen, N. (Eds.), *International public relations: A comparative analysis*. Hillsdale, NJ: Lawrence Erlbaum Associates, pp. 171–190.

Sriramesh, K. (2002). The dire need for multiculturalism in public relations education: An Asian perspective. *Journal of Communication Management*, 7(1), 54–70.

Sriramesh, K. (2004). *Public relations in Asia: An anthology*. Singapore: Thomson.

Sriramesh, K. (2006). The relationship between culture and public relations. In Toth, E. (Ed.), *Excellence in public relations and communication management: Challenges for the next generation*. Mahwah, NJ: Lawrence Erlbaum Associates, pp. 507–527.

Sriramesh, K. (2010). Globalization and public relations: Opportunities for growth and reformulation. In Heath, R. E. (Ed.), *Encyclopedia of public relations*. Thousand Oaks, CA: Sage, pp. 691–707.

Sriramesh, K. and Duhe, S. (2009). Political economy and public relations: A blueprint for future research. *Public Relations Review*, 35, 368–375.

Sriramesh, K. and Grunig, J. E. (1988, November). *Toward a cross-cultural theory of public relations: Preliminary evidence from India*. Paper presented to the panel on New Frontiers in the International Management Environment, Association for the Advancement of Policy, Research and Development in the Third World, Myrtle Beach, NC.

Sriramesh, K. and Takasaki, M. (2000). The impact of culture on Japanese public relations. *Journal of Communication Management*, 3(4), 337–352.

Sriramesh, K. and Verčič, D. (2009a). *The handbook of global public relations: Theory, research, and practice* (revised and expanded edition). New York: Routledge.

Sriramesh, K. and Verčič, D. (2009b). Mass media and public relations. In Sriramesh, K. and Verčič, D. (Eds.), *The global public relations handbook* (revised edition). New York: Routledge, pp. 62–78.

Sriramesh, K. and White, J. (1992). Societal culture and public relations. In Grunig, J. E. (Ed.), *Excellence in public relations and communications management: Contributions to effective organizations*. Hillsdale, NJ: Lawrence Erlbaum Associates, pp. 597–616.

Sriramesh, K., Grunig, J. E., and Buffington, J. (1992). Corporate culture and public relations. In Grunig, J. E. (Ed.), *Excellence in public relations and communications management: Contributions to effective organizations*. Hillsdale, NJ: Lawrence Erlbaum Associates, pp. 577–596.

Sriramesh, K., Grunig, J. E., and Dozier, D. (1996). Observation and measurement of organizational culture: Development of indices of participative and authoritarian cultures. *Journal of Public Relations Research*, 8(4), 229–262.

Stauber, J. and Rampton, S. (1995). *Toxic sludge is good for you: Lies, damn lies, and the public relations industry*. Monroe, ME: Common Courage Press.

Thussu, D. K. (2000). *International communication: Continuity and change*. London: Arnold.

Tyler, E. B. (1871). *Primitive culture*. London: Murray.

Verčič, D., Grunig, L. A. and Grunig, J. E. (1996). Global and specific principles of public relations: Evidence from Slovenia. In Culbertson, H. M. and Chen, N. (Eds.), *International public relations: A comparative analysis*. Mahwah, NJ: Lawrence Erlbaum Associates, pp. 31–66.

White, J. and Mazur, L. (1995). *Strategic communications management: Making public relations work*. Wokingham, UK: Addison-Wesley.

Yoshikawa, M. J. (1993). Japanese and American modes of communication and implications for managerial and organizational behavior. In Dissanayake, W. (Ed.), *Communication theory: The Asian perspective*. Singapore: Asian Media Information and Communication Centre, pp. 150–182.

2

WESTERN CLASSICAL RHETORICAL TRADITION AND MODERN PUBLIC RELATIONS

Culture of Citizenship

Robert L. Heath

In an era when the term *rhetoric* is rarely associated with what is good and wholesome about organizational and societal discourse, citizenship, and the enactment of political economy, it is important to realize from the outset of this chapter that such commentary is more of a reflection of contemporary culture and its views of discourse than it is about discourse as it has been encouraged and studied over the centuries. This chapter carefully examines the Western rhetorical heritage, specifically the work of selected ancient Greeks and Romans set in their cultural context, to understand how they conceived discourse and why they believed that rhetoric was essential to the viability of society. As we today believe that public relations also is vital to society, or at least here to stay, the Western rhetorical heritage can help define the rationale and set the conditions for understanding what aspects and purposes of discourse are better than others. In this sense we can view public relations as the rhetorical enactment of organizations as citizens engaged in the shaping of political economy.

Today, many of us like to use this rationale for examining, championing, theorizing, and challenging public relations to serve, through thoughtful discourse, a citizenship role that demands that words and actions serve as rhetorical enactment of organizations as they are called on to make society more fully functioning (see, for instance, Heath, 2001, 2006a, 2007, 2009; Ihlen, 2002, 2008, 2010; L'Etang, 1996, 2010; Taylor, 2009). In this tradition, two books explicitly address the complexities of rhetoric as organization-public discourse and critical inquiry. They are Toth and Heath (1992), *Rhetorical and Critical Approaches to Public Relations*, and Heath, Toth, and Waymer (2009), *Rhetorical and Critical Approaches to Public Relations II*. These themes, featured as external organizational rhetoric, are closely examined in a recent special issue of *Management Communication Quarterly*.

Public relations, as a primary voice of organizations, internally and externally, in the twenty-first century, parallels the spirit of individuals who have engaged in public dialogue, however well, ethically, and attentively to facts required for enlightened choices, the optimal outcome of responsible and productive discourse (Nichols, 1963). Given this, public relations most reflectively and responsibly enacted can help create and use infrastructures to forge shared meaning that helps society function most fully (Heath, 2006a). That goal and the process required to achieve it underpin the best of the Western rhetorical culture reaching back to ancient Greece, several centuries BC. This point of view characterizes the theory and practice of public relations as inherently rhetorical. This character is never more powerfully demonstrated than when we feature public relations as discourse oriented, as dialogue. The dialogic nature of Western rhetoric, statement and counter statement, is the essence of this chapter, which points out how that paradigm is championed by this key aspect of Western culture as the rationale for public relations.

As a vital part of Western civilization, rhetoric was inseparable from Greek and Roman cultures, government, and democratic self-rule. Citizens were expected, and even required, to speak on important matters, to address what they and other citizens wanted to know and consider. In this sense, the importance and character of the Greek rhetorical heritage was aptly captured by George Kennedy (1963, 1991): "In its origin and intention, rhetoric was natural and good; it produced clarity, vigor, and beauty, and it rose logically from the conditions and qualities of the classical mind" (Kennedy, 1963, p. 3).

One of many distinguished scholars on the Western rhetorical heritage, Kennedy set the standard by which many of us like to ground the meaning-making, social construction role of public relations. Rhetoric is often seen as a distortion of some more wholesome and honest form of discourse. Without doubt, even among classical writers, Plato was as skeptical of the ability of people to conduct reasonable and civil discourse as critics of rhetoric, and even public relations, are today. However, as Kenneth Burke (1946) mused: "How can a world with rhetoric stay decent, how a world without it can exist at all?"

As we do today, the ancients liked to believe that rhetoric was a reflection of their culture and the character of citizenship. Reason, fact, demonstration of propositions, focus on socially relevant ends, contextual challenges, emotion, ethics, statement and counter statement, and all other aspects of the human condition captured through the philosophical underpinnings of rhetoric are the preconditions of the culture of self-government. Irony is an essential part of rhetoric, and it is ironic that the very rationale for why society, community, works can also be used to explain its downfall. The ancients recognized these pitfalls and devoted an enormous amount of intellect to the culture of rhetoric, seeking to define and champion its best and prevent its worst nature. Such was the impact of their work that this line of analysis is the oldest and most resilient approach to human communication in Western culture.

Within this cultural heritage, the Greek and Roman tradition was the rationale for the American university study of speech (later speech communication) from the nineteenth century until the 1960s, when social science and textual discourse analysis broadened the view of communication studies. Eventually, and predictably, public relations would endure, as well as profit from, discussion of how it could be dysfunctional as well and could be strengthened by understanding and applying principles and ethics of rhetoric as part of what Cutlip (1994) called the Babel of society, a contest between many voices.

To explore themes outlined in this introduction, this chapter briefly sets a foundation by discussing culture, and then progresses to examine the rhetorical heritage of ancient Greece and Rome. Finally, the paper concludes by connecting the culture of citizen participation in public and private forums and the rationale for responsible and reflective practice of public relations. Within the context of public relations, what was the person as citizen is today the organization, of whatever kind, as citizen enacting a culture of dialogue.

Culture

As Sriramesh, Grunig, and Buffington (1992) observed, "The buzzword *culture* does not have a unanimously accepted definition in the field of anthropology, the field in which it originated" (p. 580). After a review of several definitions, these authors stressed how "Culture is viewed universally as a construct that reduces ambiguity and facilitates interaction in social settings" (pp. 580–581). Culture creates and frames the tensions between individualism and collectivism, between ordered behavior and randomness, between certainty and uncertainty.

From a communication studies perspective, Jandt (2009) identified four conditions for the existence, impact, durability, change, and power of culture. One is the internal identity of a community of thought and action that reproduces itself. The second is "The totality of that community's thoughts, experiences, and patterns of behavior and its assumptions, understandings, and values about life that guide behavior" (p. 397). The third dimension features the process of social transmission of these thoughts. Last, culture is enacted as people in each identifiable community "consciously identify themselves with that community—referred to as cultural identity or the identification with and acceptance into a group that has shared symbols and behavior norms" (p. 397).

Thus, culture is a means for normative identification, the shared sense of the world that is transmitted to subsequent generations as a way of knowing, as shared understanding, and as a knowable process of varying kinds of empowerment. Culture gives people in each community the vocabulary that carves reality, physical and social, into meaningful and actionable units. Frameable as narratives, it defines roles, themes/plots, morals, relationships, characters, scripts, scenes/location, morality, identities, narrators, and auditors (Heath, 1994). Culture influences behavior because it contains the *social reality* people use to know what they are expected to do—the expectations others hold—and what rewards and punishments result from individual and collective actions.

The power of culture results from shared reality that allows and even demands various enactments to fulfill others' expectations. Viewed that way, culture is not only a shared sense of reality but also the enactment of that reality. As such, it creates enactment as a bracketing activity that allows for selection and retention (Weick, 1987). Thus, it sets limits, frames, that focus attention unique to the reality shared. To keep culture alive and transmit its influence, it must be remembered.

Part of this knowability and normative retention results from icons, archetypes, and paradigms. Thus, the Western heritage of rhetoric, simply stated, is the archetype of the good person speaking well: a combination of ethics and discourse effectiveness for the collective good—whether enacted by individuals or organizations.

The Rhetorical Heritage: A Key to Understanding Western Culture

The Western rhetorical heritage grew out of a very difficult time in the history of Greece. After an era of tyranny, citizens regained much of their self-government. They could, and even were required to, speak in forums designed to re-establish property rights and other rights and responsibilities of citizenship. As mentioned above, Kennedy (1963, 1991) explored the culture of ancient Greek citizenship connecting politics (political theory and practice), ethics, and rhetoric. As Kennedy (1963) remarked, "One of the principal interests of the Greeks was rhetoric" (p. 3). "Greek society relied on oral expression" (p. 3). This was the case because other forms of communication were difficult (long before the digital age, which actually is a rhetorical Babel) and proximity of citizens to their government made speaking easy—thus necessary.

Three forums defined government: the political forum of deliberation, courts (forensic discourse), and ceremonies (the place of epideictic). Matters were resolved by the tensions of statement and counter statement to examine matters of fact, evaluation, policy, and identification. As Kennedy (1963) framed the culture, "The significance of oratory is as great in substance as in form. Wherever persuasion is the end, rhetoric is present" (p. 7). Doubt, choice, agreement, and disagreement are the rationale for rhetoric. Truth and best choices are not given, but are forged through discourse.

This section expands on that defining essence of culture and sets the stage for giving voice to the views of Plato, Aristotle, Isocrates, and Quintilian, whose works are among the most important for connecting culture with rhetoric:

public discourse as self-government. Buffeted in many ways by dramatic changes in political economy, especially through the governmental role of the church and the prevailing cultural definition of the rights of the ruler and the ruled, rhetoric was part of classical education from Roman times, continuing through European pedagogy, and into modern education in the United States and other Western countries.

If culture is a shared view of the world that can be collectively and normatively enacted and transmitted to subsequent generations, then rhetoric needs to be codified and incorporated into the education of the citizen. That was the case in Greece, Rome, and subsequent generations in Europe and the Americas. As Kennedy (1963) noted:

> The Greek word for speech is *logos*, an ambiguous and sometimes mystical concept which may refer concretely to a word, words, or an entire oration, or may be used abstractly to indicate the meaning behind a word or expression or the power of thought and organization or the rational principle of the universe or the will of God. On the human level it involves man's thought and his function in society, and it further includes artistic creativity and the power of personality.
>
> (p. 8)

With this assessment of the role of discourse in mind, Pernot (2008) reminded us that "the art of speaking exists in many civilizations, but Greek antiquity has given it a distinctive, rigorous, and rich theoretical underpinning" (p. 4257).

In our modern times, rhetoric as an element of our culture is often tainted by the rhetorical claims of 1960s activists that some statement they oppose is "mere rhetoric." It also has come to be synonymous with shallow and/or manipulative discourse. Such claims are unfortunate because they reveal a contemporary culture that has lost sight of the centrality of discourse as argumentation in the public arena. We can find the voices of television and radio political commentators railing rhetorically about the rhetoric of their targeted enemies.

Contributing one of many entries on rhetoric in the *International Encyclopedia of Communication*, van Eemeren (2008) addressed the paradoxes of argumentation as the essence of rhetoric as contested ground:

> The argument schemes that are distinguished remain for the most part close to the classical topical tradition. There are arguments with a quasi-logical argument scheme, but also arguments with a scheme that structures reality and arguments with a scheme based on the structure of reality.
>
> (p. 4217)

From ancient times, the culture of rhetoric (or the role of rhetoric in culture) has centered on the inherent and problematic tensions between words and reality, between a knowable and judgable reality and the limits of human knowledge and judgment.

As Gaines and Gronbeck (2008) observed, "The rhetorical impulse may be conceived as the desire to express one's thoughts in a way that affects the thoughts of others" (p. 4382). Such observations are tantalizingly simple and offer a siren call to champion the role of suasory discourse as the essence of any culture (as well as competing and contesting subcultures, which can be found in the array of topics covered in the *International Encyclopedia of Communication* under the heading of "rhetoric." Debate over the factors that make ethical and effective discourse reaches back at least 2,500 years to the time of Plato. Starting with his concerns, which anchor the Western heritage, through contributions by Aristotle and Isocrates, as well as Quintilian, the remainder of the chapter explores the fundamentals of the ancient rhetorical culture as tensions between politics, ethics, and discourse

Plato: A Critic of Rhetoric

The discussion to this point has stressed, however obliquely or explicitly, that ancient culture respected the responsibility and skill of citizens to achieve self-government through discourse. Plato cautioned that rhetoric is not a lofty aspect of life, but is similar to cookery, a craft in which truth is not as important as its appearance, and cleverness supplants soundness of argument. He scorned rhetoric as the use of deceit rather than a means for discovering truth, improving knowledge, or forming enlightened policy. Pointedly condemning it as a tool exploited for evil ends, he reasoned that it consisted of trickery aimed at achieving an outcome desired by one party that was indifferent and even purposefully harmful to the interest of others. He doubted that rhetoric could avoid making false accusations and using contrived evidence to achieve unethical ends.

In its place, Plato preferred dialectic to disclose truth through focused interrogation of one person by another. He assumed one party in each exchange is more knowledgeable and therefore able to lead the other party to a predetermined truth. This presumption led him to favor not the ordinary citizen but the philosopher king as the archetypal head of any political entity. Despite Kennedy's (1963) sense of ancient Greeks' love for public discourse logically crafted and eloquently presented, Plato (1952) caustically cautioned that "rhetoric is not an art at all, but the habit of a bold and ready wit, which knows how to manage mankind: this habit I sum up under the word 'flattery'" (p. 262).

By such criticism, Plato forced generations of communicators to be mindful of ethics and to worry about the relationship of truth to public discourse, but his narrowing distortion of the socio-political role of the rhetorical tradition denied people access to means of engaging democratically in public discourse to share information, propose opinions, and seek mutually beneficial solutions to collective problems. However difficult it is to tolerate counter statements, most people prefer public debate to having decisions made by management elites along the lines of Plato's philosopher king—even though, in contemporary society, talk show personalities often have influence disproportionate to their insightfulness.

Plato also posed one of the eternal challenges: what is the pathway to truth? Lunsford, Wilson, and Eberly (2009) offered insights into this eternal puzzle, "In the Western tradition, the argument between philosophy and sophistry perfectly captures competing conceptions of rhetorical knowledge, with philosophy linking Truth to dialectic and logic and the sophist linking contingent truth to rhetoric" (p. xx).

Aristotle: Blending Rhetoric, Politics and Ethics

Aristotle, a pupil of Plato, enriched the rhetorical tradition by focusing on it as the socially structured process and substance of public discourse required to achieve the good of society supported by an articulated ethos. He determined that rhetoric was strategically functional, a means to solve problems collaboratively and achieve socially required and contextualized outcomes with audiences whose opinions might differ and who might respond to different appeals. Acknowledging the reality of contingency and expedience, Aristotle launched a platform of thought that justified rhetoric and the best that can be known and said under the reality of self-government. He championed logic in discourse but also knew that decisions often were required in the absence of absolute truth.

One of his greatest achievements was the recognition that Greek culture offered three prevailing contexts: deliberative (political communication, including legislative debate), judicial (what we would call litigation), and epideictic (occasional or special situation communication). Each context was defined by its unique purpose and desired outcome. Deliberative rhetoric demonstrates the expedience of some policy, what is best to do under the circumstances. Forensic rhetoric deals with guilt and innocence. Epideictic rhetoric is concerned with matters of praise and blame (and today, therefore, becomes the rationale for crisis response).

As he studied discourse in action, Aristotle observed three major kinds of proof: logos (typically featured as the logic of fact and reasoning about facts), pathos (conceptualized as the emotionally relevant value judgments related to a case), and ethos (roughly thought of as credibility but more wisely conceived as character). Thus, the rhetor who is mounting a case is expected to focus strategic discourse on solving some problem and to recognize how different audiences may perceive and address that problem as well as respond differently to various proofs.

The rhetorical canon featured five elements of each presentation: invention, structure, substance, delivery, and mastery. How the case is built depends on the rhetor's skills at invention, knowing what could and must be said to draw each situationally appropriate conclusion. Ideas are not presented randomly, but need to follow one of several well-defined structures. Invention of a specific perspective requires knowledge of the relevant substance. All of this material needs to be effectively delivered (verbally and non-verbally), and with confidence that comes from mastery of the case. Some might call this mastery *gravitas*: communicating with authority drawn from sound character.

These functional outcomes, forms of proof, and strategic elements demanded a sound theoretical glue to hold them together and give them a laudable role in society. To produce such a glue, Aristotle (1952a) set two high ethical standards for those who engage in rhetoric. One is the need to demonstrate through evidence the factual basis for any claims advocated. As he viewed the relationship between the discovery and exposition of ideas, he reasoned that rhetoric is "the faculty of observing in any given case the available means of persuasion" (p. 595). The essence of persuasion is demonstration "since we are most fully persuaded when we consider a thing to have been demonstrated" (p. 594). In this sense, demonstration implies, or requires, sound evidence and reasoned argument with that evidence to thoughtful conclusions.

Truth as it can best be known emerges through proof and reasoning presented for others to consider. The second standard is to demonstrate through the values espoused that the communicator is a good person speaking for a good cause—the demonstration of character. The highest good is the effort to make society better, more fully functional. His inquiry led to the conclusion that persons who engage in rhetoric must have a profound understanding of the role of discourse in a society, preferably one more disposed to democratic dispute rather than royal proclamation.

As he pondered character, Aristotle stressed how the *ethos* of speakers—the predominant form of communication in the golden age of Greece—was vital to their success as well as required to achieve the wholesomeness of their social participation. Persons with more credibility are more believable and trustworthy because they associate their lives, arguments, and purposes with higher-order values: truth, morality, and virtue. What distinguishes a speaker's character? Aristotle (1952a) answered: "good sense, good moral character, and goodwill" (p. 623). Standards of each "good" are basic to rhetoric, which "exists to affect the giving of decisions" by listeners (readers or viewers) who then decide among the positions presented to them (p. 622).

He thought the openness characteristic of public discourse motivated communicators to seek the best—strongest and most ethical points of view—because public contest leads ideas to enjoy and suffer penetrating analysis. Aristotle believed the process entailed the seeking of truth through public advocacy rather than leaving truth to be known (as Plato did) by the singular and "superior" analytic efforts of a "philosopher king." As Aristotle would argue, neither side in some controversy is inherently correct or morally right, but the process of exchange can reveal the interests of both sides so they can achieve a win–win, integrative outcome based on collaborative decision making.

The culture in which people find themselves calls for collective and collaborative decisions and policy formation as a public good. In the opinion of Aristotle (1952b), "if all communities aim at some good," the best aspire to "the highest good" (p. 445). Thus, rhetoric is judged by the quality of the process and its outcomes: "A man [or woman] can confer the greatest of benefits by a right use of these [techniques], and inflict the greatest of injuries by using them wrongly" (p. 594). "Every state is a community of some kind, and every community is established with a view of some good; for mankind always acts in order to obtain that which they think 'good'" (p. 445). Good can be either prescribed by one philosopher king (elitism) or decided by the populace (democracy).

What, according to Aristotle (1952a), is the source of persuasiveness? "A statement is persuasive and credible either because it is directly self-evident or because it appears to be proved from other statements that are so" (p. 596). He reasoned, "Persuasion is achieved by the speaker's personal character when the speech is so spoken as to make us think him credible. We believe good men [and women] more fully and more readily than others" (p. 595). In this way, he believed that rhetoric should foster enlightened choice. For Aristotle (1952a), rhetoric serves to give counsel "on matters about which people deliberate; matters, namely, that ultimately depend on ourselves, and which we have it in our power to set going" (p. 599). Aristotle thought bad judgment and unsound character undo persuasion:

> Men [or women] either form a false opinion through want of good sense; or they form a true opinion, but because of their moral badness do not say what they really think; or finally, they are both sensible and upright, but not well disposed to their hearers, and may fail in consequence to recommend what they know to be the best course.
>
> (p. 623)

When a rhetor recommends a conclusion or action, he or she does so "on the ground that it will do good; if he [or she] urges its rejection, he [or she] does so on the ground that it will do harm" (Aristotle, 1952a, p. 598). People and societies are evaluated with regard to the ends to which they aspire and how that such aspiration fosters discussants toward excellence (Aristotle, 1952a, p. 608). Rhetoric is used to explore ways of achieving happiness by making choices that will do good and prevent or at least minimize harm. He observed, "When we know a thing, and have decided about it, there is no further use in speaking about it" (p. 639). This logic, crafted centuries ago, supports the rationale for public relations in our day. It can guide promotion and publicity as well as the dispute over issues, the resolution of crisis, and the ethical management of risk (Heath, 2006b).

Critics have argued that rhetoric is inherently unethical. Aristotle would have been amused at least or shocked to hear such complaint. Instead of seeing a dysfunction of ethical judgment, he embraced and examined it in his *Nicomachean Ethics* (Aristotle, 1952c): "Every art and every inquiry, and similarly every action and pursuit, is thought to aim at some good; and for this reason the good has rightly been declared to be that at which all things aim" (p. 339). "Therefore, virtue is a kind of mean, since, as we have seen, it aims at what is intermediate" (p. 352). For him, the higher ethical position was one that struck an appropriate balance between ethical extremes; some see this position as a fatal flaw in his ethics. Yet he reasoned that ethics must recognize:

> that moral virtue is a mean, then, and in what sense it is so, and that it is a mean between two vices, the one involving excess and the other deficiency, and that is such because its character is to aim at what is intermediate in passions and in actions.
>
> (p. 354)

He firmly believed that some actions and morals were bad in and of themselves: "But not every action nor every passion admits of a mean; for some have names that already imply badness, e.g. spite, shamelessness, envy, and in the case of actions adultery, theft, murder" (p. 352).

For Aristotle (1952c), "it is no easy task to be good. For in everything it is no easy task to find the middle" (p. 376). For him ethics is a balance between excess and deficit, something that is learned through thoughts and actions that pit extremes against one another. The search is for the middle between the extremes, a win–win midpoint. Critics can find in this reasoning an unwise sense of accommodation, but he was interested in the search for justice:

> We see that all men [and women] mean by justice that kind of state of character which makes people disposed to do what is just and makes them act justly and wish for what is just; and similarly by injustice that state which makes them act unjustly and wish for what is unjust.
>
> (p. 376)

Thus, the tug of ethics is the process of knowing a state and its contrary state. Thus, the state of lying and not telling the truth is known as a contrast to the state of telling the truth.

As did his study of ethics, his *Politics* (Aristotle, 1952b) frames his thoughts on rhetoric as he launched that treatise:

> Every state is a community of some kind, and every community is established with a view to some good; for mankind always act in order to obtain that which they think good. But, if all communities aim at some good, the state or political community, which is the highest of all, and which embraces all the rest, aims at good in the greater degree than any others, and at the highest good.
>
> (p. 445)

"Virtue, then, is a state of character concerned with choice" (Aristotle, 1952c, p. 352). In his *Rhetoric* (Aristotle, 1952a), he argued that:

> Rhetoric is useful (1) because things that are true and things that are just have a natural tendency to prevail over their opposites, so that if the decisions of judges are not what they ought to be, the defeat must be due to the speakers themselves, and they must be blamed accordingly.
>
> (p. 594)

However narrow or incorrect one instance of advocacy might be, it is a statement that is likely to suffer counter statement in some collective and collaborative search for truth. Aristotle's view assumed that each voice deserves to be heard and judged for its merits and deficiencies. The public relations voice of a big business, an activist group, a non-profit, or a government agency is not inherently superior to that of others. One voice should not drown out others.

> No other of the arts draws opposite conclusions: dialectic and rhetoric alone do this. Both these arts draw opposite conclusions impartially. Nevertheless, the underlying facts do not lend themselves equally well to the contrary views. No: things that are true and things that are better are, by their nature, practically always easier to prove and easier to believe in.
>
> (p. 594)

Thus, for Aristotle, the strength of any case was not its deceit but its demonstration. Through demonstration, the targets of messages determine which is best. Great good can be done by using rhetoric ethically. The opposite can lead to harm. Thus, "rhetoric is an offshoot of dialectic and also of ethical studies" (Aristotle, 1952a, p. 595).

In these ways, Aristotle offered two important lines of analysis that help us understand and appreciate the culture of rhetorical heritage and its rationale for public relations. Each communicator puts his or her character on the line by the content of what is said, the manner in which it is presented, the interests that are advanced or harmed by a case, and the way it serves or harms society. Persons (and organizations) must prove their claims and aspire to the highest values in all that they do and say. To those who claim that rhetoric is hollow statement, Aristotle would say that it can be the case, but that is not the best rhetoric, nor the reason that it is vital to society. As we are wise to, Aristotle would shun sham, spin, and the presentation of falsehood. Likewise, we are asked in matters of public relations to demonstrate our case, be of sound character, seek the public interest, and examine the statements of others as we expect them to examine the quality of our presentations.

This standard, developed as rhetorical culture, is amplified by Isocrates and Quintilian. They featured rhetoric as the responsibility and essence of citizenship. Our modern culture features organizations using public relations rather than individuals as citizens. Can ancient theory keep our culture focused on sound principles when organizations are called on to be citizens and expected to make society fully functional?

Isocrates: Rhetorical Training Depends on Social Responsibility

As did Aristotle, Isocrates' opinions on rhetoric underscored how citizens need to prepare themselves to serve society. He recognized the need for civic education, since each generation hands to each following generation the reins of governance. How men and women are educated will shape how they govern and define the culture that guides their choices and empowers their voices. If they are educated to understand the power of persuasion and appreciate its responsible role in collective decision making in the public interest, they will act accordingly when it is their turn to lead society. Such advice, explicit to public relations, is well discussed today (Marsh, 2010).

Isocrates (1929) observed that the first requirement of the effective communicator is "a mind which is capable of finding out and learning the truth and of working hard and remembering what it learns" (p. 293). Contrary to the claims of Plato, discourse is not an art (craft?) in which a facile mind and a quick wit should be the only rule; rather, a thinker devoted to truth can best serve society.

As did Aristotle, Isocrates (1929) observed that rhetoric is a responsibility of each citizen and an essential element of an effective and ethical society (Marsh, 2010). To this end, Isocrates reasoned:

> because there has been implanted in us the power to persuade each other and to make clear to each other whatever we desire, not only have we escaped the life of wild beasts, but we have come together and founded cities and made laws and invented arts; and, generally speaking there is no institution devised by man which the power of speech has not helped us

to establish. For this it is which has laid down laws concerning things just and unjust, and things honourable and base; and if it were not for these ordinances we should not be able to live with one another. It is by this also that we confute the bad and extol the good. Through this we educate the ignorant and appraise the wise; for the power to speak well is taken as the surest index of a sound understanding, and discourse which is true and lawful and just is the outward image of a good and faithful soul.

(p. 327)

The key to discourse is not its nature alone, but its role in service to society. Sham and deceit may occur in the substance and strategies used by rhetors, but time will reveal those devices and their deficiencies (Isocrates, 1929). These are principles sound enough to guide the practice of public relations as a responsible profession serving many interests and making society more fully functional (Marsh, 2010).

In Isocrates' view, society is the benefactor of the persons trained to be effective and ethical communicators. Each citizen—today, even corporate citizens—must learn and apply the principles of strategic and ethical commu-nication. That end must not narrowly serve some participant's self-interest, but the collective interest of all. Through robust dialogue, as Isocrates argued, a better, more ethical society can be crafted.

With this faculty we both contend against others on matters which are open to dispute and seek light for ourselves on things which are unknown; for the same arguments which we use in persuading others when we speak in public, we employ also when we deliberate in our own thoughts.

(p. 327)

Isocrates reasoned that no one can know with certainty what path best achieves the most desirable outcomes. Reasoning, knowledge, and the ability to communicate were, in his opinion, essential tools to that end: "I hold that man [or woman] to be wise who is able by his [or her] powers of conjecture to arrive generally at the best course" (p. 335). Education in the principles and practice of discourse is essential to be a worthy citizen:

when anyone elects to speak or write discourses which are worthy of praise and honour, it is not conceivable that he will support causes which are unjust or petty or devoted to private quarrels, and not rather those which are great and honourable, devoted to the welfare of man and our common good; for if he fails to find causes of this character, he will accomplish nothing to the purpose.

(pp. 337–338)

Not only the ends, but also the means of discourse rest on sound ethical purpose. In the matter of means, character counts:

> the man [or woman] who wishes to persuade people will not be negligent as to the matter of character; no, on the contrary, he will apply himself above all to establish a most honourable name among his fellow-citizens; for who does not know that words carry greater conviction when spoken by men [or women] of good repute than when spoken by men [or women] who live under a cloud, and that the argument which is made by a man's [or woman's] life is of more weight than that which is furnished by words.
>
> (p. 339)

The ethical challenge, one can assume Isocrates would argue, has not changed over the past 2,000 years: "Therefore, the stronger a man's [or woman's] desire to persuade his [or her] hearers, the more zealously will he [or she] strive to be honourable and to have the esteem of his fellow-citizens" (p. 339).

Citizens, Isocrates advised those of his age, need to serve the interests of others by being effective communicators. Concern for others should motivate and precede the development of rhetorical expertise. That approach is preferred to developing such expertise and then looking for interests to serve. Thus, the rhetorical culture of ancient Greece offers a template for us, as it is relevant to public relations' role in society and the manner in which it is practiced. Ours is an age of organizational rhetors, instead of individuals themselves speaking or writing for public evaluation. It is a responsibility of citizenship to participate in responsible, responsive, and reflective dialogue.

Quintilian: Teacher of Ethical Rhetoric and Ethical Speakers

Greek philosophers realized two basic facts. People must demonstrate good character and be effective rhetors to be worthy citizens. To enjoy the privilege and meet the responsibility of engaging in discourse, citizens must aspire to a culture that connects ethics, means, and ends as the burden of responsible and reflective communication. Greeks offered this legacy to the Romans who followed.

Picking up this culture, Marcus Fabius Quintilian called on each citizen first to be "good" as the foundation for speaking well. Only propositions that are justifiable and ethical can sustain themselves against the scrutiny of counter rhetoric. Today's trend for large organizations not only to achieve higher standards of corporate responsibility but to report their success fits the trend to be good, do good, and communicate well.

On this point, Quintilian (1951) was firm: "My ideal orator, then, is the true philosopher, sound in morals and with full knowledge of speaking, always striving for the highest" (p. 20). Quintilian's mission was clear and relevant to public relations' ethical standards: "My aim is to educate the true orator, who must be a good man [or woman] and must include philosophy in his studies in order to shape his character as a citizen and to equip himself to speak on ethical subjects, his special role" (p. 20).

Conclusion

As we near three millennia of careful consideration of character, purpose, responsibility, and citizenship, we can build on the rhetorical culture of ancient Greece and Rome. By that standard, discourse is expected to advance society, not singular interests at the expense of others. It is expected to bring out the best in human character. Today, that character is more corporate than personal. Nevertheless, our culture is made sound or dysfunctional by our diligent attention to principles and practices that are tested over time. Is our culture capable of advancing the sound role of discourse or must it be marred by some dysfunctional alternative?

References

Aristotle. (1952a). *Rhetoric.* (Trans. by Roberts, W. R.) In Hutchins, R. M. (Ed. in Chief), Great Books, Vol. 2. Chicago, IL: Encyclopædia Britannica, pp. 593–675.

Aristotle. (1952b). *Politics.* (Trans. by Jowett, B.). In Hutchins, R. M. (Ed. in Chief), Great Books, Vol. 2. Chicago, IL: Encyclopædia Britannica, pp. 445–548.

Aristotle. (1952c). *Nicomachean ethics.* (Trans. by Jowett, B.). In Hutchins, R. M. (Ed. in Chief), Great Books, Vol. 2. Chicago, IL: Encyclopædia Britannica.

Burke, K. (1946, October 22). [Letter to Malcolm Cowley] Kenneth Burke file, Pennsylvania State University.

Cutlip, S. M. (1994). *The unseen power: Public relations. A history.* Hillsdale, NJ: Lawrence Erlbaum Associates.

van Eemeren, F. H. (2008). Rhetoric, argument, and persuasion. In Donsbach, W. (Ed.), *International encyclopedia of communication.* Malden, MA: Blackwell Publishing, pp. 4215–4219.

Gaines, R. N., and Gronbeck, B. E. (2008). Rhetorical studies. In Donsbach, W. (Ed.), *International encyclopedia of communication.* Malden, MA, Blackwell Publishing, pp. 4382–4395.

Heath, R. L. (1994). *Management of corporate communication: From interpersonal contacts to external affairs.* Hillsdale, NJ: Lawrence Erlbaum.

Heath, R. L. (2001). A rhetorical enactment rationale for public relations: The good organization communicating well. In Heath, R. L. (Ed.), *Handbook of public relations.* Thousand Oaks, CA: Sage Publications, pp. 31–50.

Heath, R. L. (2006a). Onward into more fog: Thoughts on public relations research directions. *Journal of Public Relations Research*, 18, 93–114.

Heath, R. L. (2006b). A rhetorical approach to issues management. In Botan, C. and Hazleton, V. (Eds.), *Public relations theory II.* Mahwah, NJ: Lawrence Erlbaum Associates, pp. 499–522.

Heath, R. L. (2007). Rhetorical theory, public relations, and meaning: Giving voice to ideas. In Hansen-Horn, T. and Neff, B. D. (Eds.), *Public relations: From theory to practice*. New York: Allyn & Bacon, pp. 208–226.

Heath, R. L. (2009). The rhetorical tradition: Wrangle in the marketplace. In Heath, R. L., Toth, E. L., and Waymer, D. (Eds.), *Rhetorical and critical approaches to public relations II*. New York: Routledge, pp. 17–47.

Heath, R. L., Toth, E. L., and Waymer, D. (Eds.) (2009). *Rhetorical and critical approaches to public relations II*. New York: Routledge.

Ihlen, O. (2002). Rhetoric and resources: Notes for a new approach to public relations and issues management. *Journal of Public Affairs*, 2(4), 259–269.

Ihlen, O. (2008). Rhetorical theory of public relations. In Donsbach, W. (Ed.), *International encyclopedia of communication*. Malden, MA: Blackwell Publishing, pp. 4395–4397.

Ihlen, O. (2010). The cursed sisters: Public relations and rhetoric. In Heath, R. L. (Ed.), *SAGE handbook of public relations*. Thousand Oaks, CA: Sage, pp. 59–70.

Isocrates. (1929). *Antidosis*. (Trans. by Norlin, G.). In *Isocrates, Vol. 2*. Cambridge, MA: Harvard University Press, pp. 182–365.

Jandt, F. E. (2009). Culture. In Eadie, W. E. (Ed.), *21st century communication: A reference handbook*. Thousand Oaks, CA: Sage, pp. 396–404.

Kennedy, G. (1963). *The art of persuasion in Greece*. Princeton, NJ: Princeton University Press.

Kennedy, G. (1991). *Aristotle: A theory of civic discourse*. Oxford: Oxford University Press.

L'Etang, J. L. (1996). Public relations and rhetoric. In L'Etang, J. L. and Pieczka, M. (Eds.), *Critical perspectives in public relations*. London: International Thomson Business Press, pp. 106–123.

L'Etang, J. (2010). "Making it real": Anthropological reflections on public relations, diplomacy, and rhetoric. In Heath, R. L. (Ed.), *SAGE handbook of public relations*. Thousand Oaks, CA: Sage, pp. 145–162.

Lunsford, A. A., Wilson, K. H., and Eberly, R. A. (2009). Introduction: Rhetorics and roadmaps. In Lunsford, A. A., Wilson, K. H., and Eberly, R. A. (Eds.), *SAGE handbook of rhetorical studies*. Thousand Oaks, CA: Sage, pp. xi–xxix.

Marsh, C. (2010). Precepts of reflective public relations: An Isocratean model. *Journal of Public Relations Research*, 22, 359–377.

Nichols, M. H. (1963). *Rhetoric and criticism*. Baton Rouge: Louisiana State University Press.

Pernot, L. (2008). Rhetoric, Greek. In Donsbach, W. (Ed.), *The international encyclopedia of communication*. Malden, MA: Blackwell Publishing, pp. 4257–4260.

Plato. (1952). *Gorgias* (Trans. by Jowett, B.). In Hutchins, R. M. (Ed. in Chief), *Great Books*. Chicago, IL: Encyclopædia Britannica, pp. 252–294.

Quintilian, M. F. (1951). *The institutio oratoria of Marcus Fabius Quintilianus* (Trans. by Little, C. E.). Nashville, TN: George Peabody College for Teachers.

Sriramesh, K., Grunig, J. E., and Buffington, J. (1992). Corporate culture and public relations. In Grunig, J. E. (Ed.), *Excellence in public relations and communication management*. Hillsdale, NJ: Lawrence Erlbaum Associates, pp. 577–596.

Taylor, M. (2009). Civil society as a rhetorical public relations process. In Heath, R. L., Toth, E. L., and Waymer, D. (Eds.), *Rhetorical and critical approaches to public relations II*. New York: Routledge, pp. 76–109.

Toth, E. L. and Heath, R. L. (1992). *Rhetorical and critical approaches to public relations.* Hillsdale, NJ: Lawrence Erlbaum Associates.

Weick, K. E. (1987). Theorizing about organizational communication. In Jablin, F. M., Putnam, L. L., Roberts, K. H., and Porter L. W. (Eds.), *Handbook of organizational communication.* Newbury Park, CA: Sage, pp. 97–122.

;E OF HYBRIDITY

Globalization and the Modern Western Paradigm

Aleš Debeljak

It almost appears obscene to speak about culture during the time of the global financial, economic, and political crisis. But I persist in my intention. And I can give at least two reasons in justification of it.

The first is my conviction that, whereas an exchange of products of cultural creativity sustains a human community, it is life in a community that gives temporary meaning to our search for a better, more sophisticated, and more complete experience of reality. Each and every individual needs to search for meaning within overlapping cultural frameworks, sparkling—even if deceptively—with the thrilling beauty of our living present, the better to resist the alluring grip of banality.

The second reason is that I know, think, and sense that culture is not just a more or less convenient tool for increasing the gross national or municipal income: it is much more than that. Culture is an open space of play and criticism, imagination, and meditation. It is precisely within this open space that many particular experiences and collective visions fertilize and permeate each other, come into contact, and engage with each other, thus producing the norms of life and specific ideas about human beings, personal fulfillment and life, old age and death. Culture is in fact a grand laboratory of meaning.

But, as I do not intend to split academic hairs, I will be straightforward. What I have in mind when I say *culture* are those specificities that characterize a certain group in a certain time and space, and I use *civilization* to refer to the ideas and technologies that are not tied to one group but are transferable in time and space. In this regard, culture becomes rejuvenated by feeding on locally binding principles of thought and action, whereas civilization propels itself by improving inventions and testing their general applicability. In his *Modernity at Large*, Appadurai (1996) suggests as much by interpreting the work of imagination as a social force.

Each and every culture is based on a selection from a large, although not arbitrary, catalogue of narrative possibilities and stocks of meaning. In a culture thus perceived, the products of intellectual creativity as well as material achievements and religious ceremonies, dining habits, and lyrical monologues should find their legitimate place. Something else should be kept in mind, too: people's ability to occupy successfully the most varied niches of a living space is inseparable from their ability to perceive differences and attribute meaning to them (Appadurai, 1996).

It is precisely difference that is crucial for individual or collective self-awareness, if not self-confidence. Every shaping of identity depends on a difference—between me and the others, my family and another family, my neighborhood and the one at the other side of the city, not to mention between peoples and nations. A difference established by setting a limit, *finis*, always de-fines an individual, that is, determines and delimits her.

The basic principle of affiliation can be implemented only by inventing, maintaining, and shifting differences. Differences repeatedly establish and shift borders between *us* and *them*, be they regional, national, linguistic, or religious communities, or contemporary "urban tribes." Bauman's pair of conceptual metaphors *mixophilia* and *mixophobia* graphically illustrate such relationships in global contexts as they refer to the ways in which the city prompts the feelings of tolerance toward and fear of strangers (Bauman, 2007). Viewed from this perspective, it becomes clear that cultures, understood as systems of lived collective experiences, do not become alike or automatically uniform even if, and when, the economic circumstances of diverse living worlds become similar. Even modern information and communication technologies, which presumably represent a supreme realization of universal and global applicability, are, after all, included in particular living worlds and local communities in different manners adjusted to specific local circumstances. It is under the specific local circumstances that individuals communicate, discovering new sources of affiliation and attraction, if not solidarity (Habermas, 2001).

Modern technologies and ideas that are for better or worse used today by all communities around the globe, although in different ways, stem from the modern Western paradigm. Let me hasten to specify the claim: the contemporary package of narratives and tools by which we manage human experience that governs contemporary world was indeed born in Western Europe, but it is no longer in the exclusive possession of Western Europeans. Literally all peoples of the planet reach into this package, in various and frequently clashing and controversial manners.

The Package of Modern Ideas

The global expansion of the package of Western modernity was set in motion when Europe first established a link with the Americas. The early globalization process began when the Genoan sailor in the service of the Spanish king "discovered the new world" on his sixteenth-century transatlantic voyage to India. Globalization and modernity therefore wear the same shoes necessary to make a big leap into the unknown.

Western modernity, or the mindset of the era that was born through the midwifery of the Renaissance, humanism, Protestantism and capitalism, was actually marked by a revolutionary event: human authority replaced divine authority, human reason took the place of collective faith, and the power of a better argument gradually prevailed over hereditary privileges.

Whereas medieval Europe exacted unconditional observance of Christian dogma and the rules of the Church as the sole road to truth in the "divine order," different approaches to the search for truth gained ground under the umbrella of modernity. These were relative approaches that stemmed from the rational logic of trial and error, empirical observation, and mathematical calculation (Gellner, 1988).

The skeptical individual mind is clearly observable in, say, seventeenth-century Dutch culture. There, the defining feature of the dominant value system was anti-clericalism and anti-feudalism. No wonder: it was based on Protestant resistance to the Pope's theology and the politics of the then recently departed Spanish occupying forces. It also drew on self-confidence gained by reclaiming valuable land from the waves of the North Sea by building ingenious dams. To use the defiant folk saying: "God created the world, but the Dutch created the Netherlands." Amsterdam and other Dutch ports rapidly integrated into the transatlantic exchange of military, economic, cultural, and political products between the "old" and the "new world," and, in contrast to Spain, equally rapidly developed the capitalist principles of operation.

What does this mean? To put it simply but not incorrectly: instead of asking whether this or that thing was the will of God, the Dutch merchants and sailors rather wanted to know whether this or that thing "worked." Such a functional perception of the world could not but give birth to the recognitions that are the backbone of modern social practices: instead of suppressing diverse opinions and standpoints differing from one's own, it is more profitable to adopt a generally tolerant attitude.

To illustrate the traditional, monolithic "worldview" that dominated medieval Europe, it is perhaps sufficient to draw attention to the fact that artists of that time were not seen by their communities as being much different from skillful and mainly anonymous craftsmen, who, understandably, did not "create from nothing," as modern (particularly Romantic) tradition teaches us. In medieval times, the ability for *creatio ex nihilo* had to remain reserved for the absolute source of authority: God.

Christianity began to lose the status of absolute norm as early as the Renaissance and humanism. The educational curriculum based on a new interest in Greek and Roman authors grew from the belief that it had been

ancient (pagan) writers rather than medieval Christian scholars who represented the peak of human achievement. Although Petrarch and Boccaccio, the
pioneers of humanism, had not read much of old Greek texts, nor had they
spoken fluent classical Latin, their enthusiasm for ancient writers spread across
the old continent like prairie fire.

When the fall of Constantinople in 1453 brought an end to the Eastern
Christian, or Byzantine, Empire, many Greek-speaking Constantinopolites
found refuge in Italian city-states. Not only were they skilled speakers of
Greek, but they also brought with them many ancient manuscripts. The
ancient Greek and Latin curriculum received new impetus and was formalized
in such a way that in the sixteenth century classical Latin rather than medieval
Latin became the language of spoken and written communication among educated Europeans.

The studies of classical works, *respublica litteraria*, consisted of prescribed
subjects that were uniform across Europe and thus greatly contributed to
the emergence and reinforcement of a kind of solidarity among the educated
elites. Their thoughts, descriptions, and criticism of the world were no longer
dependent on *respublica christiana* alone, as they could turn to classical sources
for inspiration.

The emerging rejection of the absolute Christian norm came to light in
literary work. Boccaccio's *Decameron* and Petrarch's *Canzoniere* are among the
best examples of literature written in the Italian vernacular, dealing with popular topics of everyday life, love and eroticism, adventures on the open road, and
carnal insights in kitchens. In other words, the medieval world was reshaped
into the modern world through the symbolical adoption of diverse experiences
and stylization of lived attitudes.

By the end of the fifteenth century, Gutenberg's new invention, mov-
able type printing, made possible the publication of all accessible old Greek
and Latin texts, previously available only as manuscripts. European printers'
hunger for new and preferably popular products increased their interest in
authors writing in the vernaculars and dealing with popular subjects. In the
early sixteenth century, around 2,000 printing works across Europe encouraged and enabled the vertiginous diffusion of ideas, including revolutionary
ones. By that time, books by François Rabelais, Geoffrey Chaucer, and other
authors writing in the vernaculars had already accounted for the majority of all
published works (Jameson and Miyoshi, 1988: 222).

One trait shared by the best among these texts was that, although religious
in tone and perhaps even in intention, they nevertheless placed man as the
center of attention. Man, not God, became the main subject of description,
doubts, and criticism.

The anxious lure of freedom into which modern man ventured, and
not without shuddering excitement, was perhaps most lucidly explored by
Machiavelli and Luther. Each came, in his unique way, to the far-reaching

realization that the site of ethical living was no longer a community but an individual. The fragile balance of power in national affairs and the fragile balance of soul in human relations; both describe the developmental trends of Western modernity, Machiavelli in the name of national interests and Luther in the name of personal liberation.

The first condition for such a perception of the world was the separation of the Church from the state (Gellner, 1988: 93–100). In modern states, it is a constitution and legislation, not the doctrines of one religious community or another that determine the basic frameworks of coexistence in a public space. The process through which this separation was accepted led the Christians of various denominations across post-Renaissance Europe, where secular states gradually gained ground, to recognize a new principle. It is the principle of relative autonomy enjoyed by various value spheres in modernity (science, arts, ethics, religion). This is to say that, in modernity, scientific rules cannot be applied within the religious sphere without inflicting serious cognitive harm, and, by the same token, the sphere of art cannot be required to observe the religious principles of operation.

Whereas the Renaissance, humanism, Protestantism, and capitalism destroyed the metaphysical unity of the Christian world, *compleat mapa mundi*, it was the twins of Enlightenment and the French Revolution that provided the legal framework of the modern paradigm. It has to be said, though, that this rather conventional narrative has been challenged in both its Eurocentric and multiculturalist aspects, for example, by Marshall G. S. Hodgson. He argues that the ligature between Ancient Greeks and the Renaissance, including the modern times, is practically an optical illusion. Global and thus Asia-centered history can better locate the European experience in the shared histories of humanity (Hodgson, 1993).

Still: finding incentive in a fresh example of successful and complete change—the liberation of 13 American colonies from the British crown—France set the new rules of the game with the Declaration of the Rights of Man and of the Citizen, altogether unimaginable during the feudal *ancien régime*. The missionaries of the Enlightenment saw the world as based no longer on the privileges arising from blue blood and Church traditions, but on the equality of all before national law. Instead of the God-blessed monarchy, the secular state and its representative government, a parliament, became the main organizers of social life.

Civilization and Barbarism

Modern Western civilization, born as it was out of the pains of revolution is, naturally, far from being internally monolithic. This holds true, too, when it is compared with other civilizations. The late American professor, Samuel

Huntington (1996), famously saw the world as a "clash of civilizations," with the clash between the modern West and Islam presumably being in the foreground.

Yet such a perception of the world is based on a wrong assumption. The underlying error of the idea about the clash of civilizations is the premise that civilizations behave like countries. Civilizations, however, do not have material power or control over a territory, and they do not behave like singular "players."

A much more appropriate representation of a civilization is to imagine it as a cognitive framework or a package of ideas. And ideas have always traveled. Well before modern times, numerous Asian, African, and European peoples were regularly interacting and intermingling with each other. Their encounters rank among the most effective agents of change in world history, spreading technologies, ideas, beliefs, and values (Bentley, 1993).

Think of the ideas relating to law, philosophy, and politics developed by the ancient Greeks and Romans. Their huge influence on the modern West cannot be ignored. It can be observed far beyond the time and space of the community that first developed and integrated them successfully in its symbolic economy. The Armenians, Jews, Persians, Egyptians, and other peoples eagerly utilized these ideas for centuries, long after their originators had disappeared under the ruins of collapsed empires.

Borders among civilizations are neither clear-cut nor sharp. Rather, they are shifting and permeable demarcation lines traversed by the processes of cross-fertilization and cross-stimulation, acceptance and rejection. Civilizations are invariably in contact, in communication and in conflict, but by no means solely in conflict. For this reason, no civilization is "pure." All civilizations are "impure" and "hybrid." Buzan and Segal, authors of the insightful *Anticipating the Future* (Buzan and Segal, 1998) argue along similar lines as they stress that what is important about our age becomes apparent only when we view the present both as a product of the past and as the maker of the future.

In principle, all civilizations are reluctant when it comes to accepting shocking ideas that are in conflict with the dominant opinion and manner of behavior, but most absorb the inventions that promise to reinforce power, prosperity, and prestige. They differ precisely in their abilities to recognize the promises of freedom that emerge from the fertile communication between "local" and "foreign" inventions.

Skeptics are particularly numerous among the ranks of those who would like to place an equation mark between Christianity and modern Europe. The test of "authenticity" is quick and painless for anybody educated in a Western tradition: try to calculate your monthly salary using Roman numerals! Everyone will agree that this would be an awkward and time-consuming task. The expedient elegance of arabic numerals is much better. Along with the decimal system, it is an indispensable component of modern Western literacy. Make no mistake: I refer to a specific form of literacy that is particular to the modern West.

In the shaping of this specific form, Muslims played a pivotal role. The medieval Muslim reign stretched to the African and European Mediterranean in the west and to Iran, India, and China in the east. There, Muslims picked these symbols from Indian mathematicians. They brought them to Moorish Europe in the tenth century. The Western languages pay tribute by gratefully naming them "arabic numerals," although the Arabs themselves do not conceal their origin and call them "Hindu numerals." Hybridity here comes to light in a most graphic way, even though it is admittedly limited to the European collective imaginaries.

Nevertheless, when the modern West detached itself from its home anchorage by colonizing the Americas, a certain global process was set in motion. The colonists indeed arrived to the new coasts under the flag of belligerent Christianity, but they were already the children of revolutionary times. It is therefore no wonder that the globalization processes were driven by both the warrior's sword and the writer's pen. No doubt, Hernán Cortés and other conquistadores committed genocide of aboriginal peoples in the name of Christian superiority. However, other Christians, too, disembarked in the new world, bravely rejecting crime and meticulously cataloging atrocities in the name of equality of all peoples, both "civilized" Europeans and "barbarian" natives.

Bartolomé de las Casas, a contemporary of Columbus and later the first bishop of Chiapas, Mexico, arrived in Cuba as a young dandy eager for a quick profit. However, horrified at the dreadful torturing of the locals, he joined the Dominican order and then determinedly condemned colonialism and racism in *A Short Account of the Destruction of the Indies* (1552; de las Casas, 1992), which was eagerly read across Europe at that time. It is Hernán Cortés and Bartolomé de las Casas together who represent the true, that is, the Janus face of modern Western civilization.

This also means that the power of the modern West lies precisely in a skeptical reflection and reasoned critique that gave birth to a far-reaching recognition that has been repeatedly confirmed by history and, in a particularly painful manner, by the totalitarian twentieth century. Theodore H. von Laue approaches the dynamics of the twentieth century from a new perspective by proposing that the world revolution of Westernization has caused the global violence and major warfare of this century. The Siamese twins that painfully grimace into our bewildered faces today are the expansion of modern Western paradigm and the emergence of global interdependence. The global impact of these forces was severe as:

> robbed of their past freedom to go their own ways politically and culturally, non-Western peoples were subjected to a world order that perpetuated or

even deepened their helplessness. Henceforth equality could be attained only on the terms imposed by the West.

(von Laue, 1987: 4)

The Global Framework of the Modern West

The ideas conceived by the modern West are today global ideas in good and bad ways. The processes of the first globalization during the imperial sixteenth century, the second globalization during the colonial nineteenth century, and the third globalization in the corporate twenty-first century changed the world dramatically. All national groups and cultural traditions on the planet have become interdependent through the exchange of ideas and information, people and capital, goods and services.

In the course of these processes, the ideas of the modern West turned into a general framework that today governs the reasoning and operation of the contemporary world. Why do I talk about a package? Because it is not a supermarket from which one could select arbitrarily. Modernization and westernization of individual societies are Siamese twins. Those societies that had rejected the important elements of the package sooner or later encountered great obstacles, for example, the Soviet Union yesterday or North Korea today.

What does this package include? For a start, it includes the basic notions of time and space. Consider: years and longer time units are measured by the Gregorian calendar formulated in the sixteenth century by Western (Latin) Christianity. Hours and smaller time units are measured by a clock, a mechanical device based on the use of weights and transfer of force discovered by Muslim engineers in Moorish Europe and adapted to public use by the Latin Christian monks in the late Middle Ages. Gerard Mercator, a Renaissance cartographer from the Netherlands, substantially improved the spatial representation of the world through the invention of a globe. After initial resistance, which lasted a good 100 years, Mercator's projection was accepted within the Ottoman Empire, then the most powerful non-European power, and then elsewhere across the Islamic Middle East. Today, such understanding of time and space seems self-evident everywhere.

The package also includes political geography. Borders between countries must and can be drawn, and a demarcation line should be technically precise, which inevitably influences the feelings of group affiliation and membership. Such an organization of life naturally required symbolical narratives that could be used by people in their collective search for common good.

The modern West invented a number of such narratives. Among them are representative government and the rule of law, the separation of church and state, freedom of speech, media and association, nationalism and liberalism, individualism and human rights, but clericalism and communism, Nazism and fascism as well. During the colonial era, the package was transplanted, virtually in full, to the Americas and Australia. Elsewhere in the world, even the most stubborn local elites have been compelled to accept it to be able to participate in administration or gain independence.

After the end of the Cold War and the collapse of communism in the late twentieth century, capitalism, which was developed by the modern West, indisputably became the global system (Wallerstein, 1984). We have no grounds for doubting its worldwide presence. By contrast, we have good grounds for doubting its alleged responsibility for the division of the planet into the "West and the rest" (Scruton, 2003).

The idea about the two opposing camps containing all humankind is certainly appealing. The politically progressive advocates of a different, supposedly more just world find this simple division attractive because it creates room for accusatory moralizations and criticism of the exploitative West. The reactionary advocates of the clash of civilizations, from which it is the West that emerges as the threatened side, find an irresistible lure in its potential for inspiring exercises in open arrogance and hypocritical contempt for all non-Western peoples, nations, and cultures.

Westernistic Civilization

Instead of subscribing to the ideology that views the world through the fixed lens of conflict between "the West and the rest," we should try a theory that looks onto the world through the flexible lens of "Westernistic civilization."

What is involved here? I shall make use of an analogy between Hellenistic and Westernistic civilizations. In much the same way as classical Greece cannot be equated with Hellenic civilization, the modern West is not the same as Westernistic civilization (Buzan and Segal, 1988). Until the fourth century BC and the twilight of city-states, classical Greek civilization had remained within the territorial borders of the south Balkans. Similarly, the civilization of Latin Christianity or the traditional West had been firmly rooted in the western countries of Europe until the advent of modernity.

Hellenistic civilization after Alexander the Great emanated from classical Greek heritage, but territorially it stretched across practically the entire "old world," reaching to Egypt, India, Tajikistan, and Afghanistan. In the same way, Westernistic civilization arising from the modern Western heritage today comprises the entire known world.

A special fusion of Middle Eastern and Indo-Iranian cultural traditions on the one hand, and ancient Greek tradition on the other, gave rise to such forms of collective life in which the essence of classical Greek tenets represented only the backbone rather than the entire social body. Alexander the Great systematically expanded the borders of his multinational empire and borders in the minds of his multicultural subjects. He encouraged "mixed marriages" between the Greek colonists and locals with the same fervor with which he supported laboratory experiments and the merging of Greek and local technologies and ideologies.

Westernistic civilization, too, has a hybrid nature. The backbone of the basic package of ideas arises from the heritage of the modern West, but its many ribs extend to all sides of the planet, as various communities in various parts of the world adjust these ideas in their singular ways while taking into account local specificities. Elections provide an illustrative example: this form of representative democracy is today practiced in virtually all countries of the world, although we will readily agree that this process is not equally free and honest across the board.

In ancient Greece, individual identity was determined by the politics of a city-state. It embodied the center of the world. For this reason, the ancient Greeks engaging in trading and military expeditions, and especially those in overseas colonies, always invoked their homeland, their home city or *metropolis*. In Hellenistic civilization, the ethnic origin of a person was not an issue worthy of much attention. After all, ancient Greek ideas were carried to the outside world by the army under the command of a Macedonian.

Within this extensive empire that stretched across three continents, in which the journeys between regional capitals could take several years, the need for just one center gradually diminished. The idea of a metropolis was replaced with the idea about a world city or *cosmopolis*. It transcended local citizenship and offered an answer to the new need for diverse identities, obligations and loyalty. Instead of exclusive patriotic feelings incorporated in the ancient Greek differentiation between "the home and the world," the inclusive Hellenistic cosmopolitanism expresses the paradox of global awareness: "the world is the home."

Diverse identities of peoples and places in Westernistic civilization are perhaps best expressed in cosmopolises such as Marseilles and Milan, London and Lisbon, Berlin and Barcelona. All of these cities are historically and geographically rooted in the countries of the traditional West, but they have included in their symbolic and actual economy many non-Western elements. From fast food to intoxicating music, from stirring fashion styles to exciting social customs, "local" and "foreign" elements merge on this street corner and in that business office, producing new synthetic products and hybrid ideas.

A similar process has been taking place beyond the traditional West: megalopolises such as Sydney and Saigon, Cairo and Kuala Lumpur, Mexico City and Manila are the laboratories of diverse identities, where transport and trade, science and industry, communication and weaponry are unmistakably of modern Western provenance, but every local environment uses them in accordance with its own prejudices, needs, capacities, and resources. Appadurai considers the way images—of lifestyles, popular culture, and self-representation—circulate internationally through the media and are often borrowed in surprising (to their originators) and inventive ways (Appadurai, 1996).

Ancient Greek, the lingua franca of the Hellenized world, gathered many local accents and underwent (not necessarily subtle) adaptations through the babble of tribes and peoples, soldiers and diplomats, merchants and pilgrims. This process is not unlike the one currently experienced by English in the globalized capitalism of modern Westernistic civilization, as various groups and individuals make use of it in their (not necessarily subtle) exchange of ideas, goods, and services.

Westernistic civilization therefore does not imply one Western model that is uniformly imposed all over the planet in the same manner. This is the assumption of those critics who advocate the division into the "West and the rest," explaining the processes of cultural exchange as a blind alley at the end of which the victorious thief (the West) empties the purses of all the rest.

The notion of Westernistic civilization carries a cognitively different, even if politically unpromising, content. It is actually a two-way street accommodating a lively trade in ideologies and technologies that the modern West invented but no longer holds in its sole possession. This is a defining feature of globalization that Roland Robertson, one of the foremost sociologists of globalization, describes in terms of "particularisation of the universal and the universalisation of the particular" (Robertson, in Jameson and Miyoshi, 1998: xi).

To use a different illustration: the globalized ideas and technologies of the modern West are like sewing patterns that define the basic rules of clothes making but do not dictate the thickness of the material, the motif, or the color of seams.

Perhaps the most illustrative example of Westernistic civilization is Japan. The land of the rising sun began to absorb Western ideas more than a century ago, accepting administrative, military, and industrial procedures of the modern Western type. Not only did this enable it to avoid the fate of becoming a Western colony, but it itself became a regional colonial force. It uses the package of modern Western ideas in its own unique way, in accordance with thoughtful selection and adaptation, while steadily taking into account local cultural traditions.

Japan turned certain fruits of such hybridization into profitable export items. For pundits, these are anime and manga, for ordinary people karaoke and karate, and for business elites industrial miniaturization, just-in-time delivery, and the mass production of low-price high-quality electronic products. The secret of Japan's global success lies precisely in its ability to combine Western and local ideas creatively.

However, it is not possible to overlook the fact that many people at many corners of the planet seriously fear globalization. Unfortunately, the one-sided exposure of destructive consequences of global trade in services, products, and goods is frequently grist to the mill of popular fears, searches for scapegoats, and mass paranoia. A terrified mind cannot help but perceive globalization as a flood threatening to sweep away diverse and special cultural traditions.

A closer look will show that many critics of globalization unfortunately only point their moralist fingers and turn up their refined noses at one or other internationally popular style, be it teenage hip hop or Madonna's exuberant dance steps, Hollywood kitsch or hard-boiled detective movies. To be more precise: the critics of globalization frequently use cultural diversity and defense of collective (national) identities as a kind of smoke screen. It usually conceals some other agenda: in most cases, it is romantic anti-capitalism that is close to leftist zeal, or modern anti-Americanism nourishing right-wing litanies.

The actual globalization processes are controversial and complex, but the international exchange of ideas and technologies, symbols and methods of operation increases and broadens cultural diversity. If culture is understood as a laboratory of meaning, on which individual communities feed, then we have to accept the flexible process of adaptation and resistance, transformations and hybridity, in which the border between the "domestic" and the "foreign" evaporates like the smell of cheap petrol.

References

Appadurai, A. (1996). *Modernity at large: Cultural dimensions of globalization*. Minneapolis: University of Minnesota Press.

Bauman, Z. (2007). *Liquid times: Living in an age of uncertainty*. Cambridge: Polity Press.

Bentley, J. H. (1993). *Old world encounters: Cross-cultural contacts and exchanges in pre-modern times*. Oxford: Oxford University Press.

Buzan, B. and Segal, G. G. (1998). *Anticipating the future*. London: Simon & Schuster.

de las Casas, B. (1992). *A short account of the destruction of the Indies*. London: Penguin Books.

Gellner, E. (1988). *Plough, sword and book: The structure of human history*. London: Paladin.

Habermas, J. (2001). *The postnational constellation*. Cambridge: Polity Press.

Hodgson, M. G. S. (1993). *Rethinking world history: Essays on Europe, Islam and world history*. Cambridge: Cambridge University Press.

Huntington, S. (1996). *The Clash of Civilisations*. New York: Simon & Schuster.

Jameson, F. and Miyoshi, M. (Eds.). (1998). *The cultures of globalization*. Durham, NC: Duke University Press.

von Laue, T. (1987). *The world revolution of westernization: The twentieth century in global perspective*. New York: Oxford University Press.

Scruton, R. (2003). *The West and the rest: Globalization and the terrorist threat*. London: Continuum.

Wallerstein, I. (1984). *The politics of the world economy: The states, the movements and the civilizations*. Cambridge: Cambridge University Press.

4

A PUBLIC RELATIONS FRAMEWORK FOR INDIGENOUS ENGAGEMENT

Judy Motion, Jarrod Haar, and Shirley Leitch

Integrating indigenous communicative principles, protocols and practices is a complex and challenging task for public relations professionals in bicultural and multicultural nations. Within this chapter, we examine the potential of an engagement orientation for indigenous public relations efforts and suggest some approaches for appropriately navigating the complexities of indigenous cultures. Engagement is a core concept for a public relations philosophy grounded in notions of mutually beneficial relationships (Heath, 1994, 1997, 2001), which takes into account the multiple assumptions, values, emotions, beliefs and visions that publics—including indigenous publics—may hold. Mutually beneficial relationships evolve from engagement processes that involve publics in agenda setting (deciding which issues are important), decision making (determining which views ought to prevail) and policy formation (setting the context for action). Engagement processes must be explicitly designed to address issues of power and cultural differences in order to be mutually beneficial. Integrating indigenous communicative principles, protocols and practices, we contend, is therefore a challenging but vital task for public relations professionals seeking authentic and respectful engagement in bicultural and multicultural contexts. We draw upon examples from the Maori culture of the indigenous people of New Zealand to illustrate some of key principles of engagement between Western and indigenous cultures in one national context.[1] Maori use the term *whanaungatanga* to encompass communication that is oriented towards creating shared outcomes and constructing shared understandings (Bishop, 1996). As Mead (2003) highlighted, this important concept emphasises reciprocity and is, we suggest, closely aligned with the engagement principle of mutually beneficial relationships. Introducing *whanaungatanga* into public relations practice is therefore one answer to Holtzhausen's (2000) call for a more socially, culturally and politically contextualised form of public relations and to Cheney and Christensen's (2001: 182) question 'what would a non-western, non-managerial and nonrationalist form of public relations look like?'

In response to these challenges, we theorise culture as a political, strategic and positional concept and draw upon Curtin and Gaither (2005: 17), who argued that power is a central concern for public relations practice. Curtin and Gaither (2005) provided a theoretical framework for the discursive processes of constructing cultural meanings, which saw public relations practitioners as 'cultural intermediaries' operating within a 'circuit of culture' model. This discursive intermediary role for practitioners was earlier identified by Motion and Leitch (1996, 2009) as a form of 'discourse technology'—a term developed by Fairclough (1992) to explain how public relations is centrally involved in effecting social and cultural transformations. The work undertaken by public relations professionals may facilitate the achievement of socio-cultural objectives that may or may not serve the interests of indigenous peoples (Motion and Leitch, 1996, 2009). That is, public relations professionals may engage with indigenous peoples to co-produce and circulate alternative discourses or they may work to suppress such alternative discourses. Our research agenda is guided by the postcolonial work of Said (2003: xiv), who critiqued 'the difference between the will to understand for purposes of co-existence and humanistic enlargement of horizons, and the will to dominate for the purposes of control and external domination'. The aim here is to advocate for public relations processes and practices that serve to empower indigenous people.

Sriramesh (2009: 47) warned that in a rapidly globalising world public relations will ignore culture at its peril. An emerging feature of public relations engagement with indigenous people is the globalising and potentially empowering influence of social media. The rise of social media makes the suppression of ideas increasingly difficult. We draw on the recent work of Castells (2009: 36), who conceptualises culture as 'a set of values and beliefs that inform, guide, and motivate people's behaviour.' Castells's (2009) work is especially salient because it is crucial that communication with indigenous people be considered in the contemporary context of the global networked society as well as in more traditional terms. Heterogeneity and fragmentation are significant characteristics of globalised network societies and, Castells suggests, 'protocols of communication between different cultures are the critical issue for the network society, since without them there is not society; just dominant networks and resisting communes' (Castells, 2009: 37). Thus, the public relations perspective adopted in this chapter is grounded in a discursive perspective that acknowledges fundamental power relations that underpin communicative efforts—what Castells (2009) refers to as 'communication power'. Our agenda is to construct a cultural public relations framework in order to facilitate 'power-sharing' (Castells, 2009: 52). We define power sharing as a breaking down of the boundaries of organisational discourses in order to make respectful space for indigenous principles, protocols and practices and to advocate for a more influential role for indigenous peoples in society. We offer general insights into the dynamics of indigenous public relations work but specifically focus on one indigenous people, the New Zealand Maori. Lessons from New Zealand—*Aotearoa*—may be applicable for the wider global community, particularly in relation to engagement. However, we emphasise that there is no single 'indigenous culture', and indeed there are significant cultural differences within the various tribal and family groupings within Maori. Given the global need for a more sophisticated understanding of indigenous cultures we identify a significant gap in the public relations literature in this area. First, we theorise the cultural intermediary work involved in indigenous community engagement as a mode of public relations and, second, we offer a public relations framework for indigenous engagement.

Public Relations Engagement

The development of equitable, meaningful communication processes requires openness to cultural differences, and flexibility in response to different cultural priorities and protocols. Policy, organisational and public interests need to be balanced or reconciled with indigenous interests. Public relations communication strategies may include:

1 public information campaigns, which are an asymmetrical, one-way mode of conveying organisational perspectives and knowledge;
2 public consultation, which is a mode of providing or soliciting information and researching public opinion (Motion and Leitch, 1996); and
3 public engagement, which is a form of dialogical exchange and negotiation (Rowe and Frewer, 2005).

Engagement should not be conflated with dialogical approaches. As noted above, mutually beneficial relationships emerge from *whanaungatanga*, from engagement processes that involve indigenous people and communities in agenda setting, decision making and policy formation. The communication design process needs to address and resolve issues of power to the satisfaction of all those engaging. Thus, co-design and co-organization of the engagement process (see Powell and Colin, 2008) and potentially the co-production of solutions must be embarked upon (see Bovaird, 2007).

Public relations engagement processes may be deployed to enable organisations to gain a better understanding of issues of importance to indigenous peoples, as well as to manage or resolve such issues. However, our observation in a New Zealand context has been that, too often, public relations campaigns that involve communicating with indigenous people often concentrate on promoting the interests of governments and organisations by simply reinterpreting these interests in more culturally palatable ways. The challenge, then, is to move beyond this culturally attuned public information or consultation model to facilitate meaningful engagement with indigenous people. Engagement is not, however, a panacea for the multiple issues that may confront indigenous people and communities. Systemic societal change that involves power sharing is required.

The fundament question of how to develop meaningful engagement processes that facilitate power sharing, equitable participation and mutually beneficial outcomes forms the focus of this chapter.

Indigenous Contexts: Contemporary Challenges

Experiences of colonization, discrimination, severe socio-economic disadvantage, lower standards of living and health, and struggles for recognition are variously shared by indigenous peoples (Durie, 2003). International attention has more recently been focused on indigenous struggles to publicise issues, to advance opportunities and to claim the right to self-determination and sovereignty, which Maori refer to as *tino rangatiratanga* (Walker, 2004). The establishment of the *United Nations Permanent Forum on Indigenous Issues* in 2002 (Durie, 2003) has provided a global space for discussion of grievances, aspirations and development issues. Indigeneity, Durie (2003) suggests, has shifted from remonstration to negotiation as a shift in opinion and opportunities for reconciliation are opening up. The emerging global, moral imperative to act in a culturally inclusive way when engaging with indigenous people can create anxiety for those who are uninformed and may undermine efforts to communicate. It is therefore essential to establish collaborative approaches that ensure that Western organizational communication practices create spaces for and are compatible with indigenous approaches. Culturally compatible approaches evolve from mutual understanding and positive interaction.

Identifying how to communicate and engage with indigenous people may, however, be challenging for those who are unaccustomed to stepping outside Western cultural perspectives. Common problems may be as basic as not being able to identify whom to communicate with or how indigenous cultural groups are organised. For example, during a public policy engagement process, public relations practitioners wishing to communicate with Maori will not find one single individual who represents the community. Depending upon the issue involved, they will need to engage with a number of social groupings including traditional tribal affiliations, community groups, urbanised individuals or members of indigenous organisations and corporations. From a traditional Maori perspective, social grouping affiliation is linked to *whanau* (family; members are all relatives), *hapu* (kinship; extended family groups) and *iwi* (people, nation) (Mead, 2003). However, urbanisation has isolated many from traditional groupings and there is an extensive, widespread international diaspora. Maori thus shift between traditional and contemporary identities and groupings, and public relations professionals need to understand and flexibly respond to identity shifts and dynamic, possibly ambiguous social groupings in order to engage effectively. They must also take account of multiple viewpoints. Just as there is no individual who speaks for Maori, there is no single viewpoint that represents all Maori. In addition, although traditionally indigenous cultures and knowledge have been orally transmitted, they are not static. The dynamic nature of indigeneity means that the multiplicity of viewpoints within Maoridom is constantly evolving.

Recently, there has been a strong growth in Maori culture, in particular with language undergoing a renaissance: 24 per cent of Maori can hold an everyday conversation in *Te Reo Maori* (Maori language) (Statistics New Zealand, 2007). Such a renaissance has lead Maori researchers to reiterate the importance of understanding *Te Aro Maori* (the Maori world), and recognising and valuing Maori *tikanga* (customs) and traditions (Harris, 2007; Walker, 2006).

Indigenous cultures are often characterised as collective and cooperative. There have been many cross-cultural studies that have unveiled significant differences between different countries (e.g. Hill et al., 2004; Spector et al., 2007). Spector and colleagues (2007) noted that an important difference between nations is the level of collectivism or individualism. Societies that are concerned with one's self and immediate family are considered to be individualist, as they focus on independence and personal achievement (Markus and Kitayama, 1998; Hofstede, 2009). Collectivist societies are typically focused on interconnectedness with extended family groups and a broader range of social networks (Spector et al., 2007; Markus and Kitayama, 1998; Hofstede, 2009). Collectivist regions include Asia, Latin America, eastern Europe and the Pacific Islands (Spector et al., 2007; Hofstede, 2009). Although North America and western European countries are most individualist, New Zealand—in which people of European descent constitute the majority of the population—is also considered to be an individualist country (Hofstede, 2009).

In contrast, New Zealand Maori are considered to be collectivist even though they live in a individualist society that was colonised by the British more than 150 years ago (Guthrie, 2001; Hofstede, 2001; Ratima and Grant, 2007). Ratima and Grant (2007) suggested that Maori base their individuality on a connection to the past, present and future generations, whereas the Europeans of New Zealand tend to base their individuality on freedom, autonomy and self-interest. Similarly, Hook, Waaka and Raumati (2007) suggest that the fundamental difference between New Zealand Europeans and Maori is perceptions of individuality. Although Maori, Asian and Pacific peoples are more collectivistic, they are also citizens and residents of an individualistic society (New Zealand). Thus, Maori, Asian and Pacific people are likely to vary in collectivistic tendencies. Engagement with indigenous groups in a context that situates a collectivistic culture in the midst of a dominant, individualistic setting clearly creates significant challenges for public relations practice.

In this chapter we emphasise authentic, inclusive engagement as a communicative process that is more appropriate for the collectivist orientations of indigenous peoples. In New Zealand, the task of engagement with Maori communities is generally delegated to either public relations consultancies that specialise in communicating with Maori communities or Maori employees who act as cultural intermediaries for organisations. Engagement processes are therefore more likely to take cultural considerations into account but, in order to be effective, the organisational contexts in which these processes operate must also be inclusive. In the following sections we examine the implications of indigenous principles, protocols and practices for successful and respectful public relations engagement.

Principles

An understanding of cultural principles provides an insight into the foundations that guide judgements about what is important and valued by indigenous communities. Despite the fact that principles vary across communities, they are an important indication of the belief and value systems that influence engagement processes. It is therefore essential for public relations professionals to identify and understand the principles that connect and unify an indigenous community or organisation so that efforts to engage are culturally appropriate.

Within New Zealand, Maori are referred to as *tangata whenua*—the people of the land. The commonly accepted use of this term establishes the first nation principle that Maori are the indigenous people and as such have rights protected in law. In New Zealand, the 1840 Treaty of Waitangi enshrined in legislation the rights of Maori. The Waitangi Tribunal is the legislative organisation that administers the Treaty of Waitangi. Four key principles underpin the Waitangi Tribunal interpretations of the treaty: 'the principle of active protection, the tribal right to self regulation, the right of redress of past breaches and the duty to consult' (Waitangi Tribunal, 2010).

Public relations professionals working in indigenous contexts need to understand and work within the legislative principles that guide interaction. In this instance, the duty to consult is a significant principle for all interactions with Maori. The intention is to ensure that Maori are recognised as 'custodians of the land', to guarantee a governance role and to draw on the knowledge of Maori. The duty to consult has been variously interpreted as the need to inform, to establish dialogue and to actively engage with Maori to co-produce solutions. Consultation has not always been a positive or productive experience for Maori—in many cases it has been perceived as an exploitative, superficial attempt to comply with legislation rather than an attempt to genuinely engage with Maori and co-produce solutions. Consultation processes have consumed

Maori resources and time; senior Maori leaders or *kaumata* have been expected to participate in consultation processes that do not reflect Maori principles or benefit Maori people. Such practices inherently function as power relations that serve to legitimise inherently unequal processes that disproportionately benefit the powerful. They also lead to cynicism amongst Maori who have experienced engagement as neither purposeful nor useful. Public relations practitioners must be aware that such practices engender a level of reluctance and suspicion towards engagement. However, Maori have actively resisted attempts to coopt them into tokenistic engagement; one common response has been to identify themselves as consultants and charge for their time. In doing so, Maori establish that their contributions have an economic value and reclaim some power in the relationship. Clegg and colleagues (2006: 364) suggest that, as new issues and agendas emerge, decision-making processes and power distribution will be challenged. Models of consultation or engagement should not act as strategies of exclusion or exploitation. Working within the cultural principles of indigenous peoples offers the opportunity to balance public relations, power relations and ethical practices. It means that the role of indigenous people as experts is acknowledged and respected. It means that there is a more equitable distribution of power in decision-making processes, and engagement may shift from a consultation model to a partnership model.

Protocols

Observing cultural protocols—the unwritten rules or guidelines that regulate conduct in certain situations—is essential for public relations-led engagement. For Maori, cultural protocols are derived from *tikanga*. Tikanga has a wide range of meanings (Gallagher, 2008) but generally refers to Maori culture, 'customary concepts' (Mead, 2003: 1) and related knowledges (Macalister, 2005). Durie (1996: 449) defined *tikanga* as the 'values, standards, principles or norms to which the Maori community generally subscribed for the determination of appropriate conduct'. Williams (1998: 2) explained that *tikanga* is 'the Maori way of doing things—from the very mundane to the most sacred or important fields of human endeavour'. Traditionally *tikanga* was communicated orally and governed Maori political, legal, social and spiritual behaviour (Gallagher, 2008). *Tikanga* may also be understood as a discourse about cultural concepts, values and beliefs that regulates what is right and moral, communicates the values that underpin such norms and values, and establishes appropriate Maori cultural practices.

The colonisation of Maori people led to a subjugation of their culture and beliefs (Mead, 2003; Smith, 1999). Gradually, a revival of Maori *tikanga* was driven by cultural events such as internationally acclaimed exhibitions of Maori art and the *waka tua* (war canoes), followed by various influences such as the establishment of the Waitangi Tribunal, a Maori language movement and the acknowledgement and acceptance of the role of *tikanga Maori* as a normative system in certain legislation (Mead, 2003). However, the revival and role of *tikanga Maori* in New Zealand society has been partial and often highly contested. Foucault (1980: 81) suggested we are now experiencing '*an insurrection of subjugated knowledges*' (italics in the original). The term *subjugated knowledges* had two meanings for Foucault. First it referred to 'historical contents that have been buried and disguised in a functionalist coherence or formal systemisation' (Foucault, 1980: 81) and second it referred to a set of knowledges that have been disqualified—*tikanga* may be understood as a subjugated knowledge in both senses. The insurrection and re-examination of subjugated knowledges or discourses, according to Foucault (1980), provides opportunities and scope for criticism and interrogation of the power relations at play. Indigenous systems of knowledge need to be integrated into engagement protocols in order to facilitate power sharing.

Within Maori culture, communication protocols are informed by *tikanga*. Mead (2003: 13) explained that 'concepts such as *tapu* (the state of being set apart), *mana* (prestige), *noa* (neutrality), *manaakitanga* (hospitality), *take* (cause), *utu* (reciprocation), *ea* (satisfaction) and many others' all play a part in explaining customary practice. The protocols (customs and ceremonies) inherent within *tikanga* are underpinned by the principles of *whanaungatanga*, *manaakitanga* and *aroha*. These principles focus on the relational aspects of interaction and guide the customs or protocol for engaging with others. The concept of *whanaungatanga*, which was introduced above, involves a sense of relationships and kinship and focuses on the notion of collective support and mutual obligations (Macalister, 2005; Mead, 2003). Individuals are supported by the group but the collective group also expects support. The implication for public relations is that engagement practices must incorporate and integrate these collective obligations. Indigenous engagement, therefore, is not a process of circulating key messages and achieving desired organisational outcomes; instead it is a process of fostering supportive collective relationships. Furthermore, engagement with Maori should also typically include *kaumatua* and *kuia*, the elders of Maori knowledge and lore; they are viewed as repositories of knowledge and likely to be strong gate keepers and providers of acceptance. Thus, indigenous engagement may require interacting with experienced elders well versed in *tikanga Maori* even when they lack contemporary knowledge about specific topics that public relation consultants might seek to address. Similarly, *manaakitanga* is concerned with nurturing relationships and looking after people (Macalister, 2005; Mead, 2003). It establishes a protocol of being very careful about how others are treated. For example, it is essential to ensure that visitors are treated hospitably and fed. Underpinning all engagement with others is the principle of *aroha*: love, respect, and compassion (Macalister, 2005; Mead, 2003). Understanding indigenous protocols may initially occur at a more superficial level that lacks conceptual depth, but an appreciation of the foundational relational principles will partially mitigate insensitivity and lack of understanding of the nuances and subtleties of cultural knowledge and protocols.

Practices

In order to understand how to engage with indigenous people it is necessary to understand the interrelationship between principles, protocol and communication practices. The ways in which indigenous people meet and congregate, the ways that they communicate and the ways that they make decisions need to form part of the co-design of engagement practices. Engagement practices may be developed from an understanding of the practices associated with a *marae*—a Maori meeting house or place.

> A marae is a place where Maori culture can be celebrated to the fullest extent, where the language can be spoken, where Maori can meet Maori, where intertribal obligations can be met, where the customs can be explored, practised, debated, continued or amended, and where necessary ceremonies—such as welcoming visitors or farewelling the dead—can be carried out.
>
> (Mead, 2003: 110)

Participation in decision making in a *marae* is decided according to *mana*; those with prestige speak first. A *koha* (gift/money) is given to the hosts, and meetings are opened with a *mihimihi*: information sharing about genealogy, connection to spaces and places and acknowledging relationships to those who are present (Scott and Du Plessis, 2008: 110). Maori have a tradition of oration, which may take the form of traditional speeches, blending mythical and contemporary story telling. The use of speeches and story telling in engagement processes has implications for public relations engagement processes: these approaches tend to be more one-sided in nature, but may be the catalyst for discussion. Within Maori culture, a *hui* or meeting adopts a consensus-based approach to decision making: differences of opinion are aired and discussed until a consensus is reached (Tremaine, 1990). Engagement may thus be a lengthy process. However, such an engagement process would be viewed as culturally acceptable to Maori, who are thus more likely to perceive the engagement process (and those undertaking it) in a favourable light, irrespective of the actual outcome.

Traditional ways of engagement and decision-making approaches shape and influence contemporary decision making. The Internet and digital technologies, with their potential for interactivity, offer interesting possibilities for organisations that seek increased engagement with indigenous people. It may be possible to create digital spaces that accommodate collectivist principles and power sharing. For example, in New Zealand the creation of a digital *marae* could amalgamate *tikanga* and *marae* protocol and practices and be readily available to local Maori and the international diaspora. The first issue that must be addressed if public relations professionals want to trial Internet and mobile engagement process is access to technology. According to the Ministry of Social Development (2009), in 2006 46.7 per cent of Maori had access to the Internet at home, compared with 70.4 per cent of European New Zealanders. This disparity is a serious concern. However, because Maori have a younger age profile, their use of technology is comparable to young European New Zealanders and they are making more extensive use of the Internet (Statistics New Zealand, 2007). Coleman and colleagues (2008) cautioned that a high level of usability is also important. Another potential issue is that online digital public engagement may emulate the more limited traditional deliberative democracy approaches (Wiklund, 2005) and simply function as one-off exercises that are restricted by the limited number of participants (Powell and Colin, 2008). Another issue to be considered is that younger Internet users are less politically engaged and more interested in entertainment (Coleman et al., 2008). Furthermore, as suggested above, young Maori may be less likely to be deeply set in and knowledgeable and about *tikanaga Maori* than elders—*kaumatua* and *kuia*—making digital engagement likely to be less culturally demanding. Online engagement approaches such as digital story telling and alternative reality gaming may serve to re-engage and empower Maori. Digital stories are personal reflections published on the Internet that make use of 'low-cost digital cameras' to create short multimedia stories (Meadows, 2003: 189). Alternative reality games are large-scale brainstorming tools that rely on technology and teamwork to solve puzzles, problems or create future scenarios and are characterised by a high level of interactivity and 'optionality' or multiple choices (McGonigal, 2006). An interesting result of large-scale alternative reality games is that participants sometimes take control of the game and decide how it will play out and what it means. Innovative approaches such as digital stories and alternative reality games have the potential to create a democratic 'cybercommons' or 'digital *marae*' that is highly usable and creates ongoing empowering opportunities for large-scale engagement processes, inspires young people and changes the way people engage through 'conversational media' (Couldry, 2008: 387). Consequently, technology may play a role in the process of engagement with indigenous people, providing them with greater control and autonomy to thus improve their participation and perception of the process.

Conclusion

The fundament question underpinning this chapter was how to develop meaningful engagement processes that facilitate power sharing, equitable participation and mutually beneficial outcomes forms. We have sought to offer public relations practitioners and scholars some insights into the challenges and complexities of engagement with indigenous people. Our intention was to emphasise the relational, people-oriented nature of cultural engagement and the need for genuine power sharing. To illustrate the potential of an engagement orientation we have drawn upon examples related to New Zealand Maori; in particular the concept of *whanaungatanga*. It is important to stress, however, that, although indigenous peoples share many challenges in relation to equity, the principles, protocols and practices that underpin their communication may differ substantially. Public relations practice must thus be firmly rooted in particular cultural contexts. A significant issue we identify, then, is the need to develop a culturally contextualised public relations practice. Such a practice will encompass both traditional and contemporary understandings of indigenous publics and engender culturally sensitive approaches to designing engagement processes. The collaborative, collectivist nature of indigenous publics means that engagement is neither quick nor straightforward. It requires openness to the multiple cultural principles that underpin an indigenous culture, adaptability and flexibility in the adoption of indigenous protocols and a commitment to engagement processes that genuinely inform and transform public policy and societal discourses.

Note

1 Jarrod Haar is Maori of Ngati Maniapoto and Ngati Mahuta descent; Judy Motion and Shirley Leitch are descended from European migrants to New Zealand.

References

Bishop, A. (1996). *Collaborative research stories: Whakawhanaungatanga*. Palmerston North, New Zealand: Dunmore Press.

Bovaird, T. (2007). Beyond engagement and participation: User and community coproduction of public services. *Public Administration Review*, 67(5), 846–860.

Castells, M. (2009). *Communication power*. New York: Oxford.

Cheney, G., and Christensen, L. T. (2001). Public relations as contested terrain: A critical response. In Heath, R. L. (Ed.) *Handbook of public relations*. Thousand Oaks, CA: Sage, pp. 167–182.

Clegg, S. R., Courpasson, D. and Phillips, N. (2006). *Power and organizations*. London: Sage.

Coleman, R., Leiber, P., Mendelson, A. L. and Kurpius, D. D. (2008). Public life and the internet: If you build a better website, will citizens become engaged? *New Media & Society*, 10(2), 179–201.

Couldry, N. (2008). Mediatization or mediation? Alternative understandings of the mergent space of digital story-telling. *New Media & Society*, 10(3), 373–391.

Curtin, P. A. and Gaither, T. K. (2005). *International public relations: Negotiating culture, identity and power*. Thousand Oaks, CA: Sage.

Durie, E. (1996). Will the settlers settle? Cultural conciliation and law. *Otago Law Review*, 3(8), 449.

Durie, M. (2003). *Ngā kāhui pou launching Māori futures*. Wellington, Aotearoa/New Zealand: Huia.

Fairclough, N. (1992). *Discourse and social change*. Cambridge: Polity.

Foucault, M. (1980). *Power/knowledge: Selected interviews and other writings 1972–1977*. (Trans. by Gordon, C., Marshall, L., Mepham, J. and Soper, K.). New York: Pantheon.

Gallagher, T. (2008). Tikanga Maori pre 1840. *Te Kahui Kura Maori*, 0(1). Retrieved from http://www.nzetc.org/tm/scholarly/tei-corpus-tkkm.html.

Guthrie, J. P. (2001). High-involvement work practices, turnover, and productivity: Evidence from New Zealand. *Academy of Management Journal*, 44(1), 180–190.

Harris, N. T. A. (2007). *Work life balance: A Maori women's perspective*. Auckland, New Zealand: Auckland University of Technology.

Heath, R. L. (1994). *Management of corporate communication: From interpersonal contacts to external affairs*. Hillsdale, NJ: Lawrence Erlbaum.

Heath, R. L. (1997). *Strategic issues management: Organizations and public policy challenges*. Thousand Oaks, CA: Sage.

Heath, R. L. (2001). A rhetorical enactment rationale for public relations. In R. L. Heath (Ed.), *Handbook of public relations*. Thousand Oaks, CA: Sage, pp. 31–50.

Hill, E. J., Yang, C., Hawkins, A. J. and Ferris, M. (2004). A cross-cultural test of the work–family interface in 48 countries. *Journal of Marriage and Family*, 66(5), 1300–1316.

Hofstede, G. (2001). *Culture's consequences: Company values, behaviors, institutions, and organizations across nations* (2nd edition). Beverly Hills, CA: Sage.

Hofstede, G. (2009). New Zealand's cultural dimensions. Retrieved from http://www.geert-hofstede.com/hofstede_new_zealand.shtml.

Holtzhausen, D. R. (2000). Postmodern values in public relations. *Journal of Public Relations Research*, 12(1), 93–114.

Hook, G. R., Waaka, T. and Raumati, L. P. (2007). Mentoring Māori within a Pākehā framework. *MAI Review*, 3(1), 1–5.

Macalister, J. (2005). *A dictionary of Maori words in New Zealand English*. Melbourne, Australia: Oxford.

McGonigal, J. (2006). The puppet master problem: Design for real world, mission based gaming. In Harrigan, P. and Wardrip-Fruin, N. (Eds.), *Second person: Role playing and story in games and playable media*. Cambridge, MA: MIT Press.

Mead, S. (2003). *Tikanga Māori: Living by Maori values*. Wellington: Huia Publishing.

Markus, H. and Kitayama, S. (1998). The cultural psychology of personality. *Journal of Cross-Cultural Psychology*, 29(1), 67–87.

Meadows, D. (2003). Digital story-telling: Research based practice in new media. *Visual Communication*, 2(2), 189–193.

Ministry of Social Development. (2009). *The social report: Te Pūrongo oranga tangata*. Wellington, New Zealand: Ministry of Social Development. Retrieved from http://www.socialreport.msd.govt.nz/documents/social-report-2009.pdf.

Motion, J. and Leitch, S. (1996). A discursive perspective from New Zealand: Another world view. *Public Relations Review*, 22(3), 297–309.

Motion, J. and Leitch, S. (2009). On Foucault: A toolbox for public relations. In Ihlen, O., van Ruler, B. and Fredriksson, M. (Eds.), *Public relations and social theory: Key figures and concepts*. New York: Routledge, pp. 83–102.

Powell, M. C. and Colin, M. (2008). Meaningful citizen engagement in science and technology: What would it really take? *Science Communication*, 30(1), 126–136.

Ratima, M. and Grant, B. (2007). Thinking about difference across and within mentoring. *MAI Review*, 3(1), 1–5.

Rowe, G. and Frewer, L. J. (2005). A typology of public engagement mechanisms. *Science, Technology, & Human Values*, 30(2), 25–290.

Said, E. W. (2003). *Orientalism*. London: Penguin.

Scott, A. and Du Plessis, R. (2008). Eliciting situated knowledges about new technologies. *Public Understanding of Science*, 17(1), 105–119.

Smith, L. (1999). *Decolonizing methodologies: Research and indigenous peoples*. Dunedin, New Zealand: University of Otago.

Spector, P. E., Allen, T. D., Poelmans, S., Lapierre, L., Cooper, C., O'Driscoll, M., Sanchez, J., Abarca, N., Alexandrova, M., Beham, B., Brough, P., Ferreiro, P., Fraile, G., Lu, C., Lu, L., Zquez, I., Pagon, M., Pitariu, H., Salamatov, V., Shima, S., Simoni, A., Siu, Q. and Widerszal-Bazyl, M. (2007). Cross-national differences in relationships of work demands, job satisfaction, and turnover intentions with work–family conflict. *Personnel Psychology*, 60(1), 805–835.

Sriramesh, K. (2009). The relationship between public relations and culture. In Sriramesh, K. and Verčič, D. (Eds.), *The global public relations handbook: Theory, research and practice*. New York: Routledge, pp. 47–61.

Statistics New Zealand. (2007). QuickStats about Maori: Census 2006. Retrieved from http://www.stats.govt.nz/Census/2006CensusHomePage/QuickStats/quickstats-about-a-subject/maori.aspx.

Tremaine, M. (1990). Sharing from the baskets of knowledge. In Sligo, F. (Ed.), *Business communication: New Zealand perspectives*. Palmerston North, New Zealand: Software Technology, pp. 48–54.

Waitangi Tribunal—Te Rōpū Whakamana I Te Tiriti O Waitangi. (2010). *Treaty of Waitangi: Principles of the Treaty*. Retrieved from http://www.waitangi-tribunal.govt.nz/treaty/principles.asp.

Walker, R. (2004). *Ka Whawhai Tonu Matou: Struggle without end* (revised edition). Auckland, New Zealand: Penguin.

Walker, T. (2006). *Whanau is whanau: Blue skies report*. Wellington: Families Commission.

Wiklund, H. (2005). A Habermasian analysis of the deliberative democracy potential of ICT-enabled services in Swedish municipalities. *New Media & Society*, 7(2), 247–270.

Williams, J. (1998). He aha te tikanga Maori. Unpublished paper for the Law Commission.

5

IDENTITY AND CULTURE

Implications for Public Relations

Bey-Ling Sha, Natalie T. J. Tindall, and Ting-Ling Sha

Just as the phenomenon of culture may be examined at multiple levels (see Chapter 1), so can the question of identity. In this chapter, we define *identity*, relating it to *culture*. Then, we examine identity from various perspectives; these include theories of identity development, the notion of intersectionality, professional identity, and organizational and national identity. Finally, we consider various ways in which the notion of identity may be relevant for public relations scholarship and practice.

Identity Defined

In this chapter on cultural identity, we define *cultural identity* in the sense of what Cross (1987) termed "reference group orientation" or how individual identities are related to a culturally defined group.[1] According to Cross (1987), an individual's self concept actually is a combination of personal identity (PI) and group identity, which he termed reference group orientation (RGO). The latter term is more accurate because *group identity* may be confused with the concept of the identity of a group, whereas reference group orientation deals with the identity of an individual in relation to a group. Understanding the distinction between PI and RGO is critical, especially because this distinction is often confounded in research on identity (Cross, 1987).

As Cross (1987) explained, the PI sector of an individual's self concept deals with characteristics of persons as individuals; these characteristics exist in all humans universally. "PI variables are the building blocks for all personalities, with culture, class, race, ethnicity, and gender mediating . . . how much of the variable is present across cultures or different groups of people" (Cross, 1987, p. 121). In other words, PI research examines universal components of human behavior and analyzes differences in behavior in light of race or ethnicity. In PI research, racioethnicity is thus treated as an independent variable and excluded from stimulus conditions or dependent measures.

Reference group orientation research explicitly includes racioethnicity as a salient dimension of the stimulus and seeks to determine how a person feels, not in general, but regarding a specific group (Cross, 1987). In short, RGO research seeks to explain the aspects of self concept that are specific to social, ethnic, gender, and other groups of people. As Cross (1987) pointed out:

> though everyone eats food, what a person eats, how it is prepared, and the utensils involved are not the same across cultures. Likewise, every human being tends to rely on groups as a point of reference, but the specific *groups* one relies on reveal the nature of one's group identity or reference group orientation.
>
> (p. 123, emphasis added)

Approaches to the Study of Identity

Two primary approaches to the study of cultural identity are the social psychological approach and the communication approach (Sha, 1995).[2] The traditional perspective, that of social psychology, holds that identity is a personal characteristic that affects the self in its relation to society (Collier, 1994; Erikson, 1968; Waterman, 1985). Researchers in this approach attempt to find the components of this personal characteristic. For example, Rotheram and Phinney (1987) asserted that ethnic identity includes several concepts, such as ethnic awareness, ethnic self-identification, ethnic attitudes, and ethnic behaviors.

In addition to operationalizing components of racioethnic identity, much research using the social psychological approach to identity focuses on the processes by which these components are acquired or developed (Helms, 1992; Rotheram and Phinney, 1987). For example, Cross (1987) stressed that ethnic identity is a process of ego development rather than merely the acquisition of ethnicity concepts. In addition, Spencer and Markstrom-Adams (1990) defined ego identity as being "characterized by the attainment of an ever-revised sense of psychological reality that is supported by a social reality" (p. 291). Although this definition points to a linear process of identity attainment, the mention of social reality relates to the communication perspective on identity.

Whereas the social psychological perspective views identity as an ego development process, the communication perspective considers identity as the enactment of cultural communication (Hecht, Collier, and Ribeau, 1993). In other words, a cultural identity is created by the exchange of messages between interactants; it "is the particular character of the group communication system that emerges in the particular situation" (Collier, 1994, p. 39). In this view, communication is the means by which individuals and groups negotiate, co-create, reinforce, and challenge cultural identity. Furthermore, cultural identities emerge in communication contexts (Collier, 1994). When cultural identities are enacted, patterns of communicative conduct become evident.

Identity Dimensions

Various aspects of cultural identity articulated in the scholarly literature include the notion of identities as being salient, situational, multifaceted, ascribed, and avowed.[3] Collier (1989) asserted that aspects of identity vary along three dimensions: scope, salience, and intensity. Of these three identity dimensions, salience has received the greatest amount of attention in the literature (Cupach and Imahori, 1987). Cupach and Imahori (1987) defined salience as "the relative importance of a particular aspect of identity in a specific situation, relative to the other aspects of one's total identity" (p. 114).

Cupach and Imahori (1987) further asserted that identity salience is *situational* in nature (p. 115).[4] Similarly, Rotheram and Phinney (1987) pointed out that the "importance and meaning of ethnic identity varies with the specific context . . . and *will be more salient in some situations than in others*" (p. 16, emphasis added). In identity terms, the question becomes: In which situations does the individual avow a racioethnic identity rather than another identity? Alternatively, in which situations does racioethnic identity become more salient than other identities in an individual's self-concept? These questions both point to the situational nature of racioethnic identity salience.

Of course, race and ethnicity are only two components of any particular individual's identity; put another way, groups grounded in race or in ethnicity are only two of the myriad groups with which an individual may identify. Collier (2003) articulated several "cultural identity types" (p. 417), including those grounded in national and ethnic cultures, sex and gender, profession, geographic area, organizations, and physical ability or disability. In short, identities are multifaceted, and any individual may hold as many cultural identities as there exist cultural groups with which that person identifies. The act of identifying with a cultural group means that an individual is avowing a particular identity.

Avowals and Ascriptions

Indeed, one key concept in the literature on cultural identities is that some identities are assigned to us by others (called *ascribed identities*), whereas other identities are claimed by us for ourselves (called *avowed identities*). The terms *ascribed* and *avowed* are used by Collier (1994), although other scholars have likewise made this distinction using different terms. For example, Cross (1987) discussed "personal" reference group orientation (parallel to avowed identity) and "ascriptive" reference group orientation (parallel to ascribed identity).

Hecht, Collier, and Ribeau (1993) argued that an avowed identity is "internally defined," whereas an ascribed identity is "externally imposed." Similarly, Rotheram and Phinney (1987) labeled the "performance criteria" of ethnic identity as being the "extent to which one feels and acts like a group member" (p. 16) and the "ascribed criteria" of ethnic identity as being how others see an individual. This distinction between identity ascription and identity avowal is particularly important in that theories of identity development largely focus on how individuals come to avow, enact, claim, or assert a particular set of identities.

Identity Development

Literature on identity development may be found in several scholarly disciplines, including communication, child development and education, college student development, and race and ethnicity studies. Although an in-depth presentation of each area is beyond the scope of this chapter, we provide here both a broad overview of this scholarly literature and directions to additional resources for those who wish to seek them.

The relevance of this overview for public relations scholars is threefold. First, the communication perspective on cultural identity is grounded in the notion that communication provides the means for individuals to assert or to enact an identity (see Hecht, Collier, and Ribeau, 1993). Since public relations is a communication-based function, scholars and practitioners would do well to consider what identities are being asserted not only by organizational publics, but also by organizations themselves. Second, because identities are avowed by organizational publics, public relations scholars and practitioners may enhance their understanding of the identity of publics with background knowledge of identity development theories. Finally, public relations scholars may wish to extrapolate from theories of individual identity development to study the development of identities for organizations.

Child Identity Development

In individuals, identities begin to develop in the earliest life stages, so it is fitting for this chapter to examine theories from the field of child development and education. First, Erikson's (1959, 1968) identity development model included eight stages of psychosocial development marked by identity crises and movement to the next stage if successful resolutions were reached in response to each crisis (Thomas, 2000). The environment and social context in which a child lives is deemed crucial in providing experiences that allow for growth, self-awareness, and identity development. Satisfactory resolution of each stage promotes greater psychological well-being and social development.

However, unsatisfactory resolutions may not prepare individuals to meet the demands of the identity crisis in the next stage.

A second major theory related to identity is that of Piaget's (1963) cognitive development theory. This theory includes four major levels: sensorimotor, preoperational, concrete, and formal operational. Children pass through these levels at individual rates of progress, based on four factors: biological maturation, physical environmental experiences, social environmental experiences, and adaptation, an equilibrium between assimilation and accommodation (Schunk, 2004). Assimilation, the process of fitting new information into existing schemes, and accommodation, temporarily or permanently modifying schemes, interact during development and learning, and are affected by environmental factors (Thomas, 2000), as well as by the challenges and dilemmas presented by these factors. Environmental experiences are reshaped to fit pre-existing schemes during assimilation, whereas accommodation is the process of modifying schemes to fit new thinking garnered from environmental features.

Vygotsky's (1978) sociocultural theory focuses on the ways in which children engage and interact in activities and how their schemas are constructed based on these engagements. Currently in popular use among U.S. educators, Vygotsky's theory stresses social interactions with people, objects, and the environment as critical experiences for learning and thought development, as these previous experiences greatly influence how one interprets and learns in specific situations. Cognitive development is further promoted through the social interactions with others in the individual's zone of proximal development, defined as "the distance between the actual developmental level as determined by independent problem solving and the level of potential development as determined through problem solving under adult guidance or in collaboration with more capable peers" (Vygotsky, 1978, p. 86). Cognitive development occurs when children internalize their interactions with the environment and others. Vygotsky posited that children are capable of devising new problem-solving methods when faced with new challenges, and then internalizing the new resolutions to add to their existing schema. However, the cognitive development of each individual is also important, as it determines how prepared the child is to resolve each new problem. One should also remember that the child's cultural-historical background is also important, as each culture and environment provides opportunities, demands, and challenges that are unique to that specific culture.

Finally, Kohlberg's (1958) moral development model focuses on the socialization of individuals, through the process by which children learn to conform to and internalize standards and expectations set by the culture in which they grow up (Thomas, 2000). To advance through the three levels and six sub-levels (stages), an individual moves from a premoral level to a conformation level and finally a personal level. However, four principal factors are utilized to determine how far along the levels and stages an individual will progress: the individual's level of logical reasoning, the individual's motivation, the individual's opportunity to learn social roles, and the form of justice (Thomas, 2000).

College Student Identity Development[5]

Theories of identity development are not restricted to children, nor do they cease being relevant when children become adults. Indeed, among the numerous theories that explain the cognitive, moral, and psychosocial development of college students, especially those in their first year of the university experience, are several theories of identity development. The establishment of identity is seen as a crucial task for college students (Chickering and Reisser, 1993; Pascarella and Terenzini, 1991, 2005; Skipper, 2005), most of whom are on their own for the first time and thus experiencing challenges to the identities with which they grew up. Chickering and Reisser (1993), leading scholars in student development theory, articulated seven "vectors" or "journeys" that represent "major developmental tasks that students address throughout their college years" (Skipper, 2005, p. 14), and "establishing identity" is one of those vectors (p. 15).

For college students, establishing identity means working through various identity components, including body appearance, gender and sexual orientation, sense of self in relation to contextual factors and in relation to others, lifestyle choices, self-esteem, and personal stability (see Chickering and Reisser, 1993). Other researchers have found that different subgroups of college students resolve identity issues differently. For example, men often define their identities through individual achievements and activities, whereas women frequently define their identities through their connections and interpersonal interactions with others (Evans et al., 1998; Gilligan, 1982).

For women students, Helms proposed a four-stage model of gender identity development that moves from external to internal definitions of gender (Ossana et al., 1992). The Helms Womanist Identity Model borrows the term "womanist" from Black feminist scholars and parallels the first four stages of the model of racial identity development proposed by Cross (see next section). Greatly simplified, the stages of Helms's model may be explained thus: (1) pre-encounter, during which women subscribe to traditional societal views regarding gender and, often subconsciously, value men over women; (2) encounter, during which women experience an incident or new information that makes them question their own views on gender; (3) immersion–emersion, during which women idealize their own gender and form "intense affiliations with women" (Ossana et al., 1992, p. 403); and (4) internalization, during which "women incorporate a range of positive definitions of womanhood based on their own values and beliefs" (Skipper, 2005, p. 28). For other theoretical approaches to gender identity development, see the next section below.

Related to the notion of gender identity development is the concept of sexual identity development; scholarship in the latter has primarily examined how gay, lesbian, and bisexual (GLB) students develop their identities, not only in regard to their sexual activities, but also in regard to psychological and social dimensions of identity (Skipper, 2005). Proposed by Cass (1979, 1984) and empirically tested by Evans, Forney, and Guido-DiBrito (1998) is a six-stage model of homosexual identity development: (1) identity confusion; (2) identity comparison; (3) identity tolerance; (4) identity acceptance; (5) identity pride; and (6) identity synthesis. For detailed explications of each stage, see Cass (1979, 1984).

In short, models of "minority" identity development all seem to follow one basic pattern, beginning with acceptance of socially defined identities, progressing through internal conflict and assessment, experiencing pro-identity feelings to the likely rejection of attitudes held in stage 1, and concluding with an identity forged by oneself, rather than defined externally. Although these linear models of development may be rejected by postmodern scholars (see Sha, 1995), the pattern is seen in both Helms's gender identity development model for women and Cass's homosexual identity development model for GLB students. The pattern also holds for the development of minority racial identities. Indeed, a major component of identity development for college students, especially those at universities with diverse student populations, deals with race and ethnicity.

Racial Identity Development

Public relations scholarship has examined race and ethnicity to some extent (e.g., Pompper, 2004, 2005; Sha and Ford, 2007; Tindall, 2009), but not from the perspective of identity development. Racial identity "refers to a sense of group or collective identity based on one's perception that he or she shares a common heritage with a particular racial group" (Helms, 1993, p. 3). The common identifiers for racial identity are phenotypical characteristics, including skin color. According to Chavez and Guido-DiBrito (1999), "[t]he use of skin color is one of many labeling tools that allow individuals and groups to distance themselves from those they consider different from themselves" (p. 40). Ethnic identity is based on common origin and cultural traditions, values, beliefs, and language (Chavez and Guido-DiBrito, 1999); individuals identify with a societal group or community who "share segments of a common culture and who, in addition, participate in shared activities in which the common origin and culture are significant ingredients" (Yinger, 1976, p. 200). The development of a racial or ethnic identity is explained in a variety of models that outline the stage processes of identity formation and self-identity formation.

One of the most well-known models of racial identity development is Cross's (1987) Model of African American Identity Development, which challenged the idea that minority (or emerging majority) persons experienced the same racial development as majority individuals. Cross (1995) argued that this model defines the identity formation of Blacks as they "become more aware of themselves as objects of oppression, their attitudes toward themselves, their own minority group, other minority groups, and members of the dominant culture crystallize in a manner that leads to a core sense of identity" (p. 180). The model is composed of five identified stages through which an individual progresses. The healthiest stage, according to the model, is the integration stage, at which the individual is aware of the uniqueness of his or her cultural heritage and declares that the African-American identity will serve as the main reference cluster (Crawford et al., 2002; Helms, 1993). Also, Crawford and colleagues noted that, in this stage of the model, the person's core reference identity creates a buffer and protection against the elements of societal racism.

In society and in research, whiteness is the assumed and unspoken norm that other identities deviate from and pivot around (Carter and Gushue, 1994; Flagg, 1997; Frankenberg, 1993; Takaki, 1993). To challenge the vast terrain of what Flagg (1997) considered "usually unsituated assumptions that [one] culture is superior to all others" (p. 630), Helms (1990) articulated and developed the White Racial Identity Development Model, which charts the development of racial consciousness and the impact on racist behaviors, attitudes, and emotions for U.S.-born Whites. According to Helms and others (McIntosh, 1997; Morrison, 1993; Rasmussen et al., 2001), whiteness is an unacknowledged identity for many members of the majority, dominant group; this distortion and ignoring of racial consciousness is rooted in racism. Helms (1990) wrote, "The greater the extent that racism exists and is denied, the less possible it is to develop a positive White identity" (p. 49).

The first step in this development model operationalizes the contact hypothesis (Allport, 1954); here, individuals interact with members of another race with fear and trepidation. However, the longer the person interacts and makes contact with non-White persons, the less fear and caution they feel, and, "when enough of these 'socialization' experiences penetrate the White person's identity system, then he or she can enter the disintegration stage" (Helms, 1990, p. 58), the stage that triggers dissonance as the individual acknowledges the benefits of White privilege. At the reintegration stage, the individual has reconciled his or her dissonance, has reshaped cognitions, and accepts White identity. Helms considered the next stage, "pseudo-independent," as "the first stage of redefining positive White identity" (p. 61), in which the individual disavows beliefs in White superiority. The final stage is immersion–emersion or autonomy, when the individual interrogates racial identities, appreciates diversity, and challenges racism and oppression.

Gender Identity Development

Wood (2007) offered a solid overview of three theoretical approaches to gender identity development: biological, interpersonal, and cultural. The biological approach considers the chromosomal and hormonal influences that shape the development of gender identity, as well as how brain structures and brain development affect gender and its expressions. Interpersonal theories of gender identity development constitute a broad collection of ideas. These include how children's earliest relationships with their mothers affect identity (called psychodynamic theory; see Freud, 1957); how gender identity develops in response to socially approved behavioral norms (called social learning theory; see Mischel, 1966; Bandura, 2002); and how child development affects gender identity (called cognitive development theory; see section above).

Finally, culture-based theories of gender identity development consider how anthropological differences in culture inform assumptions regarding gender (e.g., Coltrane, 1996; Cronk, 1993). The cultural approach also examines how gender identity is developed in the communication process (called symbolic interactionism; see section above). Finally, Wood (2007) explained how standpoint theory (see Harding, 1998; Hegel, 1807/1910; McClish and Bacon, 2002) informs gender identity by emphasizing "how a person's location within a culture shapes his or her life" (Wood, 2007, p. 55).

Standpoint theory, which considers various identity dimensions in relation to myriad cultural factors, brings to mind what Collier (2003) called "interpellation," which "refers to the interrelationships among such cultural identities as sex, race, and class" (p. 420). These interrelationships in turn may be related to the argument of some scholars in college student development theory, who point out that processes of identity development should not be treated in isolation, with one identity dimension examined without consideration of other identity dimensions that may be undergoing simultaneous development (e.g., Jones and McEwen, 2000; Miville et al., 2005). Rather, they propose a model that encompasses multiple dimensions of identity (see Jones and McEwen, 2000), which brings our chapter to the notion of intersectionality.

Intersectionality

As explicated in our definition of cultural identity and as underscored in our review of literature on how identities develop, every individual possesses numerous cultural identities. However, research on identity often investigates one dimension to the exclusion of others. For example, in public relations, many scholars have looked at women practitioners (e.g., Grunig et al., 2001;

Toth, 1988; Wright et al., 1991; Wrigley, 2002), concentrating on their gender to the exclusion of their race, marital status, sexual orientation, and so on. Similarly, public relations scholars studying the experiences of minority practitioners (e.g., Kern-Foxworth, 1989a, 1989b; Kern-Foxworth et al., 1994; Tindall, 2009) usually focus on race or ethnicity to the exclusion of other identity dimensions.

The notion that identities have intersecting components—and that identities should be studied at those intersection points—is called "intersectionality." The key premise of intersectionality is that the confluence of invisible and visible socially constructed identities shapes the lived experiences and realities of individuals. Intersectionality is rooted in the understanding that intricate and pervasive invisible webs and systems of power and inequalities link together to create oppression and privilege between individuals and within institutions. According to Essed (1991), these dynamic systems of inequality and privilege are produced and enacted at the macro and micro levels. At the micro level, the routine and everyday social practices create inequality through the activation of "existing structural racial inequality in the [macro] system" (p. 39).

Intersectionality challenges the idea of the "unitary" bracketing of groups into specific categories because of assumed "uniform sets[s] of experiences" (Hancock, 2007, p. 65). Bowleg (2008) acknowledged this universalizing and flattening trend: "Despite an abundance of theories on social identity . . . , the prevailing view of social identities is one of unidimensionality and independence, rather than intersection" (p. 313).

Intersectionality pivots on the central idea of multiplicative identities. Traditional paradigms have treated identities as building blocks, solid cubes of identity attributes and meanings that can be stacked on top of each other. In this approach, identities are mutually exclusive. Identities, according to the summative or additive approach, are ranked and distinct, isolated and independent from other identities (see Bowleg, 2008; Collins, 1999; Weber, 2001). The additive approach produced aggregates that multiply or increase with each added identity. Thinking that identities can be added together is problematic, as Bowleg (2008) discovered in her study analyzing qualitative and quantitative approaches to intersectionality, and as Lorde (1984), Ransford and Miller (1983), Weber and Parra-Medina (2003), and others debated and questioned.

In contrast to the "additive" approach, intersectionality posits that social identities are interdependent, intertwining social locations that interact with and relate to each other to create meaning and relevance in the lived experience. Identities are simultaneously enacted and experienced. The fluidity and power of identity as evidenced in intersectionality cement the shift in the conceptualization of identity and culture. Rather than seeing identity as a category "that announces who we are and calls upon notions of nation, class, gender, and ethnicity for definition" (Yon, 2000, p. 12), identity is seen as a continuous and unfinished "process of categorization" (Hobbel and Chapman, 2009, p. 77). The consideration of intersectionality for researchers and practitioners was best articulated by Crenshaw (1995) as "the need to account for multiple grounds of identity when considering how the social world is constructed" (p. 355).

Vardeman-Winter and Tindall (2010) proposed a conceptual road map for the study of intersectionality in public relations across multiple levels, including organizational practices, organizational roles, and publics. Intersectionality acts as research paradigm and method, a theoretical construct, and practical approach to understanding the diversity of internal and external publics (Vardeman-Winter and Tindall, 2010). In short, we believe that consideration of intersectionality has the potential to raise the professionalism of public relations scholarship and practice.

Professional Identity

Professional identity can be considered in two ways. First, one may study the identity of people who practice public relations, in which case "professional identity" deals with the identity of these individuals with respect to their profession. As noted earlier in this chapter, some researchers have examined gender and race in public relations, but these studies have not considered, in depth, the extent to which practitioners may identify with a particular racial or gender group. Similarly, no studies published to date have examined the extent to which practitioners identify with the public relations profession. One recent study, however, did examine the extent to which public relations and journalism students identified with their respective future professions (see Sha and Schmitz Weiss, 2010).

A second way to study "professional identity" is to consider the identity of the public relations profession as a whole. As noted by Sha (2001), professions—like individuals—can have both avowed and ascribed identities. The public relations profession's avowed identities include being managerial (e.g., Dozier et al., 1995; Grunig, 1992), being ethical (Pearson, 1989; Public Relations Society of America, 2000; Ryan and Martinson, 1983), and being professional (Broom, 2009). However, in contrast to the managerial, ethical, and professional identities that public relations tries to avow, the field's identities—as ascribed by news media, entertainment media, and so on—are quite different. For example, news media frequently connect public relations to negative issues (Lesly, 1981), which harms the ascribed professional identity of the field. Other scholars likewise have noted that the public relations profession often is portrayed in a negative manner (e.g., Penning, 2008; Sterne, 2010), or ascribed a negative identity.

Organizational and National Identity

Just as "professional identity" may be considered at both micro and meso levels (i.e., individual and collective levels), so can "organizational identity" be related both to the identification that employees have with their employing organization and to the identity of that organization itself. Similarly, "national identity" may be examined from both the perspective of the identities of people who see themselves as belonging to specific nations, as well as the collective identity of the nation as a whole.

With respect to individual-level analyses, some research has examined the extent to which employees identify with or feel a sense of belonging to their employing organizations (e.g., Sha and Ahles, 2009; Stein, 2006; White et al., 2010) and the extent to which students identify with their universities (e.g., Sha, 2009). Other studies have examined the extent to which individuals, such as migrants or new immigrants, identify with a given national culture (e.g., Green and Power, 2006; Lacatus, 2008; Ong, 2009; Zhou, 2008) or are ascribed inaccurate identities by their host nations (e.g., Hopkins, 2008). With respect to collective-level analyses, many scholars have indeed studied the identities of organizations (e.g., Albert and Whetten, 1985; Harrison, 2000; Haslam et al., 2003; Humphreys and Brown, 2002; Ravasi and van Rekom, 2003). Others have examined the identities of nations, particularly as portrayed by news and entertainment media (e.g., Beeden and de Bruin, 2010; Ifert Johnson, 2006; McIver, 2009; Moorti, 2004; Perkins, 2010; Volčič, 2006).

However, this research has examined identity primarily[6] from what Cross (1987) would call the perspective of "personal identity," as opposed to "reference group orientation." In the latter, identity is examined as it relates to a reference group; for example, an individual's racial identity involves how that person sees himself in reference to a racial group. On the other hand, "personal identity" research examines personality characteristics of identity, such as being funny or intelligent or ethical. For example, Taylor and Kent (2006) defined "national identity" as "the conscious identification of a group of people with shared national goals" (p. 343). This clear gap in scholarship leaves much room for future public relations research on identities and cultures.

Implications and Directions for Research

Research on identity and culture has the potential to be incorporated into numerous extant streams of public relations scholarship. Thus, in closing our chapter, we discuss the implications that identity and culture have for various potential areas of public relations research.

Corporate Identity

First, to clarify, in discussing "corporate identity," we do not mean the identity of organizations that are classified as for-profit "corporations." Rather, we mean the term *corporate* in the sense of "corporal" or pertaining to the whole. Thus, corporate identity may refer to the identity of any collectivity or collective body, and we believe that this is one area of research with great potential.

As noted earlier, the literature cited in this chapter with respect to professional, organizational, and national identities emphasizes the PI dimensions of identity, as opposed to the RGO dimensions of identity (see Cross, 1987). For example, the corporate identity of BP in the wake of the explosion and oil spill in the Gulf of Mexico will no doubt be studied in terms of the company's "personality" characteristics, for example, whether it was appropriately apologetic, environmentally conscious, quintessentially British, and so forth.

However, we believe that organizational identities in public relations scholarship also should be examined with respect to an organization's "referent group": the larger collectives of which a particular organization may be a part. To that end, a study of the "corporate identity" of BP would examine the extent to which the organization was still seen as part of the larger collective identity group known as "the oil industry" or "British companies." Perhaps even more interesting would be a study of the identity of the larger system (e.g., "the oil industry") and how its identity may have been affected by the crisis faced by its subsystem (i.e., BP).

Similar studies may be undertaken with national identity, for example, with respect to how the specific nations are seen in relation to their membership in the North Atlantic Treaty Organization (NATO) or the Association of Southeast Asian Nations (ASEAN). For instance, to what extent might NATO resistance to Turkey's membership have been an issue of corporate religious identity, or how might the Asian identity of ASEAN be affected should Australia or New Zealand request to join the association?

In public relations, some practitioners and scholars have sought to claim a "professional" identity for the field, although there never has been a clear articulation regarding with which professional body or collective we seek to identify. Future research may wish to explore whether the avowal of a professional identity in public relations is the assertion of belonging to the group of practitioners who are, say, members of the Public Relations Society of America or some other national-level professional association or, say, accredited in public relations. (Some authors have already argued that public relations cannot achieve professional status without accreditation; e.g., Bernays, 1980; Brody, 1984, 1992; Hainsworth, 1993; Sha, 2011). These questions of corporate identity in the sense of reference group orientation—as opposed to in the sense of personal identity—would be quite interesting to investigate.

Reputation and Coalition Building

Organizational reputations are grounded in how an organization behaves (see Broom, 2009; Reuber and Fischer, 2010). If an organization's reputation is defined by how others see the organization in question (Claeys et al., 2010), then there is a clear connection between organizational reputation and the concept of ascribed identities. For instance, Behrend, Baker, and Thompson (2009) found that organizations avowing a pro-environmental identity earned better reputations among potential job candidates. Hong and Yang (2009) examined the connections among organizational reputation, customer–company identification, and customers' communication intentions regarding the organization.

Future research in public relations might examine reputation less from an evaluative perspective (i.e., PI) and more from a reference group perspective (i.e., RGO). This means examining reputation in terms of an organization's relationships, associations, and alliances with other organizations, rather than with organizational publics. Some research in this vein has been done with respect to coalition building (e.g., Bodensteiner, 1997; Wilson, 1994), but that area of scholarship may benefit from taking the lens of identity theories and considering how coalitions build collective identities and how those identities are perceived by others.

Message Development and Branding

Whereas ascribed identity is how others see us, avowed identity is how we articulate our own connections to various reference groups. At an organizational level, public relations is in fact about the avowal of organizational identities, in the forms of corporate messaging, branding, and dissemination of organizational viewpoints, using the Internet, news media, or institutional advertising. Just as college students establish identity by working through various identity components (see Chickering and Reisser, 1993), organizations establish identity in similar ways. Scholars may study the extent to which the public relations function participates in these corporate identity-establishing tasks, connecting such research to scholarly traditions regarding the dominant coalition (see Bowen, 2009; Grunig, 1992) or public relations manager-technician roles (see Dozier and Broom, 1995, 2006).

These identity development tasks may be particularly important for newly established organizations or organizations with unique missions, which may go through the identity stages of confusion, comparison, tolerance, acceptance, pride, and synthesis (see Cass, 1979, 1984), much like the stages experienced by some minority individuals. Public relations research could examine whether some organizations experience greater challenges than do others in the articulation of corporate identities. In a related vein, scholars may consider whether the expression of corporate identities is tempered by social expectations regarding specific types of organizations. For instance, taking some hints from theories of gender identity development, public relations scholars may examine whether organizational identity develops in response to what are perceived by organizational leaders as socially approved behavioral norms (see Bandura, 2002; Mischel, 1966; Wood, 2007), with, say, for-profit corporations expressing more aggressive, "masculine" identities and non-profit associations expressing more passive, "feminine" identities.

Identity Development

For public relations scholars, prior scholarship on identity development in children has several implications, particularly with respect to the identity development of organizations. For example, Erikson's (1959, 1968) notion that identity development moves in stages as crises in each stage are confronted and resolved may be applicable to organizations that adjust their identities in response to crises or other challenges in their environments. Public relations scholars might take a historical approach to the study of organizational identity, looking at how corporations and non-profits have responded to various crises by modifying and adjusting their identity avowals. One obvious example would be Johnson & Johnson, which managed to avow an identity as a socially responsible organization in the wake of the Tylenol poisonings, largely thanks to the astute manner in which the company faced and resolved the crisis (see Broom, 2009).

Stakeholder Segmentation

Scholarship on the development of identity in women and other minorities also should be taken in account by public relations practitioners seeking to segment organizational publics strategically. For example, the alumni office of a predominantly White university, seeking to connect with Black graduates, may need to segment those who are African-American from those who are more recent African immigrants. Furthermore, donation-seeking materials from the alumni office may need to be sensitive to the fact that some African-American graduates may be in the identity development stage of rejecting all aspects of non-African-American culture, whereas other graduates from the same demographic segment may be perfectly comfortable with their own racial culture and its location with respect to the university's overall culture.

Similarly, a U.S.-based global organization trying to acknowledge its multicultural workforce in an employee magazine might wish to keep in mind that White employees may be in different stages of Helms's (1990) White Racial

Identity Development Model. For example, some White employees, having had little contact with non-Whites, may be in the first stage of White racial identity development, in which they view non-Whites with fear and distrust; they may be very uncomfortable with photos of non-Whites in the employee magazine and wish to distance themselves from the organization. Other White employees, perhaps in the last stage of Helms's (1990) model, may be quite appreciative of racial diversity and pleased to work for a company whose employee magazine reflects a multicultural workforce.

Identifying Activists

Just as public relations researchers and practitioners may segment organizational publics by their stages of identity development, organizational stakeholders also may be segmented on grounds of their potential for activism. One public relations theory that has consistently predicted the levels of activism in organizational publics has been the situational theory of publics (see Grunig, 1997). However, more recent research has argued that the original independent variables of the situational theory—problem recognition, involvement, and constraint recognition—are insufficient predictors of active communication (e.g., Aldoory and Sha, 2007; Sha, 2006). One additional factor in predicting active communication may in fact be cultural identity (see Sha, 2006).

Another scholar (Kim, 2006) has asserted that the situational theory's original dependent variables—information seeking and information processing—are likewise insufficient to describe the range of possible communication outcomes. Arguing for multiple communication outcomes, Kim (2006) emphasized the importance of what he called "communicant activeness in problem solving" or CAPS. Specifically, this model investigates how information selection, information acquisition, and information transmission interact to enhance problem-solving abilities of communicators (Kim and Grunig, 2007).

Given this potentially fruitful area of research in public relations, Vygotsky's (1978) concept of "zone of proximal development," discussed above, becomes particularly salient. In short, combining Kim's (2006) work with Vygotsky's (1978) theory, future public relations scholars might be able to determine how organizational identity and its development are related to either an organization's or its stakeholders' ability to engage in problem-solving activities.

Social Responsibility and Ethics

Just as Vygotsky's (1978) theories of child development may inspire public relations practitioners to consider new ways to identify activist organizational stakeholders, Kohlberg's (1958) theory of moral development in children may be useful as some scholars continue to insist that the public relations function serves as the "conscience of the corporation" (see Pearson, 1989; Ryan and Martinson, 1983). Perhaps the process by which organizations become more ethical in their business practices could be related to the process by which individuals develop their internal moral compass. If so, then public relations would benefit greatly by applying Kohlberg's theory to the development of concrete guides for organizations to improve their ethical practices and their social responsibility.

On a related note regarding ethics, we urge public relations practitioners to remember that intersectionality matters. Echoing Tindall and Vardeman (2008) and Vardeman-Winter and Tindall (2010), we recommend that researchers and practitioners consider how publics process and encounter the daily micro-experiences of power, oppression, and privilege. Previous research has outlined and demonstrated the fluidity of identities, that is, that publics view their lives through a variety of identities. Some identities are more prominent and salient than are other identities in some social, everyday occurrences. Therefore, to segment stakeholders and to create messages for latent and active publics, practitioners and researchers must understand the complexities of intertwined identities to find the identity-based referent criterion that can evoke emotions and trigger behavior change. This is both an ethical imperative and a methodological challenge for public relations researchers.

Methodological Concerns

Finally, the discussion of social responsibility and ethics brings this chapter to two more methodological concerns raised by the incorporation of identity and culture into public relations theory and practice. First, we recommend that researchers, be they academics or practitioners, move beyond simple demographics in the collection of data about organizational stakeholders. Echoing Sha (2006), we call on public relations scholars to investigate the avowed identities of organizational publics, rather than merely ascribing identities to them in the arrogant belief that ascribed and avowed identities will always align with each other. To believe the latter is to make a crucial—and unethical—mistake in the process of segmenting organizational publics.

Second, we encourage future scholarship to problematize the very notion of "identity," to question its state, and to remember that identity is almost never a constant, but almost always in flux. From a methodological perspective, this means that researchers who wish to study identity must carefully conceptualize it, clearly operationalize it, and cautiously delimit the extent to which specific data sets may be useful for further explicating it. At the very least, we hope that public relations scholars will consider the various theories of identity development presented in this chapter and remember that, like "culture" itself, "identity" is ever-changing.

Conclusion

In closing, we encourage public relations scholars to continue thinking about issues related to identity and culture. We believe that the intersection of identity and culture is not only inherently fascinating, but also potentially fruitful for continued theory building and practical application in public relations. Only by extending our scholarship in these ways can the field of public relations hope to one day identify with—and be identified among—truly established disciplines in the academy.

Notes

1 The remaining sentences in this section are taken with minor edits from Sha (1995).
2 The remaining sentences in this section are taken directly from Sha (1995).
3 The remaining sentences in this paragraph are taken directly from Sha (1995).
4 This sentence and those following in this paragraph are taken directly from Sha (1995).
5 In the United States, the administration of university campuses usually separates academic affairs from student affairs. Academic programs of study, such as the teaching of public relations and other academic subjects, are housed in academic affairs, whereas such programs as student extra-curricular activities, on-campus housing, and students' social programs are housed in student affairs. This divide is unfortunate in that most professors, despite being experts in their academic areas of study, never understand important theories of student development that explicate the challenges their students are facing both in and outside the classroom. For a good primer on college student development theory, see Skipper (2005).
6 One exception is Chang and Holt (2009).

References

Albert, S. and Whetten, D. (1985). Organizational identity. In Cummings, L. L. and Staw, B. M. (Ed.), *Research in organizational behavior, vol. 7*. Greenwich, CT: JAI Press, pp. 263–295.
Aldoory, L. and Sha, B.-L. (2007). The situational theory of publics: Practical applications, methodological challenges, and theoretical horizons. In Toth, E. L. (Ed.), *The future of excellence in public relations and communication management: Challenges for the next generation*. Mahwah, NJ: Lawrence Erlbaum, pp. 339–355.
Allport, G. W. (1954). *The nature of prejudice*. Cambridge, MA: Perseus Books.
Bandura, A. (2002). Social cognitive theory of mass communication. In Bryant, J. and Zillman, D. (Eds.), *Media effects: Advances in theory and research* (2nd edn.). Mahwah, NJ: Erlbaum, pp. 121–153.
Beeden, A. and de Bruin, J. (2010). *The Office*: Articulations of national identity in television format adaptation. *Television & New Media*, 11(1), 3–19.
Behrend, T., Baker, B., and Thompson, L. (2009). Effects of pro-environmental recruiting messages: The role of organizational reputation. *Journal of Business & Psychology*, 24(3), 341–350.

Bernays, E. (1980). Viewpoint: Gaining professional status for public relations. *Public Relations Quarterly*, 25(2), 20.

Bodensteiner, C. (1997). Special interest group coalitions: Ethical standards for broad-based support efforts. *Public Relations Review*, 23(1), 31–46.

Bowen, S. (2009). What communication professionals tell us regarding dominant coalition access and gaining membership. *Journal of Applied Communication Research*, 37(4), 418–443.

Bowleg, L. (2008). When black + lesbian + woman ≠ black lesbian woman: The methodological challenges of qualitative and quantitative intersectionality research. *Sex Roles*, 59, 312–325.

Brody, E. W. (1984). The credentials of public relations: Licensing? Certification? Accreditation? An overview. *Public Relations Quarterly*, 29(2), 6–9.

Brody, E. W. (1992). We must act now to redeem PR's reputation. *Public Relations Quarterly*, 37(3), 44.

Broom, G. M. (2009). *Cutlip & Center's effective public relations* (10th edn.). Englewood Cliffs, NJ: Prentice Hall.

Carter, R. T. and Gushue, G. V. (1994). White racial identity development and work values. *Journal of Vocational Behavior*, 44, 185–197.

Cass, V. C. (1979). Homosexual identity formation: A theoretical model. *Journal of Homosexuality*, 4, 219–235.

Cass, V. C. (1984). Homosexual identity formation: Testing a theoretical model. *Journal of Sex Research*, 20, 143–167.

Chang, H. and Holt, R. (2009). "New Taiwanese": Evolution of an identity project in the narratives of United Daily News. *Journal of Asian Pacific Communication*, 19(2), 259–288.

Chavez, A. F. and Guido-DiBrito, F. (1999). Racial and ethnic identity and development. In Clark, M. C. and Caffarella, R. S. (Eds.), *An update on adult development theory: New ways of thinking about the life course*. New Directions for Adult and Continuing Education No. 84. San Francisco: Jossey-Bass, pp. 39–47.

Chickering, A. W. and Reisser, L. (1993). *Education and identity* (2nd edn.). San Francisco: Jossey-Bass.

Claeys, A., Cauberghe, V., and Vyncke, P. (2010). Restoring reputations in times of crisis: An experimental study of the Situational Crisis Communication Theory and the moderating effects of locus of control. *Public Relations Review*, 36(3), 256–262.

Collier, M. J. (1989). Cultural and intercultural communication competence: Current approaches and directions for future research. *International Journal of International Relations*, 13, 287–302.

Collier, M. J. (1994). Cultural identity and intercultural communication. In Samovar, L. A. and Porter, R. E. (Eds.), *Intercultural communication: A reader*. Belmont, CA: Wadsworth, pp. 36–45.

Collier, M. J. (2003). Understanding cultural identities in intercultural communication: A ten-step inventory. In Samovar, L. A. and Porter, R. E. (Eds.), *Intercultural communication: A reader* (10th edn.). Belmont, CA: Thomson Wadsworth, pp. 412–429.

Collins, P. H. (1999). *Black feminist thought: Knowledge, consciousness, and the politics of empowerment*. New York: Routledge.

Coltrane, S. (1996). *Family man: Fatherhood, housework, and gender equity*. New York: Oxford University Press.

Crawford, I., Allison, K. W., Zamboni, B. D., and Soto, T. (2002). The influence of dual-identity development on the psychological functions of African-American gay and bisexual men. *Journal of Sex Research*, 39, 179–189.

Crenshaw, K. W. (1995). Mapping the margins: Intersectionality, identity politics, and violence against women of color. In Thomas, K. (Ed.), *Critical race theory: The key writings that formed a movement*. New York: New Press, pp. 357–383.

Cronk, L. (1993). Parental favoritism toward daughters. *American Scientist*, 81, 272–279.

Cross, Jr., W. E. (1987). A two-factor theory of Black identity: Implications for the study of identity development in minority children. In Phinney, J. S. and Rotheram, M. J. (Eds.), *Children's ethnic socialization*. Newbury Park, CA: Sage, pp. 117–133.

Cross, Jr., W. E. (1995). The psychology of nigrescence: Revising the Cross model. In Ponterotto, J. G. and Casas, J. M. (Eds.), *Handbook of multicultural counseling*. Thousand Oaks, CA: Sage, pp. 93–122.

Cupach, W. R. and Imahori, T. T. (1987). Identity management theory: Communication competence in intercultural episodes and relationships. In Wiseman, R. L. and Koester, J. (Eds.), *Intercultural communication competence*. Newbury Park, CA: Sage, pp. 112–131.

Dozier, D. M. and Broom, G. M. (1995). Evolution of the manager role in public relations practice. *Journal of Public Relations Research*, 7(1), 3–26.

Dozier, D. M. and Broom, G. M. (2006). The centrality of practitioner roles to public relations theory. In Botan, C. H. and Hazleton, V. (Eds.), *Public relations theory II*. Mahwah, NJ: Lawrence Erlbaum, pp. 137–170.

Dozier, D. M., Grunig, L. A., and Grunig, J. E. (1995). *Manager's guide to excellence in public relations and communication management*. Mahwah, NJ: Lawrence Erlbaum.

Erikson, E. H. (1959). Identity and the life cycle. *Psychological Issues*, 1 (1, Monograph 1).

Erikson, E. H. (1968). *Identity: Youth and crisis*. New York: Norton.

Essed, P. (1991). *Understanding everyday racism: An interdisciplinary theory*. Newbury Park, CA: Sage.

Evans, N. J., Forney, D. S., and Guido-DiBrito, F. (1998). *Student development in college: Theory, research, and practice*. San Francisco: Jossey-Bass.

Flagg, B. (1997). "Was blind, but now I see": White race consciousness and the requirement of discriminatory intent. In Delgado, R. and Stefanic, J. (Eds.), *Critical White studies: Looking behind the mirror*. Philadelphia: Temple University Press, pp. 629–631.

Frankenberg, R. (1993). *The social construction of whiteness: White women, race matters*. Minneapolis: University of Minnesota Press.

Freud, S. F. (1957). *The ego and the id* (Trans. by Riviere, J.). London: Hogarth.

Gilligan, C. (1982). *In a different voice*. Cambridge, MA: Harvard University Press.

Green, A. and Power, M. (2006). Defining transnationalism boundaries: New Zealand migrants in Australia. *Australian Journal of Communication*, 33(1), 35–52.

Grunig, J. E. (Ed.). (1992). *Excellence in public relations and communication management*. Hillsdale, NJ: Lawrence Erlbaum.

Grunig, J. E. (1997). A situational theory of publics: Conceptual history, recent challenges, and new research. In Moss, D., MacManus, T., and Verčič, D. (Eds.), *Public relations research: An international perspective*. London: International Thomson Business Press, pp. 3–48.

Grunig, L. A., Toth, E. L., and Hon, L. C. (2001). *Women in public relations: How gender influences practice*. New York: Guilford Press.

Hainsworth, B. E. (1993). Commentary: Professionalism in public relations. *Public Relations Review*, 19(4), 311–314.

Hancock, A.-M. (2007). When multiplication doesn't equal quick addition: Examining intersectionality as a research paradigm. *Perspectives on Politics*, 5, 63–79.

Harding, S. (1998). *Can feminism be multicultural?* Ithaca, NY: Cornell University Press.

Harrison, J. D. (2000). Multiple imaginings of institutional identity: A case study of a large psychiatric research hospital. *Journal of Applied Behavioral Science*, 36(4), 425–455.

Haslam, S. A., Eggins, R. A., and Reynolds, K. J. (2003). The ASPIRe model: Actualizing social and personal identity resources to enhance organizational outcomes. *Journal of Occupational and Organizational Psychology*, 76(1), 83–113.

Hecht, M., Collier, M. J., and Ribeau, S. (1993). *African-American communication*. Newbury Park, CA: Sage.

Hegel, G. W. F. (1807/1910). *The phenomenology of mind* (Trans. by Baillie, J. B.). New York: Macmillan.

Helms, J. E. (Ed.). (1990). *Black and white racial identity: Theory, research, and practice*. Westport, CT: Greenwood Press.

Helms, J. E. (1992). *A race is a nice thing to have: A guide to being a White person, or, understanding the White persons in your life*. Topeka, KS: Content Communications.

Helms, J. E. (1993). *Black and white racial identity*. Westport, CT: Praeger.

Hobbel, N. and Chapman, T. K. (2009). Beyond the sole category of race: Using a CRT intersectional framework to map identity projects. *Journal of Curriculum Theorizing*, 25, 76–89.

Hong, S. and Yang, S. (2009). Effects of reputation, relational satisfaction, and customer-company identification on positive word-of-mouth intentions. *Journal of Public Relations Research*, 21(4), 381–403.

Hopkins, L. (2008). Muslim Turks and anti-Muslim discourse: The effects of media constructions of "Islamic" and "Arabic" in Australia. *Australian Journal of Communication*, 35(1), 41–55.

Humphreys, M. and Brown, A. D. (2002). Narratives of organizational identity and identification: A case study of hegemony and resistance. *Organization Studies*, 23(3), 421–447.

Ifert Johnson, D. (2006). Music videos and national identity in post-Soviet Kazakhstan. *Qualitative Research Reports in Communication*, 7(1), 9–14.

Jones, S. R. and McEwen, M. K. (2000). A conceptual model of multiple dimensions of identity. *Journal of College Student Development*, 41(4), 405–414.

Kern-Foxworth, M. (1989a). An assessment of minority female roles and status in public relations: Trying to unlock the acrylic vault and assimilate into the velvet ghetto. In Toth, E. L. and Cline, C. G. (Eds.), *Beyond the velvet ghetto*. San Francisco, CA: International Association of Business Communicators Research Foundation, pp. 241–286.

Kern-Foxworth, M. (1989b). Status and roles of minority PR practitioners. *Public Relations Review*, 15(3), 39–47.

Kern-Foxworth, M., Gandy, O., Hines, B., and Miller, D. A. (1994). Assessing the managerial roles of black female public relations practitioners using individual and organizational discriminants. *Journal of Black Studies*, 24, 416–434.

Kim, J.-N. (2006). Communicant activeness, cognitive entrepreneurship, and a situational theory of problem solving. Unpublished doctoral dissertation, University of Maryland, College Park.

Kim, J.-N. and Grunig, J. (2007, May). Explicating and validating communicant activeness in problem solving (CAPS). Paper presented to the International Communication Association, San Francisco.

Kohlberg, L. (1958). The development of modes of thinking and choices in years 10 to 16. Unpublished doctoral dissertation, University of Chicago.

Lacatus, C. (2008). What is a blatte? Migration and ethnic identity in contemporary Sweden. *Journal of Arab & Muslim Media Research*, 1(1), 79–92.

Lesly, P. (1981). The stature and role of public relations. *Public Relations Journal*, 37(1), 14.

Lorde, A. (1984). *Sister outsider: Essays and speeches*. Trumansburg, NY: Crossing.

McClish, G. and Bacon, J. (2002). "Telling the story her own way": The role of feminist standpoint theory in rhetorical studies. *Rhetoric Society Quarterly*, 32, 27–55.

McIntosh, P. (1997). White privilege and male privilege: A personal account of coming to see correspondence through work in women's studies. In Delgado, R. and Stefanic, J. (Eds.), *Critical White studies: Looking behind the mirror*. Philadelphia: Temple University Press, pp. 291–299.

McIver, D. (2009). Representing Australianness: Our national identity brought to you by Today Tonight. *Media International Australia*, 131, 46–56.

Mischel, W. (1966). A social learning view of sex differences in behavior. In Maccoby, E. E. (Ed.), *The development of sex differences*. Stanford, CA: Stanford University Press, pp. 93–106.

Miville, M. L., Darlington, P., Whitlock, B., and Mulligan, T. (2005). Integrating identities: The relationships of racial, gender, and ego identities among White college students. *Journal of College Student Development*, 46(2), 157–175.

Moorti, S. (2004). Fashioning a cosmopolitan Tamil identity: Game shows, commodities and cultural identity. *Media, Culture & Society*, 26(4), 549–567.

Morrison, T. (1993). *Playing in the dark: Whiteness and the literary imagination*. New York: Vintage.

Ong, J. (2009). Watching the nation, singing the nation: London-based Filipino migrants' identity constructions in news and karaoke practices. *Communication, Culture & Critique*, 2(2), 160–181.

Ossana, S. M., Helms, J. E., and Leonard, M. M. (1992). Do "womanist" identity attitudes influence college women's self-esteem and perceptions of environmental bias? *Journal of Counseling & Development*, 70, 402–408.

Pascarella, E. T., and Terenzini, P. T. (1991). *How college affects students: Findings from twenty years of research*. San Francisco: Jossey-Bass.

Pascarella, E. T., and Terenzini, P. T. (2005). *How college affects students, volume 2: A third decade of research*. San Francisco: Jossey-Bass.

Pearson, R. (1989). Business ethics as communication ethics: Public relations practice and the idea of dialogue. In Botan, C. H. and Hazleton, V., Jr. (Eds.), *Public relations theory*. Hillsdale, NJ: Lawrence Erlbaum, pp. 111–131.

Penning, T. (2008). First impressions: U.S. media portrayals of public relations in the 1920s. *Journal of Communication Management*, 12(4), 344–358.

Perkins, C. (2010). The banality of boundaries: Performance of the nation in a Japanese television comedy. *Television & New Media*, 11(5), 386–403.

Piaget, J. (1963). *The origins of intelligence in children* (2nd edn.). New York: Norton.

Pompper, D. (2004). Linking ethnic diversity & two-way symmetry: Modeling female African American practitioners' roles. *Journal of Public Relations Research*, 16, 269–299.

Pompper, D. (2005). "Difference" in public relations research: A case for introducing critical race theory. *Journal of Public Relations Research*, 17, 139–170.

Public Relations Society of America. (2000). *Member Code of Ethics*. Retrieved from http://www.prsa.org.

Ransford, H. E., and Miller, J. (1983). Race, sex, and feminist outlooks. *American Sociological Review*, 48, 46–59.

Rasmussen, B. B., Klinenberg, E., Nexica, I. J., and Wray, M. (Eds.). (2001). *The making and unmaking of whiteness*. Durham, NC: Duke University Press.

Ravasi, D. and van Rekom, J. (2003). Key issues in organizational identity and identification theory. *Corporate Reputation Review*, 6(2), 118–138.

Reuber, A. and Fischer, E. (2010). Organizations behaving badly: When are discreditable actions likely to damage organizational reputation? *Journal of Business Ethics*, 93(1), 39–50.

Rotheram, M. J. and Phinney, J. S. (1987). Introduction: Definitions and perspectives in the study of children's ethnic socialization. In Phinney, J. S. and Rotheram, M. J. (Eds.), *Children's ethnic socialization*. Newbury Park, CA: Sage, pp. 10–28.

Ryan, M., and Martinson, D. (1983). The PR officer as corporate conscience. *Public Relations Quarterly*, 28(2), 20.

Schunk, D. H. (2004). *Learning theories: An educational perspective* (4th edn.). Upper Saddle River, NJ: Pearson Merrill Prentice Hall.

Sha, B.-L. (1995). Intercultural public relations: Exploring cultural identity as a means of segmenting publics. Unpublished master's thesis, University of Maryland, College Park.

Sha, B.-L. (2001). The feminization of public relations: Contributing to a more ethical practice. In Toth, E. L. and Aldoory, L. (Eds.), *The gender challenge to media: Diverse voices from the field*. Cresskill, NJ: Hampton Press, pp. 153–182.

Sha, B-L. (2006). Cultural identity in the segmentation of publics: An emerging theory of intercultural public relations. *Journal of Public Relations Research*, 18, 45–65.

Sha, B.-L. (2009). Exploring the connection between organizational identity and public relations behaviors: How symmetry trumps conservation in engendering organizational identification. *Journal of Public Relations Research*, 21(3), 295–317.

Sha, B.-L. (2011). Accredited vs. non-accredited: The polarization of practitioners in the public relations profession. *Public Relations Review*, 37(2), 121–128.

Sha, B.-L. and Ahles, C. B. (2009, March). *Identity vs. survival: Communicating with employees while adjusting to the changing business environment*. Paper presented to the International Public Relations Research Conference, Miami, FL.

Sha, B.-L. and Ford, R. (2007). Redefining "requisite variety": The challenge of multiple diversities for the future of public relations. In Toth, E. L. (Ed.), *The future of excellence in public relations and communication management: Challenges for the next generation*. Mahwah, NJ: Lawrence Erlbaum, pp. 381–398.

Sha, B.-L. and Schmitz Weiss, A. (2010, August). *Pre-professional attitudes and identities: The socialization of journalism and public relations majors*. Paper presented to the Association for Education in Journalism and Mass Communication, Denver, CO.

Skipper, T. L. (2005). *Student development in the first college year: A primer for college educators*. Columbia, SC: University of South Carolina, National Resource Center for The First-Year Experience and Students in Transition.

Spencer, M. B. and Markstrom-Adams, C. (1990). Identity processes among racial and ethnic minority children in America. *Child Development*, 61(2), 290–310.

Stein, A. (2006). Employee communications and community: An exploratory study. *Journal of Public Relations Research*, 18(3), 249–264.

Sterne, G. D. (2010). Media perceptions of public relations in New Zealand. *Journal of Communication Management*, 14(1), 4–31.

Takaki, R. (1993). A different mirror: A history of multicultural America. Boston: Little, Brown.

Taylor, M. and Kent, M. L. (2006). Public relations theory and practice in nation building. In Botan, C. H. and Hazleton, V. (Eds.), *Public relations theory II*. Mahwah, NJ: Lawrence Erlbaum, pp. 341–359.

Thomas, R. M. (2000). *Comparing theories of child development* (5th edn.). Belmont, CA: Wadsworth/Thomson Learning.

Tindall, N. T. J. (2009). In search of career satisfaction: African American public relations practitioners, requisite variety, and the workplace. *Public Relations Review*, 443–445.

Tindall, N. T. J. and Vardeman, J. E. (2008, November). *Complications in segmenting campaign publics: Women of color explain their problems, involvement, and constraints in reading heart disease communication*. Paper presented to the National Communication Association, San Diego.

Toth, E. L. (1988). Making peace with gender issues in public relations. *Public Relations Review*, 14(3), 36–47.

Vardeman-Winter, J. and Tindall, N. T. J. (2010). Toward an intersectionality theory of public relations. In Heath, R. L. (Ed.), *The Sage handbook of public relations*. Thousand Oaks, CA: Sage, pp. 223–235.

Volčič, Z. (2006). Blaming the media: Serbian narratives of national(ist) identity. *Continuum: Journal of Media & Cultural Studies*, 20(3), 313–330.

Vygotsky, L. S. (1978). Interaction between learning and development. In Cole, M., John-Steiner, V., Scribner, S., and Souberman, E. (Eds.), *Mind in society: The development of higher psychological processes*. Cambridge, MA: Harvard, pp. 79–91.

Waterman, A. S. (1985). Identity in the context of adolescent psychology. In Waterman, A. S. (Ed.), *Identity in adolescence: Processes and contents*. San Francisco: Jossey-Bass, pp. 5–24.

Weber, L. (2001). *Understanding race, class, gender, and sexuality: A conceptual framework*. New York: McGraw-Hill.

Weber, L. and Parra-Medina, D. (2003). Intersectionality and women's health: Charting a path to eliminating health disparities. *Advances in Gender Research*, 7, 181–230.

White, C., Vanc, A., and Stafford, G. (2010). Internal communication, information satisfaction, and sense of community: The effect of personal influence. *Journal of Public Relations Research*, 22(1), 65–84.

Wilson, L. (1994). Excellent companies and coalition-building among the Fortune 500. *Public Relations Review*, 20(4), 333–343.

Wood, J. T. (2007). *Gendered lives: Communication, gender, and culture* (7th edn.). Belmont, CA: Thomson Wadsworth.

Wright, D. K., Grunig, L. A., Springston, J. K., and Toth, E. L. (1991). *Under the glass ceiling: An analysis of gender issues in American public relations*. New York: PRSA Foundation.

Wrigley, B. J. (2002). Glass ceiling? What glass ceiling? A qualitative study of how women view the glass ceiling in public relations and communications management. *Journal of Public Relations Research*, 14, 27–55.

Yinger, J. M. (1976). Ethnicity in complex societies. In Coser, L. A. and Larsen, O. N. (Eds.), *The uses of controversy in sociology*. New York: Free Press.

Yon, D. A. (2000). *Elusive culture: Schooling, race, and identity in global times*. Albany: State University of New York Press.

Zhou, Y. (2008, November). *National identity of expatriate Chinese in the United States*. Paper presented to the National Communication Association, San Diego, CA.

6

CULTURE AND CHINESE PUBLIC RELATIONS RESEARCH

Yi-Hui Christine Huang

The field of Chinese public relations has received extensive scholarly attention over the past three decades (Chen and Culbertson, 2009; Hung and Chen, 2009; Maynard and Tian, 2004; Tang and Li, 2009; Wang and Chang, 2004; Xue and Yu, 2009; Zhang and Benoit, 2009; Zhang and Cameron, 2003; Zhang et al., 2009). In practice, the globalized business economy and the proliferation of international trade agreements such as NAFTA, the EU, and GATT require an understanding of cross-cultural differences in the practice of public relations, especially from a Chinese perspective. In terms of research, however, scant attention has been paid to Chinese cultural factors in public relations scholarship. As Pompper (2005) noted, a very small percentage of articles published over the course of 28 years in *Public Relations Review* and *Journal of Public Relations Research* involved attention to race, ethnicity, and cultural difference.

The purpose of this paper is to articulate a theoretical framework, from a Chinese cultural perspective, for further understanding the key components contributing to typical Chinese public relations practice and for promoting an awareness of cultural differences. The basic premise of developing this framework is that such an exploration should be preceded by and rooted in a sound conceptual definition of culture (see relevant discussion in Edwards, 2009). Three notes are made concerning the scope of the topic examined.

First, this paper engages with appeals for more cultural and context-sensitive perspectives in Chinese public relations scholarship. As cross-national and comparative studies are now unavoidable in the field of public relations research, it is necessary to develop a conceptual framework that allows for valid comparisons between public relations in China and similar practices in other countries. Second, this paper provides a Chinese cultural perspective for the demonstrated problem of insensitive Western theory borrowing and suggests important implications for the future of communications research in any countries or regions where such research is also promising. Third, it is crucial to investigate Chinese public relations in a way that takes into account its societal context in order to assess the extent to which its features are culture-specific and culture-bounded. This framework could apply to interpersonal and organizational communications as well as media studies and should contribute to advancing comparative studies of Chinese communication research.

This paper will first define public relations. Then, the current status of and critics on Chinese public relations scholarship will be discussed. This paper will conclude with a framework theorizing Chinese culture and public relations research.

Defining Public Relations

Expanding on the work of J. Grunig and Hunt (1984) in which public relations is defined as the "management of communication between an organization and its publics" (p. 6), this paper adds the term *relationship management* to the concept of public relations. The emphasis on relationship management is based upon two grounds. First, serving as an "organizational boundary spanner" (Leifer and Delbecq, 1978), a public relations practitioner "works at organizations' peripheral areas or boundaries to interact with organizations' internal and external strategic publics (or stakeholders) and environments" (pp. 40–41). Thus, maintaining and cultivating relationships between an organization and the public has been an essential task. In fact, research on such relationships in the late 1990s has become increasingly extensive (Heath, 2001; Huang, 2001, 2008; Hung and Chen, 2009; Ledingham and Bruning, 2000). Second, and particularly in East Asian countries, research has demonstrated the prevalence of the personal influencing model that focuses on interpersonal relationships rather than on pure communication practice (Grunig et al., 1995; Huang, 2000, 2004; Sriramesh, Kim, and Takasaki, 1999; G. Wang and Liu, 2010).

Current Status and Critics of Chinese Public Relations Scholarship

In public relations scholarship, one consensus among scholars is that mainstream public relations research is limited by Western cultural assumptions (Choi and Cameron, 2005; Curtin and Gaither, 2005; Pompper, 2005). Similar problems occur in Chinese communication and management scholarship (Huang, 2010). On the one hand, research that is primarily built in and for a North American cultural context is a problem because it inadequately explains the communicative behavior of non-Western people (Kim, 2007; Lee, 2002). On the other hand, Miike (2007) specifically noted the following Eurocentric biases and predispositions: individuality and independence, ego-centeredness and self-enhancement, reason and rationality, rights and freedom, and pragmatism and materialism. In a similar vein, Jia (2000) specified that Orientalistic scholarship that is overly reliant on the deduction-oriented Western research tradition has the following Western biases: dichotomous thinking, linear thinking, individualism, analyticalism, absence of cosmic, historical, and moral perspectives, ignorance of relevant indigenous Chinese concepts (such as *ren* 仁, *yi* 義, *li* 禮, *chi* 智, etc.), and pervasive apathy toward Chinese communication (pp. 148–152).

Two reasons are identified for a shortage of cultural sensitivity in organizational scholarship: deliberate avoidance and careless oversight (Heath and Sitkin, 2001; Johns, 2001; Rousseau and Fried, 2001). First, scholars purposefully disregard cultural and contextual factors for a variety of reasons, including a misguided belief that context-free knowledge has greater scientific merit than contextualized knowledge (Cheng et al., 2004). Second, investigators fail to take into account relevant contextual factors because they simply do not see them. Facing the problems that research relies heavily on Western theory and a subsequent insensitivity to cultural and contextual assumptions, this study suggests that Chinese public relations scholarship should broaden and transform the field to be more comprehensive and culturally sensitive.

A Framework Proposed to Advance Chinese Public Relations Research

This section adopts Kim's (2007) decentering–recentering–integrating approach. Kim specifies three changes that should take place in the discipline of communication: "(a) cultural decentering away from Euro-American theory; (b) recentering the discipline within the cultures of interest; and (c) integrating the different cultural perspectives to move toward a truly universal theory of human communication" (pp. 279–285). The next section will first introduce Chinese culture as a method of cultural decentering away from Euro-American theory. Then the similarities and differences of cultural assumptions between and among Western and Chinese cultures will be consciously examined in response to the call for "recentering the discipline within the cultures of interest." The framework will conclude with several theoretical approaches in the existing literature that attempt to integrate different perspective so as to move toward a universal theory of human communication.

Cultural Decentering away from Euro-American Theory: Understanding Chinese Culture

Chinese culture contributes to the practice of Chinese communication (Huang, 2000). Confucian tradition, Taoism, and Buddhism are discussed in light of their pertinence to the exploration of public relations practice.

Confucian Traditions

Confucian teachings that emphasize long-term relationships, harmony, interpersonal relationships, humanism (仁, *jen*), face, loyalty, order, and harmony contribute to Chinese communication practices, relationships, and public relations. *Guanxi*, or *social relationship*, in particular is crucial for understanding Chinese behavior in social (Fried, 1969), political (Jacobs, 1979), and organizational (Walder, 1983) contexts. Bond and Hwang (1986) noted that Chinese people see other people as relational beings, socially situated and "defined within an interactive context" (quoted in Huang, 2000, p. 222). They further specified three aspects of the important role of social relations in Chinese society: "1) People exist through, and are defined by, their relationships to others; 2) these relationships are structured hierarchically; 3) social order is ensured through each party's honoring the requirements in the role of relationships" (quoted in Huang, 2000, p. 222).

Confucius' Five Cardinal Relations set rules for interpersonal relationships in ancient society. The Five Cardinal Relations denote the relationships between father and son, husband and wife, elder brother and younger brother, superior and subordinate, and friends. Because of the different roles in the Five Cardinal Relations, the values and norms emphasized between these roles vary: closeness between father and son, righteousness between superior and subordinate, differentiation between husband and wife, hierarchy between elder and younger, and trustworthiness between friends.

Outside the Five Cardinal Relations, Yang (1992) noted that Chinese people adopt familism in families and pan-familism outside families. Chinese people tend to apply the following three strictures in the practice of familism (Yang, 1992): (1) strict adherence to familial structure; (2) definition of ethics and roles in relation to familial hierarchy; and (3) interpersonal and social skills learned primarily from within the hierarchical family structure. Thus, Redding and Wong (1986) revealed that, in overseas Chinese organizations, "members of the organization enter with a set of values stressing familism, a wider collectivism, a sensitivity to interpersonal harmony, and a sense of social hierarchy" (p. 293).

Relational Orientation

In addition to the important role of *guanxi* and the Five Cardinal Relations, the following constructs derived from Confucian tradition are worthy of exploration: relational fatalism, face (面子, *mianze*; Huang, 2011), reciprocity, favor (人情, *renqing*; Huang, 2011), return (報, *bao*), and asymmetrical power structure. The theory of relational orientation (Yang, 1992) should be pertinent to understanding these notions because of its indigenous nature on one hand and its sound theoretical base on the other.

Yang (1992) stressed five core concepts representing relational orientation in Chinese society:

1 *Relational fatalism* is rooted in the Chinese concept of karma. Prior to the inception of a relationship, karma dictates the occurrence of certain patterns of interpersonal relationships and even the duration and outcomes of such a relationship.

2 *Relational determinism* refers to the characteristics of the degree of intimacy in differential order (Yang, 1992). Such characteristics define interpersonal relationships as relationships with family members, acquaintances, or strangers (Hwang, 1987), categorizing such relationships accordingly. Differential order also dictates how a person manages affairs in which other people also have a stake or an interest.

3 The term *relational role* assumes that interpersonal interactions primarily hinge on a given relationship, in which roles and related behaviors to a great extent are predesignated and fixed (i.e., the Five Cardinal Relations, the related roles, and corresponding behaviors; Yang, 1992, p. 98).

4 *Relational interdependence* (reciprocity) notes that the natures of people's corresponding roles in their social relations with others are supplementary and reciprocal. Moreover, the employment of "face" and "favor," two important resources of social exchanges in Chinese society, allow the mechanism of reciprocity function smoothly. Yang (1992) noted the characteristics of "face" and "favor" that (1) operate in interpersonal relationship networks, (2) increase and decrease in quantity, (3) can be deposited, overdrawn, or owned on credit, (4) can be given away and taken back, and (5) are transferable and can be rendered to third parties (p. 102).

5 *Relational harmony* refers to the goals pursued by the Chinese in interpersonal communication and social interaction. Yang noted that traditional Chinese people pursued interpersonal "harmony for the sake of harmony," and that there are even cases of "anxiety about disharmony" and "fear of conflicts" (Yang, 1992, p. 103).

Confucianism focuses essentially on internal discipline or cultivation of the self, which is a long-term process of individual development that occurs by internalizing ethical values such as humanness (*ren*), righteousness (*yi*), and propriety (*li*) (Hwang, 1987). These normative doctrines, directly or indirectly contributing to the preservation of the status quo, ensure an orderly society. The rights, needs, and freedoms of some particular positions or classes such as the rank-and-file people, however, were often underscored or even discounted. Discontent and failure in "self realization" then would motivate the people to turn to the other "isms," such as Taoism and Buddhism, for alternative solutions (e.g., H. Chang, 1996, 1998; I. Chang, 1998; G. Chen, 1994, 1995, 1998; Chen and Chung, 1993; Crawford, 1994; Kluver, 1998;

Kowal, 1998; Lin, 1995; Lu, 1998, 1999; Yu, 1998; see G. M. Chen, 2001, for more detailed discussion).

Alternative "Isms:" Taoism and Buddhism

Taoism and Buddhism serve as alternative philosophical groundworks to Confucianism. On one hand, Taoism provides the suppressed class "a sense of worth by directly associating them with nature" and "consolation to the lower classes in that the noble Confucian officials are not really viewed as unique in essence and in that the wealth and power they have are not represented as being really that attractive" (Shih, 1988, p. 612). On the other hand, Buddhism, which suggests a sense of afterlife and a sort of liberation from the constraint of the status quo, offers a substitute worldview that circumscribes day-to-day behavior for laypeople.

Recentering the Discipline within the Cultures of Interest: Comparison between Chinese and Eurocentric Worldviews

To sum up, Confucianism, Buddhism, and Taoism provide a vivid contrast to the Eurocentric core values, which emphasize instrumental rationality, individual liberty, calculated self-interest, material progress, and rights-consciousness (Tu, 1996). The difference between Chinese and Western worldviews, respectively, can be succinctly summarized: (1) emphasis on wholeness versus parts, (2) complex interpersonal relationships versus individuals, (3) emphasis on emotional/spiritual versus cognitive outcomes, and (4) nature of communication being intuitively and directly experienced versus language-centered.

The *contrasts between wholes and parts* and between *complex relationships and individuals* can best be understood by examining Chinese teachings involving the relations that exist among the self, others, and the universe. The Confucian teaching of *ren* underlines the fact that a person's well-being is intertwined with those of others. Moreover, the Buddhist principle of "co-cultivation" and the Taoist doctrine of *yin* and *yang* also sheds light on the interpenetration in nature of the self, family, community, society, nation, world, and cosmos (Chen, 2006; Saral, 1983). Miike (2007) gave a vivid explanation in this respect:

> It is an endless process in which people continuously locate and relocate themselves in an ever-expanding network of relationships across space and time. Constant interaction with fellow humans, nature, and the world of spirits helps us escape the illusion that we are independent individuals at a particular place and at a particular time and experience the oneness of the universe.
>
> (p. 273)

Moreover, *the emphasis on the emotional/spiritual nature of communication* can be appreciated by the ways in which humans interact with others and their natural environment. On the one hand, Chinese concepts such as *renqing* (favor) and relationship fatalism suggest that humans are not only rational animals but also emotional beings. Tu (2001) clearly spelled out that treating a person humanely is the result of emotional sensitivity and sensibility, not of reasonable and rational choice. Miike (2007) also found that:

> according to their teachings, therefore, humans ought to discipline and cultivate themselves to eliminate spatial and temporal illusions, experience the nonseparateness of the universe, and harmoniously coexist with other members of the human family, nature, and the supernatural. Communication is central to this process of self-discipline and self-cultivation.
>
> (p. 274)

Integrating the Different Cultural Perspectives to Move toward a Universal Theory of Public Relations

Much research has been conducted in the field of cross-cultural communication to observe cultural differences. Among them all, the line of research involving individualism–collectivism (Hofstede, 1980) for cultural comparison has been evident (Oyserman et al., 2002). In an attempt to overcome the limitations associated with individualism–collectivism, however, two alternative approaches—self-construal and Chinese relationalism—have been explored by several researchers (e.g., Kashima et al., 1995; Markus and Kitayama, 1991; Triandis, 1989) and recently received much research in replication and extension.

Individualism–Collectivism

Cross-cultural psychologists maintain that people in individualistic and collective cultures hold different relational orientations. This helps to shed light on cultural difference and the difficulties that arise from it. International researchers have intensively used individualism–collectivism (referred to as IND-COL hereafter; Hofstede, 1980) as an analytical framework in order to compare Western and Eastern communication (Oyserman et al., 2002). Individualism is defined by Hofstede (1980) in self–other relationships from an "individuality perspective," which maintains at the same time both a self–family relation and an ordinary self–other relation. However, self is also defined, from a collectivist point of view, from a group perspective to emphasize identification with families, parties, and groups. Oyserman, Coon, and Kemmelmeier (2002) concluded that:

with regard to relationality, definitions of collectivism imply that (a) important group memberships are ascribed and fixed, viewed as "facts of life" to which people must accommodate; (b) boundaries between in-groups and out-groups are stable, relatively impermeable, and important; and (c) in-group exchanges are based on equality or even generosity principles (U. Kim, 1994; Sayle, 1998; Triandis, 1995).

(p. 5)

IND-COL research also received widespread criticism, especially for its broad definition of collectivism and the low validity of the collectivistic scales. Low levels of consensus in definitions of IND-COL, which result in idiosyncratic operationalizations and assessments of these constructs (Oyserman et al., 2002, p. 44), have stimulated the development of new theoretical discourses. The following two theories emerge as alternative perspectives.

Interdependent or Relational Self-Construal

Examining interdependent self-construal has been a focus in the existing literature in Chinese or cross-cultural communications research (Kim, 2009). Kim (2002, 2009) pointed out that there are dramatic differences in psychological functioning and communicative behavior between independent and interdependent selves. Comparatively, Western culture equates self with the autonomous or self-sufficient individual. Independent self is thus highlighted inasmuch as relationality would usually weaken the "right" of individuality, selfhood, and autonomy. In contrast, interdependent self is more appreciated in Eastern culture because caring and relational styles of identity are characterized as the pinnacle of psychological and ethical development.

The Theory of Chinese Relationalism

On the other hand, but also in the same vein of providing an alternative approach to overcome the limitations associated with individualism–collectivism, Q. Wang and Liu (2008) assert the important implication of "relational self" and Chinese relationalism to Chinese communications research.

Q. Wang and Liu (2008) shared Brewer and Gardner's (1996) view of "trichotomization" (p. 84) and proposed to identify self in the categories of the individual self, the relational self, and the collective self. Thus relational self-construal is seen to be more pertinent. Moreover, G. Wang and Liu (2010) also suggest that Chinese relationalism should more closely reflect the way self relates to others in Chinese societies based upon the following three observations. First, the individualism–collectivism model was developed "within the individualistic cultural framework, but considered as a universal construct and pertinent across cultures" (p. 45). Second, there have been many conflicting findings on collectivism that have led researchers to question its applicability across cultures, especially concerning the meaning of "collective" (p. 42). Third, Confucius's teaching in fact includes individualistic and collectivistic values.

G. Wang and Liu (2010) assert that individuals

> in a relational culture define themselves according to their relative position in the interpersonal networks. The position is both culturally/socially ascribed, according to the role of the self vis-a-vis that of the others, and fluid, constantly revised by reciprocal interactions.
>
> (p. 56)

Theories derived from or related to Chinese relationalism include differential order (Fei, 1948), relational orientation (Ho, 1998), social orientation (Yang, 1981a,b, 1992, 1995), model of face and favor (Huang, 2011; Hwang, 1987, 2011), model of conflicts (Hwang, 1997), and a series of research related to the concept of face (Zhu, 1991; Chou and Ho, 1992).

Conclusion

Cross-national and comparative studies are now unavoidable in the field of communications research. As a result we should be increasingly wary of the implications that Western social theory, imported unquestioningly into research on Far Eastern communicative practices, has for the way that research is conducted and the conclusions to which it may come. Whereas most critics of Western theory borrowing advance the alternative of indigenous theory, this chapter focuses on making theory borrowing more culturally sensitive instead of promoting its outright proscription. The conceptual challenges scholars face when comparing Chinese cultural contexts and communication practices with communication elsewhere necessitate that researchers should not overlook the importance of developing a framework that allows for valid comparisons between cultural context and communication in China and other countries. The framework outlined here engages with recent calls for more culturally sensitive perspectives in Chinese public relations research (Huang, 2010). This framework should help advance theoretical approaches in Chinese public relations research in a way that takes into account Chinese cultural context in order to assess the extent to which its features are culturally defined.

References

Bond, M. H. and Hwang, K. K. (1986). The social psychology of the Chinese people. In Bond, M. H. (Ed.), *The psychology of the Chinese people.* Hong Kong: Oxford University Press.

Brewer, M. B. and Gardner, W. (1996). Who is this "we"? Levels of collective identity and self representations. *Journal of Personality and Social Psychology*, 71, 83–93.

Chang, H. C. (1996, November). *Language and words: Communication in the Analects of Confucius*. Paper presented at the annual meeting of Speech Communication Association, San Diego, California.

Chang, H. C. (1998, November). *Constructing Chinese communication theory: A proposed agenda*. Paper presented at the annual meeting of National Communication Association, San Diego, California.

Chang, I. S. (1998, November). *The rhetoric of Taoism: The futility of argumentation*. Paper presented at the annual meeting of National Communication Association, San Diego, California.

Chen, G. M. (1994, November). *A conceptualization and measurement of communication competence: A Chinese perspective*. Paper presented at the annual convention of the Speech Communication Association, New Orleans, Louisiana.

Chen, G. M. (1995, August). *A Chinese model of human relationship development*. Paper presented at the 5th International Conference on Cross-Cultural Communication: East and West, Harbin, China.

Chen, G. M. (1998, November). *A Chinese model of human communication*. Paper presented at the annual meeting of National Communication Association, San Diego, California.

Chen, G. M. (2001). An examination of overseas Chinese communication studies. *Mass Communication Research*, 69, 1–28.

Chen, G. M. (2006). Asian communication studies: What and where to now. *Review of Communication*, 6(4), 295–311.

Chen, G. M. and Chung, J. (1993, November). *Preventive communication cost in Confucianism-influenced organizations*. Paper presented at the annual convention of the Speech Communication Association, Miami, Florida.

Chen, N. and Culbertson, H. M. (2009). Public relations in Mainland China: An adolescent with growing pains. In Sriramesh, K. and Verčič, D. (Eds.) *The global public relations handbook: Theory, research and practice*. New York: Routledge.

Cheng, B. S., Chou, L. F., Wu, T. Y., Huang, M. P., and Farh, J. L. (2004). Paternalistic leadership and subordinate response: Establishing a leadership model in Chinese organizations. *Asian Journal of Social Psychology*, 7, 89–117.

Choi, Y. and Cameron, G. T. (2005). Overcoming ethnocentrisms: The role of identity in contingent practice of international public relations. *Journal of Public Relations Research*, 17(2), 171–189.

Chou, M. L. and Ho, Y. H. (1992). The essence of face and its operation in social interaction. In Yang, K. S. and Yu, A. B. (Eds.), *Chinese psychology and behavior: Methodological and conceptual considerations* (in Chinese). Taipei: Guiguan Book Co., pp. 205–254.

Crawford, L. (1994). Colorado Tao: Construing behavior in a commune. *Massachusetts Journal of Communication*, 12, 1–6.

Curtin, P. A. and Gaither, T. K. (2005). Privileging identity, difference, and power: The circuit of culture as a basis for public relations theory. *Journal of Public Relations Research*, 17(2), 91–115.

Edwards, L. (2009). Symbolic power and public relations practice: Locating individual practitioners in their social context. *Journal of Public Relations Research*, 21(3), 251–272.

Fei, S. T. (1948). *Rural China* (in Chinese). Shanghai: Observer.

Fried, M. H. (1969). *The fabric of Chinese society: A study of the social life of a Chinese county seat*. New York: Octagon.

Grunig, J. E. and Hunt, T. (1984). *Managing public relations*. New York: Holt, Rinehart & Winston.

Grunig, J. E., Grunig, L. A., Sriramesh, K., Huang, Y., and Lyra, A. (1995). Models of public relations in an international setting. *Journal of Public Relations Research*, 7(3), 163–187.

Heath, R. L. (2001). Shifting foundations: Public relations as relationship building. In Heath, R. L. (Ed.), *Handbook of public relations*. Thousand Oaks, CA: Sage, pp. 1–10.

Heath, C. and Sitkin, S. B. (2001). Big-b versus big-o: What is organizational about organizational behavior? *Journal of Organizational Behavior*, 22(1): 43–58.

Ho, D. Y. F. (1998). Interpersonal relationships and relationship dominance: Analysis based on methodological relationalism. *Asian Journal of Social Psychology*, 1, 1–16.

Hofstede, G. (1980). *Culture's consequences: International differences in work-related values*. Newbury Park, CA: Sage.

Huang, Y. H. (2000). The personal influence model and "gao guanxi" in Taiwan Chinese public relations. *Public Relations Review*, 26(2), 216–239.

Huang, Y. H. (2001). OPRA: A cross-cultural, multiple-item scale for measuring organization-public relationships. *Journal of Public Relations Research*, 13(1), 61–91.

Huang, Y. H. (2004). PRSA: Scale development for exploring the cross-cultural impetus of public relations strategies. *Journalism and Mass Communication Quarterly*, 81(2): 307–326.

Huang, Y. H. (2008). Trust and relational commitment in corporate crises: The effects of crisis communicative strategy and form of crisis response. *Journal of Public Relations Research*, 20, 297–327.

Huang, Y. H. (2010). Theorizing Chinese communication research: A holistic framework for comparative studies. *Chinese Journal of Communication*, 3(1), pp. 95–113.

Huang, Y. H. (2011). Favor (*Renqing*): Characteristics and practice from a resource-based perspective. *China Media Research*, 7(4), 34–43.

Hung, C.-J. F. and Chen, Y.-R. R. (2009). Types and dimensions of organization–public relationships in greater China. *Public Relations Review*, 35, 181–186.

Hwang, K. (1987). Face and favor: The Chinese power game. *American Journal of Sociology*, 92(4), 944–974.

Hwang, K. K. (1997). Guanxi and mientze: Conflict resolution in Chinese society. *Intercultural Communication Studies*, 7(1), 17–37.

Hwang, K. K. (2011). Face dynamism in Confucian society. *China Media Research*, 7(4), 13–24.

Jacobs, B. J. (1979). A preliminary model of particularistic ties in Chinese political alliances: Ran-ching and Kuan-his in a rural Taiwanese township. *China Quarterly*, 78, 232–273.

Jia, W. (2000). Chinese communication scholarship as an expansion of the communication and culture paradigm. In Heisey, D. R. (Ed.), *Chinese perspectives in rhetoric and communication*. Stamford, CT: Ablex Publishing Corporation, pp. 139–161.

Johns, G. (2001). In praise of context. *Journal of Organizational Behavior*, 22(1): 31–42.

Kashima, Y., Yamaguchi, S., Kim, U., Choi, S., Gelfand, M., and Yuki, M. (1995). Culture, gender and self: A perspective from individualism–collectivism research. *Journal of Personality and Social Psychology*, 69, 925–937.

Kim, M. S. (2002). *Non-Western perspectives on human communication: Implications for theory and research*. Thousand Oaks, CA: Sage.

Kim, M. S. (2007). The four cultures of cultural research. *Communication Monographs*, 74(2), 279–285.

Kim, M. S. (2009). Cultural bias in communication science: Challenges of overcoming ethnocentric paradigms in Asia. *Asian Journal of Communication*, 19(4), 412–421.

Kim, U. (1994). Individualism and collectivism: Conceptual clarification and elaboration. In Kim, U., Triandis, H. C., Kagitcibasi, C., Choi, S. C., and Yoon, G. (Eds.), *Individualism and collectivism: Theory, method, and applications*. London: Sage, pp. 19–40.

Kluver, R. (1998, November). *The impact of Confucianism on Chinese political discourse*. Paper presented at the annual meeting of National Communication Association, San Diego, California.

Kowal, D. M. (1998, November). *Lessons from the Chinese art of gun fu: Towards the development of a nonconfrontational rhetoric*. Paper presented at the annual meeting of National Communication Association, San Diego, California.

Ledingham, J. A. and Bruning, S. D. (2000). Concept and theory of organization–public relationships. In Ledingham, J. A. and Bruning, S. D. (Eds.), *Public relations as relationship management: A relational approach to the study and practice of public relations*. Hillsdale, NJ: Lawrence Erlbaum Associates, pp. 3–22.

Lee, P. S. N. (2002). The observation and thinking of communication in China. In Zhang, G. and Huang, X. (Eds.), *Chinese communication: Rethink and prediction* (in Chinese). Shanghai: Fudan University Press, pp. 125–145.

Leifer, R. and Delbecq, A. (1978). Organizational/environmental interchange: A model of boundary spanning activity. *Academy of Management Review*, 20, 40–50.

Lin, J. (1995, November). *An exploration of Hsun Tzu's perspectives on persuasion and argumentation*. Paper presented at the annual meeting of Speech Communication Association, San Antonio, Texas.

Lu, S. (1998, November). *Chinese perspective on communication*. Paper presented at the annual meeting of National Communication Association, San Diego, California.

Lu, S. (1999, November). *Native terms for Chinese small talk and implications for communication theory*. Paper presented at the annual meeting of National Communication Association, Chicago, Illinois.

Markus, H. R. and Kitayama, S. (1991). Culture and the self: Implications for cognition, emotion, and motivation. *Psychological Review*, 98, 224–253.

Maynard, M. and Tian, Y. (2004). Between global and glocal: content analysis of the Chinese web sites of the 100 top global brands. *Public Relations Review*, 30(3), 285–291.

Miike, Y. (2007). An Asiacentric reflection on Eurocentric bias in communication theory. *Communication Monographs*, 74(2), 272–278.

Oyserman, D., Coon, M. H., and Kemmelmeier, M. (2002). Rethinking individualism and collectivism: Evaluation of theoretical assumptions and meta-analysis. *Psychological Bulletin*, 128, 3–72.

Pompper, D. (2005). "Difference" in public relations research: A case for introducing critical race theory. *Journal of Public Relations Research*, 17(2), 139–169.

Redding, G. and Wong, G. Y. Y. (1986). The psychology of Chinese organizational behavior. In Bong, M. H. (Ed.), *The psychology of the Chinese people*. New York: Oxford University Press, pp. 267–295.

Rousseau, D. M. and Fried, Y. (2001). Location, location, location: Contextualizing organizational research. *Journal of Organizational Behavior*, 22, 1–13.

Saral, T. B. (1983). Hindu philosophy of communication. *Communication*, 8(1), 47–58.

Sayle, A. H. (1998). Can quality calm the roar of the stricken Asian tiger? *Quality World*, April, 38–40.

Shih, C.-Y. (1988). National role conception as foreign policy motivation: The psychocultural bases of Chinese diplomacy. *Political Psychology*, 9(4), 599–631.

Sriramesh, K., Kim, Y., and Takasaki, M. (1999). Public relations in three Asian cultures: An analysis. *Journal of Public Relations Research*, 11(4), 271–292.

Tang, L. and Li, H. (2009). Corporate social responsibility communication of Chinese and global corporations in China. *Public Relations Review*, 35(3), 199–212.

Triandis, H. C. (1989). The self and social behavior in differing cultural contexts. *Psychological Review*, 96, 506–520.

Triandis, H. C. (1995). *Individualism and collectivism*. Boulder, CA: Westview Press.

Tu, W. (1996). Global community as lived reality: Exploring spiritual resources for social development. *Social Policy and Social Progress*, 1(1), 39–51.

Tu, W.-M. (2001). Mutual learning as an agenda for social development. In Baudot, J. (Ed.), *Building a world community: Globalization and the common good*. Copenhagen, Denmark: Royal Danish Ministry of Foreign Affairs, pp. 253–260.

Walder, A. G. (1983). Organized dependency and cultures of authority in Chinese industry. *Journal of Asian Studies*, 63, 51–75.

Wang, G. and Liu, Z. B. (2010). What collective? Collectivism and relationalism from a Chinese perspective. *Chinese Journal of Communication*, 3(1), 42–63.

Wang, J. and Chang, T. K. (2004). Strategic public diplomacy and local press: how a high-profile "head-of-state" visit was covered in America's heartland. *Public Relations Review*, 30(1), 11–24.

Wang, Q. and Liu, Z. B. (2008, December). *What is the collective? A review of individualism, collectivism and guanxi from Chinese culture*. Paper presented at the conference of Imagining Chinese Communication Research, Hong Kong, China.

Xue, K. and Yu, M. (2009). A content analysis of public relations literatures from 1999 to 2008 in China. *Public Relations Review*, 35(3), 171–180.

Yang, K. S. (1981a). Chinese personality and behavior: Formation and change (in Chinese). *Chinese Journal of Psychology*, 23, 39–55.

Yang, K. S. (1981b). Social orientation and individual modernity among Chinese students in Taiwan. *Journal of Social Psychology*, 113, 159–170.

Yang, K. S. (1992). Chinese social orientation: A social interactional approach. In Yang, K. S. and Yu, A. B. (Eds.), *Chinese psychology and behavior: Methodological and conceptual considerations* (in Chinese). Taipei: Guiguan Book Co., pp. 87–142.

Yang, K. S. (1995). Chinese social orientation: An integrative analysis. In Tseng, W. S., Lin, T. Y., and Yeh, Y. K. (Eds.), *Chinese societies and mental health*. Hong Kong: Oxford University Press, pp. 19–39.

Yu, X. (1998, November). The influence of Confucianism on Chinese conceptions of power, authority, and the rule of law. Paper presented at the annual meeting of National Communication Association, San Diego, California.

Zhang, A., Shen, H., and Jiang, H. (2009). Culture and Chinese public relations: A multi-method "inside out" approach. *Public Relations Review*, 35(3), 226–231.

Zhang, E. and Benoit, W. L. (2009). Former Minister Zhang's discourse on SARS: Government's image restoration or destruction? *Public Relations Review*, 35(3), 240–246.

Zhang, J. and Cameron, G. T. (2003). China's agenda building and image polishing in the US: assessing an international public relations campaign. *Public Relations Review*, 29(1), 13–28.

Zhu, R. L. (1991). Face pressure and the reaction behavior. *National Science Council Journal: Humanity and Social Science*, 1(1), 14–31.

7

MAGO MAGO

Nigeria, Petroleum and a History of Mismanaged Community Relations

Julia Jahansoozi, Kingsley Eyita, and Nnadozie Izidor

This chapter explores the context of the petroleum industry and its approaches to community relationships within the Nigerian cultural context. Interest in exploring the petroleum industry and culture has come from the authors' previous and ongoing research into the petroleum industry in Nigeria and Canada. Although both locations share issues concerning community engagement, environmental impact, sustainability and corporate social responsibility, the petroleum industry's approach has been markedly different, even within the same petroleum operators, and has very different results. Whereas global petroleum companies (e.g. Shell, Chevron, Exxon, Mobil, Total) have international business principles there are significant differences in the way these principles are translated into local practice. At the same time there is a drive to minimise the global level of operations from a cost perspective and yet government access largely depends upon the global reputation, not the local one; thus the well-being of the locals is often put last or ignored. Internally within petroleum companies this 'problem' is referred to as the issue of double standards. As oil is getting harder to find and more expensive to produce, the 'oil economy' problems faced in many countries will get worse, and bribery and corruption, far from being on the decline, in some places will actually increase.

There are cultural differences at play that influence how the petroleum operators engage with the country and local communities where they are causing the direct impact as well, but these are sometimes used to legitimise double standards, leading to an ethical slippery slope. Much behaviour is down to the individual managers in the local areas and how they are coping and resolving issues and conflicts at the local and even community level, which is why an understanding of the historical relational context and local culture is critical (Jahansoozi, 2007). Also, there is a continuing problem of colonialism as Western business models are being exported to countries that are the most vulnerable because they do not have a strong economy or established Western-style business culture. The 'plundering' continues, although now it is done with a smile and a hospital and often labelled as corporate social responsibility (CSR). It was this perceived difference in approach and outcomes regarding the behaviour of petroleum operators around the world that led to the development of this chapter.

In this chapter we attempt to present the Nigerian cultural context, the petroleum industry context in Nigeria and its current public relations/community relations practice. Culture is something that cannot be ignored in public relations practice; as Curtin and Gaither (2007, p. 12) explain: 'cultural constructs don't affect public relations practice, they are the essence of public relations practice.' So we need to consider the impact of culture and subcultures on numerous levels, including national, local (community) and organisational levels, when viewing public relations practice. International public relations scholarship has increased, especially within the comparative research setting, leading to the 'illumination on the different practices, assumptions and expectations of those involved in public relations in both global and local contexts' (Daymon and Hodges, 2009, p. 429).

Over time and space, culture, as an integrated social/human phenomenon, appears to have assumed a more self-asserting definition and importance, traversing other boundaries—geography and industry—with profound influence on business, politics, economy and every other aspect of our life and environment. Indeed, it has become the road map for progress.

Culture, long recognised as a significant factor that can influence public relations practice, has been defined in various ways by different researchers (Grunig et al., 1995, pp. 163–186). From the anthropological school:

> it consists in patterned ways of thinking, feeling and reacting; it is acquired and transmitted mainly by . . . human groups, including their embodiments in artifacts; the essential core of culture consists of traditional ideas and especially their attached values.
>
> (Kluckhohn, 1951, p. 86)

Like Kluckhohn, Hofstede has done extensive research on culture as a factor that can swing the practice of public relations. Hofstede introduced the concept of 'national culture' into the discourse. He defines national culture as 'the collective programming of the mind that distinguishes the members of one group or category of people from another' (Hofstede, 2001, p. 9). Although there are a number of empirical studies in other climes on how culture could improve or influence the practice of public relations (Hofstede, 2001; Burns and Stalker, 1961; Taylor, 2000, pp. 277–293), the situation is different in

Nigeria, as it most probably is in other African countries where research commands no important consideration (Rensburg, 2008, pp. 1–2).

The limitations to this chapter are many, as it is difficult to sufficiently cover the plethora of cultures involved, which at a minimum include political, media, ethnic, social, occupational, organisational and activism cultures (see Chapter 13 below), all of which are highly relevant for the Nigerian petroleum sector.

The Nigerian Cultural Context

Nigeria is the most populous country in Africa and has a population of approximately 140 million (2006 national census). It has over 250 ethnic groups, with three major tribes accounting for 40 per cent of the population: the Hausa, Yoruba, and Igbo. Although the official language is English there are approximately 374 dialects. Most Nigerians speak or understand Pidgin English (Koper et al., 2009, p. 289). Nigeria is a developing country with diverse cultural background, which at a minimum can be described as a tripod of ethnicity, regionalism and religion (Muhammad, 2003, p. 40).

Nigeria has struggled with its identity since it came into existence in 1914 following the unpopular amalgamation of the southern and northern protectorates into one umbrella with the name Nigeria. Matthew Hassan Kukah, Chairman of the National Secretariat of the Nigerian Roman Catholic Church and a highly respected public commentator with very strong views on issues concerning Nigeria and its corporate survival and existence, commented on Nigeria, Nigerians and their national identity: 'every Nigerian carries an excess luggage of identity . . . even in our common quest for social justice, we are constantly negotiating with the others on behalf of a religion, an ethnic group or a state' (Maringues, 1996, p. 22, cited in ICG, 2006, p. 2). The actual name *Nigeria* was coined by Flora Lewis, the colonial editor of the British newspaper *The Times*, in 1897 to describe the "amalgamation" of the Niger River and the surrounding areas (Niger + area). After she married Lord Frederick Lugard, the first governor-general of the amalgamated British colony, the territory was 'christened' Nigeria (ICG, 2006, p. 1; Peel, 2009, p. 41). Despite a level of discomfort the name has stuck although the national anthem has changed.

Many agree that Nigeria's problems are traceable to the unification of three very different ethnic groups by the British colonial government of the time (Falola and Heaton, 2008; Peel, 2009). The Igbo, Yoruba, and Hausa-Fulani, which constitute the majority population in the Eastern, Western, and Northern regions respectively, were brought under one administration under the 1914 amalgamation. Whereas the Hausa-Fulani are predominantly Muslim, with cultural values that are markedly different from those of other regions, and were happy to be ruled under the emirate structure fashioned under the Sokoto caliphate structure, the same could not be said of the

Eastern and Western regions. Their differences were and are still very clear; why the British colonialists chose to down-play these differences and went ahead to force these different regions together can be explained only from the perspective of the vested political and economic interests of the colonial administration.

Details of actions and reactions which followed that unpopular action are outside the scope of this chapter. Suffice it to stress that, theoretically, the British ruled the pre-independence Nigeria as a single political unit. In practice the administrations of the regions were distinct and independent in recognition of their inherent cultural differences. For instance, there was no central representative institution to unify the country's political forces; thus each unit was administered and run along its unique cultural values. This continued until after the Second World War when, under pressure from nationalist politicians, constitutional development led to the adoption of a truly federal system of government. Under that arrangement, the different regions had considerable autonomy (Forrest, 1993, p. 17). However, the spirit and letter of true federalism have since been diluted or 'nationalised' by political forces from the majority ethnic groups; thus what Nigeria now has in place in the name of federalism can better be experienced than described. As Augustine Ikein expressed it, the government tends to protect favoured groups or special interest groups rather than general welfare of the people; as a result, 'federalism has worked chiefly to the advantage of elites, capitalists . . .' (Ikein, 1990, p. 38).

Region and ethnicity play varying important factors in the running of Nigeria, which now comprises 36 states and the federal capital territory of Abuja. As Tom Forest highlighted, 'Patron–client ties provide much of the social fabric for informal and party politics in Nigeria. [Such] patronage flows along personal networks based on kinship, community, ethnic associations, and religious affiliations' (Forrest, 1996, p. 5). It is on the basis of these multiple networks that, in their insatiable appetite to hold on to political power, wealthy and powerful regional, religious and ethnic champions deplore mobilising support for the 68 per cent (CIA, 2010) who are illiterate and impoverished rural dwellers.

Nigeria achieved independence from the British in 1960 and gained the status of a republic in 1963. Before independence Nigeria's economy was heavily based on agriculture. However, as soon as petroleum reserves were discovered and exploited the economy switched and became overly dependent on petroleum resources. This has led to the neglect of agricultural development. Despite the huge wealth petroleum brings, Nigeria has a disintegrating infrastructure and widespread corruption, with wealth not being distributed (Koper et al., 2009, p. 298). The lack of enforced regulation of the petroleum sector has led to civil unrest and sabotage of petroleum facilities, attacks on petroleum employees, kidnappings and extortion. However, it appears that it is still more profitable for the foreign petroleum multinational corporations

(MNCs) to ignore the communities they operate within than to engage with them in the form of community relations.

In rural Nigeria, the concept of culture revolves around activities based on people's ways of life expressed as artefacts, colourful festivals, religious beliefs, dresses, names and language, for example. Culture binds the Nigerian people and their values very strongly together with no provision for compromise. Against this backdrop, public relations practice in such a diverse culture and important economic sector is not only an exciting challenge; it is also innovative, requiring much more than textbook theories and business approaches imported from Western countries. Even considering the difficulties the foreign MNCs have encountered in extracting the petroleum wealth they are smiling all the way to the bank because business is good, really good—or, as the previous President, Chief Obasanjo, would say, 'Nigeria de kamkpe' (meaning Nigeria is all right), at least for those who are benefiting from the wealth petroleum has brought to the country.

The Nigerian Petroleum Industry Context

The beginning of the Nigerian oil sector can be traced back to 1906 (Ebeku, 2001), when a German MNC, the Nigerian Bitumen Corporation, commenced exploration activities in the Araromi area, in the southwest of Nigeria (NNPC, 2010). This first oil exploration operation hurriedly ended with the outbreak of the First World War in 1914, but began again in 1937 when Shell D'Arcy (now Shell) gained the sole concessionary rights covering the whole territory of Nigeria for oil exploration. Shell D'Arcy's activities were also halted by the Second World War, until 1947. It was in 1956 that Shell D'Arcy's exploration led to the first commercial discovery of oil at Oloibiri (in Bayelsa State) in the Niger Delta region. In 1958 when oil was first exported to Europe, Oloibiri was already producing 5,100 barrels per day (NNPC, 2010). This first oil exportation opened up the petroleum sector in 1961, bringing in other foreign petroleum MNCs such as Mobil, Tenneco (now Texaco), Safrap (now Total), Agip, Amoseas (now Chevron) and others. This scramble for oil in Nigeria created the need to liberalise the oil concessionary rights previously monopolised by Shell (NNPC, 2010; Ebeku, 2001).

By 1965, with the introduction of the off-shore fields, oil production leapt to 27,500 barrels per day and by the early 1970s oil production was at 2.06 million barrels per day, and it has kept increasing (Ebeku, 2001). Oil production increased to 420,000 barrels prior to the Nigerian civil war (1967–1970). The civil war (also known as the Biafra war) did not seem to stop petroleum extraction activities. The Nigerian civil war started when the Eastern region (which has the Igbo majority ethnic group) declared independence from the rest of Nigeria and formed the Biafran republic.

Petroleum became an inducement for external interference. Michael

Peel (2009, p. 54) in his fascinating book *Swamp Full of Dollars: Pipelines and Paramilitaries at Nigeria's Oil Frontier* describes how Shell supported the federal government, which was unelected, during this war and pressured the British government to keep supplying arms to it. Shell executives also lobbied British Foreign Office officials as they were concerned about what a change in the Nigerian government would mean regarding petroleum policy, given that it was the Eastern region that had declared its independence. Peel documents Shell's view that any change in regime would be disastrous for the company's future in Nigeria. It is interesting to reflect that, according to Ebeku (2001), whereas the two World Wars halted oil activities in Nigeria, it did not seem that the horrific Nigerian civil war significantly affected oil production as the million barrels daily mark was passed in 1970 and by 1973 production had doubled to 2.06 million per day. The Nigerian National Petroleum Corporation (NNPC) identified that, while the civil war was drawing to an end, the global oil price was rising (owing to the Middle East oil crisis of 1973), and Nigeria was able to reap instant riches from its oil production.

In 1971, Nigeria became a member of the Organization of the Petroleum Exporting Countries (OPEC), and by decree 33 the Nigerian National Petroleum Corporation (NNPC) was established in 1977. The NNPC, as a government-owned and -controlled entity, manages the upstream (exploration and production) and downstream (marketing, export, retail, and research and development) aspects of the Nigerian oil sector. As stated in its mission statement, the responsibility of the NNPC is 'to engage in adding value to the country's hydrocarbon resources for the benefit of all Nigerians and other stakeholders' (NNPC, 2010). Between 1978 and 1989, the NNPC constructed new refineries in Port Harcourt, Warri and Kaduna, and then took over the first refinery in Nigeria, previously controlled by Shell since its establishment in 1965.

As previously mentioned, petroleum activities are broadly categorised into the upstream and downstream subsectors. The majority of the big petroleum companies in the Nigerian upstream subsector are foreign MNCs, or 'Alien oil MNCs', as referred to by Olsen (2002) and Collingsworth (2006). These operations are done in joint partnerships between the NNPC and the major oil MNCs (for example Shell, Mobile, Total, Chevron, Texaco and Agip), under Joint Operating Agreements (JOAs) or Production Sharing Contracts (PSCs). These MNCs are operating predominantly in the onshore Niger Delta, coastal offshore areas and more recently offshore in deep water (Ebeku, 2001; Olsen, 2002; Dhir, 2007; NNPC, 2010). The downstream subsector includes all operations done at the refinery. Operators here include the government-owned NNPC, foreign oil companies and private indigenous oil companies.

The existing refineries have a history of not operating at full capacity and there is no clear explanation for this. Year after year, government after government ensures that several millions of U.S. dollars are earmarked for the maintenance of the refineries. To date, there is very little to show for it as all the refineries remain troublesome despite the huge amount of money said to have been spent on them. The Economic and Financial Crime Commission (EFCC) under the leadership of Malam Nuhu Ribadu revealed in 2005 that 'as much as $120 billion has been siphoned from the Nigerian treasury and moved into coded bank accounts offshore by dishonest politicians since 1960' (Financial Standard, 2005, p. d). Recently there has been mention of privatising the refineries.

The corruption and mismanagement of resources by top Nigerian politicians and their business counterparts are responsible for the NNPC's inability to refine enough crude oil even for local consumption, which, considering that Nigeria ranks among the top 15 oil-producing countries, is astonishing (US EIA, 2010). As a way out, the country exports the raw product abroad (at great expense), and then imports the refined petroleum products back into Nigeria for domestic use and at a higher cost (EIA, 2009). In February 2009, the U.S. Energy Information Administration report revealed that only one of the Nigerian refineries was operational and it was running below capacity; hence the country is currently importing almost 85 per cent of refined products. Problems in the refining operation are attributed to corruption, poor maintenance and theft (Braide, 2003; EIA, 2009). The present government is making arrangements to fully privatise these refineries, which has led to a backlash by some critics as it is questionable whether corruption, poor maintenance and theft will be reduced once the refineries are privatised (Braide, 2003).

The Niger Delta Region and Oil Production in Nigeria

The Niger Delta region is the home base of the Nigerian oil exploration activities (Dhir, 2007; Ebeku, 2001; CIA, 2010). Ironically, the people of the Niger Delta region still live in abject poverty and have little to no access to basic social amenities meant to be provided by the federal government, even though they are surrounded by the oil wealth of Southern Nigeria (Dhir, 2007; Ebeku, 2001). The World Bank estimated in 2002 that about 66 per cent of the population struggled to survive on less than $1 a day. The situation has worsened over the years. Even today, the people of the Niger Delta live where there is no development in terms of reliable health services, education, road networks, electricity, running water and telecommunication systems. Yet Nigeria is estimated to have earned about $280 billion from oil over the past three decades. Hence, the key underlying cause of recent civil unrest and activism in Nigeria is the inequity of the petroleum wealth distribution and the sustained hazardous impact on the Niger Delta environment from the petroleum extraction. This impact includes environmental degradation and damage to local livelihoods, and the continued lack of development in the region (Dhir, 2007; Ebeku, 2001).

The Niger Delta communities have been in contact with the MNCs since the discovery of oil in Nigeria in 1956 (Ebeku, 2001). Stakeholder groups in Nigeria are complex and highly integrated, with both the state and the non-state actors fully involved (Fiakpa, 2009). In addition there are some very powerful individuals within the community stakeholder groups (whose opinions and demands are as powerful as the stakeholder group itself and sometimes quite different from it), which makes stakeholder engagement efforts difficult to deal with.

Dhir (2007) noted that two major issues surround the ongoing civil unrest in Nigeria. One is the unequal allocation of the country's oil revenues among its population, and the other involves the environmental responsibilities of the oil MNCs (Mbendi, 2010). The Niger Delta protests in the past have been not only against the MNCs, but also against the Nigerian government, which is viewed as a collaborator in the system of exploitation and corruption (Dhir, 2007). There is evidence that the MNCs depend upon the Nigerian military provided by the federal government in quelling protests from the host communities and essentially acting as 'hired guns' (Goodman and Scahill, 1998, p. 9). Frynas and Mellahi (2003, p. 557) add that the MNCs occasionally summon government security forces 'in preference to negotiations with the local people' in exchange for financial contributions and equipment (helicopters and boats), as well as having their own security forces recruited from the Nigerian police. It would appear that nothing is off limits when it comes to protecting the petroleum production and the shared economic interests.

Poverty in the Niger Delta region is believed to be caused by two specific factors: (1) forced seizure of family or communal land by the federal government in favour of the MNCs; and (2) pollution of adjoining lands, creeks, rivers and the sea, which most of the people depend on to survive (Dhir, 2007). Ebeku (2001) postulated that the origin of deprivation and poverty in the Niger Delta region started with the Petroleum Act of 1969 and the Land Use Act of 1978 enacted by the then military regime(s), which gave all rights to the ownership of land (both surface and subsurface) to the federal government. The result is that the federal government has the absolute right to and control over all petroleum resources in the country, which happen to be found only in the Niger Delta. The federal government gave the petroleum mining rights to the MNCs and in exchange receives rent for the lands and royalties from petroleum extraction (Ebeku, 2001). Critics believe that these laws play vital roles in the Niger Delta case as the local communities have no land rights and this has led to activism in the region.

In addition to the views articulated above by Dhir (2007), there are two additional factors resulting from the often ignored background cultural context, which has changed over time, which are also very important reasons for the endemic crisis. The first relates to the advent of private media ownership. People of Niger Delta extraction own major private national media in Nigeria. This includes both print and electronic media. These media have very successfully highlighted the plight of the region, bringing the wanton degradation to the national court of public opinion. The second change in the cultural context is that Niger Delta indigenes who had for decades lived and worked in the home countries of these MNCs have retired and returned home. They are irritated that these companies have different community relations policies and principles from their home countries and an entirely different set of rules (if any) for the Niger Delta communities. This clear discrepancy does not sit well.

The relationship between the MNCs and the local host communities has been characterised by distrust and a predatory and exploitative nature rather than one of exchange (Ebeku, 2001; Dhir, 2007). Whereas the MNCs claim that the host communities are asking for too much after they (the MNCs) have paid their rents, taxes and royalties to the Nigerian government, the host communities feel that the MNCs are taking advantage of the corrupt nature of the Nigerian government by not correcting the environmental damages and the social unrest they helped to create (Ebeku, 2001; Dhir, 2007). Within the host communities, traditional leaders, youth groups (which also play key roles in Nigerian society) and women's associations are involved in politicking and jostling for their demands to be heard (Okafor, 2003). From the early 1970s until now, petroleum production has increased (Ebeku, 2001), but the Nigerian government continues to face the daunting task of reforming a petroleum-based economy, whose revenues are critical but have caused great tension in both the economic and social environments of Nigeria (CIA, 2010).

The Petroleum Industry's Approach to Community Relations

In the Nigerian petroleum industry context there is already research exploring paradigms for community engagement (Evuleocha, 2005; Ite, 2004; Amaeshi et al., 2006; Turner and Brownhill, 2004; Idemudia, 2007). Much of this research relates to the philanthropic model, which is expressed through community assistance and community compassion. This approach portrays the host community with a bowl in hand begging for crumbs to be dropped for its survival. The problems with this model are numerous. For example:

1 When the giver defaults for whatever reason, tension sets in.
2 An imagery of master–servant relationship is created whereby the recipient (servant) has to constantly do the behest of the giver (master).
3 There is no guarantee that what is dropped in the bowl by the master will not be abused by the servant.

4 Counting on the power and goodwill of his gifts, the giver is not morally bound to show restraint in plundering the servant's environment; that may harm the servant severely.

5 Given the present trends, whereby community needs are no longer static, the giver, irrespective of any fluctuation in his income level, must consistently increase the size and amount of gifts to meet the expanding community needs.

6 Finally, the giver is not interested in how the gifts are used for mass community benefits. Any failure leads to tension and crisis in the corporate–community relationship.

This understanding and philanthropic approach to community relations in Nigeria is not working as it is apparent that many MNCs are not getting their community relations 'right' (Blowfield and Frynas, 2005, pp. 502–504). Blowfield and Frynas (2005) attribute part of the problem to the conceptual vagueness of community relations as a practice.

Empirically, the concept of community relations recognises and integrates the following:

1 Organisations have a responsibility for the impact of their operations on society and its natural environment. This responsibility goes beyond legal compliance.

2 They have a responsibility for the behaviour of others with whom they relate for business purposes.

3 As corporate citizens, they have need to manage all segments of their relationship with host communities for the sake of reputation and as a way of adding value to society.

4 The concept should not be restricted to altruistic philanthropy.

5 Communities, as stakeholders, have to contribute to the success of a mutually beneficial relationship.

The petroleum operators need to move beyond the philanthropic model in order to have community relationships that potentially could be 'mutually beneficial' and help to legitimise their social licence to operate, which is currently being vigorously contested by means of the kidnappings of petroleum employees, sabotage incidences and levels of general insecurity. This approach encompasses all the financial and non-financial responsibilities including the prevention of harm, institutionalisation of a regular dialogic communication process, and honest efforts by the MNCs to preserve the aesthetics (cultures) of the community as a responsible corporate citizen (Skinner et al., 2007). If properly invested in and coordinated these organisations could obtain their 'social licenses to operate' (Burke, 1999, p. 28).

Community Relations: Historical Context

How do all of these paradigms interrelate and conspire to influence the notion of community relations and, by extension, public relations practice of the MNCs in the Niger Delta? The petroleum MNCs arrived in the Niger Delta in the early 1950s. The then relatively serene communities, dotted with many unpolluted creeks abundant with aquatic life, had mere infinitesimal needs which the companies could easily meet without convening a board meeting to formulate policies. Omole (1998, pp. 2–3) outlines the features of those early days:

- Demands from host communities were simply fulfilled by offering scholarships for secondary and tertiary education, which the industry liberally granted.
- Environmental awareness both internationally and in Nigeria was lower.
- Concerns for human rights in host communities where oil exploration went on was very minimal.
- Nigeria was not subject to the kind of international scrutiny being witnessed today.
- Industry–community relationships were characterised by respectful deference and calm.

In such a peaceful, largely illiterate and rural operating environment, these companies probably failed then to:

1 interpret the prevailing socio-political and economic culture that weighed heavily against the oil rich Niger Delta communities;
2 predict how such culture would evolve in the future to influence their public relations strategy and organisational culture(s).

Besides these failures on the part of the MNCs they also did not recognise that the Niger Delta communities as part of their culture cherished a collective approach to problem solving. This approach to problem solving as a way of life evolved from the common bonds within their extended family system, reinforced by a strong village community orientation. Also, they are indicative of an inherently socially responsible race of people—the African version. However, the advent of military rule with an elite ruling class reinforced the culture of coercion and force first introduced into Nigeria by the British colonialists.

The MNCs failed to ask what was important to the communities they were operating within, which was a critical error because what motivates CSR in a developing country such as Nigeria is quite different from in Europe and

North America. In their home countries the pressure for community relations is exerted by governments through their regulatory frameworks, which provide a clear indication of the 'expected standard' of corporate behaviour. In that case CSR initiatives become part of the commercial business process with philanthropy as business tradition. For example, the experience gained by many of the MNCs in Canada[1] was that writing cheques was not enough and that communities wanted a level of engagement that enabled them to participate in the decision-making processes regarding decisions that had an impact on their quality of life. The reverse is the case in Nigeria where CSR activities are motivated by sustained failures of government on service delivery. Unbridled corruption and ineptness on the part of officials have become institutionalised. Some MNCs take advantage of the host communities through clever manipulation of weak public service structures.

In their empirical research into factors that can promise success or failure for public relations practitioners on international assignments, Burns and Stalker (1961, cited in Diaz et al., 2009) theorised that organisational culture makes critical inputs into the processes of determining organisational structure. That includes public relations. They used the terms *organic* and *mechanistic* to define organisational structure. The "organic" organisational structure (which most petroleum MNCs use) is characterised by:

- little emphasis on the chain of command (managers can assess and react to new developments without recourse to head office);
- divisional-type division of work (divisions are different but are linked strategically);
- continually adjusted or flexible job descriptions (subject to quick changes as need arises);
- lateral communication style (which covers community relations models);
- employee commitment to the organisation's goals and tasks.

The mechanistic organisational structure is very popular in government, especially in developing countries, and has been adapted for Nigeria's situation depends on the following features:

- close adherence to the chain of command (no flexibility); the political elites and the military who ruled Nigeria then adopted this structure with its built-in coercion model: force mentality as a compliance-gaining strategy;[2]
- functional division of work ('A' cannot and must not do the work of 'B' without rigorous authorisation and clearance processes);
- specialised task (a typical civil servant in Nigeria is not easily adaptable);
- vertical communication style (only the boss should talk for he knows all and is above mistakes); and

- top-down decision making (the infallibility of the head; ideas come only from the top).

These two structures—organic and mechanistic—differ in their value systems. If one has loopholes, the other can take full advantage and exploit the weaknesses to its advantage. For instance, traditional Nigerian persuasive strategies were deeply ingrained in coercive theory, as Professors Opubor (1985) and Nwuneli (1987) have observed. Modern Nigerian persuasive ideology is not yet free from various forms of coercion as compliance-gaining strategies. That explains why terms such as 'obey before complain', 'with military alacrity', 'with immediate effect' and many others are still relevant in Nigerian parlance. Even personnel in the military and paramilitary organisations display their stickers, berets, uniforms, even horse-whips (known in local terminology as *koboko*) in and on their cars, all to scare the public and gain advantage over others on the roads and other public interface points. In tandem with the culture of force, in Nigeria anyone in the military, police and such other institutions holds the mentality of a superior species and is next only to God. Within this context civilians are vulnerable when they demand due process as the power-distance between authority figures and ordinary civilians is vast (Hofstede, 2001). The power-distance cultural variable extends beyond authority figures to include individuals perceived as being in powerful or successful roles. The result is that following the 'laws of the land' is a theoretical or superficial concept. Government officials and members of parliament regularly accept gifts from MNCs and without transparency the exchange of favours allows injustice to continue.

The MNCs have taken full advantage of the apparent weaknesses in the mechanistic culture by abdicating their responsibilities toward their host communities. As Omotola (2006, pp. 16–19) and Manby (1999, p. 15) discovered, they work with the government to deploy heavily armed soldiers to quell community protests that could have been handled through simple explanations, respect, dialogue and relationship building. So culture, indeed, influences the depth of PR practice in Nigeria.

Part of the problem is that the host communities are populated by ethnic minorities, which do not have representation and access to political elites. Within Nigeria the three majority ethnic groups mentioned previously have benefited the most from the petroleum extraction. Even though the petroleum resources are located in the Niger Delta region the local population, which is an ethnic minority within Nigeria, has not benefited.

The majority ethnic groups determine the political and economic fortune (culture) for Nigeria and have supported the petroleum revenue-sharing formula that distributes the petroleum income across the country, which benefits their regions but not that of the Niger Delta.

An observation by Nash (1977) succinctly portrays this issue and the implications and is therefore quoted here in full:

> The Nigerian state's unfair policy toward the oil areas may be consistent
> with this observation by critics of federalism that the state tends to protect
> favoured groups or special interest groups rather than general welfare
> of the people . . . federalism has worked chiefly to the advantage of the
> elites, capitalists, absentee corporate owners and their surrogate elitist
> representatives.
>
> (Nash, 1977, pp. 10–24)

It is this political gerrymandering that has lacerated Nigeria's political and
economic cultural space, and is responsible for the problems the host communities have with the MNCs. Essentially the MNCs have realised that
the host communities are powerless and do not 'count' within the Nigerian
political and economic equation despite living where the country's wealth is
derived. The host communities are made up of minority groups and are not
adequately represented in government, and therefore are distant from political
power sources and are thus not 'protected', nor are their interests advocated
as the majority ethnic groups focus on their own needs. The MNCs have col-
laborated with those in political power and have their support in suppressing
dissent within their host communities. Finally, the Nigerians employed by the
MNCs tend to come from the majority ethnic groups and not from the local
host communities. This approach has led the MNCs to abdicate their community relations responsibilities and engagement without being challenged by
the government (Manby, 1999, pp. 95–98; Omotola, 2006, pp. 12–17; Frynas,
2005, pp. 585–588; Idemudia, 2007, pp. 1–3; NDDC, 2004).

Facilitated by the Nigerian political culture as explained earlier, the MNCs
deliberately evaded many responsibilities. For them that approach was com-
mercially convenient until recently. This can be looked at from a different
perspective: much of the literature on the Niger Delta with regard to stakeholder and community relations contains the phrase "decades of neglect"
(Idemudia, 2007, p. 3; Omotola, 2006, p. 9). It is hard not to question why
these communities were neglected for decades and if it was possible that the
multinationals did not know how to obtain and retain what Burke (1999,
p. 28) calls the community's 'social license to operate'.

In the early 1950s there was no community relations-focused legislation
in Nigeria (there is still none today) but the notion of effective community
relations begins where legislation stops. Counting on their 'international
orientation', the absence of legislation cannot and should not be an excuse
given that the same MNCs are engaged in community relations with very
different outcomes in other parts of the world. The simple answer, however,
is that the surrounding culture encouraged them to devise a public relations
approach fit for such an environment. In response to this lack of community
engagement and CSR the local communities formed activist militia groups
(Omotola, 2006, pp. 4–5, 12–13). To many analysts this has been a clear sign of

a public relations disaster facilitated by the prevailing culture in the operating environment.

The concept of community relations has to shift in response to changing community expectations (Burke, 1999, p. 28). Burke argues that it has to shift from voluntary philanthropy to a principle about the way a company should behave in a community. Companies now need to act in ways that build community trust and loyalty in order to become neighbours of choice.

In agreement with Burke, Sola Omole, a senior manager in Chevron Nigeria Limited's public affairs, drawing from his long experience in the oil and gas industry, stated that 'public relations cannot continue to be practiced as it always was when the world was a different place; when the international community was more tolerant of independent indulgences of each component member' (Omole, 1998, p. 2). In the light of all this Omole (1998) offers some suggestions that may help the practitioners to cope with the overwhelming dynamics of the twenty-first century and beyond:

> The challenge for the public relations practitioner will not be how best to successfully launder image, but how well he (she) can expose superior performance, and how credibly he or she can manage and explain contemporary challenges and emerging issues . . . the manager will not be hired to clean up the mess resulting from bad policy or unacceptable behaviour—as such unwholesome events would be exposed sooner than later given the pervasive nature of global information technology—he/she will be hired to enhance the ability of the employer to formulate good policies and behave in a manner acceptable to the now small, more open and prying world of the 21st century.
>
> (Omole, 1998, pp. 2–3)

Today and in the future, successful community relations in the Niger Delta will emphasise the strategic rather than tactical. Marshall McLuhan's catchphrase, 'the medium is the message', cautions us as public relations academics and practitioners, that the tools we choose to pitch our messages have a significant impact on the extent of the coverage we receive. For example Pidgin English is a popular and powerful medium (culture in language) in the Niger Delta region but so far public relations practitioners appear to underplay or disdain this language medium because, by the standard of their organisational culture, Pidgin English is *infra dig*. In contrast to this, public relations practice today requires the flexibility and ability to adopt and adapt in order to develop positive relationships with key stakeholder groups, which is also vital in gaining competitive advantage. Another potential feature of this 'new' approach to community relations will be transparency, corporate performance and behaviour. That means companies have to dilute their cultural bias against public disclosure and accept that communities expect to participate in the decision-making processes that have an impact upon them. When problems arise, they should be honestly acknowledged and solutions developed in collaboration with the community, which would improve trust and credibility (Doorley and Garcia, 2007, p. 375; Jahansoozi, 2007).

Currently the communication coming from the MNCs has been elitist in approach. In fact Michael Porter and Mark Kramer have questioned who constitutes the audience of their community journals and their publications. They are usually produced in high-quality gloss, in digital print and written in 'the Queen's English' (Porter and Kramer, 2006, p. 1). In the case of the Niger Delta, where the literacy level in rural communities is low, it does not appear that the MNCs are actively trying to communicate with their local communities.

Public relations initiatives must aim at creating values in the relationships within and outside organisations. With the enormous potential benefits for the organisation and society, but without the enabling cultural space in the operating environment, they will remain sheer fairy tales.

Conclusion

All along the argument has been that the oil and gas multinationals in Nigeria should have done better in their community relations strategies, given their international orientation and learning from practice elsewhere. Added to this is the fact that these companies employ public relations professionals who need to learn from the MNCs' organisational experiences regarding community relations and then apply and adapt the 'best practice' approaches to community relations in Nigeria. Part of the reason why this has not happened can be found in the negative influence of ethnicity, regionalism and religion, which rules Nigeria's cultural space. This has constituted a major hindrance to a participative approach to community relations.

There are many reasons why, after over 50 years of oil exploitation, the host communities still endure poverty, lack of infrastructure and environmental degradation that would not be tolerated in the MNCs' 'home' countries. These reasons cannot be discussed in a single chapter. It is, however, in the interests of the MNCs to work in an environment where host communities have access to equal opportunities, land rights (at least surface rights) and education.

As a result of the Internet and social networking sites the global village is now a modern reality. People and/or interest groups in distant countries and continents now have instant access and chances to learn, interact, exchange and share ideas with others as time and space have shrunk. It is no longer acceptable for the global petroleum operators to hide behind the excuse of culture as the reason why they are not able to engage in participative community relations approaches. Instead they need to adapt these approaches so that the local culture facilitates engagement. Without this change the unhappiness and dissatisfaction experienced by local communities will continue.

Notes

1 The Sundre Petroleum Operators' Group in Sundre, Canada, is an excellent example of a dynamic industry–community relationship in which community members have a significant input into the decisions regarding petroleum extraction activities in their area (Jahansoozi, 2008).

2 Reflecting on the dominance of coercive power in Nigeria, Professor Alfred Opubor wrote: 'If you want to guarantee success, don't give people any alternatives. Through legislations, economic and political sanctions, constrain everybody to adopt the ideas or practices you have introduced' (Opubor, 1985, p. 162).

Professor Onuora Nwuneli also noted that 'our youths are mobilised by age grades. Every level of development in the life of the child is associated with specific indoctrination on the expectation of the society from the individual. Failures to comply with indoctrinating messages are met with sanctions, some wild, others very steep' (Nwuneli, 1987, p. 2).

References

Amaeshi, K. M., Adi, B. C., Ogbechie, C. and Amao, O. O. (2006). Corporate social responsibility in Nigeria: Western mimicry or indigenous influences? *Journal of Corporate Citizenship*, 24, 83–99.

Blowfield, M. and Frynas, J. G. (2005). Setting new agendas: critical perspectives on corporate social responsibility in the developing world. *International Affairs*, 81(3), 499–513.

Braide, M. K. (2003). Modes of deregulation in the downstream sector of the Nigerian petroleum industry. Retrieved from http://www.nigerdeltacongress.com/marticles/modes_of_deregulation_in_the_dow.htm.

Burke, E. M. (1999). *Corporate community relations: The principle of the neighbour of choice.* Westport, CT: Praeger.

Burns, T. and Stalker, G. M. (1961). *The management of innovation.* London: Tavistock.

CIA (Central Intelligence Agency). (2010). The world factbook: Nigeria. Retrieved from https://www.cia.gov/library/publications/the-world-factbook/geos/ni.html.

Collingsworth, T. (2006). Beyond public relations: Bringing the rule of law to corporate codes of conduct in the global economy. *Corporate Governance*, 6(3), 250–260.

Curtin, P. A. and Gaither, T. K. (2007). *International public relations: Negotiating culture, identity, and power.* Thousand Oaks, CA: Sage.

Daymon, C. and Hodges, C. (2009). Researching the occupational culture of public relations in Mexico. *Public Relations Review*, 35, 429–433.

Diaz, V., Abratt, R., Clarke, R. and Bendixen, M. (2009). PR practitioners in international assignments: An assessment of success and the influence of organisational and national cultures. *Corporate Communications: An International Journal*, 14(1), 78–100.

Dhir, K. S. (2007). Stakeholder activism through nonviolence. *Corporate Communications: An International Journal*, 12(1), 75–93.

Doorley, J. and Garcia, H. F. (2007). *Reputation management: The key to successful public relations and corporate communication.* New York: Routledge.

Ebeku, K. S. A. (2001). Oil and the Niger Delta people: The injustice of the Land Use Act. *Centre for Energy, Petroleum and Mineral Law and Policy (CEPMLP) Journal*, 9, Article 14. Retrieved from http://www.dundee.ac.uk/cepmlp/journal/html/vol9/article9-14.html.

EIA (Energy Information Administration). (2009). Country analysis brief: Nigeria. Retrieved from http://tonto.eia.doe.gov/country/country_energy_data. cfm?fips=NI.

Evuleocha, S. U. (2005). Managing indigenous relations: Corporate social responsibility in a new age of activism. *Corporate Communications*, 10(4), 328–340.

Falola, T. and Heaton, M. M. (2008). *A history of Nigeria*. Cambridge: Cambridge University Press.

Fiakpa, L. (2009). Fidelity Bank adopts unique CSR model in Nigeria. *Vanguard Newspaper* (Nigeria), 28 June.

Financial Standard. (2005). $120bn stolen from Nigerian treasury, says EFCC, Lagos. 18 April, p. d.

Forrest, T. (1993). *Politics and economic development in Nigeria*. Boulder, Co: Westview Press.

Forrest, T. (1996). *The making of Nigerian indigenous enterprises*. Oxford: Oxford University Press.

Frynas, J. G. (2005). The false developmental promise of corporate social responsibility: Evidence from multinational oil companies. *International Affairs*, 81(3), 581–598.

Frynas, J. G. and Mellahi, K. (2003). Political risks as firm-specific (dis)advantages: Evidence on transnational oil firms in Nigeria. *Thunderbird International Business Review*, 45(5), 541–565.

Goodman, A. and Scahill, J. (1998). Drilling and killing: The hidden face of Chevron Nigeria Limited. Radio documentary. Transcript retrieved from http://www.democracynow.org/1998/9/30/drilling_and_killing_chevron_and_nigerias.

Grunig, J. E., Grunig, L. A., Sriramesh, K., Huangi, Y. H. and Lyra, A. (1995). Models of Public Relations in an international setting. *Journal of Public Relations Research*, 7, 163.

Hofstede, G. H. (2001). *Culture's consequences: Comparing values, behaviours, institutions and organisations* (2nd edn.). Thousand Oaks, CA: Sage.

ICG (International Crisis Group). (2006). *Nigeria: Africa Report: Want in the midst of plenty*. Report Number 113. Retrieved from http://www.crisisgroup.org/~/media/Files/africa/west-africa/nigeria/Nigeria%20Want%20in%20the%20Midst%20of%20Plenty.pdf.

Idemudia, U. (2007). *Corporate partnerships and community development in the Nigerian oil industry: Strength and limitations*. Geneva: United Nations Research Institute for Social Development.

Ikein, A. A. (1990). *The impact of oil on a developing country: The case of Nigeria*. New York: Praeger.

Ite, U. E. (2004). Multinationals and corporate social responsibility in developing countries: A case study of Nigeria. *Corporate Social Responsibility and Environmental Management*, 11, 1–11.

Jahansoozi, J. (2007). Organization–public relationships: An exploration of the Sundre Petroleum Operators Group. *Public Relations Review*, 33(4), 398–406.

Jahansoozi, J. (2008). When interests collide: The story of an industry–community relationship. Unpublished PhD thesis, University of Stirling, UK.

Kluckhohn, C. (1951). The study of culture. In Lerner, D. and Lasswell, H. D. (Eds.) *Policy sciences*. Stanford, CA: Stanford University Press.

Koper, E., Babaleye, T. and Jahansoozi, J. (2009). Public relations in Nigeria. In Sriramesh, K. and Verčič, D. (Eds.) *The global public relations handbook expanded and revised edition*. New York: Routledge.

Manby, B. (1999). *The price of oil: Corporate responsibility and human rights violations in Nigeria's oil producing communities*. New York: Human Rights Watch.

Maringues, M. (1996). *Nigeria, Guerrilla Journalism*. Reporters Sans Frontieres: Paris.

Mbendi. (2010). Nigeria: oil and gas industry. *Mbendi: Information for Africa*. Retrieved from www.mbendi.co.za/indy/oilg/af/ng/p0005.htm.

Muhammad, B. Y. (2003). *Echo of reforms*. Zaria, Nigeria: Open Press.

Nash, A. E.K. (1977). *Oil production and public interest*. Berkeley: Institute of Government Studies, University of California.

NDDC (Niger Delta Development Commission). (2004). *Niger Delta regional development master plan: Draft 3*. Port Harcourt, Nigeria: NDDC Directorate of Planning.

NNPC (Nigerian National Petroleum Corporation). (2010). Oil and gas in Nigeria: Nigerian profile, history and development. Retrieved from http://www.nnpcgroup. com/NNPCBusiness/BusinessInformation/OilGasinNigeria/IndustryHistory.aspx.

Nwuneli, O. E. (1987, February). Communication as a management and development tool. Paper presented at the Institute of Policy and Strategic Studies, Kuru, Jos, Nigeria.

Okafor, L. (2003). *Enhancing business–community relations: Elf Petroleum Nigeria Limited, (UNDP-UN Volunteers)*. Special report. New Academy of Business, United Kingdom.

Olsen, J. E. (2002). Global ethics and the Alien Tort Claims Act: A summary of three cases within the oil and gas industry. *Management Decision (Journal)*, 40(7), 720–724.

Omole, S. (1998). *New dimensions in community relations*. Paper presented at the Nigerian Institute of Public Relations (NIPR), Abuja, Nigeria, November 26.

Omotola, S. (2006). *The next Gulf? Oil politics, environmental apocalypse and rising tension in the Niger Delta*. Durban, South Africa: Accord.

Opubor, A. E. (1985). Mass communication and modern development in Nigeria. In Nwuneli, O. E. (Ed.) *Mass communication in Nigeria: A book of reading*. Enugu, Nigeria: Fourth Dimension.

Peel, M. (2009). *Swamp full of dollars: Pipelines and paramilitaries at Nigeria's oil frontier*. London: I. B. Tauris.

Porter, M. E. and Kramer, M. R. (2006). Strategy & society: the link between competitive advantage and corporate social responsibility. *Harvard Business Review*, 84(12), 1–15.

Rensburg, R. (2008). Public relations research and evaluation in Africa. In Ruler, B. V., Verčič, A. T. and Verčič, D. J. (Eds.) *PR metrics: Research and evaluation*. New York: Routledge.

Skinner, C., Essen, L. V., Mersham, G. and Motau, S. (2007). *Handbook of public relations* (8th edn.). Cape Town, South Africa: Oxford University Press.

Taylor, M. (2000). Culture variances as a challenge to global public relations: A case study of the Coca-Cola scare in Europe. *Public Relations Review*, 26, 277–293.

Turner, T. E. and Brownhill, L. S. (2004). Why women are at war with Chevron: Nigerian subsistence struggles against the international oil industry. *Journal of Asian and African Studies*, 39(1/2), 63–93.

US EIA (Energy Information Administration). (2010). *Country analysis brief: Nigeria*. Retrieved from http://www.eia.doe.gov/country/index.cfm.

8

PUBLIC RELATIONS AND CULTURE IN GERMANY

Between the "Iron Cage" and Deliberative Democracy

Günter Bentele and Jens Seiffert

Introduction

In the following essay, the key question is twofold. First, we are asking what makes German corporate culture different from corporate culture in other countries. Second, we want to find out how German societal culture and corporate culture(s) in Germany influence each other. The answers to both questions will give us the opportunity to draw conclusions concerning the special relationship between public relations and culture in Germany.

We argue that the development of the relations between culture and PR is characterized by breakpoints and continuities. The reference to history allows us to analyze the interdependency between both phenomena according to political or economic events in the past. Regarding political, economical, and societal settings, recent German history provides a strong basis for a discussion concerning specific public relations cultures.

Furthermore, in consideration of Sriramesh's analytical framework (Sriramesh, 2009, p. 48), and as elaborated by him in Chapter 1 of this book, we agree that not only does societal culture affect PR, but PR also affects culture. Because of processes such as globalization, fragmentation, and regionalization and the emergence of an information and communication society, the phenomenon "culture" turns constantly into a reflected and conscious field of research. Nowadays, culture is in need of translation and mediation (Lüddemann, 2010) and has become a subject in the evolving field of culture management and PR.

Based on the assumption that PR and culture are interdependent on a societal level, we claim, lastly, that this assumption can be assigned to the corporate and the individual level as well (Huck, 2003). As Huck explored, in an organization, the state of the art of PR, whether regarding managerial or technical innovation, is determined by the different levels of culture.

According to Sriramesh and Verčič's conclusion—"both corporate and societal culture has significant impact on communication in general and Public Relations in particular" (Sriramesh and Verčič, 2009, p. 13)—we have to ask how this impact is shaped in the German case. Their diagnosis that "only in the last decade . . . Public Relations scholars have attempted to study the impact of culture on organizational processes" (Sriramesh and Verčič, 2009, p. 9) can be fully approved for German PR research.[1] Therefore, we use the proposed distinction between societal and corporate culture for our considerations and apply this distinction to the German case by following culture and PR in German history since the middle of the nineteenth century.

Concepts of Culture

By the term *culture* we refer to an extended concept (Voigt, 2004). Hence, we consider culture as a way of life (Junge, 2009, p. 10) that differs from society to society. Further, it is the precondition and form of social action (Rehberg, 2003, p. 65) at the same time. Rehberg defines culture as the entity of learned norms and values, of knowledge, artifacts, speech, and symbols, that are permanently exchanged between men sharing the same way of living (Rehberg, 2003, p. 68). Central to our chapter are two concepts of culture that refer to the macro level and the meso level of society. Almond and Verba developed in 1963 a concept of political culture and defined the term as follows:

> When we speak of the political culture of a society, we refer to the political system as internalized in the cognitions, feelings, and evaluations of its population. People are inducted into it just as they are socialized into nonpolitical roles and social systems.
>
> (Almond and Verba, 1963, p. 14)

Leaning on this definition, Almond and Verba also state that speaking of political culture could mean speaking of economic culture as well. It is always "a set of orientations toward a special set of social objects and processes" (Almond and Verba, 1963, p. 13). The reason for us to stick more to the term *political culture* is the aforementioned assumption that the constitution of Germany's political system, more than any other factor, influenced the set of orientations towards social objects during the last two centuries.

When we consider, looking from a neo-institutional perspective, that organizations are "part of a larger system that must adapt in order to survive" (Prechel, 2008, p. 71), we can assume that "coercive pressures emerge from political and cultural influences" (ibid.). These pressures are one agent that "causes organizations to become homogeneous" (ibid.). According to our hypothesis, this "weak form" of the environment–organization relation is the dominant form that evolved in Germany with the beginning of the industrial revolution and kept being dominant until the second half of the twentieth century. "In contrast, the 'strong form' of the organization–environment hypothesis suggests that companies and other organizations are capable of influencing public policies that are designated to control and regulate them" (ibid., p. 72).

The German term *Kultur*, developed in Germany in the nineteenth century, is almost synonymous with "civilization" (Panourgiá, 2008, p. 202). It was Johann Gottfried von Herder who "observed that the slippery nature of the two terms denoted the slippery understanding of 'culture' and 'civilization' and the frequent conflation of the two" (ibid.) Taking Herder's idea of "culture-in-the-plural" (ibid.) as a bottom line, it is obvious why it might be useful to develop a specific German view on the relationships between culture and PR. The distinct use of the term *culture* also emphasizes the special relation of culture and PR every society has in different parts of the western hemisphere.

Framing the Relationships between PR and Culture: History as a Guideline

Cultural Influences on an Emerging Profession

The first half of the nineteenth century can be seen the first period of German PR history. Its importance for the relationship of PR and culture should not be underestimated. Probably the first full time "press officer" in Germany was Karl August Vamhagen van Ense (1785–1858), who worked for the Prussian state during the Congress of Vienna. The Prussian *Ministerial-Zeitungsbüro* (governmental news bureau), established in 1841, has to be seen as the first organized PR department in the German countries. Its tasks were not only the monitoring of newspaper contents, but also producing information about what happened nationwide and internationally. Further, the bureau informed the Prussian government about political issues such as controlling the spread of liberal ideas that seven years later led to the March revolution of 1848. Consequently, the bureau started to carry out direct press censorship.

The French hegemony over Europe (and Germany[2]) ended with the defeat of Napoleon at Waterloo in 1815. The reforms and thoughts that spread out from the French Revolution had already found their way into the German cultural consciousness after a decade of occupation. As the Carlsbad Decrees of 1819 marked the beginning of an unfolding distinction in German political culture, a pervasive relationship between PR and culture in Germany emerged.

From the beginning of the nineteenth century until the end of World War I, social and political development was driven by the *Obrigkeit* (authority), excluding a short period of the revolution in 1848/49. All in all, continental absolutism was able to preserve the barriers between gentry and bourgeoisie longer than anywhere else in the West (Habermas, 1990, p. 139).

In his historical approach, Bentele defines the first period of German PR history as reaching from the beginning of the nineteenth century to the end of World War I (Bentele, 1997a, p. 161). Whereas the field of public relations was set in motion by economic means, but also political forces, in the end politics launched the first PR campaign in German history. The fleet campaign, for example, a campaign to create public support for enlarging the German naval forces, was conducted by the *Reichsmarineamt* (Imperial Naval Office) (Bentele and Wehmeier, 2009).

Although the Prussian Central Agency for Press Affairs was an instrument to control communication, the governmental attitude towards communication changed at World War I to an active use of communication for matters of war, exemplified by the setting up of the *Kriegspresseamt* (War Press Office) in 1915 (Szyszka, 1997, p. 324). In addition, German authorities were able to effectively prevent—in a modern way by using PR, not censorship—the emergence of *Öffentlichkeit* (the public sphere) until the end of World War I. Since the end of the eighteenth century a new consciousness of culture concerning PR had begun to develop as an alternative to the authoritarian approach.

The shifting from direct control to a more subtle influence on the press since the middle of the nineteenth century can be interpreted as a growing impact of liberal ideas during this century. As a result the democratic experiment of 1848/49 had shown that the revolution had failed because a full restoration of the Carlsbad regime was not possible.

Within this shift from censorship to subtle influence, we can notice an important move for the development of PR in the context of German political culture. Hence, German elites learned from the revolution in 1848 that the oppression of liberal ideas by direct censorship did not weaken the movement. It seems that this "lesson" was a formative experience that placed one of the cornerstones for the development of propaganda and mass persuasion, which was the dominant form of PR in the first half of the twentieth century in Germany.

Culture and PR from Upstart to Propaganda: The Weimar Republic

We assume that the discontinuities in German history have led to breakpoints in the relationships between PR and the German cultural consciousness.

By using techniques of PR to stabilize the system from the top,[3] the nation-state of Germany remained under authoritarian control. In the time of the Weimar Republic (*Weimarer Republik*) there was an open confrontation between authoritarian and deliberative approaches in public communication.

The administration of public and private institutions and organizations was still under the heavy influence of an authoritarian culture, while the political constitution of the state was democratic.

With the beginning of World War I, the foundations for the emerging field were established. Though under the strong influence of the political sphere, such industrial entrepreneurs as "Alfred Krupp, Emil Rathenau and Werner von Siemens simultaneously became leading businessmen as well as architects of Public Relations in the 19th century" (Bentele and Wehmeier, 2009, p. 444; Wolbring, 2000; Zipfel, 1997).

Moreover, the relationship between PR and culture oscillates between the metaphor of the "Iron Cage" coined by Max Weber and the concept of "deliberative democracy" by Joseph M. Bessette.[4] Here, we emphasize the idea behind the concept more than the concept itself. By being counter-factual especially, the deliberative approach is far from describing the reality of the relation between culture and PR. We are neither tied to an "iron cage" nor living in a fully deliberate society. Nevertheless, the emergence of approaches such as the "two-way symmetrical model" indicates that PR theory and practice offer an orientation within the field.

According to Steinvorth (1999, p. 251) Weber gives three reasons why there is no escape from the "Iron Cage." First, the material goods of the world take control over the people. Second, modern states and companies are administrated by a bureaucracy that can be characterized by inescapable procedures, by rational and professional specialization, and by socialization. Third, the people are overwhelmed by the ideologies in the world, captured in struggle with each other, leaving the people stunned and unable to escape the "Iron Cage" (Steinvorth, 1999; Weber, 1995)."What we saw was the 'Iron Cage' hailed and lamented by Max Weber as limiting the selfish actions of individuals in the most rational type of government, the bureaucracy, was nested in a grand project, namely the nation-state" (Bentele and Nothhaft, 2010, p. 104)

When the Nazis took over the state power in Germany 1933, the dominance of the cultural paradigm of the "Iron Cage" was seen in the relationship between Public Relations and culture at that time. Despite the democratic interplay between 1919 and 1933, the hegemony of authoritarian culture remained the driving cultural force until 1945.

Mitzman noted in his critical introduction to Weber that his idea was closely connected to the culture within the system in Germany:

> At the heart of Weber's vision lies only the truth of his epoch, his country and his station, the truth of a bourgeois scholar in Imperial Germany. It was developed under agonizing personal pressures, themselves exerted and maintained by the dilemmas of family, social milieu, and historical position.
>
> (Mitzman, 2002, p. 3)

The Nazi Period

During 1933 and 1945, the German National Socialist Party ideologically dominated press relations within a frame of political propaganda. The political conditions included a centralized, dictatorial, state-controlled, and state-organized media system. The Nazis, represented by Dr. Josef Goebbels, the state minister for propaganda, controlled all forms of public information and communication such as newspapers, radio, film, big political events, art exhibitions, music, and other forms of culture (Sösemann, 2002, p. 136). Consequently, Nazi propaganda was unidirectional in the political field and consisted of persuasive communication that subordinated or deliberately negated truthful and accurate information. The typical communication tools of propaganda were strong penetration, repetition, simple stereotypes, clear evaluations, no separation of information and opinion, often emotionalized and—this was very important—working with concepts of a concrete enemy: the Jews, the Jewish. Propaganda, also, was in a position to select relevant issues unilaterally and to manage and distort social reality.

Besides these forms of state propaganda, there was also PR in today's sense as in the context of internal communications and in the area of press relations of cultural and economic organizations. Political propaganda of state organizations was structured not only as a model of a top-down style in which the state controls the information. In Germany this propaganda style in the system of "public communication" had impacts on the societal everyday culture as insisting on (anticipatory) obedience. Making people submissive was an aim of the Nazi party and the state societal organizations.

Zero Hour and Restart: 1945–1958

The cultural conditions in Germany slowly began to change with the end of the Nazi regime in 1945 and the founding of the Federal Republic of Germany in 1949. In the postwar period the first German textbooks concerning PR were published (Hundhausen, 1951; Korte, 1954). Simultaneously, the institutionalization of the field accelerated and culminated in the founding of the German Public Relations Society (DPRG) in 1958.

Overall, the first 13 years after World War II can be characterized as an emancipation from the previous propagandistic style of PR during the Nazi regime.

Almond and Verba stated in 1963 their first study researching the Civic Culture for Germany: "What we may be observing in our data is the persistence of this authoritarian subject culture, which involves imparting legitimacy to authority and bureaucracy, but not to political parties and competitive elections" (Almond and Verba, 1963, p. 15). However, Almond revisited the Civic Culture later and indicated: "the problem child of democracy—Germany—was showing strong signs of an emerging civic culture" (Almond, 2002, p. 212).

Learning from new ideas of U.S. public relations was necessary in order to "free" PR from the "Iron Cage" and to push the development of professional self-confidence (Bentele, 1997a). The rapid evolution, especially in the economy, indicated a cultural shift from a mainly national culture to an emerging influence of corporate culture on PR.

The Period of Consolidation and Boom: 1959–1985

The oscillation between flat and top-down hierarchies was a trait of not only German national culture, but German corporate culture as well.

As did researchers before (Hofstede, 1979; Lammers and Hickson, 1979), Bartölke and colleagues (1982), among others, found evidence for the thesis of a centralizing culture of power in German companies: "Support for this interpretation is provided by studies that demonstrate the comparatively centralized problem-definition and problem-solving processes in Germany . . . , thus indicating that Germans, more than other nationalities, are accustomed to and perhaps more receptive to centralization" (Bartölke et al., 1982, p. 395). In their study the authors stated earlier that "the hierarchical distribution of control occurs in all plants[5] whether relatively more participative or not, and is reported by all groups of respondents" (Bartölke et al., 1982, p. 393).

Kocka argues in the same way when he states that:

> When Krupp and Siemens in the 1970s tried to get a grip on the rapidly growing information and control problem by general decrees and rules of procedures; when the big companies treat their managers in terms of personal politics as public officials; and when the railways between 1835 and 1875 became the pioneers of systematic management . . . —then in all these cases archetypes, basic principles, techniques, and mentalities . . . taken out of the public administration in Germany, played a major role.
> (Kocka, 1999, p. 141)

The differences of German corporate culture from the US are best observed in the development of corporate rationality types (Guenther, 2007, p. 171). Guenther argues on the basis of U.S. cultural patterns that a rationality type of "best practice" had been developed, whereas German cultural patterns generate a basis for the evolvement of "best principles" as a rationality type (Guenther, 2007, p. 171). Therefore, differences in cultural patterns of both societies lead to different ways of innovation within the organization.[6] Guenther thereby wants to show how "on the one hand an incremental innovation is made of a rationality type that constitutes a good basis to legitimize radical innovations and on the other hand how a rationality type emerged out of German cultural patterns of best principles" (Guenther, 2007, p. 171). Through the different proceedings in the innovation process the communication of innovations needs to be different as well. The same assumption counts for other fields of PR within an organization. The procedures of organizational politics,[7] based on general cultural patterns, have an influence on, for example, internal communication processes. A strongly hierarchically structured organization will conduct its internal communication differently from organizations with flat structures.

Based on the works on deliberative democracy, Jürgen Habermas developed his theory of communicative action (Habermas, 1981). His approach was and is the result of what Bentele and Nothhaft called the "Age of Reason" (Bentele and Nothhaft, 2010, p. 102). Michelman defines deliberative politics as a "certain attitude toward social cooperation, namely, that of openness to persuasion by reasons referring to the claims of others as well as one's own" (Michelman, 1989, p. 259)

The deliberative approach was the basis for a development of a bunch of theories, of which Burkart's Consensus-Orientated Public Relations (see Burkart and Probst, 1993; Burkart, 2008) approach is an example. This type of PR can be seen as fitting very well in a German cultural tradition that began to develop at the end of the eighteenth century with the bourgeoisie longing "to form Öffentlichkeit as a reasoning public" (Habermas, 1990, p. 140).

Other than the authoritarian use of PR, which was discredited after 1945, the deliberative culture, the culture of reasoning, uses PR[8] to establish procedures that allow mutual understanding within society.

Overall, PR provides some linkages to the symmetrical model of PR (Grunig and Hunt, 1984), although mutual understanding in the sense of the Habermasian theory of communicative action is different from the approach of Grunig and Hunt. What the deliberative concept rendered possible was the opportunity for PR to communicate not only to publics, be they internal or external, but with its publics as well.

Professionalization, Germany Inc. and Globalization: From 1985 to Present

Though Rhineland capitalism was a successful model during the years of the *Wirtschaftswunder* (economic miracle), weak organizations began to develop into strong organizations until the end of the 1980s, forming what was called *Deutschland AG*—Germany Inc., a similar concept to "Corporate America." The cultural shift in Germany after World War II was a transfer of power between the political authorities, organizations, and corporations. During recent decades, German companies, like trade unions, non-governmental organizations, or other players, gained a remarkably strong influence on the processes of throughput and output of the political system. The influence of organizations on politics by means of Public Affairs has led to a reversal of the relationship between the two. In the present state, the power of organizations influencing the legislation process seems to be stronger than before. German politics has lost its "iron grip" on organizations in many societal systems, especially in the economic system.

Furthermore, we assume that there was a second shift taking place at the same time touching the relation between organizations and individuals.

In the recent past, some German companies such as Telekom, LIDL, or Deutsche Bank have been accused publicly of spying on their employees. The idea of familiarity and mutual trust, distinguishing organizational culture during the time of the *Wirtschaftswunder* from Germany Inc., seems to be in retreat. The lessening trust people have in political and economic institutions, already stated by Coleman for the US in 1982 (Coleman, 1982), seems to be taking place in Germany as well (Bentele, 1993, 1994).

For Guenther, culture contributes an acting frame for individuals within collectives (Guenther, 2007, p. 166).

> Collectives need a lively, dynamic culture to access a common, coherent cosmos of meaning. Only through a lively, dynamic culture is understanding enabled, orientation mediated, and players made capable of acting. If there is no lively, dynamic culture, values lose their prevalence and rules their abidingness.
>
> (Guenther, 2007, p. 166)

In her explorative study on the relation between culture and PR of organizations, Huck was able to find arguments for the existence of cultural influence on the basis of Hofstede's dimensions.

On the macro level the study could show that there is a specific relation between each of the four tested dimensions of culture: individualism/collectivism, power distance, masculinity/femininity, and uncertainty avoidance. However, the study did not provide concrete findings concerning the nature of this relation and therefore argues for further research (Huck, 2003, p. 229). Huck summarizes on the relation between corporate culture and PR in the researched German organizations:

> Whereas participative corporate cultures show a strong management orientation, in which the two-way symmetrical model dominates and the employees of the company represent the core target group, authoritarian corporate cultures show a correlation with a rather technical understanding and execution of public relations.
>
> (Huck, 2003, p. 233)

In the individual culture, Huck sees a much more influential role for PR than corporate culture. "In contrast to corporate culture, the individual culture of the PR practitioner presumably presents the core influencing factor for her work, because of shaping the occurrence of PR elements" (Huck, 2003, p. 238). This result of Huck's study can be placed within the context of the collective–individual dichotomy. Zerfass remarks that "culture as a connecting element of common practice is accompanied by the uniqueness of concrete actions that qualified protagonists execute on the basis of their particular abilities" (Zerfass, 1996, p. 105).

In the first place, the results of the study seem to be astonishing. Sriramesh, Grunig, and Dozier argued that corporate culture is one of the most important influencing factors for PR (see Sriramesh et al., 1996). However, taking the German characteristics into account, the lower impact of corporate culture on PR can be explained without revising their thesis. Unlike in the US for example, the field of PR is very young. Many German organizations implemented PR in their organizational structure only a few years ago. It takes time for them to become aware of the necessity of professional communication.

Excursus: The German Democratic Republic

During a first period from 1949 to 1965, the field of PR developed in a "normal" way in the German Democratic Republic (GDR). The instruments were very similar to that used in West Germany. Political PR, however, took the form of political propaganda: one-way communication and a top-down model. In 1965, a model of *sozialistische Öffentlichkeitsarbeit* (socialist PR) developed (Bentele and Peter, 1996) that had—on an instrumental level—very much in common with the type of PR in West Germany. The commonalities between socialist PR and its western counterpart showed that the reasons for organizations to communicate with the public were the same. The differentiated use of instruments (media relations, event organizations, instruments of evaluation), as well, was similar. Differences between eastern and western PR, however, showed that every PR department in the GDR had to fulfill political plans, with political-ideological aims and a propagandistic communication style (Bentele, 2008; Liebert, 1998). In contrast to West Germany, the GDR with a totalitarian political system and a strong party dictatorship kept characteristics of the old Prussian state. The "old Prussian style" was obvious not only in military rules such as the (military) goose-step, but also in many examples of everyday behavior of policemen, custom officials, and members of the political administration or university administration. The political propaganda of the GDR also carried this "Prussian style" of communication: top-down, authoritarian, not dialogue oriented, deliberative.

Culture and Public Relations: Implications of the German Case

The high impact of concepts and theories of integrated corporate communication (Bruhn, 1992; Zerfass, 2004) in the German-speaking countries indicates that the influence of culture on the development of theories and practices of PR is different from the situation in the US. The U.S. tradition in PR research focuses more on culture as a contributing factor to excellence (Sriramesh et al., 1996). In Germany, culture is more relevant in terms of how to conduct PR, how to change the set of orientations towards a social phenomenon, and how to organize the process of PR.

Jan Assmann's concepts of the communicative and the cultural memory may explain why the integration of communication is often stressed in German PR. According to him "the cultural memory centers on fixed points in the past . . . the past clots here rather to symbolic figures, on which remembrance is pinned" (Assmann, 2007, p. 52). Assmann states further: "By remembrance history becomes myth. History thereby does not become unreal, but in the contrary reality in the sense of an ongoing, normative and formative force" (Assmann, 2007, p. 52).

The Germans, being "separated" within dozens of small states from the founding of the Holy Roman Empire[9] in 962 until the German Empire in 1871, stored the experience of fragmentation, as we suppose, over centuries within their cultural memory.

Bentele's definition of PR (Bentele, 1997b), building upon Grunig and Hunt's definition (Grunig and Hunt, 1984), includes some special features: *organizational and societal functions*. The primary and secondary functions of PR, especially on an organizational and societal level, are mentioned and defined as "monitoring, information, communication, persuasion (primary functions), image building, *continuous building of trust*, *management of conflicts*, the building *of social consensus*" (Bentele, 1997b, pp. 22). The terms in italic letters represent those functions of PR that either pursue the forming of community (building trust, generate social consensus) or prevent the disintegration of society (management of conflicts). Taking this into consideration, we can argue that the development of theory and practice of PR in Germany is in a certain way a consequence of the constitution of the German cultural memory during history.

Culture and Public Relations in Germany: A Historical Model

Based on the examination of the emergence of public relations in Germany and the influence of national and corporate culture on PR, we developed a historical model showing the impact of the three forms of culture (national, corporate, individual) on PR in Germany during four periods (Table 8.1). This model is contrasted by the development of the profession as modeled by Bentele (Bentele, 1997a; Bentele and Wehmeier, 2009, p. 408).

TABLE 8.1 German History of Culture and Public Relations: A Periodical Model

Political Period	Public Relations Period	Cultural Period	Impact of National Culture	Impact of Corporate Culture	Impact of Individual Culture
German Empire and World War I (1871–1918)	Emergence of the occupational field (beginning of nineteenth century to 1918)	Period of Emergence (1841–1894): cultural influence on PR starts to unfold	Moderate (increasing)	Low (increasing)	Low (stable)
Weimar Republic (1918–1933)	Consolidation and growth (1918–1933)	Period of Dominance (1894–1949): era of the "Iron Cage"; PR under dominance of national and organizational culture	High (stable)	High (stable)	Low (stable)
Nazi dictatorship and World War II (1933–1945)	Nazi propaganda and propagandistic media relations, internal relations, etc. (1933–1945)				
The two German states (1949–1989)	New beginning and upturn (1945–1958)	Period of Change (1949–1990/96): beginning of the pluralistic era of PR, rise of the influence of individual culture	High (decreasing)	High (decreasing)	Moderate (increasing)
	Consolidation of the profession (1958–1985) in Federal Republic of Germany, establishment of socialist PR in the GDR (1965–1989)				
Re-united Germany (1989–today)	Boom of the field and professionalization (1985–today)	Period of Fragmentation (1990/96–today): loss of dominance of the "great stories," era of individualization	Moderate: (stable)	Moderate (decreasing)	High (increasing)

The first period, the period of emergence, reaches from the beginning of PR at the beginning of the nineteenth century until 1894 with the beginning of the German fleet campaign. This period of emergence is marked by the development of PR procedures that culminated in the first strategically planned and conducted big communication campaign in German history (Kunczik, 2006). At this time PR evolved as a technique that was used not only to inform publics and observe their information media, but also to control the public, to repress liberal and revolutionary ideas, by state authorities and bureaucracy. Concerning the economic system, it was in 1851 that Alfred Krupp presented his steel block at the Great Exhibition in London, it was in 1870 that he looked for a full-time "literate person" (Wolbring, 2000, p. 160) to work as a public relations officer in his company, and it was in 1890 that a news bureau was installed in this company (Wolbring, 2000, pp. 226–228).

The period of dominance lasts from 1894 until 1949 and is characterized by the full impact of national culture on PR. Even though the first German democracy, the Weimar Republic, is part of this period, we see more continuity than a break with the past in this episode between the Empire and the Third Reich. First "tested" in World War I, propaganda and mass persuasion reached its peak in this period thanks to the arising of modern mass media. The process of institutionalization had already provided the emergence of a critical mass of press bureaus in public administrations and the economic sector.

With the founding of the two German states in 1949, PR in culture started to change in the Federal Republic of Germany. In the German Democratic Republic, the period of dominance lasted longer. The years of the *Wirtschaftswunder* were accompanied by the development of the foundations of "Germany, Inc.," while the impact of national culture on PR, be it economic or administrative, was still strong. The student movement of 1968 marked a change within the whole society. Societal and organizational culture can be seen as the decline of the "Iron Cage" mentality.[10]

The fall of the Berlin Wall, German reunification, and the last years of the chancellorship of Helmut Kohl form the last turning point so far. At the end of the millennium, the process of globalization reached a new peak, which was marked for Germany by the end of "Germany, Inc." The high degree of corporate integration between German companies started to decrease from the middle of the 1990s. The effects of globalization have led to a weakening of the traditional understanding of economic activity, earlier described by the ideas of "best principles" and "incremental innovation" (Guenther, 2007).

Nowadays, the mutual relationships between culture and PR are not as stable as during the twentieth century. Although the end of the Nazi regime marked historically a new beginning, the process of culture took longer to enable change. Today, German institutions are still interpenetrated by the Weberian vision of the "Iron Cage," but to a much lesser extent than 60 years ago. The impacts of national and corporate culture, however, do not show parallel developments as they did before.

The model helps to show the relations between culture and PR for further research, which should include empirical and historical research besides theoretical approaches.

The Influence of Public Relations on German Culture

As shown before, German national culture influences PR and corporate culture. However, as suggested in the introduction, we assume that this relationship between culture and PR is mutual. On the one hand, culture influences the way and the styles in which we communicate. On the other hand, nowadays the system of culture is reproducing itself through communication. Since "culture [gained] autonomy from the material basics of our existence" (Castells, 2001, p. 536), patterns of society are now "purely culturally—and thereby communicatively—constructed" (Zerfass, 2004, p. 417).

Public relations campaigns are the way organizations "re-enter" society.[11] Lüddemann remarks that the "guiding aspect is the insight that culture needs concrete implementations, but, to become visible, needs to be able to be experienced and learnable" (Lüddemann, 2010, p. 65). Public relations can be seen as one of the forces that provides opportunities of experiencing and learning culture. Applying the concept of the communicative memory, we argue that the field of PR is one important contributory factor to the constitution of the communicative memory of organizations (Assmann, 2007). "The communicative memory contains memories, referring to the recent past" (Assmann, 2007, p. 50). Employees of organizations form what Assmann would call a "remembering community." Owing to the ongoing process of fragmentation in society, the field of PR substitutes the role of the collective as the constructor of communicative memory. This reduced connection between organization and employee results in what Richard Sennett (2007) called "flexible capitalism." "Employees are wanted to behave more flexibly, to be open for changes in the short term, to perpetually take risks and to become less dependent on rules and formal procedures" (Sennett, 2007, p. 10). Sennett argues further: "The experience of unsettled times threatens people's ability to form their character as an ongoing narrative" (Sennett, 2007, p. 37). It might be a result of the unsettled time that PR itself still seems to be overburdened with the role of implementing culture in society and organizations.

Conclusion

Regarding the relationship between culture and PR in the German case, it might be surprising to argue that it is not the corporate culture that is one of the most influencing factors for PR, but the national and individual German culture (see Huck, 2003). This of course has to do with the fact that PR cannot be seen only and sufficiently as a function of organization but must be interpreted also as a phenomenon in society as a whole.

German society, though individualistic, leans on the interplay between national cultural procedures and individual cultural procedures when it comes to carrying out PR. Corporate culture, however, remains "an important variable that may help explain the communication and Public Relations activities of organizations" (Sriramesh et al., 1996, p. 238). The question is how important this variable really is, and this seems to be an empirical question as well.

Furthermore, we assume that the influence of corporate culture on PR was stronger in the days of Germany Inc., but is now in decline. As people are employed in German companies for shorter lengths of time, the time for corporate culture to display its effects might be decreasing as well. As the retreat of "family" approaches to corporate management[12] leads to a shrinking impact of corporate culture, employees have stopped identifying themselves with their company.

Even the influence of national culture is on retreat. The ongoing fragmentation of German society into subcultures and the ongoing decrease of trust in organizations and social macro-systems (such as the political party system, the health system, and the pension system) make it likely that the dominant cultural variable is that of the subculture the individual is connected to.

The relationship between culture and PR in Germany, oscillating between the poles of the "Iron Cage" and deliberation, seems currently to be stuck somewhere in between.

Notes

1 Huck-Sandhu's empirical study of the impact of culture on PR in companies (Huck, 2003) was the first work that explicitly examined this issue.
2 "Germany" at the end of the Napoleonic wars was fragmented into 39 independent states, associated by the federal institution of the Deutscher Bund which was under the dominance of the Austrian Empire.
3 Which does not mean that propaganda or persuasive communication was not used in Germany.
4 The concept was further developed by, among others, Jürgen Habermas.
5 "The study reports on the implication of workers' participation for the exercise of control as perceived by members of ten German companies" (Bartölke et al., 1982, p. 380).
6 Rehberg's view, that "innovations are not only dependent of the creativity of individuals, they are the result of social interactions and general institutional frameworks" (Rehberg, 2003, p. 84), supports the assumption that innovation patterns are highly dependent on culture.
7 We do refer to the other two dimensions of politics, polity and policy, as well.
8 We have to admit that Habermas himself saw PR already as a threat to deliberative democracy in his *Strukturwandel der Öffentlichkeit* (Habermas, 1990).

9 The strength of the imperial authority differed from emperor to emperor. However, in contrast to France, Germany never became a centralized state before 1871. The rulers of the German states were able to defend their relative independence against the emperor. Still today Germany is characterized by a strongly federal constitution, granting the federal states many freedoms and rights towards the central government.

10 However, it would be a mistake to say that the "Iron Cage" has vanished nowadays. In contrast to the time of Max Weber, one could argue that the walls of the cage are just not visible any more. Sloterdijk speaks of the crystal palace the people of the Western world are living in (Sloterdijk, 2006).

11 For the concept of "re-entry" in a social theoretical context see Luhmann (1995).

12 As organizations have become more and more complex since the beginning of the Industrial Revolution, they can no longer be managed by only a few people, who integrate the organization as leading "parental figures."

References

Almond, G. A. (2002). *Ventures in political science: Narratives and reflections*. Boulder, CO: Lynne Rienner Publishers.

Almond, G. A. and Verba, S. (1963). *The civic culture: Political attitudes and democracy in five states*. Princeton, NJ: Princeton University Press.

Assmann, J. (2007). *Das kulturelle Gedächtnis: Schrift, Erinnerung und politische Identität in frühen Hochkulturen* (6th Edn.). Munich: C.H. Beck.

Bartölke, K., Eschweiler, W., Flechsenberger, D., and Tannenbaum, A. S. (1982). Workers participation and the distribution of control as perceived by members of ten German companies. *Administrative Science Quarterly*, 27, 380–397.

Bentele, G. (1993). Immer weniger öffentliches Vertrauen. *Bertelsmann Briefe*, 129, 39–43.

Bentele, G. (1994). Öffentliches Vertrauen: Normative und soziale Grundlage für Public Relations. In Armbrecht, W. and Zabel, U. (Eds.), *Normative Aspekte der Public Relations: Grundlagen und Perspektiven. Eine Einführung*. Opladen: Westdeutscher Verlag, pp. 131–158.

Bentele, G. (1997a). PR-Historiographie und funktional-integrative Schichtung: Ein neuer Ansatz zur PR-Geschichtsschreibung. In Szyszka, P. (Ed.), *Auf der Suche nach Identität: PR-Geschichte als Theoriebaustein*. Berlin: Vistas, pp. 137–169.

Bentele, G. (1997b). Grundlagen der Public Relations: Positionsbestimmung und einige Thesen. In Donsbach, W. (Ed.), *Public Relations in Theorie und Praxis: Grundlagen und Arbeitsweise der Öffentlichkeitsarbeit in verschiedenen Funktionen*. Munich: Reinhard Fischer, pp. 21–36.

Bentele, G. (2008). Sozialistische Öffentlichkeitsarbeit in der DDR. In Bentele, G., Fröhlich, R. and Szyszka, P. (Eds.), *Handbuch der Public Relations: Wissenschaftliche Grundlagen und berufliches Handeln. Mit Lexikon* (2nd edn.). Wiesbaden: VS Verlag für Sozialwissenschaften, pp. 415–430.

Bentele, G. and Nothhaft, H. (2010). Strategic communication and the public sphere from an European perspective. *International Journal of Strategic Communication*, 4, 93–116.

Bentele, G., and Peter, G.-M. (1996). Public relations in the German Democratic Republic and the new federal German states. In Culbertson, H. M. and Chen, N. (Eds.), *International public relations: A comparative analysis*. Mahwah, NJ: Lawrence Erlbaum Associates, pp. 349–350.

Bentele, G. and Wehmeier, S. (2009). From literary bureaus to a modern profession: The development and current structure of Public Relations in Germany. In Sriramesh, K. and Verčič, D. (Eds.), *The global public relations handbook: Theory, research, and practice*. New York: Routledge, pp. 441–465.

Bruhn, M. (1992). *Integrierte Unternehmenskommunikation: Ansatzpunkte für eine strategische und operative Umsetzung integrierter Kommunikationsarbeit*. Stuttgart: Poeschel.

Burkart, R. (2008). Verständigungsorientierte Öffentlichkeitsarbeit. In Bentele, G., Fröhlich, R., and Szyszka, P. (Eds.), *Handbuch der Public Relations: Wissenschaftliche Grundlagen und berufliches Handeln. Mit Lexikon* (2nd edn.). Wiesbaden: VS Verlag für Sozialwissenschaften, pp. 223–240.

Burkart, R. and Probst, S. (1993). *Public Relations als Konfliktmanagement: Ein Konzept für verständigungsorientierte Öffentlichkeitsarbeit; untersucht am Beispiel der Planung einer Sonderabfalldeponie in Niederösterreich*. Vienna: Braumüller.

Castells, M. (2001). *Der Aufstieg der Netzwerkgesellschaft: Das Informationszeitalter*. Opladen: Leske + Budrich.

Coleman, J. S. (1982). Systems of trust: A rough theoretical framework. *Angewandte Sozialforschung*, 10, 277–299.

Guenther, T. (2007). *Struktur- und Kulturwandel international tätiger Deutscher Unternehmen: Das Beispiel des Bayer-Konzerns*. Wiesbaden: DUV.

Grunig, J. and Hunt, T. (1984). *Managing public relations*. New York: Holt, Rinehart and Winston.

Habermas, J. (1981). *Theorie des kommunikativen Handelns*. Frankfurt am Main: Suhrkamp.

Habermas, J. (1990). *Strukturwandel der Öffentlichkeit*. Frankfurt am Main: Suhrkamp.

Hofstede, G. (1979). Hierarchical power distance in forty countries. In Lammers, C. J. and Hickson, D. J. (Eds.), *Organizations Alike and Unlike*. London: Routledge, pp. 97–119.

Huck, S. (2003). *Public Relations ohne Grenzen? Eine explorative Analyse der Beziehung zwischen Kultur und Öffentlichkeitsarbeit von Unternehmen*. Wiesbaden: VS.

Hundhausen, C. (1951). *Werbung um öffentliches Vertrauen*. Essen: Girardet.

Junge, M. (2009). *Kultursoziologie: Eine Einführung in die Theorien*. Konstanz: UVK.

Kocka, J. (1999). Management in der Industrialisierung: Die Entstehung und Entwicklung des klassischen Musters. *Zeitschrift für Unternehmensgeschichte*, 44, 135–149.

Korte, F. H. (1955). *Über den Umgang mit der Öffentlichkeit*. n.p.: Kulturbuch-Verlag.

Kunczik, M. (2006). Geschichte der staatlichen Öffentlichkeitsarbeit in Deutschland: Regierungs-PR von gestern bis heute. In Köhler, M. M. and Schuster, C. H. (Eds.), *Handbuch Regierungs-PR: Öffentlichkeitsarbeit von Bundesregierungen und deren Beratern*. Wiesbaden: VS, pp. 35–48.

Lammers, C. J. and Hickson, D. J. (1979). Are organizations culture bound? In Lammers, C. J. and Hickson, D. J. (Eds.), *Organizations Alike and Unlike*. London: Routledge, pp. 402–419.

Liebert, T. (Ed.) (1998). *Public Relations in der DDR: Befunde und Positionen zu Öffentlichkeitsarbeit und Propaganda*. Leipziger Skripten für Public Relations und Kommunikationsmanagement, 3. Leipzig: Universität Leipzig.

Lüddemann, S. (2010). *Kultur: Eine Einführung*. Wiesbaden: VS.

Luhmann, N. (1995). *Social systems*. Stanford, CA: Stanford University Press. (First edition 1984 in German as *Soziale Systeme: Grundbegriffe einer allgemeinen Theorie*. Frankfurt am Main: Suhrkamp.)

Michelman, F. I. (1989). Conceptions of democracy in American constitutional argument: The case of pornography regulation. *Tennessee Law Review*, 56, 291–309.

Mitzman, A. (2002). *The "Iron Cage": An historical interpretation of Max Weber*. New Brunswick, NJ: Transaction Publishers (first published in 1931).

Panourgiá, N. (2008). Culture. In Darity, W. A. Jr. (Ed.), *International encyclopedia of the social sciences, vol. 2* (2nd edn.). Detroit: Macmillan, pp. 202–204.

Prechel, H. (2008). Organizations. In Darity, W. A. Jr. (Ed.), *International encyclopedia of the social sciences, vol. 6* (2nd edn.). Detroit: Macmillan, pp. 71–74.

Rehberg, K.-S. (2003). Kultur. In Joas, H. (Ed.), *Lehrbuch der Soziologie*. Frankfurt: Campus, pp. 63–92.

Sennett, R. (2007). *Der flexible Mensch*. Berlin: BvT. (Originally published in English as *The Corrosion of Character*.)

Sloterdijk, P. (2006). *Im Weltinnenraum des Kapitals: Für eine philosophische Theorie der Globalisierung*. Frankfurt am Main: Suhrkamp.

Sösemann, B. (2002). Propaganda und Öffentlichkeit in der "Volksgemeinschaft." In Sösemann, B. (Ed.), *Der Nationalsozialismus und die deutsche Gesellschaft: Einführung und Überblick*. Stuttgart/Munich: Deutsche Verlags-Anstalt, pp. 114–154.

Sriramesh, K. (2009). The relationship between culture and public relations. In Sriramesh, K. and Verčič, D. (Eds.), *The global public relations handbook: Theory, research, and practice* (2nd edn.). New York: Routledge, pp. 52–67.

Sriramesh, K., Grunig, J. E., and Dozier, D. (1996). Observation and measurement of two dimensions of organizational culture and their relationship to public relations. *Journal of Public Relations Research*, 8, 229–261.

Sriramesh, K. and Verčič, D. (2009). A theoretical framework for global public relations research and practice. In Sriramesh, K. and Verčič, D. (Eds.), *The global public relations handbook: Theory, research, and practice* (2nd edn.). New York: Routledge, pp. 3–24.

Steinvorth, U. (1999). *Gleiche Freiheit: Politische Philosophie*. Berlin: Akademischer Verlag.

Szyszka, P. (1997). *Annalen zur Geschichte der Öffentlichkeitsarbeit*. In Szyszka, P. (Ed.), *Auf der Suche nach Identität: PR-Geschichte als Theoriebaustein*. Berlin: Vistas, pp. 319–329.

Vogt, L. (2004). Culture and civilization. In Ritzer, G. (Ed.), *Encyclopedia of social theory*. Retrieved from http://www.sage-ereference.com/socialtheory/Article_n69.html, 24.06.2010.

Weber, M. (1995). *Parlament und Regierung im neugeordneten Deutschland: Zur politischen Kritik des Beamtentums und Parteiwesens*. Schutterwald: Wissenschaftlicher Verlag.

Wolbring, B. (2000). *Krupp und die Öffentlichkeit im 19. Jahrhundert*. Munich: C. H. Beck.

Zerfass, A. (2004). *Unternehmensführung und Öffentlichkeitsarbeit: Grundlegung einer Theorie der Unternehmenskommunikation und Public Relations*. Wiesbaden: VS.

Zipfel, A. (1997). *Public Relations in der Elektroindustrie: Die Firmen Siemens und AEG 1847 bis 1939*. Cologne: Böhlau.

9

PUBLIC RELATIONS' OCCUPATIONAL CULTURE

Habitus, Exclusion and Resistance in the UK Context

Lee Edwards

This chapter addresses the broad topic of the book from the perspective of public relations (PR) as a site of cultural practices. I draw on the professionalisation literature to understand the function of these practices in sustaining PR as a legitimate profession. Particularly important in this is the interconnectedness of what are commonly recognised as structural artifacts (education, professional qualifications, formal training) with social and cultural professional norms, and the way this affects the public relations professional project. I draw on the work of Pierre Bourdieu to explain these dynamics. The theoretical argument is illustrated using empirical data from research conducted in the UK during 2009–10, and I conclude by reflecting on the implications of this perspective of public relations' culture for future scholarship.

Professional Projects, Structure and Habitus

Critical sociological work on professions has revealed the nature of professional fields as elite status projects (Abbott, 1988, p. 16), stratified in terms of gender, class, race and other 'primary social definers' (Atewologun and Singh, 2010; Anthias, 2001; Sommerlad and Sanderson, 1998; Atkinson and Delamont, 1990; Bagilhole and Goode, 2001). Public relations is an aspiring profession (Wilensky, 1964; Goode, 1969; Bolton and Muzio, 2008), still establishing its professional jurisdiction and legitimacy after half a century of formal practice (Pieczka and L'Etang, 2006). As part of this professionalisation process, PR practitioners engage in their own professional project, a 'systematic attempt by occupations to translate a scarce set of cultural and technical resources into a secure and institutionalized system of occupational and financial rewards so as to pave the way for collective mobility and social advancement' (Bolton and

Muzio, 2008, p. 284). Fundamental to establishing this 'system of occupational and financial rewards' is the profession's claim to legitimacy, or right to exist. Successfully claiming a right to exist is particularly important in aspiring professions such as PR because they are less established than older professions such as law, medicine or accounting (Goode, 1969; Wilensky, 1964). For example, in the case of PR, territorial challenges regularly come from marketing and human resources functions, and evaluation is a constant issue for practitioners who must justify their PR budgets on the same grounds as less nebulous and more easily measurable disciplines such as advertising and direct marketing.

Establishing legitimacy includes processes of occupational closure: the means by which the boundaries of the profession are defined, its jurisdiction delimited and its practitioners' identity established. All occupations employ structural and cultural mechanisms to achieve occupational closure (Abbott, 1988). Structures include specific entry qualifications, strong professional bodies that can act as self-regulatory mechanisms, and internal professional training requirements (Goode, 1969; Johnson, 1972). These enable the occupations to demonstrate superiority and expertise and justify territorial claims based on 'objective' criteria such as the academic ability of their practitioners and the formal qualifications that demonstrate the profession's specialist knowledge.

In general, the exclusionary function of structural mechanisms has become increasingly compromised as a result of changing social norms that recognise and challenge the systemic discrimination that characterises both education and professional fields. For example, equal opportunities legislation in the UK has made explicit discrimination illegal along a range of social categories (Home Office, 2010), while widening participation in higher education and the growing incidence of merit-based qualifications among women and members of minoritised ethnic groups have increased their participation in professional workforces (Muzio and Ackroyd, 2005; Sommerlad and Sanderson, 2008; Davidson and Burke, 2004; Atewologun and Singh, 2010). Simultaneously, policy arguments for the desirability of increased diversity in professional bodies (e.g. Panel on Fair Access to the Professions, 2009) have prompted professions to consider or engage with programmes aimed at increasing the range of backgrounds from which their members originate (Arts Council England, 2008; Law Society, 2009; British Medical Association, 2009; Farmbrough, 2009).

In some occupations, this increasing permeability of structures is exacerbated by their status as aspiring professions. Because their jurisdiction is relatively new and may still be imprecisely defined, practice is more fluid and entry may be possible without profession-specific qualifications, making structural protection difficult to achieve and vertical segregation more problematic. Other structural mechanisms such as formal training processes or hierarchies of specialist practice may not be as entrenched as they are in older professions, and may not even be compulsory (Wilensky, 1964). In PR, for example, no specific degree is required for entry into the profession, nor is there a formal career path of the kind found in law, medicine, accounting or engineering. Anecdotal evidence in the UK suggests that PR degrees themselves are less respected than more general degrees, given that they tend to be taught at less prestigious 'post-1992 institutions' (Byrne, 2008). Membership of the professional body, the Chartered Institute of Public Relations (CIPR) is not compulsory and the institute has no formal authority over its members' practices, other than adherence to a Code of Conduct (Chartered Institute of Public Relations, 2012). The total number of professionals in the UK is over 60,000 and the CIPR membership makes up only a small portion of this number (*PR Week*, 2011). Although it does offer training programmes, they are neither compulsory nor essential to be able to practise. The usefulness of structures as an exclusionary mechanism in PR, through which territory can be defined and protected, is therefore limited.

The advent of 'outsiders' into an occupational field through these more fluid mechanisms has important consequences for incipient professional projects. In the context of professions that remain segregated and discriminatory, it represents a challenge to the symbolic power of existing professional elites that draw on the dominance of white patriarchy in wider society to justify their position (Bolton and Muzio, 2007; Bourdieu, 1991). This power is derived from the ability to argue, based on wider social norms, that white males are best suited to carry out the highest-status professional tasks. However, if social norms evolve to recognise the ability and entitlement of outsiders to join the professional field, then the white patriarchal superiority in the professional environment is open to question. This in turn increases the fragility of the structural foundations for the dominance of a professional elite; structures, as a tool to achieve occupational closure, become less reliable.

It might be expected that more fluid structures would tie an aspiring profession less rigidly to wider social hierarchies and allow for a more diverse professional body as a matter of course. However, because aspiring professions claim the same status as established, elite professions, they must use the same criteria as those elite professions when constructing their arguments for legitimacy. From this perspective, more fluid structures are a disadvantage, since they cannot be used to exclude 'lower-status' individuals such as women or members of minoritised ethnic groups, nor to allocate these newcomers into subordinate levels of the professional hierarchy. However, to include them has the potential of devaluing the profession in relation to other occupational groups in which the membership is more exclusive and stratified (Frohlich and Peters, 2007; Bolton and Muzio, 2007; Sommerlad, 2009; Hon et al., 1992). Certainly, despite the increased presence of more diverse individuals in professional fields, professions are still marked by stratification based on a range of primary social definers including gender, 'race' and class, which suggests that closure continues to operate. Here, the role of professional cultural norms and practices, or habitus, are an important explanatory factor.

The Importance of Habitus to Professional Projects

Bourdieu (1990) defines habitus as the set of durable dispositions that both structure and are structured by the objective conditions (structures) of a field. For individuals, habitus is inculcated over time, largely through family and education, but it also evolves in particular fields such as professional fields or organisations. Professional habitus draws on the wider social values, attitudes and behaviours that characterise the overarching field of power, within which Bourdieu argues all other fields are encompassed and which position individuals and groups in wider society based on 'race', class, gender and other categories (Bourdieu, 1999, 2000). The particular assumptions drawn on in a professional context will relate to attributes deemed to be important by elite members of that profession: intellectual ability, dress, comportment or gendered norms, for example (Thornton, 1996). These shape profession-specific elements of habitus, including the different forms of social, economic and cultural capital required in that particular field (Bourdieu, 1997).

Professional habitus underpins the *doxa*, the rules of the professional 'game' that practitioners follow instinctively and reproduce through practice. Because it is so fundamental to the professional *doxa*, habitus can be used as an effective criteria for entry into the profession, since it demonstrates the ability of an individual to commit to the profession's requirements. As Bourdieu (2000, p. 100) argues, acceptance into a field depends on the apparent potential of an individual to embody habitus:

> In reality, what the new entrant must bring to the game is not the habitus that is tacitly and explicitly demanded there, but a habitus that is practically compatible, or sufficiently close, and above all, malleable and capable of being converted into the required habitus, in short congruent and docile, amenable to restructuring. That is why operations of co-option [. . .] are so attentive not only to the signs of competence, but also to the barely perceptible indices, generally corporeal ones—dress, bearing, manners—of dispositions to be, and above all, to become, one of us.

Entry into professional fields is facilitated by individuals' tendency to seek out occupations in which the *doxa* resonates with their personal habitus, because it reinforces their view of the world (Bourdieu, 2000). In the process, they also reinforce the 'rightness' of that *doxa* and of the habitus that underpins it. All other things being equal, then, habitus will remain stable and provides an exclusionary mechanism that can substitute for or complement structures.

However, habitus and structures are interconnected rather than separate: Bourdieu (1999) argues that habitus both shapes *and is shaped by* the structures that frame the context for its enactment. Therefore, if structures change, particularly in a way that contests social norms about the legitimacy of elite groups, one might expect an effect on professional habitus, and this may have an impact on its availability as an effective mechanism for occupational closure.

Bourdieu argues that changes to habitus occur as a result of repeated exposure to difference that undermines the accepted view of the world: 'These practical principles of organization of the given are constructed from the experience of frequently encountered situations and can be revised and rejected in the event of repeated failure' (Bourdieu, 2000, p. 136). In other words, new information must be available that creates a basis for reviewing existing norms. One source of new information for professional habitus, prompted by structural change, is a more diverse professional body made up of individuals drawing on a range of personal habitus that produces interpretations of the status, role and jurisdiction of the occupation that may differ from the white patriarchal *doxa*.

However, the effectiveness of this new information as an impetus for change is not guaranteed. First, because individuals tend to seek similarity with their own habitus, rather than difference, the frequency with which this happens may be relatively low and individuals from diverse backgrounds who do try to enter the profession may find it difficult if elements of their identity suggest a habitus that is not 'sufficiently close' to the professional norm. Second, such professionals may not be interested in challenging the status quo; as professionals, they have bought into the professional 'game' and will be focused, at least in part, on developing their own career based on established 'rules'. Third, the norms and values of the professional habitus are perpetuated through the symbolic power of professional elites to dictate the professional *doxa*. These elites are actively engaged with the professional project, since it pertains directly to their own privilege. Consequently, their interest is in consolidation rather than openness, in order to present a strong and unified identity to the outside world; neither new information nor new professionals are pertinent to the professional project. Indeed, accepting more diverse professionals would implicitly question the validity of their claim to superiority and therefore constitutes a high-risk strategy.

Thus, the natural tendency of habitus is towards inertia rather than change, reinforcing existing structures and creating a potentially effective mechanism for occupational closure. In this way, whereas structures may have limited utility as closure mechanisms, habitus has the potential to become a central tool through which aspiring professions execute their professional project. Habitus establishes not only *what* is practised, but *how* it is practised and *who* may practise. Efforts to create and present a unified, elite professional habitus become central to the struggle for professional status (Abbott, 1988; Muzio and Ackroyd, 2005; Hodgson, 2002).

Nonetheless, cultures are fluid, shaped by and through the identity of their members (Du Gay et al., 1997); increasing diversity in a professional community will by definition open that community up to change. Evidence for this can be seen in groups and associations set up by and catering to the specific requirements of 'non-traditional' professionals (see, for example, Black Solicitors Network, 2012; Ignite, 2012; National Black Public Relations Society, 2012). The existence of such groups in itself represents a form of contestation of existing norms, an assertion that difference matters in professional cultures, and may not be argued away by dominant groups.

In the remainder of this chapter I reflect on these processes of domination and resistance in the context of the UK PR profession. I examine the normative habitus as presented by professional bodies, leading PR agencies and the trade press, and contrast this with alternative readings of this culture as articulated and lived by practitioners from minoritised ethnic groups. Although other dimensions of identity may also produce resistance in the professional context, this study was focused primarily on ethnicity; consequently, it remains the main focus in this chapter.

Background: The Structure of PR in the UK

In the UK, the PR profession is still overwhelmingly white: members of other ethnic groups make up only 4 per cent of the professional body (Chartered Institute of Public Relations, 2009). This compares with 12 per cent in the adult working population of England and Wales, and 31 per cent in London, the heart of the PR industry (Office for National Statistics, 2009). As in other countries, it is also gendered: female participation increased during the latter decades of the twentieth century and now PR is regarded as a feminised profession, with 64 per cent female practitioners (*PR Week*, 2011; Aldoory and Toth, 2002). However, although no official statistics exist, evidence suggests that men are over-represented at senior levels. In *The PR Power Book 2008* (*PR Week*, 2008), 69 per cent of the 457 practitioners listed were male, an over-representation based on their overall participation of 38 per cent.

Public relations in the UK is also classed, made up of relatively wealthy individuals whose average salary is £46,200 (Centre for Economics and Business Research, 2005). In addition to economic indicators, class is reflected in cultural capital in the form of education and cultural knowledge (Bourdieu, 1997). Seventy-six per cent of PR practitioners have a university degree compared with 11 per cent of the eligible population in England and Wales (Office for National Statistics, 2004), and an exploratory survey of UK PR practitioners (Edwards, 2008) showed that their patterns of cultural taste, knowledge and activity corresponded to those associated with relatively privileged social classes in the UK (Gayo-Cal et al., 2006). Given that habitus is inherently linked to structures, the PR habitus in the UK profession will also reflect these characteristics.

Method

The data were gathered as part of a wider study about the professional experiences of Black and other minority ethnic (BME) PR practitioners in the UK.[1] The normative professional habitus was explored through a critical discourse analysis (Wood and Kroger, 2000) of texts chosen for their role as representative of the profession. These included:

- the CIPR website;
- *The FrontLine Guide to a Career in PR* (Public Relations Consultants Association, 2009), a booklet for prospective entrants produced by the Public Relations Consultants Association (PRCA);
- the websites of the top 10 consultancies from the *PR Week 150 Top Consultancies 2009*.

Within these texts, those pages were included that helped present an image of PR to the reader. Generally, they were those that described the organisation, the services provided, the PR consultants working in the organisation, and career opportunities. In addition to these texts, 12 professional profiles from *PR Week,* the main UK trade publication, were analysed. These weekly double-page spreads feature senior practitioners whose success is explained in terms of their personal background, career history, networks and personal philosophies about public relations. In other words, the articles implicitly present different aspects of the practitioners' habitus as the basis of their success, characteristics that an 'ideal' practitioner may be expected to possess. Given that *PR Week* has a circulation of 13,678, plus 120,000 monthly unique users of its website (*PR Week*, 2012), it is reasonable to assume that these profiles also help consolidate the profession's habitus in that their definitions of a typical, and successful, PR practitioner circulate extensively throughout the industry.

To understand how this normative habitus is perceived and contested by practitioners who differ from this norm, 34 individual and seven group interviews with BME practitioners were conducted with a total of 50 different participants. They were aged from 20 to 52 and classified their ethnicity using 20 different descriptors.[2] Their professional experience ranged from six months to 30 years. Individual interviews lasted from 45 to 90 minutes; group interviews were 2–2.5 hours and had between two and six participants.

Initial qualitative thematic coding of the texts and transcripts was done using NVIVO 7 (Richards, 2005) to establish the different themes in the documents that related to habitus. These were then analysed in more detail and their connections and relationships explored. The three most prominent and contested areas of the professional habitus that emerged from this process were embodiment, social capital and cultural capital. In the following section, I explore each of these, first examining their normative presentation and then presenting an alternative reading of this presentation, as articulated by the respondents in the study.

Findings: Dominance and Resistance

Embodiment

Bourdieu (1991, p. 51) describes embodiment as the 'modalities of practices, the ways of looking, sitting, standing, keeping silent, or even of speaking'. It includes physical appearance, demeanour (confidence, sociability, speech etc.), personality, accessories and other physical aspects of practice, and is one indicator of belonging, a powerful marker by which professions implicitly specify who may practise their discipline.

Normative forms of embodiment were narrated in the *PR Week* profiles and enhanced by photographs. The gendered nature of embodiment is clear (women's physical appearance is noted in detail, men's is not), as is its link to cultural and social capital.

> Davies' coat—'It's not fur', she adds quickly—is an elegant twist on the one football commentator John Motson used to be seen wearing on freezing Saturdays at Anfield. This is appropriate: her father is Motty's fellow sports commentator Barry Davies.
>
> His daughter looks younger than 39 and posses cheekbones on which one could cut diamonds. This may be why the recruiter who put her up for interview with the IOC told her she 'lacked gravitas'. Davies, who read economics at Cambridge and speaks fluent French, was not amused.
>
> (Hill, 2009, p. 16)

> Breakfast is served at the Wolseley and Mandi Lennard looks out of place amid the restaurant's understated, business-suited clientele. Her long, bright blue nails are embossed with the Nike logo and she wears a jacket printed with a screaming face and accessorised with huge designer necklaces.
>
> Lennard looks too young and edgy to be a traditional fashion PR professional. Not for her the Gaultier suits and Louboutin courts one might expect of someone in their early forties who counts among her clients

designers Gareth Pugh and Roksanda Ilincic, style title *Love* and make-up giant MAC.

'If I did not work in this industry I would not give a shit,' she says candidly. 'The designer stuff I am into actually looks fake. It looks like I got it from a market.'

(Wallace, 2009, p. 16)

In these descriptions, embodiment is linked to success, exclusive networks, a confident, anti-establishment personality and intelligence. These attributes are echoed in the organisational 'personality' that consultancies portray on their web sites.

Our clients tell us that if the people working on their account are proven and successful in their own business, then it says something about the quality of those people. This is important for us. It keeps us alert, competitive and hungry for success—and that gets passed on to our clients in the form of great ideas, advice and service.

(Bell-Pottinger, 2010)

Do we have a corporate vision? Well there must be one around here somewhere . . . But just between us, you're not going to get it (much less believe it) by reading a website.

[. . .]

Sorry about the vision thing, but lots of other agencies will give you that kind of stuff. And anyway for us it's more of an attitude. Ask the difficult questions; think smarter, and then think again; fine is not OK; make it matter; effect outcomes not output; find the way because there always is one; did it really work?; do it better next time; the client is everything.

(Freud Communications, 2010)

This 'personality' and these forms of embodiment are presented as part of the normative professional identity, but simultaneously claim to be unique and a rationale for the success of practitioners and organisations alike. However, diverse participants contested these stereotypical presentations, recognising them as artificial constructs that served professional interests in terms of presenting the 'right' image for clients and peers. One practitioner gave the following narration of her drawing of a 'typical PR practitioner' during a group interview:

Mine is a blonde lady with quite evil-looking blue eyes—they're not meant to be that evil (laughter). She's on her BlackBerry talking a lot, um, there's a lot of . . . there's a lot of hot air, very little substance. Nice handbag, the nice shoes, the credit cards are maxed out, because people in PR are not paid very much money, but you've got to have the look. You've gotta have the look.

Group interview 5, female

The exclusionary function of embodiment as part of the professional project was obvious to participants who felt marked as outsiders because of its role as a tool to assess 'fit' during the recruitment process. This happened not only within the profession, but also through specialist PR recruitment agencies.

In the years that I've lived here I've probably been to about two thirds of [specialist PR recruiters], I have never seen a recruiter of a diverse background. [. . .] It's just much easier for them to place people who look and are like them. And to be honest, PR recruitment is very, it's very blond.

Group interview 2, female

Practitioners also challenged the association of embodiment with success. They recognised that their ethnicity meant that other aspects of their identity were judged differently and shaped perceptions of their ability, often in ways that were disadvantageous. Gender and race frequently operated as primary social divisions (Anthias, 2001) without practitioners having a choice about how such categorisations were made. Because whiteness is the normative PR identity, non-White practitioners' ethnicity was one aspect of their embodiment that they could not escape, and did not always work in their favour.

It's a marker, it's a differential and also people sometimes just don't hear you, you know, they don't want to hear your ideas because of who you are rather than listening to the idea and then considering it.

Interview 11, male

The hereditary nature of embodiment as part of habitus was also recognised by practitioners, who argued that it was easy to demonstrate if one had grown up with the right habitus, but difficult to claim without this foundation.

I think [PR] started with the whites and they, they said that's the standard, that you have to be polished, you have to come from this background and so by the time the next generation came, it's their children who had learnt that and so they also got it from them and they went to good universities, their accent, they don't have accent, you know. [At the] internship it was about you know even how to talk, just the mannerism, how to talk, how to conduct ourselves in meetings and that, that's when it becomes a reality how different you are and you're told that if you have to fit you have to start consciously getting to that mannerism to get there and feel comfortable and fit in otherwise you will always feel like an outsider.

Group interview 1, female participant

A black British would have even been able to fit in better, but a black African with a strong African accent, I think the challenges for me are even more than the black British that was born and bred here, lived here. It's easier for them to fit in than for me.

Interview 27, male

Social Capital

Bourdieu (1997: 51) defines social capital as:

the actual or potential resources which are linked to possession of a durable network of . . . relationships of mutual acquaintance and recognition . . . which provides each of its members with the backing of the collectively-owned capital, a 'credential' which entitles them to credit, in the various senses of the word.

Social capital is accumulated through networks, and networking activity is central to PR, so much so that the ability to socialise is listed under the section 'PR Skills' in the PRCA booklet, *The Frontline Guide to a Career in PR.*

The best way to build relationships with clients and journalists is often out of the office, in a social setting. You need to be someone who finds it easy to get along with people you don't know and make conversation. Building up a network of contacts is vital if you want to excel in this profession.

(Public Relations Consultants Association, 2009, p. 5)

Being sociable is also mentioned in the *PR Week* profiles as a necessary characteristic of successful practitioners:

Whitehorn does not possess the bubbly persona of his boss. On the contrary, he seems rather intense. Former City diarist and PR consultant Damien McCrystal, who has known him for 30 years, says: 'All his school and university friends always said he would end up as the chairman of ICI, but now it no longer exists he never got the chance. He has an amazing mind that retains every fact he hears.'

But an industry insider says 'while there are traces of geekiness about him', he is actually 'a late-night party animal who likes fine wine and shooting.'

(Magee, 2009a, p. 14)

Brands such as Levi's, Coca Cola and Globe-Trotter have worked with the agency for a number of years and are effusive in their praise for Shah. Globe-Trotter director Gary Bott says: 'Raoul is quite simply one of those rare individuals who understands and respects each and every brand with which he works.' And it appears Shah is not averse to having a good time. Bott adds: 'Apparently the rule is: what happens in Vegas stays in Vegas. Although there could have been a bottle of vodka involved. And a camel . . .'

(O'Reilly, 2009, p. 16)

Because such comments are made in conjunction with remarks about practitioners' professional acumen, they reinforce the professional relevance of social capital. However, the types of social capital that are highlighted reveal the elite nature of this aspect of habitus. 'Fine wine and shooting' is associated with white, upper-class males in the UK, and socialising in Las Vegas as part of an exclusive group requires adequate leisure time, substantial disposable income and freedom from the day-to-day constraints of family and work life that most people must negotiate.

On agency websites, social capital and socialising were used as evidence of consultants' approachable nature, as well as of organisations being good places to work. Again, in this context, the discursive theme of socialising is intertwined with that of professional excellence and creativity:

Our people are an eclectic bunch, with diverse backgrounds including advertising, research, journalism, banking, politics, consultancy and in-house communications. All are united by a passion and flair for communications, as well as a sense of hard-work and fun.

(Fishburn Hedges, 2010)

We have completely changed our way of working, breaking the desk-bound culture. In June 2008, we moved into our new home in Victoria which was featured in CNBC Healthy Horizons in December 2008. Designed with a touch of British eccentricity, it is full of quirky retreats to provide space for informal meetings and creative stimulation. Our cafe and bar are also a focal point for get togethers.

(Edelman, 2010)

The importance of social capital was also reflected in the symbolic value associated with practitioners' contacts, frequently from the political, media or celebrity world.

Allan remains close to his former Downing Street colleagues, many of whom are now in the cabinet. In particular, work and pensions secretary James Purnell was best man at his wedding and remains his closest friend.

Many senior journalists also know him well. *The Sun*'s George Pascoe-Watson, a regular golfing chum, says: 'He used to firefight in Downing Street and knows the players—he totally understands the system. He also gets newspapers and TV and the way in which journalists work on stories. He likes journalists. That's a big plus.'

(Singleton, 2009, p. 16)

This presentation of social capital implicitly underlines its important role as a means of career development, opening doors to opportunity. However, as Yosso (2005) notes, not all forms of capital are equally regarded across all groups and, in PR, diverse practitioners recognise the specificity of normative social capital: only certain types of network help. Their own connections are not always valued because in PR, and particularly in consultancies, only networks that have clear potential to generate business are useful for entry and progression. Lacking these connections can limit career development, as one senior practitioner discovered, who had come to the UK from overseas.

I'd be expected to walk in the door and immediately have a black book full of contacts who I'd get on the phone to and call up. And I think that's always been a consideration with jobs that I haven't been considered for. And it was why a few years ago it was recommended to me that I move in-house because this whole issue of winning new business wouldn't be an issue, and also big companies have quotas, they have to hire people who are diverse. So it was seen as an easier route in through the door and I could spend some time in-house, building up a particular area of expertise which would then make me more marketable and that's exactly what happened.

Group interview 6, female

The intersection of gender, race and class in PR networking was also clearly recognised by participants in one group interview.

Participant 1: [i]t was [an] old boys' network. You know, Friday afternoon meetings on the golf course and either you play or you don't have your meeting . . . or hold the clubs and we'll play. And it's like 'Are you kidding me (laughter) show up on Monday ten o'clock or else.' Erm, so, so there is definitely a lot of that and . . .

Participant 2: Yeah. I mean, you know, I, I have found that the men will help the men and I'm not even sure whether we, we get into the realms of will white women help, you know, ethnic women, I don't even know I've had very mixed experiences.

Group interview 2, females

Correspondingly, the importance of professional relationships, often in the form of mentoring, were recognised as an actively constructed and crucial part of networking, one of the reasons that those with a habitus that 'fitted' professional norms progressed more quickly than 'other' practitioners:

> In my last organisation I sought a mentor who was a white male . . . because the chief executive looked on him quite highly and he was, he was around the board table and I was around the board table as well. . . . I mean, take *PR Week*, every week they have the interview and the interviewer always asks, you know, 'Who is your mentor? Who was the person who helped you there?' It's extremely important whatever colour you are in any, in any career, but much more so in an area where you don't see anyone like yourself, and you . . . want to make sure you're not out of the loop because you might be excluded in some way. So you need that, someone who's got good inside information, good experience and can give you good direction and advice.
>
> Group interview 5, female

Cultural Capital

Bourdieu (1997) emphasises family and education as major sources of cultural capital for an individual, providing an unconscious training in the ways and habits of a particular group of people. In PR, cultural capital encompasses these aspects of practitioners' upbringing and is incorporated into assessments of 'fit' at entry level. Education is particularly valued, and elite education, rather than vocational PR study, attracts greater symbolic value. As the following quote illustrates, PR degrees are not regarded in the same category as 'a good degree and an excellent academic record':

> Do I need a PR degree?
>
> Definitely not. The PR industry attracts people from lots of different backgrounds, ranging from management and marketing to engineering. If you want to specialise in a certain field of PR then it helps to have a related degree, but the most important thing is to have a good degree and an excellent academic record.
>
> However, PR degrees can offer useful on-the-job experience as part of the course, which will stand in you in good stead when looking for your first role.
>
> (Public Relations Consultants Association, 2009, p. 8)

This pattern is echoed elsewhere in the other professional texts in the dataset. On one agency website, for example, 11 out of the 16 director profiles mentioned the university and subject of their degree, and another two mentioned just the subject. All but one of the universities mentioned were institutions from the elite Russell Group of universities in the UK, and four directors had attended Oxford or Cambridge (Finsbury, 2010).

In the *PR Week* profiles, biographical snapshots were included that reflected the practitioners' cultural background, sometimes from their personal lives, but occasionally also drawing on aspects of their professional experience. These added to the symbolic value associated with their cultural capital by making the practitioner seem interesting and unusual but positioning them as privileged or unique in relation to the wider population.

> He has a deep and genuine passion for space and technology, and points out that without space technologies such as GPS (to trace global food movements) and farmers being able to access instant weather updates, more than a billion people across the globe would be starving.
>
> This interest in technology developed at an early age. As a child he used to regularly make his parents sit in a café in Edinburgh Airport 'while I had my nose pressed up to glass watching every single plane that moved.' It is also in his genes. He claims his grandfather invented the first petrol–electric car in 1927, a technology that ran all the London buses in the 30s. 'But it was abandoned because no-one could understand why they would need to be more fuel efficient in the future. My grandfather died pretty much a penniless man,' he says, a hint of injustice creeping into his voice.
>
> (Magee, 2009a, p. 16)

> [H]is most bizarre stories emanate from his time at Ladbrokes. He played poker with Boyzone and got the Playboy Bunnies to stop traffic in Piccadilly at the same time as writing documents about deregulating the gambling industry.
>
> When he was setting up the world's largest poker game 'it went from the sublime to the ridiculous. I would get a call in the pub and I would be saying things like "yeah, slims, I'm not sure if the Devil Fish and the Hendon Mob agree with that, but I'll see what I can do."'
>
> (Magee, 2009b, p. 14)

Elsewhere, general cultural knowledge is presented as crucial for professional interactions.

> PR practitioners need to be aware of current trends and issues. Keeping up to date with the world around you is vital when advising clients or brainstorming campaign ideas. . . . PR practitioners must be confident talking to a wide range of people—for example, your role may involve

presenting to clients, dealing with journalists and meeting with groups of people important to your organisation or client.

(Chartered Institute of Public Relations, 2011)

Although different forms of cultural capital were normalised in mainstream professional discourses, research participants recognised some of these, too, as exclusionary mechanisms. For example, they understood the importance of *where* one went to university, rather than simply having a degree, for entering and progressing through the professional field.

> I found that there are lots of different reasons why different people couldn't be hired by certain firms and it started with education. Two firms I worked for, it was outside of their comfort zone to hire people who either didn't go to Oxford or Cambridge or didn't go to, at least to have gone to a recognisable public school or to Sandhurst.
>
> Group interview 6, female

The common cultural capital derived from similar educational backgrounds leads to a good 'fit' with colleagues and this in turn leads to greater confidence, a trait that is repeatedly mentioned as a typical characteristic of PR practitioners in industry literature but is recognised by 'non-traditional' practitioners as a benefit that is serendipitous rather than earned.

> I think it's your upbringing as well, you know, if you come from a secure type of well-educated background, you tend to be more confident and you know what you want.
>
> Interview 1, male

> I think for the person that I'm talking about it's . . . it's a real asset for them, especially when you think of the other things. So I'm educated, I am sitting in front of somebody who I am like, so my confidence level . . . it's not hard for me to have a confidence level.
>
> Group interview 4, female

The Importance of Merit as a Tool for Resistance

The data presented here show how the participants in the study understood the occupational exclusion that accompanies the professional project and the dynamic of habitus that seeks similarity rather than difference. However, these practitioners were also successful individuals who felt they had as much right as anyone to be part of PR's professional body. They used the fluid status of PR as an aspiring profession, and particularly its more open structures, to facilitate their entry and challenge exclusion. Because practitioners had access to structural resources such as education and professional qualifications, they contextualised their right to belong in terms of the merit-based discourses of skills and experience that formed part of the structural boundaries of the profession and permeated professional discourses. Such discourses were coopted to challenge the 'othering' that the professional habitus effected.

> I kind of used to go into the room and think, 'Oh. I'm the only Asian person here', type of thing. But it didn't go any further than that. Because I think . . . maybe I've got my head in the clouds or whatever, but I just . . . I'd think of it and then I'd think, 'Oh well, that doesn't matter', because I've got . . . I'm here as a person with the skills, etcetera, that demonstrate who I am. Not the colour of my skin.
>
> Interview 9, male

Practitioners not only drew on formal structural criteria for their professional status, but also redefined the value of social and cultural capital in a way that highlighted the value of their own networks and knowledge.

> We knew we were going to work with children and young people from all sorts of backgrounds, with all sorts of issues, and having typically the Oxbridge white middle-class male sitting there, spouting the benefits of what the work we were going to do was . . . when you're actually physically going to go out and meet the said young people and the families that you're trying to affect, it doesn't really work because they're just thinking, 'Oh, you're coming here and just telling us we're disadvantaged.'
>
> Interview 15, female

> When we're talking about climate change here and who can help and, you know, there's a third sector group coming up, I'll think of faith groups or, you know, other associated groups I've worked with in that scenario, whereas others here wouldn't naturally do that; they think immediately of the other green NGOs. So that I think is an advantage for them, you know, I come from a very different place.
>
> Interview 8, male

In this way, whereas the professional habitus operated as a mechanism for the exclusion of 'non-traditional' professionals in many subtle ways, the fluid structures associated with PR created avenues into the profession for those same people, and permitted them to accumulate merit. They were able to define merit in terms of professional experience, which was easier for some of them to demonstrate than elite education or family networks. At the same time, PR's relatively vague jurisdiction meant that the symbolic value associated with traditionally elite forms of capital, which mirrored corporate and public sector clients, could be defined as irrelevant in the context of an alternative professional purpose of reaching diverse audiences. These two dynamics in particular helped practitioners define their professional importance and value in the overall field of PR. In the process, they introduced new arguments about what could and should be valued in the professional context.

Conclusion

This chapter has offered an initial exploration of the complex processes of dominance and resistance that are enacted through the structures and cultural norms, values and practices of PR in the UK context. The theoretical arguments and empirical data show how, in the absence of strong structural mechanisms for closure, PR's habitus operates through informal discourses and practices to limit outsider entry into and progression through a professional career. However, these efforts are not uncontested. 'Non-traditional' practitioners understand these processes, reveal their exclusionary effects, challenge and redefine the values associated with the normative habitus, and thereby introduce new discourses into the professional field. These, in turn, have the potential to become part of the struggle for symbolic power within the profession. As such, they form part of the 'new information' that Bourdieu argues is required for a habitus to change.

The ideas presented here offer a range of new ways to understand and conceptualise culture in relation to PR and lead in particular to questions about power and/in culture. Bourdieu's framework, for example, prompts us to examine who defines the culture of a profession, who is perceived as knowledgable and authoritative, and whose knowledge is relegated to lower positions in the professional hierarchy. Understanding public relations as a professional field prompts us to examine how its culture may be affected by other fields with which it interacts: government, for example, or particular industry sectors such as health or technology. How do these interactions change the hierarchy within the PR profession and, more specifically, within individual PR consultancies or in in-house contexts? These, and many other questions, arise from the fundamental recognition, evident in this collection, that PR itself is a socio-cultural, rather than purely organisational, phenomenon. As a locus of transactions between social entities (Edwards and Hodges, 2011) it both produces and is produced by the cultural contexts in which it is enacted. Consequently, research is required that engages with both the overarching norms and the detailed practices that characterise PR. Only through such work can the various dimensions of PR as a cultural practice be understood.

Notes

1 'The experiences of BME PR practitioners in the UK: An exploratory study' was conducted during 2009–10 and was funded by the ESRC (RES 000–22–3143) and by a Promising Researcher Fellowship from Leeds Metropolitan University in the UK.
2 Participants used their own words to describe their ethnicity; this resulted in the 20 different terms.

References

Abbott, A. (1988). *The system of professions: An essay on the division of expert labour*. Chicago: University of Chicago Press.

Aldoory, L. and Toth, E. (2002). Gender discrepancies in a gendered profession: A developing theory for public relations. *Journal of Public Relations Research*, 14(2), 103–126.

Anthias, F. (2001). The concept of 'social division' and theorising social stratification: Looking at ethnicity and class. *Sociology*, 35(4), 835–854.

Arts Council England. (2008). *Diversity in publishing programme evaluation*. London: Arts Council England.

Atewologun, D. and Singh, V. (2010). Challenging ethnic and gender identities: An exploration of UK Black professionals' identity construction. *Equality, Diversity and Inclusion: An International Journal*, 29(4), 332–347.

Atkinson, P. and Delamont, S. (1990). Professions and powerlessness: Female marginality in the learned occupations. *Sociological Review*, 38(1): 90–110.

Bagilhole, B. and Goode, J. (2001). The contradiction of the myth of individual merit and the reality of a patriarchal support system in academic careers: A feminist investigation. *European Journal of Women's Studies*, 8(2), 161–180.

Bell-Pottinger. (2010). *Collaboration*. London: Bell-Pottinger. Retrieved from http://www.bell-pottinger.co.uk/how_we_work.html.

Black Solicitors Network. (2012). *Welcome to the Black Solicitors Network*. London: Black Solicitors Network. Retrieved from http://www.blacksolicitorsnetwork.co.uk/.

Bolton, S. and Muzio, D. (2007). Can't live with 'em; can't live without 'em: Gendered segmentation in the legal profession. *Sociology*, 41(1), 47–64.

Bolton, S. and Muzio, D. (2008). The paradoxical processes of feminization in the professions: The case of established, aspiring and semi-professions. *Work, Employment and Society*, 22(2), 281–299.

Bourdieu, P. (1990). *The logic of practice*. Cambridge: Polity Press.

Bourdieu, P. (1991). *Language and symbolic power*. Cambridge: Polity Press.

Bourdieu, P. (1997). The forms of capital. In Halsey, A. H., Lauder, H., Brown, P. and Stuart Wells, A. (Eds.), *Education, culture, economy, society*. Oxford: Oxford University Press.

Bourdieu, P. (1999). *The weight of the world: Social suffering in contemporary society*. Cambridge: Polity Press.

Bourdieu, P. (2000). *Pascalian meditations*. Stanford, CA: Stanford University Press.

British Medical Association. (2009). *Equality and diversity in UK medical schools*. London: British Medical Association.

Byrne, C. (2008). Industry needs to reflect social diversity. *PR Week*, 7 March, 18.

Centre for Economics and Business Research. (2005). *PR today: 48,000 professionals; £6.5 billion turnover*. London: Centre for Economics and Business Research.

Chartered Institute of Public Relations. (2009). *2009 CIPR membership survey: The state of the PR profession*. London: Chartered Institute of Public Relations.

Chartered Institute Of Public Relations. (2011). *Is PR for you?* London: Chartered Institute of Public Relations. Retrieved from http://www.cipr.co.uk/content/careers/careers-advice.

Chartered Institute Of Public Relations. (2012). *Code of Conduct*. London: Chartered Institute of Public Relations. Retrieved from http://www.cipr.co.uk/content/about-us/about-cipr/code-conduct/.

Davidson, M. J. and Burke, R. J. (2004). Women in management worldwide: Facts, figures and analysis—an overview. In Davidson, M. J. and Burke, R. J. (Eds.) *Women in management worldwide: Facts, figures and analysis*. Aldershot: Ashgate.

Du Gay, P., Hall, S., Janes, L., Mackay, H. and Negus, K. (1997). *Doing cultural studies: The story of the Sony Walkman*. London: Sage.

Edelman. (2010). *People and Culture*. London: Edelman. Retrieved from http://www.edelman.co.uk/careers.

Edwards, L. (2008). PR practitioners' cultural capital: An initial study and implications for research and practice. *Public Relations Review*, 34, 367–372.

Edwards, L. and Hodges, C. (2011). Introduction: Implications of a (radical) socio-cultural 'turn' in public relations scholarship. In Edwards, L. and Hodges, C. (Eds.), *Public relations, society and culture: Theoretical and empirical explorations*. Abingdon, Oxon: Routledge.

Farmbrough, H. (2009). It does matter. *Accountancy Magazine*, 3 February, 22–23.

Finsbury. (2010). *Our partners*. London: Finsbury. Retrieved from http://www.finsbury.com.

Fishburn Hedges. (2010). *People*. London: Fishburn Hedges. Retrieved from http://www.fishburn-hedges.com/aboutus/people/.

Freud Communications. (2010). *Freud Group*. London: Freud Communications. Retrieved from http://www.freud.com/.

Frohlich, R. and Peters, S. (2007). PR bunnies caught in the agency ghetto? Gender stereotypes, organizational factors and women's careers in PR agencies. *Journal of Public Relations Research*, 19(3), 229–254.

Gayo-Cal, M., Savage, M. and Warde, A. (2006). A cultural map of the United Kingdom, 2003. *Cultural Trends*, 15(2/3), 213–237.

Goode, W. (1969). The theoretical limits of professionalization. In Etzioni, A. (Ed.), *The semi-professions and their organization*. New York: Free Press.

Hill, A. (2009). Coming in from the cold. *PR Week*, 9 January, 16–17.

Hodgson, D. (2002). Disciplining the professional: The case of project management. *Journal of Management Studies*, 39(6), 803–821.

Home Office. (2010). *Equality Act*. London: The Stationery Office.

Hon, L. C., Grunig, L. A. and Dozier, D. M. (1992). Women in public relations: Problems and opportunities. In Grunig, J. E. and Grunig, L. A. (Eds.), *Excellence in public relations and communication management*. Hillsdale, NJ: Lawrence Erlbaum.

Ignite. (2012). *Ignite: Promoting cultural diversity in PR*. London: Ignite. Retrieved from http://www.ignitepr.org.uk/.

Johnson, T. J. (1972). *Professions and power*. London: Macmillan.

Law Society. (2009). Response to the call for evidence on fair access to the professions: A submission on the solicitors' profession by the Law Society. London: The Law Society.

Magee, K. (2009a). Galactic enterprise. *PR Week*, 19 June, 14–15.

Magee, K. (2009b). Easy hospitality. *PR Week*, 20 March, 14–15.

Muzio, D. and Ackroyd, S. (2005). On the consequences of defensive professionalism: Recent changes in the legal labour process. *Journal of Law and Society*, 32(4), 615–642.

National Black Public Relations Society. (2012). *Welcome to the National Black Public Relations Society*. Van Nuys, CA: The National Black Public Relations Society. Retrieved from http://nbprs.org/2012.

O'Reilly, G. (2009). The natural networker. *PR Week*, 6 November, 16–17.

Office for National Statistics. (2004). *All types of qualification held by people aged 16–74: England and Wales*. London: Office for National Statistics.

Office for National Statistics. (2009). *Population estimates by ethnic group mid-2007*. Cardiff: Office for National Statistics.

Panel on Fair Access to the Professions. (2009). *Phase 1 report: An analysis of the trends and issues relating to fair access to the professions*. London: Cabinet Office.

Pieczka, M. and L'Etang, J. (2006). Public relations and the question of professionalism. In L'Etang, J. and Pieczka, M. (Eds.), *Public relations: Critical debates and contemporary practice*. Mahwah, NJ: Lawrence Erlbaum Associates.

PR Week. (2008). *The PR Week Power Book*. London: Haymarket.

PR Week. (2011). PR census: How the PR industry looks today. *PR Week*, 14 July. Retrieved from http://www.prweek.com/go/prcensus.

PR Week. (2012). *About us*. London: Haymarket. Retrieved from http://www.prweek.com/uk/go/aboutus.

Public Relations Consultants Association. (2009). *The frontline guide to a career in PR*. London: Public Relations Consultants Association.

Richards, L. (2005). *Handling qualitative data: A practical guide*. London: Sage.

Singleton, D. (2009). Leaving Blair behind. *PR Week*, 15 May.

Sommerlad, H. (2009). That obscure object of desire: Sex equality and the legal profession. In Hunter, R. (Ed.), *Rethinking equality projects*. Oxford: Hart Publishing.

Sommerlad, H. and Sanderson, P. (1998). *Gender, choice and commitment: Women solicitors in England and Wales and the struggle for equal status*. Farnham, Surrey: Ashgate Publishing.

Sommerlad, H. and Sanderson, P. (2008). Professions, intersectionality and cultural capital: Understanding choice and constraint in occupational fields. Paper presented to the 3rd International Legal Ethics Conference, Queensland, Australia.

Thornton, M. (1996). *Dissonance and distrust: Women in the legal profession*. Melbourne: Oxford University Press.

Wallace, C. (2009). London loves Lennard. *PR Week*, 18 September, 16–17.

Wilensky, H. (1964). The professionalization of everyone? *American Journal of Sociology*, 70(2), 137–158.

Wood, L. A. and Kroger, R. O. (2000). *Doing discourse analysis: Methods for studying action in talk and text*. Thousand Oaks, CA: Sage.

Yosso, T. J. (2005). Whose culture has capital? A critical race theory discussion of community cultural wealth. *Race, Ethnicity and Education*, 8(1): 69–91.

10

PUBLIC RELATIONS IN MEXICO

Culture and Challenges vis-à-vis Globalization

María Antonieta Rebeil Corella and Marco V. Herrera B.

Introduction

Public relations, both as a discipline and as a profession, has been scarcely studied among communication scholars. As a result, Mexico has a wide variety of ways of understanding the public relations concept itself and there is an even broader spectrum of shapes and expressions that it undertakes in its application as a profession. The analysis of the impact of globalization and how it all has influenced the culture of public relations practice in the country posits challenging questions such as: How have the Mexican way of doing things and the economic and political realms influenced the culture of public relations industry? Is it the other way around? How has globalization penetrated the Mexican spectrum, as it manifests itself in the public relations profession? Have the uses and applications of public relations in the country introduced still other cultural forms, given the international companies that have established themselves in the midst of the Mexican public relations Industry? Furthermore, have the so-called *international standards* demanded of public relations application in the country given way to a more globalized influence on its strategies and practice?

The purpose of this chapter is to provide answers to these questions as well as to posit the evolution of the public relations industry given the country's most recent economic, political, and social development. The methodology employed by the authors consists of: (1) a review of the most recent literature published on the subject; (2) the empirical research carried out so far, by the Mexican government and associations such as Confederación de la Industria de la Comunicación y la Mercadotecnia (CICOM) and Asociación Mexicana de Profesionales de Relaciones Públicas (ProRP); (3) qualitative research carried out through a series of semi-structured interviews with some of the leading public relations providers in the country who are also members of ProRP; and (4) a set of semi-structured dialogues and consultations to public relations clients.

Professionalization/Institutionalization of the Discipline in Mexico

The institutionalization of a discipline is a difficult subject. According to Gustavo León Duarte, an expert on communication theory, for institutionalization of a discipline to take place, three things are needed: public relations has to be established in the three different realms of analysis/practice mentioned below (León Duarte, 2009).

1   Construction of a body of theory on the subject: public relations theorizing is the activity of trying to understand the nature and causes of human, organizational, and societal relations. To this, another condition should be added: it has to be taught as a formal subject within universities.
2   Empirical research and its ample diffusion: public relations knowledge not only has to be produced empirically but has to be made public.
3   Application: the practical side of public relations is doing or carrying out that which makes human beings, groups, organizations, and society maintain fruitful relations and agreement. This should also include the formal establishment of professional associations on the matter.

Given the three categories or conditions mentioned above, the authors proceed to analyze the development of these within Mexican reality. The application of the profession started in Mexico even before 1940. The practice of the occupation within an agency in Mexico began as early as 1949. However, it is a well-known fact that journalists and retired journalists were doing related jobs before that time. Theorizing, on the other hand, began as late as 1963, when Federico Sanchez Fogerty wrote *Apuntes para la historia de las relaciones públicas en México* (Sanchez Fogerty, 1963).[1] The empirical research part began as late as 2005, with an overall study carried out by CICOM and followed by ProRP's annual reports starting from 2006 on. Thus, it can be said that, as far as the issue of the institutionalization of public relations, the field of study contains the elements needed to consider it an institutionalized field of study in the wider field of organizational communication.

Summarizing the public relations concept, the authors of this chapter contend that public relations is a field of study within the broader field of organizational communication. The latter comprehends the fields of study related to communication within organizations: (1) marketing, (2) corporate (also called institutional communication), and (3) internal, also known as organizational communication (Grunig, 1992; Rebeil and RuizSandoval, 1998; Rebeil, 2006; Rebeil et al., 2009; Costa, 2009; Sánchez Uribe, 2010). The public relations field of study includes portions of corporate/institutional and internal communication because it has to do with good image, reputation and relations with both internal and external publics. Thus, public relations is an art and an occupation, which professionals and organizations employ in order to create, enhance, maintain, and restore in case of crisis, the good image and reputation of a person, a project, an organization, or a country. In order to achieve this, communication and interpersonal strategies and activities are scientifically designed, carried out, monitored, and evaluated. The purpose of these endeavors is to provide the necessary legitimacy that clients need in order to maintain and increase their operations in society. The basic purpose of public relations in society is to do its job within the realm of ethics and social responsibility (Rebeil et al., 2009).

The Formal Practice of Public Relations in Mexico

The public relations sub-discipline (from here on it will be referred to as a discipline for clarity) has been developing over the last seven decades in the country. The first agency, Mexican PR Agency (Agencia Mexicana de Relaciones Públicas) was founded in 1949 by Federico Sanchez Fogerty. Twenty-two years later (1971), Grupo PROM was created. A few years later, Advertising and Promotion (1978) was founded, followed by Marketing and Promotion in 1979 and Cosmic in 1980. ProRP reports that 12 percent of the existing Mexican agencies were created during or before the 1980s (ProRP, 2007). Forty-two percent were founded in the 1990s, especially between 1995 and 2000. An additional 19 percent were created during the year 2000. The remaining 27 percent have appeared from 2001 to the present.

The formal practice of public relations in Mexico, as in most Latin American countries, began its professionalization in the 1970s. At that point, the Mexican government, given its capitalist development model, had to seek new ways to distribute the wealth of the nation among all the sectors of the population through the allocation of diverse types of services and social welfare benefits to its citizens. Consequently, the federal government realized that it needed to create a positive image of itself. The reason for this was that it was engaged in a series of efforts intended to providing public benefits such as education, health, and pensions and the people knew very little about the actions being undertaken to fight poverty. The government departments (known as Secretarías de Estado in Mexico) that were bestowing these services to the population needed to create social communication units in their offices to do the job (Hernandez, 1995). For this reason, the administration of President José López Portillo (1976–82) initiated a legal reform of the Organic Law of the Federal Public Administration (LAOPF for its initials in Spanish) in which it is stated that the departments had to develop administrative units and communication systems:

> The public service handbooks should contain the procedures and type of organization needed for the operation of the organizational structure of the dependent units as well as the functions of these units, and their communication systems and forms of coordination, and their major administrative procedures established.
>
> (LOAPF, 1982, Article 19)

Months later, on July 1, 1977, a Federal Agreement was published by which President López Portillo created the General Direction of Information and Public Relations of the Department of the Interior (Dirección General de Información y Relaciones Públicas de la Secretaría de Gobernación). This unit´s reason for being was that "the right to information of citizens is a prerequisite for the exercise of their political and social freedom" and therefore "knowledge of all of the federal, state and local governments'" actions is a fundamental factor to the practice of these liberties (Hernandez, 1995). This new government information model led to increased budget allocations for social communications programs, creating areas for professional activities and supporting the growth and practice of communication in all of the governments' administrative units and investment in media services, endorsing the existing demand for professional communication and public relations services.

The latest legal amendment by President López Portillo was on June 21, 1982, when the Department of Information and Public Relations, through a Presidential Agreement, became the General Coordination of Social Communication and was set directly under the authority of the Office of the Presidency of the Republic. In the following presidential term, on January 31, 1983, this Coordination became the General Direction of Social Communication of the Presidency of the Republic (Dirección General de Comunicación Social de la Presidencia de la República).

Since the creation of the first social communication model within the federal government, each department opened its own Office of Social Communication, Diffusion, and Public Relations, at different levels: in some cases at directorial level, sometimes at management level. The functions that were identified as the General Direction of the Presidency are those listed below. It is important to note that these, in turn, were assumed by each of the departments (Secretarías de Estado). These government organizational reforms have created a very important communication culture in the country and have significantly affected the evolution of communication in Mexico, its practice, the need to renew professional education, and the bottom-line reform: development and new paths for the media. The four objectives and responsibilities of this communication model for these new communication units are to:

I. Inform on the activities performed by the Chief Executive and, in general, the public sector, and promote its most effective diffusion.

II. Strengthen public sector Communications, including the process and the creation of an efficient State information system that not only guides its communication activities, but also assess the needs of citizens, receives new propositions, stimulates participation the diverse entities that compose the country's Federal Public Administration but also the various sectors of the Nation.

III. Coordinate, among the different public sector units, the activities of information disclosure, advertising, and public relations.

IV. Plan, prepare, and operate advertising campaigns in the media, to enable or support the actions of the Federal Government and other public sector entities.

(LOAPF, 1982, Article 27)

Francisco Hernández (1995), mentions that the factors influencing this new scheme of government policy were two: (a) the debate on the new information and communication order and (b) the general social expectations aroused by the impending Mexican political reform establishing political parties in the nation as public interest entities. Therefore, they became organisms with the responsibility to inform the nation on their operations and expenditures. Thus, communications and public relations practices had to increase.

At this time there was a set of public policies that enhanced the development of communication activities throughout the government institutions. As a result of this, more schools and careers began to focus on communication studies as the government demanded more communication services from professionals. Both factors fostered the growth of media and the advertising industry.

One of the most recurrent practices in the offices of social communication, advertising and public relations (as they were frequently called) was the incorporation of journalists to head these new departments. Journalists, at that time, were considered the best option for handling these communication departments given their experience in handling the media. In the minds of government officials at that time, social communication had mainly to do with what renowned journalists could do. They were seen as people who knew the media and their authorities, producers, and anchormen as well as reporters. Thus, they had the know-how and the means to create favorable images of politicians and their jobs.

Another common practice was that these posts were occupied by persons who were able to do well in high social circles, both entrepreneurial and political. Over time, this is one of the main factors that have determined the public relations culture that even today is difficult to uproot. The public relations profession was thought of as a handful of social activities, parties, cocktails, events. This situation has had a definite effect on the profession, specifically affecting women public relations professionals even to this day.

Notwithstanding the wide spread of communication and public relations activities being displayed in the public institutions, these political decisions set a new path for public relations practices in the private sector. In response to these governmental practices, and in the need to find a new balance of power within Mexican society, private organizations began to develop their own departments of communication and public relations, giving way to the strengthening and further development of the independent practice of the profession. The Mexican Association of Professional Public Relations Professionals first prepared a study on the market value of the industry in 2006, and has been repeating it annually ever since. By 2009, ProRP found that, among the existing private consulting communication and public relations agencies active in Mexico, the market value of the industry was 2,520 million pesos, and there were 159 public relations agencies (ProRP, 2009). Some of these were founded between 1980 and 1982.

The Culture of Public Relations in Mexico from the Late 1980s to the Early 2000s

Needless to say, the momentum given to public relations and communication by the Federal Government in the 1980s was a determining factor for the industry. It is important to mention here the misconceptions about public relations as a factor that greatly influenced the profession throughout the country for many years. The problem is that, rather than a profession requiring high skills and strategic thought, it was seen as an activity that anyone, even those without a degree, could do just by being excellent hosts or hostesses or attending social reunions and parties and carrying on light conversations. This image affected women especially, who were the perfect choice to be hired.

This fact marked the culture of the profession for many years, until, with the signing of the North American Free Trade Agreement (NAFTA) in 1994, a new model of public relations penetrated Mexican society. New and more sophisticated ways of doing public relations were introduced at a greater speed than before, given the presence of more and more diverse multinational corporations demanding communication and public relations services. They demanded services with international standards from the local public relations agencies. They also preferred that these services be provided by international communication and public relations agencies which could more adequately provide projects with an international vision.

Notwithstanding, local public relations agencies and communication

experts have proven their worth with the knowledge and the e
have in doing their job within Mexican culture. Some nationa
survived in spite of the internationalization trend either by join
with multinational colleges and consulting firms or by having
trained to high standards either within local prestigious universities or abroad.

The Globalization of Public Relations in Mexico

Because the worldwide processes of globalization at the end of the twentieth century and the beginning of the twenty-first included Mexico, a general
breakthrough in the development of culture of public relations occurred in the
country. In many ways like other parts of the world, the idea of international
public relations has penetrated the Mexican culture of communication. The
effects of globalization in the political, economic, and socio-cultural dimensions of the country constitute a specialized framework for the development of
public relations (Moreno and Molleda, 2005–2006). The capacity to combine
both, understanding of local culture as well as knowledge of standardized
ways of carrying out public relations strategies, has represented a boost for
some agencies in the country. In Mexico, the new century has brought about
accelerated processes of globalization and internationalization, including that
of public relations.

Two main issues should be mentioned at this point:

1 In a regime change after 70 years of political domination by the
   Revolutionary Political Party (Partido Revolucionario Institucional, PRI),
   the results of the presidential campaign of 2000 elected the National
   Action Party's (Partido de Acción Nacional, PAN) candidate as President
   of the Republic. This moved the PAN administration in power as the
   Mexican government to engage in a series of communication campaigns
   in order to minimize the effects of political change.
2 With the introduction of the Internet, a whole new array of globalized
   corporations began to demand communication and public relations services to be provided by highly specialized both national but preferably
   international communications and public relations agencies. The scene
   for the public relations industry changed as it needed to employ more
   and more specialized professionals and experts in the operations of virtual
   interchange (Newsom et al., 2000).

The Growth of the Public Relations Industry in the Country

To provide information on the growth of the public relations industry along
with its process of internationalization, the following statistics may be helpful.
In 2005, the study on the industry carried out by CICOM marks that there

were a total of 56 agencies in the country dedicated specifically to public relations (CICOM, 2006).

In 2006, the industry reported a total of 98 public relations consulting firms active in the country participating in the ProRP research. In 2007 there were 109 and in 2008 the report shows a total of 132 (a 135.7% increase with respect to 2006) communication and public relations agencies (ProRP, 2007, 2008, 2009; CICA, 2010).

In 2005, the total investment in PR services was 1,216 million pesos (US$112,592,593[2]) (Figure 10.1). In 2006, the industry's value accounted for 1,753 million pesos (US$162,314,815). In 2007, it was 1,940 million pesos (US$179,629,630). By 2008, the agencies' invoicing had reached 2,270 million pesos (US$210,185,185), a 17 percent increase from 2007. In 2009, the agencies invoiced 2,520 million pesos (US$233,333,333), an 11 percent increase from 2008. Invoicing for the public relations industry has been steadily growing in the country (ProRP, 2007, 2008, 2009, 2010).

In 2006, 2,252 people were employed in public relations; in 2007, 3,130; in 2008, 3,630; and in 2009 there were 4,065 people employed in public relations activities within Mexico, an 80.1 percent increase from 2006. The employment

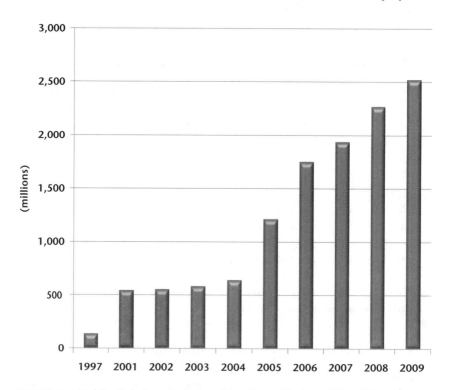

FIGURE 10.1 Public Relations Industry Growth in Mexico 1997–2009 (Mexican pesos). *Sources*: CICA (2010) and Ríos (2007).

capacity growth of the industry is very significant for the four-year span being considered (ProRP, 2007, 2008, 2009, 2010).

Along with labor prospects growing from year to year in public relations, the fact of the matter is that it is a mostly feminine business. The related percentages of women and men employed are 63 percent women and 37 percent men in 2006; 62 percent women and 38 percent men in 2007; 63 percent women and 37 percent men 2008; 61 percent women and 39 percent men in 2009. Although the labor force is basically feminine, it shows a more or less stable tendency in the last four years. The large majority of these jobs are full time.

It is interesting to note that in 2007, out of every 10 public relations clients, six were transnational or non-Mexican corporations. In 2008, the relationship remained the same; in 2009, out of every 10 PR clients, five were transnational or non-Mexican corporations. The data presented above provide an idea of the way the public relations industry is growingly internationalized, with an interesting reduction for 2009. Needless to say, a similar phenomenon is occurring with the large-scale businesses in the country; also the many industrial as well as commercial and services sectors have the same tendency.

Besides the United States, 28 percent of Mexican agencies' alliances were with European firms and 8 percent with Canadian businesses. The remaining ventures were carried out with other Latin American companies. Joint ventures of this kind are highly profitable for the public relations agencies, providing them with the capacity to serve in other countries as well and not only in Mexico (ProRP, 2008). As of 2009, the public relations industry was more fully integrated with other countries. As many as 82 percent of PR companies had some form of relationship with similar agencies outside the country (ProRP, 2009). Of those that have international relationships, 46 percent are part of an international network involved in multinational projects, 14 percent are associated with an agency of another country and even act as stakeholders of the foreign firm, and the remaining 40 percent work as a franchise in Mexico. Many of these alliances are carried out with Latin American countries, Canada, and the United States. However, some Asian countries are also represented.

At present, the culture of public relations is growing in Mexico under the influence of multinational companies and definitely globalization. Today, most foreign companies in the country have communication and public relations departments linked, in most cases, to their international corporations in another country, mainly, as mentioned before, from Latin America and the United States. The larger national firms also have their own communication and public relations departments.

On the other hand, private companies are increasingly managed with an international vision. This has linked public relations and communications practices to the international practice of public relations. This tendency has moved the Mexican public relations agencies to engage in partnerships with globalized networks of specialized agencies. Also, national public relations agencies are moving their businesses into servicing foreign companies seeking to do business in Mexico or Mexican companies that want to do business abroad.

Another aspect that has contributed to the internationalization of the public relations culture is the expansion and outreach of communication and information technology as well as the increasing operations of social networks. This has also had an impact on some democratic processes within the country, where computers, the Internet, and cellular phones are increasingly accessible to many socio-economic segments. These changes have motivated reforms within the academic sector in the creation of new subjects and methodologies for communication and public relations. As of today, teaching public relations is unthinkable without personalized techniques carried out through the Internet and the cellular phones and without an international view being preeminent.

Bottom-line questions remain: Is this truly beneficial to the country as a whole? Is this process creating an even wider gap between socio-economic sectors? Are these disparities being carried into other fields of Mexican society, creating even wider economic, cultural, and technological gaps?

The Practice of Public Relations in the Different Regions of Mexico

The growth and development of the public relations industry in Mexico is not a uniform phenomenon throughout the country. This has been highly determined by the economic, political, social, and cultural circumstances of each region within the country. Taking this fact into account, communication and public relations activities are carried out within the cities where commercial activity, business, government, and the media are more concentrated. Public relations activities also coincide within the urban areas containing the best communication schools and public relations programs. The highest concentration of communication and public relations agencies have best flourished within the five most densely populated metropolitan areas in the country: Mexico City (14,000,9758 people); Guadalajara, in the State of Jalisco (6,753,113); Monterrey, in Nuevo León (4,199,292); Puebla, in the State of Puebla, together with Tlaxcala, in Tlaxcala (3,451,340 inhabitants); and the city of Toluca, in the State of México (747,512 people) (INEGI, 2010).

These urban areas also centralize the main operations and practices of public relations. These cities also contain the country's largest concentrations of government agencies, industries, national companies, and multinationals with activities of communication and public relations. Also, in these urban areas, one can find the largest number of private public relations agencies in the nation.

A second block where the culture of communications and public relations is highly centralized is the more touristic areas of the country. The development of large tourist resorts where a large influx of international hotel investment and tourists from all over the world as well as local tourists are found has presented fertile soil for communication and public relations. These are the cities most commonly known worldwide for their abundant natural resources, beautiful beaches, and a combination of an international atmosphere with the more folk culture, music, arts, and culinary tradition, which means they are mainly areas for tourism. These cities are: Veracruz, in the State of Veracruz (8,110,294); Puerto Vallarta, in Jalisco (7,762,113); Acapulco, in Guerrero (6,116,395); Mérida, in Yucatán (1,918,942); Cancún, in Quintana Roo (1,138,309); and Los Cabos, in Baja California Sur (818,170) (INEGI, 2010).

In these cities, the culture of public relations practice has been developed mainly with purposes such as total quality and guest services. In recent years, major climatic changes and natural disasters, such as hurricanes, have affected some of these tourist areas. The communication crisis management approach has been largely and effectively implemented in order to recover from diminishing levels of tourist flow. Also, the country's image of insecurity has been greatly affected by the growth of organized crime. To this end, communication and public relations strategies have been and are being put into service in order to promote the idea of Mexico as a safer country.

A third block of incipient development in public relations culture and practice can be found in cities with more than 1 million inhabitants and where state governments are settled and their governmental strategies have a definite focus on foreign investment. We can mention cities in the northern part of the country, within the States bordering the United States. However, there are also other cities in the inner parts of the country that are a considerable size, where industry has flourished, and whose assets are very attractive, again, to tourists both local and from all over the world. These are Chihuahua and Ciudad Juarez, in Chihuahua (4,252,444); León, in Guanajuato (4,942,812); Tijuana and La Paz, in North and South Baja California, respectively (3,844,469); Reynosa, in Tamaulipas (3,324,238); Hermosillo, Nogales, and Puerto Peñasco, in Sonora (2,498,861); Saltillo and Piedras Negras, in Coahuila (2,495,300); Aguascalientes, in Aguascalientes (2,065,416); and Querétaro, in Querétaro (1,598,289) (INEGI, 2010). Some of these metropolitan areas are State capital cities, thus having an abundance of political activity.

To this day, the expansion of the public relations industry continues under three main patterns in the country: (1) development of the industry is uneven in the diverse regions; (2) public relations, in a sense, goes where certain types of industry and services develop and where a good image and reputation need to be established; (3) densely concentrated urban areas and intense political and economic activities are good predictors for the presence of public relations and communication services.

As far as the concept or general idea of public relations, smaller-scale cities continue to practice public relations within the paradigm of the *old concept*, which basically refers to the public relations practice conceived as interpersonal attention and services provided by ways of *being nice* or *agreeable* to clients, based upon the belief that those attitudes will favor sales, bring new business opportunities, and create a good image or the promotion of persons, organizations, or projects. Therefore, public relations clients hire people who demonstrate this disposition to *be friendly*, instead of strategic communicators and public relations experts.

Changes Brought About by Information Technology

In Mexico, the new information technologies (Internet and email, cellular phones and others) have emerged as regular business tools. This occurred more intensely in 1998 and 1999. As a necessary component of globalization, the new technologies began to reshape communication and public relations work. New ways of doing business appeared mainly through virtual strategies, revolutionizing with this the employment spectrum and organizational strategies. Within public relations agencies, huge transformations were taking place, including big changes in the collective and group communication strategies, which become better triggered, more personalized one-to-one activities. Thus a new public relations culture is arising.

With time, this has become known to be more effective, given the learned capacity to segment and target strategic market opportunities. Mexico became fully involved in the transformation of information management and customer demand for electronic files, press clippings sent by email, or summary information reported to the international corporations.

The evolution of technology, the growth of the Internet, high-speed document imaging, data processing, and audience segmentation were decisive in the culture of the profession. The growth of the agencies or public relations units is more and more determined by human resources departments and their training activities. Suddenly, technology became the common denominator, the decision-making factor determining which agencies were preferred in the national arena.

In early 2000, some of the largest multinational companies had specific requirements of information technology and communication infrastructure in order to maintain constant interaction on similar platforms all over the world. This is true especially in situations where handling case crisis is of vital importance. Constant communication and speed is the number one factor determining the success of the operations. These aspects forced the multinational companies and agencies to be always aware of the latest technological advances in order to satisfy the highest demands of any national or international customer. It can be said that the practice of public relations in Mexico is set on a non-stop road into technology. This is true not only because they are new working and communication tools, but also because they represent new forms of liaison with the different audiences, and on account of the changes in the mass communication media.

Nowadays, the CEOs of the world's major multinational companies look to Mexico as an important country for their businesses' incursions. Their contacts, visits, and all strategic communication have been supported by public relations professionals in both the internal departments of the national corporations as well as the independent public relations agencies. This tendency has also provoked job mobility among Mexican professionals today. Some of these professionals (unfortunately, a small number of them) have been climbing positions both in corporate communication units of national firms as well as within the international structures of the major global agencies.

Another major factor affected by the change in information technology is social interaction. From the standpoint of public relations, Internet growth, and email in particular, has given the communication and public relations professional increasing power. The possibility of reaching more and more diverse audiences in less time and at a lower cost has favored public institutions as well as private companies.

Another important change was that communication and public relations clients are at present a lot more educated, knowledgeable, and informed. Today, they are the immediate and main social group with which the public relations professionals have to carry on challenging dialogues. They also have to convince and serve them efficiently, including the production of evident/measurable results. Communication and public relations clients are the number one guards to their own interests and money. Today's public relations clients are in a hurry, demanding, and thorough. Public relations and communication clients have changed the *modus operandi* of corporations, determining the way of doing public relations and communication strategies in the world and in Mexico. Also government and public institutions, somewhat lagging behind the dynamic private sector, are dealing with change and the needs of Mexican citizens.

Communication and public relations professionals face new challenges also because they are slowly but surely becoming the permanent eyes and ears between companies and the media. Given the fact that social networks have the possibility to destroy the reputation of companies and their products at such a speed that it is sometimes hard to react fast enough, it is the job of public relations professionals to keep a watchful eye on the upcoming threats to corporations and to create and carry out insightful communication strategies on the spot.

Also, today's widespread influence of social networks and electronic multi-interactions has provoked a sharp turn to the practice of public relations in

Mexico. In 2009, communication professionals began to refer to *Public Relations 2.0*. The sudden growth of this virtual phenomenon is testing the stamina and temperance of the communication and public relations profession as a whole. Needless to say, communication and PR professionals have whole new ways of doing their jobs and strategies triggered at crisis challenges. Furthermore, communication schools and faculties around the nation are changing their programs and updating their professors. Universities, as a matter of fact, prefer communication and public relations professionals to come in and teach their students the more practical courses.

Another important aspect with ramifications into public relations culture is that the traditional media themselves (radio, broadcast television, newspapers, and the cinema) are also undergoing changes, given the new ways in which information and opinions flow through the new technologies. Traditional media in the country are fully into online transmissions, with their own web pages and their own social network pages on Facebook, Twitter, MySpace, Youtube, or elsewhere. The use of mobile communication has also come into the scene. Mobile communication is a tool that provides the possibility of sending brief notes to segmented audiences on the move. It is now being widely used by the large media corporations to send out their messages. Such is the case of SMS (short message service), STM (short text message), Bluetooth, multimedia messaging system (MMS), and others. On one hand these phenomena have provided the public relations practice with more and more efficient platforms for extra penetration and outreach to different audiences. On the other hand, it has forced public relations experts and professionals to do their job on a multidimensional level. Their communication tasks have to be done attending to a wide array of media, and their media follow-ups also have to be as diverse as the wide spectrum of options has to offer. Each message created requires a plan, every media selected for the job demands a different stratagem, but also the different publics or audience segments addressed each call for a specific communication approach. Thus, there is a growing need for highly special-ized communication and public relations professionals and, therefore, the challenge on higher education institutions and universities is to make better courses and be updated on the changes in society.

The practice of public relations in Mexican society is significant, but no one has measured to date its extent and power. Public relations and commu-nication work is to some extent almost invisible. Notwithstanding that, the power they have in building brands and constructing the power base, image, and reputation of businesses is undeniable. Also, for public organisms and government offices and political leaders, communication and public relations have proven to be a key factor determining success or failure. in addition, communication and public relations have slowly begun to produce more and better understanding of corporations, public institutions, and civic society and their clients, consumers, and citizens.

Changes in Mexican Media and Public Relations

The media are also a determining factor for the public relations profession. Throughout the evolution of the profession, changes in the media have also coincided with the main public relations transformations. The changes brought about by the new technologies, bandwidth, and triple-play are transforming the rules of the game. New economic and cultural balances are coming to play in the country. Public opinion making is no longer the property and concern of the traditional media, as in old times. In Mexico, the media face the challenge of integration into the information society as the real name of the game of public opinion.

As the business of public relations grows in the country, one can find journalist groups who complain about this phenomenon on account of the fact that (according to them) public relations professionals limit journalists, who, at other times, had free and abundant access to information. On the other hand, one can find some journalists who are grateful to public relations agencies as well as to the public relations and communication departments within large corporations, because their editorial work is now being made a lot easier by them.

Opinion leaders such as the news anchormen and women and newspaper, radio, and television editorial writers and reporters working in the main communication networks throughout the country have begun to lose credibility among the population. Among other reasons, this phenomenon is also due to the digitalization of the media, technological change, and the expansion of social networks on the Internet, whereby audiences have conversations and comments among themselves, at great speed. The public thus manages to question their credibility and discovers the real economic, political and cultural alliances and interests they serve. In short, what is said in the media is confronted with the people's knowledge and points of view.

On the other hand, the image of enterprises as well as public institutions had to find new ways of creating their legitimacy among the country's audiences. Marketing specialists, under pressure to *show results*, penetrated the news programs themselves. Instead of open and straightforward advertising, they began to include advertising and sales strategies by acquiring time slots within the news programs themselves. They use that time for advertising through *information capsules* that contain *news notes* or *editorials* in which an enterprise, a project or a person is seen as doing something for the benefit of society. This, in certain ways, new communication culture is widely used around the country as elsewhere.

Currently, whenever a communication professional seeks to interview a client, the answer can be a negative, depending on whether or not that client happens to be a business partner of the specific medium in which he/she chooses to be interviewed. Thus, some television networks in the country may deny an interview if the interviewee is someone who also buys advertising time on the channel. In other cases the news program director simply passes the call to the sales department of the specific media outlet. This has closed opportunities for a sound and ethical public relations practice.

Furthermore, since 2008, the process of acquiring media time for politicians to carry out their campaigns is now regulated. Political parties can acquire time for campaigns in the media only through the Federal Institute for Elections (Instituto Federal Electoral, IFE). This regulation was designed as a way to keep the groups in the nation who have more economic clout and buying power from paying for media time in favor of the candidates of their choice. Communication and public relations professionals have had to learn their way through new laws and rules of the game in order to serve their clients well and to keep their activities within the realm of social responsibility and ethics.

On the other hand, journalists themselves still have a big hand in taking the place of public relations experts. They provide services such as media coaching for the higher-ranking managers and CEOs in firms, as well as for politicians. This has led to assigning public relations work directly to journalists themselves, overlooking the more comprehensive and expert services that public relations and communication professionals can provide.

Final Comments

Given the development of the public relations industry in the country, it can be said that it has grown mainly within the large urban areas in the country, the state capitals, and the tourist areas. Professionalized public relations and communication services are required in the places where economic, political, and cultural activities concentrate the most. The public relations industry contends that it is useful to private enterprises but also to public organisms and government institutions. Public relations is a definite component of today's dynamic society.

The profession of public relations is slowly but surely gaining ground in the difficult process of changing the old perception of the profession. This perception had basically to do with the carrying out of specific tasks (at times not even conceived of as professional) that anyone who possessed interpersonal links with the media and opinion leaders and who went to a lot of functions and cocktail parties could do. The main objective of attending social occasions had to do with managing to obtain the trust of high-ranking officials, CEOs, and the like, and thus facilitate and extend their clients' interests.

As the process of globalization has expanded in Mexican society, public relations agencies have more and more become the intermediary agents between multinational corporations and local society and consumers. Through these activities, local enterprises and institutions themselves have undertaken important changes in their organizational culture and management. Many are now trying to match international standards not only within the realm of communication and public relations, but also within the realm of the organization as a whole.

Public relations and communication professionals are rapidly acquiring more relevant roles in Mexican politics, since the late 1970s, when massive government and political information to citizens was finally agreed to be a need and an obligation of the federal, state, and municipal governments and all the public institutions.

From the last decade and a half on, public relations experts have carried out communications projects at an international level with very good results. This has been favored by the presence of multinational corporations and NAFTA. Although good for individual employees, it is a widely recognized fact that NAFTA has not been good for the country's economy as a whole.

An interesting point is that many public relations and communications tactics, initially conceived of and carried out within the country, are later implemented among Hispanic audiences in the United States. This stratagem is not always the best way to reach diverse Hispanic audiences, given the wide cultural differences existing between Mexicans living in Mexico and Hispanics (Mexican, Spanish, Salvadoreans, Venezuelans, Chileans, etc.) who live within the United States of America.

Audiences, consumers, citizens, have become specialized, informed, critical, and harder to convince. The public relations professionals, usually serving as the link between these publics and government institutions and private enterprises, have also become more sophisticated, more efficient, and able to prove results.

As the globalization process occurs, so does change take place in Mexican cultural and PR trends. Change in information technologies has marked deep transformations in the public relations industry. Information flows are moving at greater speeds than ever before. The public relations professional has to cope with change in his/her daily practice and creating new schemes in order to be efficient and respond at great speed to clients' demands and needs.

Mexico is a very good example of how public relations professionals work to adopt and survive the changes of globalization. However, the professionalism of the discipline and the evolution of the education process in the universities can do more in order not to lag behind the speed of change in everyday communication and public relations applications.

Notes

1 It should be said that a landmark book for the profession is by Bonilla (1988).
2 Throughout this paragraph, exchange rate at 10.80 Mexican pesos per U.S. dollar, Banco de Mexico (2007).

Bibliography

Arvizu, A. (2009, October 25). About public relations. (M. Herrera, interviewer.)

Banco de Mexico. (2007). Convertidor de tipo de cambio. Retrieved October 15, 2007, from http://www.banxico.gob.mx/PortalesEspecializados/tiposCambio/indicadores. html.

Bonilla, C. (1998). *La comunicación: Función básica de las relaciones públicas*. Mexico: Trillas.

Carreño, L. (2009, February 17). About public relations. (M. Herrera, interviewer.)

Castro, J. (2009, September 9). About public relations. (M. Herrera, interviewer.)

CICA (Centro de Investigación en Comunicación Aplicada). (2010). Extract of information. México: Universidad Anáhuac.

CICOM. (2006). Estudio del valor del mercado de la comunicación comercial en México, datos 2005. Retrieved from http://cicom.org.mx.

Corzo, L. (2009, November 27). About public relations. (M. Herrera, interviewer.)

Costa, J. (2009). *Imagen corporativa en el siglo XXI* (4th edn.). Buenos Aires: La Crujía.

De la Barreda, P. (2009, August 25). About public relations. (M. Herrera, interviewer.)

García, L. (2009, June). Public relations. (M. Herrera, interviewer.)

Grunig, J. (Ed.) (1992). *Excellence in public relations and communication management*. Hillsdale, NJ: Lawrence Erlbaum Associates.

Hernandez, F. (1995). Las oficinas de Comunicación en México. *Comunicación y Sociedad Magazine*. Guadalajara: DECS Universidad de Guadalajara. Retrieved from http://ccdoc.iteso.mx/acervo/cat.aspx?cmn=download&ID=2924&N=1.

Herrera, Y. (2009, July 29). Public relations. (M. Herrera, interviewer.).

INEGI. (National Institute of Statistics and Geography). (2006, January 1). *General Population Census 2005*. Retrieved from http://www.inegi.org.mx/est/contenidos/proyectos/ccpv/cpv2005/Default.aspx.

León Duarte, G. A. (2009). *Sobre la institucionalización de la comunicación en América Latina*. Sonora, Mexico: Pearson.

LOAPF. (1982). *Ley Orgánica de la Administración Pública Federal*. Retrieved from http://www.cddhcu.gob.mx/LeyesBiblio/ref/loapf.htm.

Moreno, A. and Molleda, J. (2005–06). Las relaciones públicas en México: Contextos económico, político y mediático en un proceso histórico de cambios. *Razón y Palabra*, 48(11). Retrieved from http://www.www.razonypalabra.org.mx/anteriores/n48/morenomolleda.html.

Newson, D., Turk, J., and Kruckeberg, D. (2000). This are PR: The realities of public relations. In *International PR: Emerging Challenges for the 21st Century*. Miami: IPRRC Annual Congress, pp. 11–14.

ProRP. (Mexican Association of Professional Public Relations). (2007). *Study Report on the Public Relations Industry 2006*. Mexico, D. F.: PRORP.

ProRP. (2008). *2nd Annual Industry Survey of Public Relations 2007*. Mexico, D. F.: PRORP.

ProRP. (2009). *2008 Annual Survey of Public Relations Industry in Mexico*. Mexico, D. F.: PRORP.

ProRP. (2010). *4th Annual Industry Survey of Public Relations 2009*. Mexico, D. F.: PRORP.

Rebeil, M. A. (2006). *Comunicación estratégica en las organizaciones*. México: Trillas.

Rebeil, M. A. and RuizSandoval, C. (Eds.) (1998). *El poder de la comunicación en las organizaciones*. México: Plaza & Valdés.

Rebeil, M. A., Montoya, A., and Hidalgo, J. (2009). The public relations industry in Mexico: From amateurship to the construction of a discipline. In Sriramesh, K.

and Verčič, D. (Eds.), *The global public relations handbook: Theory, research and practice* (revised and expanded edition). New York: Routledge.

Ríos, M. A. (2007, August). El avance casi completo. *Merca 2.0*, 64, 58–64.

Ríos, M. A. (2007, September). Respeto por la disciplina. *Merca 2.0*, 65, 85.

Sanchez Fogarty, F. (1963). *Apuntes para la historia de las relaciones públicas en México*. Mexico: Asociación Mexicana de Profesionales en Relaciones Públicas.

Sánchez Uribe, C. (2010, April 25). About public relations. (M. A. Rebeil, interviewer.)

Stone, J. (2000). Public relations. In *International PR: Emerging Challenges for the 21st Century*. Miami: IPRRC Annual Congress, pp. 11–14.

11

WHEN CULTURES COLLIDE

Theoretical Issues in Global Public Relations

Matthew R. Allen[1] and David M. Dozier

When Cultures Collide: Theoretical Issues in Global Public Relations

This chapter addresses broad theoretical issues surrounding the practice of public relations on a global scale. Special attention is focused on the role of culture when organizations seek to build and maintain relationships with publics that are culturally distinct from those of the organization. In doing so, a quantitative case study is described in some detail. The case study illustrates the value of using existing measures of key concepts (e.g., relationship satisfaction) in a cross-cultural context. At the same time, the case study illustrates the importance and challenge of instrument refinement. Such refinement is needed to account for cultural differences when using universal measures in cultural contexts that differ from the context used for initial instrument design. The case study also demonstrates the value of incorporating culturally specific measures of constructs that are relevant in some culture contexts but not others. In this manner, scholars of global public relations can better understand universal aspects that are relevant to all organizations and all publics. At the same time, culturally specific measures can help illuminate and understand areas where cultures collide in the context of global public relations. After detailing the case study, this chapter closes with a discussion of implications for scholars of global public relations, as well as implications for the practice.

Defining Key Concepts

Clear explanation of key concepts provides greater clarity with regard to subsequent discussions. Fundamental to any discussion of global public relations is explication of public relations itself. Grunig and Hunt (1984) defined public relations as the "management of communication between an organization and its publics" (p. 6). Cutlip, Center, and Broom (2006) provide a more detailed definition that de-emphasizes the primacy of communication and shifts the emphasis from processes and outputs (communication) to outcomes (relationships). They define public relations as the "management function that establishes and maintains mutually beneficial relationships between an organization and the publics on whom its success or failure depends" (p. 5). Seeking to explicitly address issues of culture in global public relations, Sriramesh and Verčič (2009) define public relations as "the strategic communication that different types of organizations use for establishing and maintaining symbiotic relationships with relevant publics, many of whom are increasingly becoming culturally diverse" (p. xxxiv).

This chapter favors the Sriramesh and Verčič definition because it implicitly recognizes communication as a key tool in building relationships, but gives primacy to symbiotic relationships as the outcome of such efforts. Further, the Sriramesh and Verčič definition highlights the tensions between worldviews constructed within boundaries of organizations and differing worldviews of publics outside organizational boundaries. These tensions increase exponentially when cultural differences are introduced.

Organizational Representations of Environments

When an organization makes decisions, the decision-makers do so based on a representation of the organization and its environment. This *representation* is a "set of shared perceptions of the organization and its environment that organization members use to make decisions" (White and Dozier, 1992, p. 92). Members of organizations develop perceptions of their organization and its environment by selectively attending to some inputs from the environment while ignoring other inputs, a process called *enactment*. This internal construction of reality is often self-serving, reflected in the notion that problems with publics would go away if publics simply understood the organization better. As boundary spanners, with one foot inside the organization and the other outside in the environment, public relations practitioners play a crucial role in helping organizational decision-makers realize that publics do not necessarily share management's enactments of the organization itself or of the organization's environment.

Central to a discussion of global public relations is a working definition of culture. As Sriramesh (2009) noted, 164 definitions of culture and over 300 variations on that definition are reported in the extant literature. For the purposes of this chapter, *culture* is defined as "that complex whole which includes knowledge, belief, art, morals, custom, and any other capabilities and habits acquired by man as a member of society" (Kroeber and Kluckhohn, 1952, p. 1). Culture embraces the totality of learned knowledge, attitudes, and behavioral predispositions that may differ, to varying degrees, within nations, between similar nation states (e.g., the United States vs. Canada), and across different regions of the globe (e.g., Japan/South Korea/Taiwan vs. the European Union). Because culture is so ubiquitous—because people assume that arbitrary aspects of their own culture are universally shared—the challenges to effective public relations increase exponentially as cultural differences between organizations and publics become more pronounced.

Two-Way Communication

Two-way communication is crucial to best practices in public relations. An effective public relations manager serves not only as the mouthpiece (e.g., spokesperson) for the organization, but also as its eyes and ears. This is accomplished through research to scan the environment and evaluate public relations programs. The expertise to conduct such research constitutes the *knowledge core* identified in the Excellence Study as a necessary condition of communication excellence (Dozier et al., 1995).

Two-way communication is easier to execute when cultural differences between organizations and publics are small. One can assert the following as a proposition: As cultural differences become more pronounced, the opportunities for misunderstandings and unintended consequences increase.

Action and Communication Strategies

The above proposition applies to both action and communication strategies. *Action strategies* are behaviors of organizations that affect relationships with publics. These include the policies, procedures, and plans that organizations use to pursue their objectives. As Cutlip, Center, and Broom (2006) affirmed, actions speak louder than words; effective public relations requires that organizations synchronize what they *say* (communication strategies) with what organizations *do* (action strategies). Excellent public relations managers must influence the behavior of the organization to reduce conflicts with publics in order for an effective communication strategy to be executed.

Participation in Decision Making

To mesh organizational actions with communication, public relations managers must participate in organizational decision making, influencing behaviors of the organization to reduce the gap between the interests of the organization and key publics. However, as empirically supported by the Excellence Study (Dozier et al., 1995; Grunig et al., 2002), public relations managers are more likely to be included in the dominant coalition informally, based on the specialized expertise that practitioners bring to the decision-making table. That

specialized expertise includes an understanding of the organizational environment and its publics, as well as the ability to anticipate how publics are likely
to react when the organization behaves in a particular manner. Public relations
managers can informally advise the dominant coalition regarding strategic
choices. The public relations manager's ability to provide that expertise is
severely reduced when cultural differences exist between the practitioner and
key publics.

A Dearth of Empirical Research

In their seminal work on global public relations, Sriramesh and Verčič (2009)
detailed a number of theories about culture and global public relations.
However, they noted that little empirical research has been conducted to date
to (1) test these theories and (2) build a body of knowledge in global public
relations that (3) rests on a solid empirical foundation. The following case
study provides a useful set of empirical findings. Further, the methodological
and theoretical challenges addressed in this case study are relevant to other
scholars attempting to conduct similar studies.

Cultures collide when an organization nested in one cultural framework
interacts with publics nested in a different cultural framework. This is the
case when transnational corporations seek to establish new markets in different cultural contexts or when they seek raw materials in areas inhabited by
cultures unfamiliar to the organization's management. Cultures collide when
international non-governmental organizations (INGOs) seek to provide assistance to people embedded in cultures different from that of the leadership
of the INGO. Most strikingly, cultures collide when nations with different
cultural frameworks are at war. The quantitative case study that follows provides a microcosm of the challenges and opportunities that researchers and
practitioners both face when conducting global public relations under adverse
conditions.

A Case Study of U.S. Military Public Affairs Officers and Arab Journalists

Here are the findings of a quantitative case study of the relationships between
public affairs officers (PAOs) serving in the U.S. military in the Middle East
and Arab journalists who worked with them. On the U.S. side of the relationship, the Department of Defense seeks to professionalize its public affairs
community. Reflective of the American experience and cultural norms, the
U.S. Department of Defense seeks to move away from traditional "seat of the
pants" practices of old-style practitioners in and out of the military and toward
an increasingly professionalized public affairs community. On the other side
of this relationship, as documented by Badran, Turk, and Walters (2003) and

Alanazi (1996), Arab journalists in the Middle East are embedded in cultures that, despite their many differences, place special importance on kinship and the interconnectedness of community. This, in turn, affects how Arab journalists manage their relationships with Western (essentially American) public affairs officers. Public affairs officers are trained to standards dictated by Western culture, emphasizing individualism and a professional, business-like approach to the practice; Arab journalists live and work in a collectivist culture. These cultural differences are posited to frame different worldviews of the nature of organization–public relationships.

Exchange and Communal Worldviews

Hon and Grunig (1999) explicated the concept of relationships and provided operational measures in the form of various scales and subscales. Most relevant here are two conceptualizations of the overall nature of the relationship between an organization (e.g., U.S. Department of Defense) and a key public (e.g., Arab journalists). Arab journalists are an important public for the U.S. Department of Defense in particular and U.S. foreign policy in general because these journalists provide access to other publics (Arab readers and viewers) on whom U.S. foreign policy is focused. We use the term *worldview* in a manner that parallels its use in cultivation theory; a *worldview* is a pervasive way of looking at the relationships between an organization and its publics. Worldview is what Hon and Grunig explicated as outcomes. Having originally developed the concepts of exchange relationship and communal relationship from work in individual psychology, Hon and Grunig (1999) incorporated them as relational outcomes specific to the public relations community.

An *exchange relationship* is characterized by one party giving benefits to the other only because the other has provided benefits in the past or is expected to do so in the future. Marketing fosters exchange relationships; goods are given for something in return. Although exchange relationships are appropriate to marketing, Hon and Grunig (1999) argued that public relations seeks to build relationships that are more enduring.

Hon and Grunig defined communal relationships as those where "both parties provide benefits to the other because they are concerned for the welfare of the other—even when they get nothing in return" (Hon and Grunig, 1999, p. 21). For most public relations activities, communal relationships with key constituencies arguably are more valuable and more enduring than exchange relationships.

Exchange and Communal Worldviews in Two Dimensions

On a single continuum, exchange relationships anchor one end, representing relationships based on the utilitarian needs of one party. At the other end, communal relationships depend on communication as dialog and the gratification of needs. However, communal and exchange worldviews also can be viewed as more or less orthogonal in two-dimensional space (see Figure 11.1). As shown, a relationship can be regarded as *strictly exchange* (A); *strictly communal* (B); *saturated* (C), wherein the relationship is rated highly on both exchange and communal measures; or *indifferent* (D), wherein the relationship receives low ratings on both exchange and communal measures.

Indeed, data from the present case study suggest that communal and exchange outcomes or worldviews are more orthogonal than not, as shown in Figure 11.1. Among PAOs, the correlation between exchange and communal outcomes is $r = -0.06$, indicating that communal and exchange worldviews are not opposite ends of a single conceptual continuum. The relationship is slightly stronger for Arab journalists ($r = -0.15$), but note limitations (discussed below) regarding the reliability of these indices for Arab journalists.

The Role of Honor in Relationship Quality

Hon and Grunig (1999) provided useful measures of relationship qualities and outcomes, but their measures did not address other aspects of relationships that are important in other, non-Western cultures. Specifically, the Hon and Grunig measures do not account for the role and value placed in Arab cultures on *honor*. For purposes of this study, *honor* is defined as the communicator's

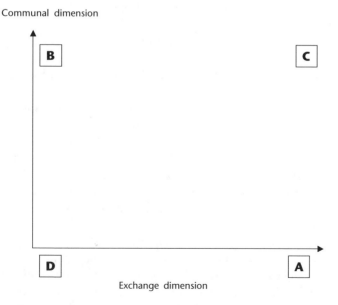

FIGURE 11.1 Conceptualizing Exchange and Communal Worldviews of Relationships in Two-Dimensional Space.

perceived understanding of family and cultural esteem, as well providing proper responses to emotional facts.

Hon and Grunig's measures of communal and exchange relationships have utility outside the English-speaking, Western world. These measures of relational worldviews provide the baseline for additional cross-cultural studies. Nevertheless, these indices are based on norms prevalent in Western cultures that cannot fully account for variations that other cultures may require.

Knowing this, global public relations practitioners should seek ways to identify and bridge these cultural differences. According to Ferreira da Cruz, the global practitioner "can be defined as a negotiator between his own cultural, social, and political identifications, and representations with those of the other" (Ferreira da Cruz, 2008, pp. 99–100). Military public affairs officers often find themselves enacting this role of cultural negotiator. In such situations, a strong background in communication theories, such as the coorientation model (Broom and Dozier, 1990), is helpful. However, an understanding of the other culture, and the tools to effectively measure these relationships in a culturally sensitive way, will provide several additional benefits.

Creating the Allen Honor Index (AHI)

Construction of the honor index was based on the extant literature specific to Arab cultures and how Arab audiences interact with media content. The first step in creating the index was to examine prior research about non-Western cultures. Huang (2000) provided the first of these expansions by creating a specific measure of favor and face for utilization within Confucian cultures of the Far East. *Favor* was defined as "a mode of conduct in which individuals stay in contact with influential parties" (p. 10). *Face* was described as a resource along the lines of pride or respect. Following this same approach of developing specific measures for use in specialized cultural contexts, this study developed an index of *honor* for utilization with Arab audiences.

Arab cultures throughout the Middle East share several values in common that differ from those found in the West. Highlighting the first of these differences, Yin (2008) contrasted "Western libertarian philosophy [that] values the independence and rights of each individual" with collectivist Eastern cultures that "focus on the state and family" (p. 40). Career choices, marriages, business dealings, and even conflicts are processed through the prism of family identity. This, in turn, impacts decisions made by Arab audiences.

Arab collectivist tendencies extend to their communication behaviors. Studying the television, radio, and newspaper habits of Arab citizens, Zayani (2005) found that these activities are family and community affairs. Coming together in living rooms or coffee shops, Arab citizens engage in lively and emotional discussions about topics of the day. News stories are debated within the frame of their impact on—and relationship to—the family or group.

Looking deeper at the relational component described in Arab communication behavior, Zayani (2005) found that these audiences are not concerned with the isolated facts that are communicated through media channels; Arab audiences are concerned with the relationship presented. According to Zayani (2005), "in Arab culture, metaphors and analogies that suggest important relationships are much more persuasive than impersonal 'facts'" (p. 191). For example, a story about a new business deal could generate much discussion, but discourse would not focus solely on the particulars of the deal. Among Arab audiences, facts such as how much money was exchanged or how many jobs were created would be given less salience than the inter- or intra-group relationships that the deal might affect.

In addition to relational importance, Zayani (2005) reported the impact of emotional responses during communication with an Arab audience. Emotions are an important part of communication; the absence of an appropriate emotional response (a detachment valued in the objective style of Western journalism) causes Arab audiences to regard the message with suspicion. Describing this culturally specific communication trait, Zayani said, "emotions are part of the story. The soul of the news lies in the emotion. Emotion is the most important fact" (Zayani, 2005, p. 194). Zayani suggested that the acceptance by Arab audiences of gross exaggerations during communication reflects the high value such audiences place on the emotional impact of communications. Highlighting the tendency of Arab news outlets to vastly overstate death tolls resulting from Israeli military actions, Zayani stated that these exaggerated numbers do not reflect reality; they are meant to relay the extent of the emotional response the deaths created. The ability to discern *emotional facts* embedded in messages communicated, as well as provide appropriate emotion-laden responses, will assist global public relations practitioners to increase the quality of relationships with Arab audiences.

The final relevant communication trait is the magnitude of the culture's historical importance as reported by Arab publics (Witteborn, 2007). Witteborn studied how the Arab families living in the United States maintained their collective identities. During the course of the interviews, researchers learned that family and cultural history were important aspects of collective identity. When asked whether they were *Arab* or *Arab-American*, one participant replied "I'm Arab. I want to identify as Arab. I don't want to be Arab-American. We have a long history, and I wanna bring it with me. Why should we have the hyphen?" (Witteborn, 2007, p. 564). Responses such as these indicate that the history and achievements of the Arab culture are important components of individual and collective esteem. Understanding how this esteem is generated is paramount to effective relationship management in the Arab world.

Challenges Faced by Public Affairs Officers

Although communal worldviews or outcomes are desired, several factors militate against communal worldviews among military public affairs officers. The major contributing factor that reduces opportunities for PAOs to develop communal relationships with Arab journalists is their relatively short tours of duty in the Middle East. Currently, each of the separate uniformed services maintains a different tour length. U.S. Army PAOs serve the longest deployments, with some tours lasting a year or more. U.S. Air Force PAOs are deployed for the shortest tours, lasting only four months. These relatively short tours exacerbate two interrelated problems. First, newly arrived PAOs may not have the requisite cultural knowledge to communicate as effectively as they might, because they do not understand the honor traits that Arab journalists associate with communal relations. Despite this knowledge deficit and the subsequent lack of attention to issues of "honor" specific to this cultural context, their leaders expect PAOs to gain immediate results. Immediacy is a trait of Hon and Grunig's exchange relationship. These situational characteristics of the PAO work setting provide support for the proposition that PAOs will view their relationships with Arab journalists as exchange relationships, even if their training as public affairs officers would lead them to favor communal relationships as an ideal.

Subscales for Measuring Qualities of Relationships

Hon and Grunig (1999) developed reliable indices for four qualities of organization–public relationships. The construct of honor is posited as a friendly addition to Hon and Grunig's measurements of relationship quality; the construct is specifically designed for use in Arab cultures.

Control mutuality is defined as the degree to which parties agree on who has the rightful power to influence one another. Although some imbalance is natural, stable relationships require that organizations and publics each have some control over the other. A relationship where one of the parties felt they had no say would be destined to failure.

Trust is revealed by one party's level of confidence in, and willingness to open oneself, to the other party. Hon and Grunig (1999) argued that trust includes three dimensions. The first dimension is *integrity*, which they defined as the belief that an organization is fair and just. *Dependability* is the belief that an organization will do what it says it will do. *Competence* was defined as the belief that an organization has the ability to do what it says it will do.

Satisfaction was described as the extent to which each party feels favorably toward the other because positive expectations about the relationship are reinforced. A satisfying relationship is one in which the benefits outweigh the costs. An unsatisfying relationship is short-term and characterized by unmet goals. Without sufficient resources exchanged or protection provided, most groups will no longer find a necessity to associate.

Commitment was described as the extent to which each party believes that the relationship is worth spending energy to maintain and promote. As with trust, Hon and Grunig (1999) provided subcomponents of commitment, which they referred to as *continuance* and *affirmative*. *Continuance* refers to maintaining a certain line of action. This is a utilitarian view of the commitment, whereas *affirmative* refers to the emotional orientation. In other words, the relationship will endure because of the participant's desire to maintain a beneficial series of actions that result in material benefits (continuance), or the relationship will endure to maintain an emotional connection (affirmative).

Honor is defined as the communicator's perceived understanding of family and cultural esteem, as well as providing proper responses to emotional facts. Yin (2008), Zayani (2005), and Witteborn (2007) highlighted the distinct communication traits associated with family, relationships, emotions, and history that are important to Arab audiences. High levels of honor would be indicated by communicating admiration for cultural, group, or family esteem, and appropriate incorporation of emotion in cross-cultural responses. Providing inappropriate responses to emotional facts, as well as disregard for family, group, or cultural esteem, could reflect low levels of honor. These expressions of esteem and understanding are independent of Arabic language aptitude, but wholly dependent on the communicator's understanding of family importance, relationship formation, emotional facts, and cultural esteem.

Hypotheses

Based on the extant literature reviewed above, the following seven hypotheses are posed:

H_1: U.S. public affairs officers will report higher agreement with the exchange worldview of the PAO–Arab journalist relationship than will Arab journalists.

H_2: Arab journalists will report higher agreement with the communal world-view of the PAO–Arab journalist relationship than will U.S. public affairs officers.

H_3: Arab journalists will report higher agreement with the value of honor in the PAO–Arab journalist relationship than will U.S. public affairs officers.

H_4: For U.S. public affairs officers, agreement with the exchange world-view of the PAO–Arab journalist relationship will be positively related with higher levels of satisfaction, commitment, control mutuality, and honor.

H_5: For Arab journalists, agreement with the exchange worldview of the PAO–Arab journalist relationship will be negatively related to satisfaction, commitment, control mutuality, trust, and honor.

H_6: For U.S. public affairs officers, agreement with the communal worldview of the PAO–Arab journalist relationship will be negatively related to satisfaction, commitment, control mutuality, trust, and honor.

H_7: For Arab journalists, agreement with the exchange worldview of the PAO–Arab journalist relationship will be negatively related to satisfaction, commitment, control mutuality, trust, and honor.

Methods

Two purposive/judgmental samples were drawn: Arab media personnel and military spokespersons. The Arab media sample comprised Arab media representatives then working with military media operation centers in Iraq, Qatar, the United Arab Emirates, and Afghanistan. The sample of military spokespersons was composed of military-trained PAOs who were serving or who had served recently in these same locations. Data were collected during the spring of 2009. A total of 34 U.S. military public affairs officers and 44 Arab media journalists completed the questionnaire.

Because the present research involved a purposive or judgmental sampling strategy, quantitative relationships are not tested by statistical inferences from samples to populations. Rather, the researchers utilized the decision rules previously reported by Kafka and Dozier (2009).

Decision Rules

First, the correlation must be in the direction hypothesized. If a relationship is posited to be positive, then a negative relationship disconfirms the hypothesis. Second, if the relationship is in the direction posited in the hypothesis, the hypothesis is rejected if the independent variable accounts for less than 5 percent of the variance in the dependent variable. Third, if the independent variable accounts for 5 percent or more of the variance in the independent variable but less than 10 percent of variance, then the hypothesis is confirmed and denoted as a *weak* relationship. Fourth, if the independent variable accounts for 10 percent or more of the variance in the dependent variable, but less than 20 percent of variance, the hypothesis is confirmed and denoted as a *moderate* relationship. Fifth, if the independent variable accounts for 20 percent or more of the variance in the dependent variable, the hypothesis is confirmed and denoted as a *strong* relationship. In this manner, quantitative rigor can be brought to the study of small populations (see Kafka and Dozier, 2009) or to purposive/judgmental samples such as those used in this case study. The goal is not to generalize to a larger population from a sample, as is explicitly done when tests of statistical significance are used. Rather, the goal is to assess the relative strength of relationships for a particular population or non-representative sample (in the statistical sense) and to make judgments about relationships that are interesting to pursue in future studies.

Reliability Coefficients

The reliability coefficients of the various measures of relationships were generally higher for U.S. public affairs officers than their Arab counterparts in the media. This was not unexpected, since the indices developed by Hon and Grunig (1999) were developed and tested in the United States on two American corporations (General Electric and Microsoft), two non-government organizations (National Rifle Association and the Red Cross), and a government agency (Social Security Administration). For public affairs officers, reliability coefficients for the seven scales ranged from 0.54 to 0.70. For Arab journalists participating in the study, reliability coefficients ranged from 0.21 to 0.67 (see Table 11.1). Most troubling were the reliability coefficients for the measures of relational worldviews of Arab journalists. The three-item exchange worldview index posted a reliability coefficient of 0.30; the two-item communal worldview index posted a Cronbach's alpha of only 0.21. Neither would be acceptable outside an exploratory case study such as this. The results of this study must be interpreted with these limitations in mind.

Results

Hypothesis 1 stated that PAOs would report higher levels of agreement than Arab journalists with the exchange worldview of relationships. This hypothesis was confirmed. PAOs averaged 3.47 on a five-point agree–disagree scale, where a score of 5 meant high agreement. Arab journalists averaged 2.76 on

TABLE 11.1 Cronbach's Reliability Coefficients for Measures of Relationships for Arab Journalists and Military Public Affairs Officers (PAOs)

Arab Journalists	Military PAOs
Satisfaction = 0.57	Satisfaction = 0.67
Commitment = 0.55	Commitment = 0.65
Control mutuality = 0.51	Control mutuality = 0.54
Honor = 0.63	Honor = 0.76
Trust = 0.67	Trust = 0.69
Exchange = 0.30	Exchange = 0.64
Communal = 0.21	Communal = 0.70

the same scale. Converting eta-square to percentage form, the independent variable (PAOs vs. Arab journalists) accounted for 10.3 percent of the variance in agreement with the exchange worldview of the PAO–Arab journalist relationship. This is a moderate relationship, according to the decision rules.

Hypothesis 2 stated that Arab journalists would report higher levels of agreement than PAOs with the communal worldview of relationships. This hypothesis was also confirmed. PAOs averaged 2.43 on a five-point agree–disagree scale, where a score of 5 meant high agreement. Arab journalist averaged 2.91 on the same scale. Converting eta-square to percentage form, the independent variable (PAOs vs. Arab journalists) accounted for 6.2 percent of the variance in agreement with the communal worldview of the PAO–Arab journalist relationship. This is a weak relationship, according to the decision rules.

Hypothesis 3 stated that Arab journalists would report higher levels of agreement than PAOs with the value of honor in the PAO–Arab journalist relationship. This hypothesis was confirmed. PAOs averaged 2.62 on a five-point agree–disagree scale, where a score of 5 meant high agreement. Arab journalists averaged 3.52 on the same scale. Converting eta-square to percentage form, the independent variable (PAOs vs. Arab journalists) accounted for 17.1 percent of the variance in the value of honor in the PAO–Arab journalist relationship. This is a moderate relationship, according to the decision rules.

Hypothesis 4 stated that, for PAOs analyzed separately, agreement with the exchange worldview would be positively related to various qualities of the relationship with Arab journalists, including satisfaction, commitment, control mutuality, trust, and honor. Table 11.2 reports the bivariate correlation

TABLE 11.2 Correlations between Exchange and Communal Overviews with Other Measures of Relationships for Arab Journalists and Military Public Affairs Officers (PAOs)

Worldview of Relationship	Arab Journalists	Military PAOs
Exchange	Satisfaction: $r = -0.12$	Satisfaction: $r = 0.19$
	Commitment: $r = -0.57$	Commitment: $r = 0.25$
	Control mutuality: $r = -0.27$	Control mutuality: $r = 0.13$
	Honor: $r = -0.28$	Honor: $r = 0.09$
	Trust: $r = -0.25$	Trust: $r = -0.19$
Communal	Satisfaction: $r = 0.16$	Satisfaction: $r = 0.13$
	Commitment: $r = 0.20$	Commitment: $r = 0.02$
	Control mutuality: $r = 0.18$	Control mutuality: $r = -0.16$
	Honor: $r = -0.02$	Honor: $r = 0.17$
	Trust: $r = 0.42$	Trust: $r = 0.19$

coefficients and Table 11.3 reports the explained variance in percentage form. As shown in Table 11.3, four of the five relationships were in the direction predicted by the hypothesis (trust was negatively related to the exchange worldview); however, only commitment accounted for more than 5 percent of the explained variance. Hypothesis 4 was mostly disconfirmed.

Hypothesis 5 stated that, for Arab journalists analyzed separately, agreement with the exchange worldview would be negatively related to various qualities of the relationship with PAOs, including satisfaction, commitment, control mutuality, trust, and honor. As shown in Table 11.3, all five relationships were in the direction predicted by the hypothesis. A strong negative relationship was detected between commitment and the exchange worldview. Weak relationships were detected between the exchange worldview and control mutuality, honor, and trust. Only satisfaction accounted for less than 5 percent of the explained variance. Hypothesis 5 was mostly confirmed.

Hypothesis 6 stated that, for PAOs analyzed separately, agreement with the communal worldview would be negatively related to various qualities of the relationship with Arab journalists, including satisfaction, commitment, control mutuality, trust, and honor. As shown in Table 11.3, only two of the five relationships were in the direction predicted by the hypothesis; none

TABLE 11.3 Explained Variance of Exchange and Communal Overviews with Other Measures of Relationships for Arab Journalists and Military Public Affairs Officers (PAOs)

Worldview of Relationship	Arab Journalists	Military PAOs
Exchange	[a]Satisfaction: EV = 1.4% (–)	[a]Satisfaction: EV = 3.5% (+)
	[d]Commitment: EV = 32.8% (–)	[b]Commitment: EV = 6.1% (+)
	[b]Control mutuality: EV = 7.0% (–)	[a]Control mutuality: EV = 1.6% (+)
	[b]Honor: EV = 8.9% (–)	[a]Honor: EV = 0.9% (+)
	[b]Trust: EV = 6.7% (–)	[a]Trust: EV = 3.7% (–)
Communal	[a]Satisfaction: EV = > 0.1% (–)	[a]Satisfaction: EV = 2.7% (+)
	[a]Commitment: EV = 4.1% (+)	[a]Commitment: EV = > 0.1% (+)
	[a]Control mutuality: EV = 3.1% (+)	[a]Control mutuality: EV = 2.5% (–)
	[a]Honor: EV = >0.1% (+)	[a]Honor: EV = 2.7% (+)
	[a]Trust: EV = 3.1% (+)	[a]Trust: EV = 2.5% (–)

Notes
a, null; b, weak; c, moderate; d, strong

accounted for more than 5 percent of the explained variance. Hypothesis 6 was disconfirmed.

Hypothesis 7 stated that, for Arab journalists analyzed separately, agreement with the communal worldview would be positively related to various qualities of the relationship with PAOs, including satisfaction, commitment, control mutuality, trust, and honor. As shown in Table 11.3, four relationships were in the direction predicted by the hypothesis (satisfaction was negatively related to the communal worldview). None of the relationships accounted for more than 5 percent of the explained variance. Hypothesis 7 was likewise disconfirmed.

Discussion

As predicted, U.S. military public affairs officers tend to regard their relationship with the Arab media as an exchange relationship. This reflects both the specifics of their assignments in the Middle East (e.g., relatively short deployments in a foreign culture) and the individualistic nature of American culture. This runs counter to Hon and Grunig (1999), who provided a strong normative case for a communal worldview of relationships. Nevertheless, communalism implies a level of connectedness that runs counter to the institutional imperatives placed upon individual public affairs officers.

Moreover, the situation is not specific to the U.S. military. Large, transnational corporations face similar challenges in building and maintaining mutually beneficial relationships across nations, regions, and cultures. This challenge is especially acute for corporations based in North America and Europe (populated by managers steeped in the individualistic cultures of Europe, the United States, and Canada) as they enter markets in the Middle East, Asia, and South America.

As predicted, Arab journalists tend to regard their relationship as a communal relationship. Again, this reflects both the specifics of the work of Arab journalists (pursuing long-term careers in the Middle East), as well as the collectivist culture in which they are embedded.

The value of honor—defined as perceived understanding of family and cultural esteem, as well as providing proper responses to emotional facts—is much more important to Arab journalists than to the PAOs studied. Once again, the practical significance of this finding is not isolated to the U.S. military. Large transnational corporations will benefit from understanding and respecting the value of honor—as specifically defined here—in their relationships with the Arab media, as well as the publics that such organizations can reach through the Arab media.

When the qualities of relationships are analyzed in terms of the exchange versus communal overview, the test of hypotheses obscures the forest through the trees. Specifically, the tests of hypotheses (H_4–H_7) were mixed. However, when the exchange worldview of the relationship is examined at arm's length, the results are quite striking. For PAOs, the more they regard their relationship with Arab journalists as an exchange relationship, the greater their satisfaction, commitment, and control mutuality. Only trust is negatively related to this worldview of the relationship. For PAOs, the value of honor is positively related to the exchange worldview.

For Arab journalists, the opposite holds true. The more that Arab journalists view their relationship with PAOs as an exchange relationship, the less their satisfaction, commitment, control mutuality, and trust. For Arab journalists, the value of honor is also negatively related to the exchange worldview. The results are muddled for the communal worldview. This finding, however, may have more to do with operationalization than with difficulties at the theoretical level.

Limitations of the Study

Two key limitations should be kept in mind while reviewing this study. First, the two samples used (PAOs and Arab journalists) were purposive/judgmental samples. Therefore, statistical generalizations to the larger populations from which these samples were drawn cannot be made. We have carefully positioned our study as a quantitative case study and limit our test of hypotheses to the participating respondents. Second, the reliability coefficients for the communal and exchange indices were low for Arab journalists. Thus, the conclusions of this case study must be filtered with this limitation in mind.

Implications for Theory and Methods

The quantitative case study above serves as a useful heuristic for a larger discussion about the body of knowledge in global public relations and the role of culture as a central concept. Regarding the specifics of the case study, the first author developed the Allen Honor Index (AHI), a measure of the construct of honor specific to Arab cultures. The index posted a Cronbach's reliability coefficient of 0.76 for American public affairs officers and 0.63 for Arab journalists. The index has strong face validity. The index also has construct validity, since Arab journalists placed greater importance on honor (as culturally defined and operationalized here) than did American public affairs officers. That is, the index performed in a manner consistent with theory.

Developing Culturally Specific Indices

The development of culture-specific indices, such as the AHI, provides a basis for empirical studies that aspire to cultural sensitivity. With regard to Chinese culture, for example, Huang (2000) explicated the construct of *gao guanxi*, the utilization of interpersonal relationships or network connections to achieve personal objectives. Similarly, in Japanese culture, Raz (2002) discussed the construct of *onjoshugi* or managerial paternalism. Culture-specific constructs require operationalization in the form of indices designed for use within specific cultural contexts. The resulting indices can be used in conjunction with cross-cultural measures to conduct rigorous cross-cultural studies and build robust theories that rest on strong empirical foundations.

Developing Cross-Cultural Indices

The quantitative case study also identified a problem of universal measures such as Hon and Grunig's (1999) measures of exchange and communal worldviews. Although these instruments performed reliably when used on Americans, they proved quite unreliable when used on Arab journalists. Such results are not surprising, since these measures were developed and tested on employees from five American organizations. In order to develop reliable and valid measures of such cross-cultural concepts as exchange and communal worldviews, instrument development must seek to include respondents from a wide variety of cultural settings. The rigor of quantitative measures depends on the construction of indices that are appropriate for all populations and subpopulations studied.

Curtin and Gaither (2007) suggest a more radical approach. They argue for the "privileging of ethnographic methods" by using such observational techniques as participant observation, depth interviews, and focus groups. They argue that measuring "awareness or attitudes on pretest and posttest surveys presents a partial picture at best" (p. 142).

There is much merit to this argument. Specifically, inductive techniques and case study methods are powerful and appropriate when little is known or understood about the phenomena of interest. Certainly the clash of cultures in global public relations fits this description of an underdeveloped theoretical and empirical domain. That said, strong empirical foundations for the study of culture in global public relations also require the rigor of replication, as well as the possibility to falsify hypotheses through rigorous statistical tests. We favor a mixed-methods approach. Empirical generalizations that flow from the research paradigm suggested by Curtin and Gaither (2007) provide a strong basis for theory construction and testing, using deductive logic and hypothesis testing.

The quantitative case study described above serves as a pragmatic bridge between ethnographic case studies and tests of hypotheses using probability-sampling techniques (external validity) and experimental designs (internal validity). This quantitative case study (1) permitted the development of the AHI and demonstrated its reliability and validity, (2) identified instrument reliability problems with Hon and Grunig's (1999) indices of exchange and communal worldviews, and (3) provided empirical test of hypothesized relationships using appropriate statistical protocols.

That is, this quantitative case study avoided the misuse of inferential statistics. The extant literature in communication studies is replete with the flagrant abuse of statistical significance tests on non-probability samples. Such statistical analysis is misleading at best. As shown here, such misuse of inferential statistics is not necessary.

Implications for Practice

When cultures clash, as often happens in times of conflict, how can the global public relations practitioner anticipate the unintended consequences of cultural differences? Specific to the case study presented above, tours of public affairs officers in the Middle East could be extended to provide sufficient experience on the ground to become knowledgeable and appreciative of such culturally specific constructs as honor. More realistically, public affairs officers could be provided with more intensive training in cultural issues they will face in the Middle East.

Lessons learned for the practice are not restricted to military public affairs and Arab journalists in the Middle East. Any large corporation or NGO with a global reach must deal with the same challenges as faced by military public affairs officers. When one is navigating cultures that are different from one's own, unintended consequences can occur at any time. Because culture is taken for granted, because culture provides shortcuts for how people should treat each other, cultures are bound to collide when these taken-for-granted cultural rules are not shared.

One theoretical concept of great utility to the practice of global public relations is requisite variety. First conceptualized by Weick (1979) and incorporated into the Excellence Theory at the outset of the study (Grunig et al., 1992), the theory of requisite variety states that organizations selectively respond to some environmental inputs while ignoring others. The organization enacts a representation of itself and its environment that is not objective. Rather, that enactment reflects the biases, prejudices, and wishful thinking of dominant coalitions; such enactments are reinforced through mechanisms of social control within the organization. In order to be effective, the principle of *requisite variety* states that "there must be at least as much variety—or [cultural] diversity—inside the organization as outside for the organization to build effective relationships" (Grunig et al., 1992, p. 84). This is especially true for the public relations department in an organization with publics around the globe.

As boundary spanners, practitioners face the awkward and seemingly disloyal task of helping the dominant coalition understand that enactments within the organization are not congruent with those of key publics. The leadership of many traditional transnational corporations and other large organizations are relatively homogeneous (e.g., white males from North America or Europe). To be effective, the public relations department needs to reflect the diversity of the various publics on whom the organization's success or failure depends. Although such diversity embraces principles of social justice, the principle of requisite variety is more directly concerned with organizational effectiveness.

This implies that public relations departments must reflect the cultural diversity of the publics that affect organizational survival and growth. As an organization deals with increasing cultural diversity among its publics on a global scale, the public relations department must increase the diversity of its staff. This permits the department to effectively span organizational boundaries.

The principle of requisite diversity is sometimes criticized as a mechanism for *tokenism*, the hiring of a few people from diverse backgrounds into highly visible public relations positions, in order to give the appearance of greater diversity than actually exists in the organization. Indeed, this may be true in some cases. However, for the principle of requisite variety to increase organizational effectiveness, global practitioners from diverse cultural backgrounds need to participate in management decision making. Only then will organizations avoid the collisions of cultures that make them less effective.

Note

1 The opinions expressed herein are those of the author and do not necessarily reflect those of the U.S. Navy, the Department of Defense, or the U.S. Government.

References

Alanazi, A. (1996). Public relations in the Middle East: The case of Saudi Arabia. In Culbertson, H. M. and Chen, N. (Eds.), *International public relations: A comparative analysis*. Mahwah, NJ: Lawrence Erlbaum, pp. 239–256.

Badran, B. A., Turk, J. V., and Walters, T. N. (2003). Sharing the transformation: Public relations and the UAE come of age. In Sriramesh, K. and Verčič, D. (Eds.), *The global public relations handbook*. Mahwah, NJ: Lawrence Erlbaum, pp. 46–67.

Broom, G. M. and Dozier, D. M. (1990). *Using research in public relations*. Upper Saddle River, NJ: Pearson Prentice Hall.

Cutlip, S. M., Center, A. H., and Broom, G. M. (2006). *Effective public relations* (9th edn.). Upper Saddle River, NJ: Pearson Prentice Hall.

Curtin, P. A. and Gaither, T. K. (2007). *International public relations: Negotiating culture, identity, and power*. Thousand Oaks, CA: Sage.

Dozier, D. M., Grunig, L. A., and Grunig, J. E. (1995). *Manager's guide to excellence in public relations and communication management*. Mahwah, NJ: Lawrence Erlbaum.

Ferreira da Cruz, M. (2008). Intercultural cybercommunication: Negotiation of representations of languages and cultures in multilingual chatrooms. *Journal of Multicultural Discourses*, 3(2), 98–113.

Grunig, J. E. and Hunt, T. (1984). *Managing public relations.* New York: Holt, Rineha and Winston.

Grunig, L. A., Grunig, J. E., and Ehling, W. P. (1992). What is an effective organization? In Grunig, J. E. (Ed.), *Excellence in public relations and communication management.* Hillsdale, NJ: Lawrence Erlbaum, pp. 65–90.

Grunig, L. A., Grunig, J. E., and Dozier, D. M. (2002). *Excellent public relations and effective organizations: A study of communication management in three countries.* Mahwah, NJ: Lawrence Erlbaum.

Hon, L. and Grunig, J. (1999). *Guidelines for measuring relationships in public relations.* Gainesville, FL: Institute of Public Relations.

Huang, Y. H. (2000). The personal influence model and *gao quanxi* in Taiwan Chinese public relations. *Public Relations Review*, 26(2), 219–236.

Kafka, W. M. and Dozier, D. M. (2009, March). Shared expectations revisited: A test of the Excellence Theory in a population study of U.S. aircraft carriers. Paper presented at the meeting of the International Public Relations Research Conference, Miami, FL.

Kroeber, A. L. and Kluckhohn, C. (1952). *Culture: A critical review of concepts and definitions.* Papers of the Peabody Museum of American Archeology and Ethnology, 47. Cambridge, MA: Harvard University Press.

Raz, A. E. (2002). *Emotions at work: Normative control, organizations, and culture in Japan and America.* London: Harvard University Press.

Sriramesh, K. (2009). The relationship between culture and public relations. In Sriramesh, K. and Verčič, D. (Eds.), *The global public relations handbook.* New York: Routledge, pp. 47–61.

Sriramesh, K. and Verčič, D. (Eds.) (2009). *The global public relations handbook.* New York: Routledge.

Weick, K. E. (1979). *The social psychology of organizing* (2nd edn.). Reading, MA: Addison-Wesley.

White, J. and Dozier, D. M. (1992). Public relations and management decision making. In Grunig, J. E. (Ed.), *Excellence in public relations and communication management.* Hillsdale, NJ: Lawrence Erlbaum, pp. 91–108.

Witteborn, S. (2007). The situated expression of Arab collective identities in the United States. *Journal of Communication*, 57(3), 556–575.

Yin, J. (2008). Beyond the four theories of the press: A new model for the Asian & the world press. *Journalism & Communication Monographs*, 10(1), 3–62.

Zayani, M. (2005). *The Al Jazeera phenomenon.* Boulder, CO: Paradigm.

INTERROGATIONS OF GLOBAL PUBLIC RELATIONS

Power, Culture, and Agency

Mohan Jyoti Dutta

Critical Interrogations of Global Public Relations: Power, Culture, and Agency

The global flow of goods, services, and labor across national boundaries is managed through the global flow of communications, constituted in the form of strategic public relations activities engaged in by transnational corporations (TNCs), international financial institutions (IFIs) such as the International Monetary Fund (IMF) and the World Bank (WB), transnational policy organizations, and national governments (Dutta and Pal, in pressa,b; Pal and Dutta, 2008a,b). Public relations has emerged on the political economy of transnational capitalism as a key actor in the management of public opinion, public policies, and resources at a global level. At the core of contemporary globalization processes are the principles of neoliberalism, emphasizing the promotion of a free market economy that operates on the basis of the minimization of trade-related tariffs and barriers and the privatization of global resources facilitated through structural adjustment programs (SAPs), and carried out through the representative politics of public relations (Dutta, 2009; Dutta and Pal, in pressa; Pal and Dutta, 2008a,b; D. Harvey, 2005).

In this essay, I propose the argument that the pervasiveness of neoliberalism is achieved through specific public relations activities carried out by transnational hegemony, comprising the interplay among powerful TNCs, nation-states, IFIs, and international policy-making actors, played out in the form of knowledge claims made at globally connected sites of knowledge production (Pal and Dutta, 2008a,b). Furthermore, the establishment of the neoliberal order on a global scale serves as the justification then of forms of power and control that carry out the agendas of transnational hegemony on a global scale. A critical stance toward public relations in the backdrop of neoliberalism creates entry points for examining the neocolonial foundations of contemporary economic configurations and forms of governance, drawing attention to the oppressions and exploitations of the subaltern sectors of the globe carried out through the rhetoric of progress, development, modernization, and emancipation, embodied in the public relations activities of transnational hegemony (Dutta, 2008a; Munshi, 1999; Munshi and Kurian, 2005).

It is on the foundations of deconstruction that a culture-centered reading of public relations articulates entry points for alternative theorizing and praxis of public relations, rooted in culturally based epistemologies from the global South that have historically been treated as backward and erased from the dominant discursive spaces of knowledge production and representation (Dutta-Bergman, 2005; de Sousa Santos, 2008; Shiva, 2001, 2008). Culture-centered theorizing of public relations foregrounds the resistive capacity of public relations practices that participate in dialogue with the subaltern sectors to co-create alternative representations of truth claims that resist neoliberalism (Kim, 2008; Pal, 2008).

Critical Interrogations: Power, Structure, and Margins

Public relations practices carry out the strategic interests of neoliberalism through the production and dissemination of knowledge, through the co-optation of local communities as sites of neoliberal governance, through the minimization of opportunities for monitoring and evaluation of TNCs, and through the continual exploitation of the global South.

Knowledge Production and Representation

Increasingly, the global position of transnational capitalism is consolidated through the representation and circulation of information and knowledge, articulated through the centers of power in academia, powerful think tanks, lobbies, legislative bodies, and international institutions such as the World Bank, the IMF, World Trade Organization (WTO), United Nations (UN), and World Health Organisation (WHO) (Dutta, 2011). For example, the WB positions itself as the key global institution working on issues of economics, development, and poverty, and serving as the core knowledge-producing organization in the global arena of poverty reduction. The knowledge that is filtered through the gate-keeping function of the WB is utilized to frame and shape global, national, and local policies, ultimately influencing the political and economic landscape of the globe (Rastogi and Dutta, 2010).

Similarly, the economic and political agendas of neoliberalism are achieved through the structural adjustment programs that are imposed upon countries as conditions for lending from the WB and IMF (D. Harvey, 2005). Large-scale economic restructurings of nation-states such as Chile, Mexico, and Nicaragua have been achieved through the imposition of structural adjustment programs (SAPs) by the IFIs, framed under the logic of development, progress, and modernization (Dutta, 2011; Dutta-Bergman, 2005). Knowledge here has emerged as the core constituent in the articulation and dominance of a hegemonic configuration of economic and political organizing that favors the global penetration and control of TNCs, and is central to the project of neo-imperialism (Dutta, 2011). The production and representation of knowledge is itself a public relations exercise as it selectively frames specific types of knowledge toward the goals of promoting neoliberalism and its rationality of the free market as modes of governance. Specific linkages between knowledge production and neo-imperialism become particularly evident in the sponsoring of anthropological projects such as the "Iraq Tribal Study" by the Pentagon, directed at finding ways to manage and manipulate Iraqi tribes in order to serve the interests of the U.S. occupation of Iraq (Gonzalez, 2008). Yet another elucidation of the militarization of knowledge production is evident in the U.S. military funding of the project "Mexico Indigena" that seeks to map indigenous lands in Oaxaca, Mexico, without the prior informed consent of the local indigenous communities, and with the goal of developing counterinsurgency knowledge and understanding the communities' resistance to privatization (Mychalejko and Ryan, 2009). Here, knowledge funded by the military is directed toward serving the political economic interests of transnational hegemony, making explicit the revolving doors among neoliberalism, neo-imperialism, and knowledge production. In both of these instances, the production of knowledge is a public relations function that promotes a specific form of governance across the globe, favoring the privatization of resources and seeking to erase collective forms of ownership and participation.

Furthermore, the production of knowledge in academic circuits is complemented by knowledge production by the private sector in the form of large-scale consulting firms, which themselves operate as TNCs, shaping global policies and forms of governance. Private knowledge-producing bodies construct and recirculate knowledge about neoliberal governance in the form of policy reports. For example, McKinsey publishes the *McKinsey Quarterly* and consults global organizations on a variety of topical areas, operating within the frameworks of neoliberalism. The McKinsey report titled "Stabilizing Iraq: Conversation with Paul Brinkley" demonstrates this linkage between neoliberalism and neo-imperialism, articulating the business decisions underlying the occupation of Iraq. The report goes on to discuss the role of economic revitalization as a core defense function, narrated in the form of an interview with Paul Brinkley, the chief architect of the Task Force for Business and Stability Operations (TFBSO) in Iraq: "We all agree—and the Iraqis agree—that the end state in Iraq should be a free-market economy" (Dowdy, 2010, p. 47).

The production, reproduction, and representation of knowledge therefore are situated within the broader agendas of transnational capitalism, carrying out the West-centric and neocolonial goals of consolidating power in the hands of neoliberal hegemony. Although the emergence of neoliberal hegemony draws attention to the spatial location of centers of power across nation states, it is also worth noting that a large proportion of the powerful TNCs on the global landscape are situated in the global North/West. Furthermore, the ontology and epistemology guiding the discourses of development in neoliberalism are guided by West-centric notions of development and modernization, guided by the logics of efficiency and effectiveness, and founded on the reductionist principles of controlling nature in order to optimize the exploitation of resources (Shiva, 1988). Furthermore, West-centric notions of individualism and private property guide the agendas of democracy production, community building, and knowledge production, based upon the privileging of West-centric ideas of social, political, and community organizing (Dutta-Bergman, 2005). Knowledge of and about communication is constructed within West-centric (read Eurocentric and US-centric) academic structures, playing out to specific agendas of transnational hegemony, privileging certain sets of values and simultaneously undermining values from elsewhere (the Third/Southern/underdeveloped sectors) to justify neocolonial interventions carried out through public relations activities.

Community, Empowerment, and Neoliberal Governmentality

The community has emerged as a key factor in the neoliberal configuration, with emphasis placed on fostering the participatory, emancipatory, and entrepreneurial capacities of communities to serve as agents for participating in the market economics of neoliberalism (see, for instance, Heath and Palenchar, 2009). First, through community relations activities, TNCs have increased their global penetration of markets across the globe, positioned under the premises of development and emancipation (Dutta, 2011; Dutta-Bergman, 2005). The participatory capacity of communities is increasingly framed under the market-based appeal of local communities as profitable resources (Dutta and Pal, in pressa). Community relations activities have emerged as tools for legitimizing the presence of global corporations in local communities. Individuals and communities are framed as having a great deal of power, and this power is realized through the participation of these individuals and communities in the market economics of neoliberalism, through the purchasing of products, the proceeds from the sale of which go toward serving community needs.

The community relations functions of TNCs have increased the reach of TNCs within distant markets, creating entry points for TNCs to push their products and services. The development of private–public partnerships toward the goals of solving specific health problems such as HIV/AIDS has increased the reach of private corporations within globally dispersed local communities.

In serving a specific community need in the area of health, TNCs have also created and fostered a specific niche and a specific market for the promotion of their products. In the context of breast cancer, for example, the Susan G. Komen Foundation has emerged as a conduit for partnerships with TNCs such as 3M and Kentucky Fried Chicken (KFC) for promoting their products under the guise of health promotion. The *Warriors in Pink* program sponsored by Ford under a partnership with the Komen Foundation is a powerful public relations tool for Ford that utilizes the avenue of breast cancer to promote the purchase of Ford vehicles (for example, the Warriors in Pink website also promotes the new Ford vehicles, the 2010 Ford Fusion Hybrid and the 2011 Mustang; http://www.fordvehicles.com/warriorsinpink/).

In projects of development promoted by SAPs, community relations activities have been folded into corporate social responsibility programs, portraying the façade of dialogue in order to legitimize the displacement of the subaltern sectors in the name of development. For example, community relations activities have been promoted by mining projects in order to create spaces of public support for mining operations and minimize resistance against the displacement of subaltern communities (Statham, 2009). Although promoted communicatively as attempts at creating inclusive spaces for listening to community voices in projects that would have an immense impact on communities, such community relations dialogues are fundamentally co-optive and oppressive as they are guided toward utilizing the façade of dialogue to enlist the support of local communities toward serving the corporate agendas. The framing of dialogue in such instances often hides the oppressive, coercive, and exploitative strategies that are deployed by TNCs and local and state government actors to displace local communities so that projects of mining, industrialization, and development may be carried out.

Also, community relations activities aimed at promoting social capital in local communities utilize the rhetoric of local empowerment to shift the provision of basic services into the hands of local actors and private providers, and simultaneously limit the responsibility of governments and public sectors to provide for the fundamental needs of underserved communities (Sharma, 2008). In such instances, the paradoxical nature of community relations lies in the disempowering function of empowering discourse, which achieves its hegemony through the rhetorical emphasis on empowering local communities. The so-called empowerment of local communities is carried out through the simultaneous depletion of local resources available to communities and the minimization of public support programs for communities in need. For example, the shifting of emphasis of delivering healthcare into the hands of local communities through self-help programs minimizes the role of the government in the provision of health services. Critical interrogations, therefore, ought to continually draw attention to the agendas served by so-called projects of community empowerment, community participation, and community relations.

Geography, Public Relations, and Neocolonialism

Critical interrogations of neoliberal hegemony draw attention to the continual recirculation of neocolonial tropes in order to justify the power and control of TNCs in global markets through the framing of the free market ideology under the premises of development. The notion of the free market is attached to development and modernization based on the argument that free market economies are also modernized economies. Although postcolonial critiques increasingly draw attention to the dispersed spaces of power and the intertwined sites of control and resistance in neoliberal spaces, also worth noting amidst the material inequities of neoliberalism are the spatial differentials in the distribution of resources.

These spatial differentials fundamentally underlie the communicative differentials such that those with points of access to resources are also the ones with access to communicative structures for participating in discourses and for circulating specific ideologies that are connected to specific cultural values. Therefore, critical interrogations fundamentally draw attention to the cultural roots of so-called universal values of development and modernization. Furthermore, the spatiality of the neoliberal logic lies in the West-centric articulations of modernity, which then are circulated as universals in order to justify the political economy of neoliberal interventions. Especially worth interrogating are the West-centric roots of the values underlying the development framework that plays out in the public information campaigns run by West-centric agencies such as the United States Agency for International Development (USAID) and Oxfam International.

Essential to the diffusion of neoliberalism is the privileging of Western ontology and epistemology as universal standards for measuring progress and development (Rabasa, 2001; Shiva, 2000). For example, the participation of the WB in supporting the building of dams globally is based on a West-centric epistemology of reductionist science that operates on the premise of controlling nature in order to achieve progress (articulated in the form of controlling water flows in order to generate resources for industrialized economies) (Shiva, 2000). The references to science made under the neoliberal logic are references ultimately to a parochial West-centric ideology that operates on the basis of the Western values of reductionism, individualism, private property, efficiency, and profit. The ideas of development, therefore, that continue to be perpetuated globally by neoliberal institutions are West-centric ideas that utilize the rhetoric of altruism in development in order to open up markets for TNCs, a large majority of which are located in the global North/West. Attention needs to be paid to interrogating the cultural values attached to the evaluation of development and modernization.

The location of so-called universals within West-centric values is perpetuated also through the production of knowledge about public relations, public information, public diplomacy, and so on. For example, fundamentally West-centric notions of civil society and democracy based on the capitalist conceptualization of property-owning individuals are central to the democracy promotion, nation-building, civil society promotion, and modernization efforts run by the US through media relations and community relations activities globally (Dutta-Bergman, 2004). Also worth noting in the discursive spaces of the communication and public relations literature are the privileging of West-centric ideals and values as the foundations of knowledge. Such privileging is seen across the various paradigms (post-positivist, interpretive, and critical), with the articulations being made under West-centric values. It is worth noting here that, even within critical scholarship, the emphasis is on circulating West-centric values, tied to West-centric notions of empowerment, power, agency, and resistance, continuing to reify the neo-imperial agendas of public relations knowledge (see, for instance, Dutta, 2009, 2011; Mignolo, 2000; Portillo, 2009; Robinson, 2009; Spirak, 1999; Wood, 2005; Shome and Hegde, 2002). Culture-centered calls for constituting public relations knowledge point toward the fundamentally colonizing missions of West-centric knowledge structures, thus urging scholars and practitioners to participate in journeys of solidarity with subaltern sectors across the globe so that alternative rationalities from elsewhere emerge into the discursive spaces of neoliberal organizing to offer entry points for hope and structural transformation (Dellacioppa, 2009; Olivera, 2004; Shiva, 1988, 1989, 1991, 2001, 2002, 2007, 2008, 2010; Shiva and Bedi, 2002; de Sousa Santos, Nunes, and Meneses, 2008; Starr, 1998, 2005).

Culture-Centered Approach to Public Relations

Responding to the criticism of the West-centric roots of public relations as a neocolonial tool that carries out the agendas of neoliberal hegemony, the culture-centered approach to public relations foregrounds the role of dialogue as an entry point for co-constructing knowledge from elsewhere that has historically been erased from the dominant spaces of knowledge production, situated within the agendas of transnational capitalism (Dutta-Bergman, 2005; Esteva, 2005; Esteva and Prakesh, 1998). In co-creating entry points for social change, culture-centered public relations emphasizes the agency of local cultures in producing knowledge that is meaningful to the lived experiences of the local communities, and that is responsive to these lived experiences as entry points for constituting action on a global scale.

The relationship-building role of public relations emerges as a foundational element in the development of networks of solidarity among local points of articulation that seek to create global spaces of change through the voicing of alternative rationalities that are locally situated. The theorization of dialogue in the culture-centered approach turns toward the emancipatory capacity of "listening to the other" in bringing about structural transformations in global public spheres. It is through dialogue then that the public relations scholar/ activist participates in the foregrounding of alternative rationalities in global platforms that challenge the hegemony of neoliberalism. For example, the dialogic co-constructions with farmers in India participating in the *Navdanya* movement creates alternative meanings of agriculture, foregrounding the rights of farmers to the seed, to retaining seeds, and to growing them the next season as opposed to the neoliberal co-optation of agriculture under the market framework of monoculture seeds to be purchased by farmers from TNCs (Shiva, 2008, 2010).

Dialogue and Resistance

Culture-centered theorizing of dialogue disrupts the apolitical West-centric treatment of dialogue (Cloud, 2004, 2007; Dutta, 2011; McPhail, 2004; Anderson and Cissna, 2008) as rational and apolitical communication among equals that is directed toward the production of some imagined symmetry between the organization and its publics, situated within the modernist structures of West-centric epistemology (Dutta and Pal, in pressa). In contrast, culture-centered treatment of dialogue begins with a skeptical stance toward the intent of seemingly dialogic platforms that are initiated by and situated within organizational agendas of neoliberalism. That the veneer of dialogue has often been used by transnational hegemony to perpetuate the interests of TNCs creates an entry point for interrogating the intention, nature, and location of dialogue within the neoliberal project (Dutta, 2006, 2007, 2008b,c; Dutta-Bergman, 2005). The situation of dialogic spaces within the domain of dominant organizational structures precludes the possibilities of authentic dialogue with the subaltern sectors by turning dialogue into a strategic tool directed at carrying out the agendas of dominant power structures (see Dutta, 2008b,c). In this sense, authenticity in dialogue is tied to the intent and location of dialogue, juxtaposed in the backdrop of dominant power structures. For example, the indigenous–mining dialogue group set up by the Australian Uranium Association to bridge the gap between Aboriginal Australians and uranium mining industries is constituted within the agendas of the mining industry to usurp indigenous land to build mines (Statham, 2009). Who gets to participate in dialogue is dictated by the interests of the system in sustaining itself as an economic enterprise. Furthermore, the rules, roles, and principles of dialogue are determined by the dominant power structures that dictate the process, nature, and content of the dialogic spaces.

Culture-centered interpretations of dialogue take the very nature of dialogue to task (Dutta and Pal, in pressa). What, for instance, is the meaning of dialogue when the call for dialogue is situated within the agendas of the UN and the dialogic platforms are situated within the structures of the UN? What then are the possibilities of listening to the subaltern "other" who has been turned into the source of profiteering under neoliberalism through seemingly dialogic exercises initiated by the dominant power structures? The strategic use of dialogue to achieve social change and to resist neoliberal structures of dominance and exploitation is achieved through the continual return to the question of authenticity. Culture-centered dialogues are entry points for listening to the "other" from elsewhere such that epistemologies from elsewhere emerge as entry points for disrupting and fragmenting the hegemonic control of the neoliberal order. Knowledge from the subaltern sectors enters into the discursive space to render impure the categories that serve as the foundations of the dominant structure.

The act of listening to the other through culture-centered dialogues creates entry points for foregrounding alternative rationalities and alternative modes of organizing that challenge the political and economic agendas of neoliberalism (Beverly, 2004a,b). For example, global dialogic co-constructions with the Zapatista Army of National Liberation (EZLN) movement in Mexico, reiterated in the form of transnational movements of solidarity with EZLN, brings forth the alternative rationality of subaltern organizing that operates on the basis of autonomy, local organization, participation, and consensus-based decision making (Dellacioppa, 2009; Olesen, 2005a,b). Dialogic engagements of global non-governmental organizations and activist movements with EZLN create entry points for the emergence of "Zapatismo" on the global stage in the form of models for activism globally. Through dialogues constituted in the global solidarity networks of activist organizing, a locally situated cosmology of resistance emerges into the global arena, thus creating an alternative space for resisting neoliberalism. Furthermore, carrying forth the theme of subaltern dialogue, EZLN initiated dialogues among transnational activist movements against neoliberalism by creating global meetings and platforms that brought together activist groups from across the globe (Olesen, 2005a,b). Similarly, dialogic opportunities created by the World Social Forum and Social Forums in various countries across the globe create alternative spaces for organizing and for voicing alternative visions of global organizing that challenge the logics of efficiency and economic effectiveness under neoliberalism (see, for instance, http://www.ussf2010.org/).

Solidarity, Community, and Resistance

Solidarity with local communities lies at the heart of culture-centered public relations because it seeks to co-create local narratives that have otherwise been erased from the mainstream public spheres (de Sousa Santos, Nunes, and Meneses, 2008). Local voices offer entry points for co-creating narratives that have otherwise been erased. It is through the re-appropriation of the community as a site of resistance as opposed to a site of neoliberal governance that new meaning structures are articulated (Beverly, 2004a,b; Spivak, 1988a,b; Tihuwai

Smith, 2006). It is through these new meanings narrated at local community levels that the scientific modernist discourses of neoliberalism are disrupted. For instance, to the large-scale funding of the Human Genome Diversity Project (HGDP) with the goal of mapping genetic variations in indigenous samples across the globe, indigenous collectives and activists responded by questioning the fundamental violation of the indigenous worldview, the continued colonization of indigenous spaces, and the political economy of exploitation of indigenous spaces to create knowledge resources that could then be used by TNCs (Wood, Hall, and Hasian, 2008). Indigenous communities organized around the issue came together in solidarity at a collective meeting of several interested indigenous organizations, and put forth "The Declaration of Indigenous Peoples of the Western Hemisphere Regarding the Human Genome Diversity Project," stating:

> In the long history of destruction which has accompanied western colonization we have come to realize that the agenda of the non-indigenous forces has been to appropriate and manipulate the natural order for the purposes of profit, power and control. To negate the complexity of any life form by isolating and reducing it to its minute parts, western science and technologies diminishes its identity as a precious and unique life form, and alters its relationship to the natural order. Genetic technologies which manipulate and change the fundamental core and identity of any life form is an absolute violation of these principles, and creates the potential for unpredictable and therefore dangerous consequences. Therefore, we the Indigenous Peoples and Organizations participating in this meeting from North, Central and South America reject all programs involving genetic technology. We particularly oppose the Human Genome Diversity Project which intends to collect, and make available our genetic materials which may be used for commercial, scientific and military purposes. We oppose the patenting of all natural genetic materials. We hold that life cannot be bought, owned, sold, discovered or patented, even in its smallest form.
>
> (http://www.ipcb.org/resolutions/htmls/dec_phx.html)

Here, the solidarity of indigenous communities locates science in the backdrop of its colonial agendas, fundamentally pointing out the value-laden nature of scientific knowledge that is directed at conquering nature, and alternatively noting the subaltern cosmology that life cannot be owned or traded (Dutta, in press; Shiva, 2010). Resistance is constituted in the challenging of logics of the neoliberal structure, and pointing toward the necessity for co-constructing alternative logics (Shiva, 2008, 2010). The resistive capacity of subaltern communities is situated amidst the articulation of the erasures of subaltern voices that are achieved through the state and corporate apparatuses of neoliberalism.

Resistance is fundamentally constituted in the reframing of the mainstream ontologies and epistemologies and in the opening up of the taken-for-granted assumptions that represented the value structures of mainstream configurations. The articulation of the erasures of subaltern voices through the representative politics of public relations knowledge production in mainstream public spheres creates openings for redefining the meanings of scholarly and practitioner engagement with local communities. The epistemology shifts from the emphasis on the outside observer, who provides expert knowledge, to a sojourner, who participates in co-creating stories so that these stories might open up new ways of imagining social, political, and economic systems (Godalof, 1999). The persuasive rhetorical approach to public relations that defines public relations in terms of persuasion is redefined in terms of the role of public relations as dialogue and understanding, situated amidst a reflexive politics of structural transformation (Dutta, 2007, 2008a). Worth noting here is the fundamental disjuncture between the conceptualization of public relations as persuasive rhetoric and the redefinition of public relations as listening and dialogue. When public relations is understood as listening, the emphasis shifts from one that attempts to persuade target audiences (who are assumed to be in need of changing their behavior, attitude, or beliefs) to one that attempts to co-create entry points for understanding.

It is through the communicative act of listening that entry points are created in mainstream discourses for bringing forth the voices of subaltern communities that have historically been treated as target audiences of campaigns and interventions. For example, the Via Campesina movement (http://viacampesina.org/en/index.php) is a transnational movement made up of several local organizations of peasants, farmers, farm workers, indigenous agrarian communities, and rural women spread across the globe that seek to offer alternative meanings of development and agriculture, challenging the neoliberal framework of agricultural development (Desmarais, 2007; Heath, 2007; Hegde, 1998, 2005). The alternative framing of development emerges at the core of the collective organizing processes of Via Campesina.

The roots of the movement are situated in the Managua Declarations that emerged out of the discussions among representatives of eight farm organizations from Central America, the Caribbean, Europe, Canada and the United States:

> Neoliberal policies represent a dramatic constraint on farmers throughout the world, bringing us to the brink of irredeemable extinction and further aggravating the irreparable damage which has been caused to our rural environs . . . We note that GATT affects farmers in poor countries and as well impoverishes farmers in rich countries to the benefit of monopolies and transnational corporations. Trade and international exchange should have as their fundamental goal, justice, and cooperation rather

than competition and the survival of the fittest. We as producers need to be guaranteed sufficient income to cover as a minimum our costs of production. This, to date, has not been a concern of the negotiators of the GATT. We reject policies which promote low prices, liberalized markets, the export of surpluses, dumping and other export subsidies. Sustainable agricultural production is fundamental and strategic to social life and cannot be reduced to a simple question of trade.

(Managua Declaration, 1992, as cited in Desmarais, 2007, p. 76)

The foundations of the social change process in the Via Campesina movement are based upon the critique of neoliberal hegemony and the widespread narrative of neoliberalism that promises uncontrolled development through privatization, allocation of land for large-scale development projects, displacement of farming communities, and liberalization. The grand narrative of neoliberalism that promises economic growth and a trickle-down effect is challenged through the articulation of an alternative frame that reinterprets the goals of trade and international exchange in the realm of social justice and cooperation. The competition-based framework of neoliberalism is challenged by an alternative framework of cooperation and sustainability. Trade is juxtaposed with social life in driving the criteria for the measurement of the effectiveness of a development model, thus disrupting the taken-for-granted ideologies underlying the articulations of development in mainstream globalization processes.

Conclusion

This chapter set out to offer a critical reading of public relations in the backdrop of globalization. At the heart of the arguments proposed in this chapter are questions of truth and accountability in the free market principles of neoliberalism that are circulated as ideals for universal progress and economic growth. A critical reading of public relations practices in neoliberal governance draws attention to the political and economic agendas that are served by structures that produce knowledge, specially attending to the public relations function of knowledge claims in reifying and reproducing certain forms of oppression and marginalization. Furthermore, a critical approach to public relations points out the ways in which the community is co-opted to serve the interests of transnational hegemony. It is in this backdrop that a culture-centered approach to public relations envisions the politics of social change through resistive practices of relationship building that are directed toward challenging and changing unequal social structures. Ultimately, the culture-centered approach envisions projects of solidarity that work toward creating spaces of structural transformation through local grassroots collaborations with communities in the subaltern sectors of the globe.

References

Anderson, R. and Cissna, K. N. (2008). Fresh perspectives in dialogue theory. *Communication Theory*, 18, 1–4.

Beverly, J. (2004a). *Subalternity and representation: Arguments in cultural theory*. Durham, NC: Duke University Press.

Beverly, J. (2004b). *Testimonio: On the politics of truth*. Minneapolis: University of Minnesota Press.

Cloud, D. (2004). "To veil the threat of terror": Afghan women and the <clash of civilization> in the imagery of the U.S. war on terrorism. *Quarterly Journal of Speech*, 90, 285–306.

Cloud, D. (2007). Corporate social responsibility as oxymoron: Universalization and exploitation at Boeing. In May, S., Cheney, G., and Roper, J. (Eds.), *The debate over corporate social responsibility*. New York: Oxford University Press, pp. 219–231.

Dellacioppa, K. Z. (2009). *This bridge called Zapatismo: Building alternative political cultures in Mexico city, Los Angeles, and beyond*. Lanham, MD: Rowman & Littlefield Publishers.

Desmarais, A. (2007). *La Via Campesina: Globalization and the power of the peasants*. Halifax: Fernwood Publishing.

Dowdy, J. (2010). Stabilising Iraq: A conversation with Paul Brinkley. McKinsey Consulting Company.

Dutta, M. (2006). Theoretical approaches to entertainment education: A subaltern critique. *Health Communication*, 20, 221–231.

Dutta, M. (2007). Communicating about culture and health: Theorizing culture-centered and cultural-sensitivity approaches. *Communication Theory*, 17, 304–328.

Dutta, M. (2008a). *Communicating health: A culture-centered approach*. London: Polity Press.

Dutta, M. (2008b). Participatory communication in entertainment education: A critical analysis. *Communication for Development and Social Change: A Global Journal*, 2, 53–72.

Dutta, M. (2008c). A critical response to Storey and Jacobson: The co-optive possibilities of participatory discourse. *Communication for Development and Social Change: A Global Journal*, 2, 81–90.

Dutta, M. (2009). Theorizing resistance: Applying Gayatri Chakravorty Spivak in public relations. In Ihlen, Ø., van Ruler, B., and Fredrikson, M. (Eds.), *Social theory on public relations*. New York: Routledge, pp. 67–76.

Dutta, M. (2011). *Communicating social change: Structure, culture, agency*. New York: Routledge.

Dutta, M. and Pal, M. (in pressa). Dialogue theory in marginalized settings: A subaltern studies approach. *Communication Theory*.

Dutta, M. and Pal, N. (in pressb). Public relations and marginalization in a global context: A postcolonial critique. In Bardhan, N. and Weaver, C. K. (Eds.), *Public relations in global cultural contexts*. New York: Routledge.

Dutta-Bergman, M. J. (2004). The unheard voices of Santalis: Communicating about health from the margins of India. *Communication Theory*, 14, 237–263.

Dutta-Bergman, M. J. (2005). Civil society and public relations: Not so civil after all. *Journal of Public Relations Research*, 17, 267–289.

Esteva, G. (2005). Celebration of Zapatismo. *Humboldt Journal of Social Relations*, 29, 127–167.

Esteva, G. and Prakash, M. S. (1998). *Grassroots postmodernism: Remaking the soils of cultures*. London: Zed Books.

Godalof, I. (1999). *Against purity: Rethinking identity with Indian and Western feminisms*. New York: Routledge.

Gonzalez, R. J. (2008). Bribing the "tribes." *Z Magazine*. Retrieved from http://www.zcommunications.org.

Harvey, D. (2005). *A brief history of neoliberalism*. London: Oxford University Press.

Heath, R. L. (2007). Management through advocacy. In Toth, E. L. (Ed.), *The future of excellence in public relations and communication management: Challenges for the next generation*. Mahwah, NJ: Lawrence Erlbaum Associates, pp. 41–65.

Heath, R. and Palenchar, M. (2009). *Strategic issues management: Organizations and public policy challenges*. Los Angeles: Sage.

Hegde, R. (1998). A view from elsewhere: Locating difference and the politics of representation from a transnational feminist perspective. *Communication Theory*, 8, 271–297.

Hegde, R. (2005). Disciplinary spaces and globalization: A postcolonial unsettling. *Global Media and Communication*, 1, 59–62.

Kim, I. (2008). Voices from the margin: A culture-centered look at public relations of resistance. Unpublished doctoral dissertation, Purdue University, West Lafayette, IN.

McPhail, M. L. (2004). Race and the (im)possibility of dialogue. In Anderson, R., Baxter, L. A. and Cissna, K. N. (Eds.), *Dialogue: Theorizing difference in communication studies*. Thousand Oaks, CA: Sage, pp. 209–224.

Mignolo, W. (2000). *Local histories/global designs: Coloniality, subaltern knowledges, and border thinking*. Princeton, NJ: Princeton University Press.

Munshi, D. (1999). Requisitioning variety: Photographic metaphors, ethnocentric lenses, and the divided colours of public relations. *Asia Pacific Public Relations Journal*, 1, 39–51.

Munshi, D. and Kurian, P. (2005). Imperializing spin cycles: A postcolonial look at public relations, greenwashing and the separation of publics. *Public Relations Review*, 31, 513–520.

Mychalejko, C. and Ryan, R. (2009). U.S. military funded mapping project in Oaxaca. *Z Magazine*. Retrieved from http://www.zcommunications.org.

Olesen, T. (2005a). Mixing scales: Neo-liberalism and the transnational Zapatista Solidarity Network. *Humboldt Journal of Social Relations*, 29, 84–126.

Olesen, T. (2005b). *International Zapatismo: The construction of solidarity in the age of globalization*. New York: Zed Press.

Olivera, O. (2004). *Cochabamba: Water war in Bolivia*. Cambridge, MA: South End Press.

Olivera, O. and Lewis, T. (2004). *Cochabamba: Water war in Bolivia*. Cambridge, MA: South End Press.

Pal, M. (2008). Fighting from and for the margin: Local activism in the realm of global politics. Unpublished doctoral dissertation, Purdue University, West Lafayette, IN.

Pal, M. and Dutta, M. (2008a). Public relations in a global context: The relevance of critical modernism as a theoretical lens. *Journal of Public Relations Research*, 20, 159–179.

Pal, M. and Dutta, M. (2008b). Theorizing resistance in a global context: Processes, strategies and tactics in communication scholarship. *Communication Yearbook*, 32, 41–87.

Portillo, Z. (2009, January 21). Peruvian region outlaws biopiracy. Retrieved from http://www.scidev.net/en/news/peruvian-region-outlaws-biopiracy.html.

Rabasa, J. (2001). Beyond representation: The impossibility of the local (Notes on Subaltern Studies in light of a rebellion in Tepoztlan, Morelos). In Rodriguez, I. (Ed.), *The Latin American subaltern studies reader*. Durham, NC: Duke University Press, pp. 191–210.

Rastogi, R. and Dutta, M. (2010). Deconstructing the poverty reduction strategy of the World Bank: A critical interrogation. Paper presented at the National Communication Association Annual Convention.

Robinson, D. (2009). Biopiracy concerns heat up over chilli pepper. *BiosRes Review, 3*, 6–7.

Sharma, A. (2008). *Logics of empowerment: Development, gender, and governance in neoliberal India*. Minneapolis, MN: University of Minnesota Press.

Shiva, V. (1988). Reductionist science as epistemic violence. In Nandy, A. (Ed.), *Science, hegemony, and violence*. New Delhi, India: Oxford University Press, pp. 161–178.

Shiva, V. (1989). *Staying alive: Women, ecology, and development*. London: Zed Books.

Shiva, V. (1991). *The violence of the green revolution: Third World agriculture, ecology and politics*. London: Zed Books.

Shiva, V. (2001). Democratizing biology: Reinventing biology from a feminist, ecological, and Third World perspective. In Lederman, M. and Bartsch, I. (Eds.), *The gender and science reader*. London: Routledge, pp. 447–465.

Shiva, V. (2002). Seeds of suicide: The ecological and human cost of globalization of agriculture. In Shiva, V. and Bedi, G. (Eds.), *Sustainable agriculture and food security: The impact of globalization*. New Delhi: Sage Publications, pp. 169–183.

Shiva, V. (2007). *Wheat biopiracy: The real issues the government is avoiding*. Retrieved from www.zcommunications.org/wheat-biopiracy-the-real-issues-the-government-is-avoiding-by-vandana2-shiva.pdf.

Shiva, V. (2008). Biodiversity, intellectual property rights, and globalization. In de Sousa Santos, B. (Ed.), *Another knowledge is possible: Beyond Northern epistemologies*. London: Verso, pp. 272–287.

Shiva, V. (2010, January 12). Press statement on Bt. Brinjal and GM foods. Retrieved from http://www.navdanya.org/news/81-press-statement-on-bt-brinjal-a-gm-foods.

Shiva, V. and Bedi, G. (2002). *Sustainable agriculture and food security: The impact of globalization*. New Delhi: Sage Publications.

Shome, R. and Hegde, S. R. (2002). Postcolonial approaches to communication: Charting the terrain, engaging the intersections. *Communication Theory, 12*, 249–270.

de Sousa Santos, B. (Ed.). (2008). *Another knowledge is possible: Beyond Northern epistemologies*. London: Verso.

de Sousa Santos, B., Nunes, J. A., and Meneses, M. P. (2008). Introduction: Opening up the canon of knowledge and recognition of difference. In de Sousa Santos, B. (Ed.), *Another knowledge is possible: Beyond Northern epistemologies*. London: Verso, pp. ix–lxii.

Spivak, C. G. (1988a). Subaltern studies: Deconstructing historiography. In Guha, R. and Spivak, G. C. (Eds.), *Selected subaltern studies*. New York: Oxford University Press, pp. 3–36.

Spivak, G. C. (1988b). Can the subaltern speak? In Nelson, C. and Grossberg, L. (Eds.), *Marxism and the interpretation of culture*. Basingstoke: Macmillan, pp. 271–313.

Spivak, G. C. (1999). *A critique of postcolonial reason: Toward a history of the vanishing present*. Cambridge, MA: Harvard University Press.

Starr, A. (1998). *Naming the enemy: Anticorporate movements against globalization*. London: Zed Books.

Starr, A. (2005). *Global revolt: A guide to the movements against globalization*. London: Zed Books.

Statham, L. (2009, February 20). Indigenous mining dialogue group not a silver bullet. *The Independent Weekly*. Retrieved from http://www.independentweekly.com.au/news/local/news/general/indigenousminning-dialogue-group-not-a-silver-bullet-acf/1439732.aspx?storypage=0.

Tihuwai Smith, L. (2006). *Decolonizing methodologies: Research and indigenous peoples*. New York: Zed Books.

Wood, L. J. (2005). Bridging the chasms: The case of people's global action. In Bandy, J. and Smith, J. (Eds.), *Coalitions across borders: Transnational protest and the neo-liberal order*. New York: Rowman & Littlefield, pp. 51–65.

Wood, R., Hall, D. and Hasian Jr., M. (2008). Globalization, social justice movements, and the human genome diversity debates: A case study in health activism. In Zoller, H. and Dutta, M. (Eds.), *Emerging perspectives in health communication: Interpretive, critical and cultural approaches*. New York: Routledge, pp. 431–446.

13

THINKING ABOUT PUBLIC RELATIONS AND CULTURE

Anthropological Insights and Ethnographic Futures

Jacquie L'Etang

Introduction

In this chapter I reflect on the potential that anthropology and its distinguishing research approach—that of ethnography—have for public relations. I argue that this approach could generate new and diverse readings of public relations activities *in* local, regional, national and international cultures, and *as* occupational cultures.

I begin with a definitional discussion of the public relations role in cultural exchanges and intercultural communication and a review of literature in the public relations field that has engaged with culture. This is followed by a summary discussion of anthropology and ethnographic practice, making reference to their applications in fields immediately adjacent to public relations practice: marketing, media and management. Finally, it is suggested that anthropology and ethnography offer considerable potential to widen the research agenda in the field. The crux of the argument is that prior research has tended to focus on cross-cultural comparisons linked to normative (U.S.) models, leaving a gap in terms of basic anthropological and ethnographic research that would yield unique in-depth data. Furthermore, existing research on public relations and culture has not addressed the occupational culture(s) of public relations or its role in organisational cultures from an ethnographic perspective. Again the existing focus on the normative, the ideal and the aspirational leaves exciting terrain unexplored.

'Boundary Spanners' and 'Border Crossings'

Public relations work requires its practitioners to criss-cross cultures within and between organisations and communities (on and off-line). Public relations practitioners are 'culture-workers'—and not only when they are involved in culture-change programmes. Public relations is also a feature of the development of a specialised 'promotional culture' (Wernick, 1991), a consequence of late twentieth-century consumerism and commodification, which has produced a particular form of discourse, values and expectations. Promotional culture is a global phenomenon, part of the standardisation processes of globalisation (Ritzer, 2000, 2002).

Public relations enacts intercultural communications between different organisations, media and international stakeholders and publics located in various countries. The term *international public relations* appears to be less popular than formerly, and one might speculate whether its relationship to political communication and diplomacy has led to associations with power and propaganda. Perhaps, for some, 'global PR' sounds more 'neutral' and less problematic. However, the use of the term *global* positions PR practice as a significant role-player in, and beneficiary of, technological changes in communications that have contributed to more rapid globalisation. Globalisation is a controversial and politicised process in which public relations international agencies play a role worthy of further study in relation to its impacts. Globalised organisations are powerful, transcend national boundaries and may be difficult to challenge in terms of transparency and governance (as became apparent at the end of 2010 in relation to FIFA, the International Federation of Association Football). They also engage in public diplomacy and public and political affairs in an international, multi- and inter-cultural context. Necessarily, public relations is at the forefront of intercultural exchanges and negotiated constructions of organisational policies and positions, since ethnic, organisational and occupational cultures frame communication, just as communication reflects those cultures' values and practices.

Public relations operates 'between the hyphens' or in the interstices of cultures, hence the importance of sensitivity to this concept and its processes of enactment. A consideration of public relations and culture is not a question of political correctness, conventions or manners but an awareness and ability to acknowledge, research and read cultural practice and to understand its significance in terms of participants—'from the native's point of view', to use the anthropological and ethnographic discourse.

Public relations may be seen as a specific occupational sub- or microculture comprising largely female labour. Public relations practice comprises multiple occupational cultures, for example 'consultancy culture' or 'in-house culture', or even more specified as in 'Hill & Knowlton culture'. These cultures have not, to date, been the subject of much research (but see Hodges 2005, 2006; Pieczka, 2002, 2006a, 2006b). This is partly the consequence of research agendas that have focused on building an occupational identity and role within a strategic management paradigm and thus have tended towards a rather homogenous view. It is time to explore the particular and to encounter difference and distinctiveness.

Public Relations and Culture: A Critical Perspective

Existing research and collections of research have tended to take a comparative cross-cultural approach to the subject based on nation-states. Furthermore, much influential research has been historically derived from the Excellence Project and its normative principles.

In an influential contribution to the literature Sriramesh and White (1992) revealed a quantitative methodological bias when, in the context of a discussion about ideology, they commented that:

> The ideological domain of any culture is extremely difficult to decipher, let alone quantify. In most cases, the people of a culture themselves may not be able to verbalize some of their ideologies and worldviews. Ideological entities such as values, themes and ethos are identified largely by the subjective perception of the ethnographer based on observed patterns of behaviors. With an increase in the extent of personal interpretation, there is a corresponding decrease in empirical controls. This is the biggest methodological problem that an anthropologist faces and one that theorists applying these concepts to organizational settings should be wary about.
>
> (Sriramesh and White, 1992, p. 606).

Because of their methodological inclinations, and because *Excellence* has been such an influential book, their chapter has been immensely influential in shaping the nature of enquiry into public relations and culture. Sriramesh and White proceeded to adopt the determinants outlined by Hofstede (1980), and this framework has shaped most discussions of public relations and culture ever since. Such a strategy allows for surveys and generalisation and avoids the messy unquantifiable aspects, which form the rich texture of our daily lives. The application of such rigid frameworks may permit some level of cross-cultural comparison, but the evasion of 'lived experience' and cultural detail means that such approaches may not be so useful for in-depth understanding of practice cultures and intercultural communication at organisational, community, societal and international levels.

Many studies, if not most, have been quantitative, employing Hofstede as a framework (Chen, 1996; Kanso, 1996; Ekachai and Komolsevin, 1996). Sriramesh's 'ethnographic study of Southern Indian organisations' did employ qualitative methods in a sample of 18 organisations, but inevitably had to compromise by limiting the time spent in those organisations (four to eight days), which some anthropologists might regard as 'blitzkrieg ethnography'.

Another much-cited study (Verčič, Grunig and Grunig, 1996) explored the impact of Slovenian culture on public relations through the lens of Hofstede and three interviews (one of them with a co-author) and required interviewees to assign numerical values to Hofstede's indices, from which generalisations were then made about Slovenian culture. Culbertson and Chen (1996) took a cross-cultural approach comparing political, economic and cultural climates in relation to public relations work. They and their contributors variously used Hofstede and the framework of symmetrical communication drawn from 'the' four models of public relations conceptualised from one version of U.S. history. Tilson and Alozie's (2004) collection also used Excellence and Hofstede as frameworks for the analysis of national data. Van Ruler and Verčič's (2004) collection took a step in a different direction since it aimed to produce work 'written from an insider's perspective' although in some cases authors were themselves constructed by the dominant paradigm.

In 2009 Sriramesh and Verčič edited a landmark volume that took a cross-cultural approach employing a standard framework to facilitate comparison: classification of political arrangements, economic development, activism, legal system, culture and media. By taking this approach, culture is essentially reduced to the status of a variable, as illustrated in the following two quotes:

> Cross-national theorising should also explore how contextual variables external to the organization influence public relations activities in various parts of the world.
>
> (Sriramesh, 2009a, p. xxxiii)

> We thought it would be best to design individual studies that break down societal culture into manageable parts and study its impact on public relations in some depth.
>
> (Sriramesh, 2009b, p. 50)

These approaches avoid the rich and messy 'lived experience' that forms the textures of daily work and living, and thus deprive us of in-depth understanding of public relations practice cultures and their interplays in organisational, community, societal and international cultures.

Reviewing the methodologies adopted in the country-specific studies in Culbertson and Chen (1996) is instructive. Chen (1996) conducted a survey among 475 members of practitioner associations testing hypotheses drawn from the dominant U.S. paradigm eliciting cultural differences and concepts such as *li* and *guanxi,* but then interpreting these with the dominant frameworks; for example '*guanxi* seems asymmetrical at first glance with its emphasis on status and preordained relationships, but it embodies principles implied in symmetry when viewed in its depth' (Chen, 1996, p. 147). Concepts of symmetry and asymmetry also shaped quantitative research into practice in Thailand (Ekechai and Komolsevin, 1996), Saudi Arabia (Alanazi, 1996), Norway (Coombs, Halladay, Hasenauer, and Signitzer, 1994, cited in Mortensen, 1996, p. 325), Romania (VanSlyke Turk, 1996) and Korea (Kim, 1996; Rhee, 2002; both cited in Kim, 2009); and qualitative research in Japan (Cooper-Chen, 1996), Costa Rica (Gonzalez and Akel, 1996) and Bulgaria (Braun, 2007). Ideological/moral values were attributed to symmetry, in that the text was written in a way that encourages the reader to see symmetry as a desirable goal. It is also noticeable that the emergence of public relations was presented as a recent phenomenon unconnected to earlier historical public communications practices of government or earlier regimes. This reinforced the idea that the US was the original source of public relations and that the practice was subsequently exported elsewhere.

Although Sriramesh and Verčič (2009) encouraged their authors to apply Hofstede's framework, already noted as a model that has its limits, some authors characterised culture in a generalised and occasionally stereotypical fashion. Examples of this process of stereotyping are shown in the following quotations:

> The characteristics that are most often connected with the Finns is reticence and shyness . . . it is a paradox that the silent Finns today belong to the most frequent users of the mobile phone in the world.
>
> (Lehtonen, 2004, p. 108)

> It is said that the Dutch were as successful as they were because they has to overcome the poor level of Holland's natural resources, and therefore developed an earthy nature, strict working ethics and a very strong propensity to negotiation and consensus. At the same time the Dutch have built the questionable reputation of pretending to know how people in other societies in the world should behave.
>
> (van Ruler, 2004, p. 262)

> According to Norwegians' self-image, Norwegians are mainly a nation of fishermen and farmers who live close to nature, they're simple and bucolic, and they tend to act awkwardly and clumsily when travelling abroad. This national–romantic image gas little to do with reality.
>
> (Horsle, 2004, p. 278)

> The UK could be considered as a brand with national symbols, such as its flag, Queen and Anthem, cultural stereotypes related to a class society, music (Beatles, Rolling Stones), film, drama (Shakespeare), humour (Monty Python, Mr Bean) and eccentric behaviour, and political, economic and industrial power.
>
> (Koper, 2004, p. 467)

Characteristics of British social life and conversation are understatement and irony.

(White et al., 2009, p. 400)

As Curtin and Gaither (2005) pointed out, 'Care must be taken not to let the cultural indexes serve as procedural shorthand which results in cultural stereotyping' (p. 105).

The difficulty in the statements shown above is not so much that they may caricature, rather than characterise, or that they are not based on cultural authenticity, but that the data upon which the generalisations are made are not necessarily made apparent. In other words, the evidence for claims is not presented; neither is the research process of observation and coding that is required to underpin such judgements (if they are not to be rendered solely subjective) laid bare. In short, the analysis is not transparent. This may have come about because qualitative work has tended to take second place in public relations scholarship and there simply is not the tradition of publishing articles which contain detailed descriptions of qualitative data and analysis.

Signs of Life?

Despite a remarkable uniformity in approaches to culture, there have been contributions that have indicated the importance of ethnography (Watson, 2005; Pieczka, 1997, 2002, 2006a,b; Curtin and Gaither, 2005, 2007; Hodges, 2005, 2006; Terry, 2005) and some more recent lobbying (L'Etang, 2010, 2011, forthcoming; Vujinovic and Kruckeberg, 2010). However, it is fair to say that little ethnographic work has been published, perhaps because such work is perceived as too long for current outlets, so that public relations academics never get to see the value of this type of data. However, it is to be hoped that a forthcoming issue of *Public Relations Review* specialising in anthropology and ethnography will begin to address the gap (L'Etang, Hodges and Pieczka, forthcoming). It is clear that there is room for considerably more engagement with fluctuating micro cultures and evolving relationships (Pal and Dutta, 2008, pp. 167–168). There are therefore signs that anthropology and ethnography may indeed be taken up by a critical mass of scholars to shift debates and the research agenda into new directions.

Anthropology

Anthropology has been defined as:

> The study of humankind in terms of scientific inquiry and logical presentation. It strives for a comprehensive and coherent view of our own species within dynamic nature, organic evolution, and socio-cultural development

. . . The anthropological quest aims for a better understanding of, and proper appreciation for the evolutionary history, sociocultural diversity, and biological unity of humankind. Anthropologists see the human being as a dynamic and complex product of both inherited genetic information and learned social behaviour within a cultural milieu; symbolic language as articulate speech distinguishes our species from the great apes.

(Birx, 2005, p. xvii)

Thus anthropology is a holistic discipline that incorporates science, social science and the humanities. Public relations fits into anthropology as part of the human story, especially in relation to culture and communication.

The historical origins of anthropology are usually identified with nineteenth-century explorers, missionaries and colonial administrators (Denzin and Lincoln, 2000, pp. 11–18; Vidich and Lyman, 2000, pp. 40–43). Such travellers typically spent long periods of time in cultures other than their own, typically learning local languages and gaining a deep, but outsider's, understanding of cultural practices.

Anthropology was not, however, merely voyeuristic. The realisation, for those from predominantly Christian lands, that there was a multiplicity of other faiths and beliefs challenged their own view of the world and its divine order (Vidich and Lyman, 2000, p. 11). Thus, although anthropology has been extensively criticised for its alignment with colonial powers, exploitation and domination; it is also the case that anthropological excursions forced a reflexivity within the breasts of travelling observers.

Most accounts of the development of anthropology as a distinct discipline highlight the significance of Polish-born, but British-based, Bronislaw Malinowski (1884–1942), whose work in New Guinea is conventionally supposed to have been the catalyst for the emergence of British anthropology (Macdonald, 2001, pp. 60–61), and Radcliffe-Brown (1881–1955), both of whom had a strong interest in the structure and function of social systems, although their approaches differed. Malinowski sought to determine general laws and to specify the purpose and function of cultural practices within a particular social context (Macdonald, 2001, pp. 61–62). Radcliffe-Brown saw societies as:

ordered systems whose constituent parts play a role in maintaining equilibrium, and he also introduced a diagnostic element that sought to specify the key elements that apparently revealed otherwise hidden meanings in social practice, whereas Malinowksi's approach was more empirical.

(Macdonald, 2001, p. 64)

Structural-functionalism was largely concerned with social ordering and conflict resolution in societies that were sometimes presented by anthropologists as being stable and static (Macdonald, 2001, p. 66).

A significant intervention was made by Evans-Pritchard, when he argued that language practices, such as the use of metaphor and symbolism in particular contexts, can produce specific situational meaning. This shifted the discipline to meaning-orientated explorations, rather than those seeking structure and function (Macdonald, 2001, p. 64). Thus the construction and interpretation of meaning became foregrounded (Macdonald, 2001, p. 65). Evans-Pritchard's approach is useful in reconsidering the application of systems theory to public relations and the extent to which anthropological origins and perspectives have been acknowledged and taken into account. For Evans-Pritchard:

> The system . . . is not so much like a *real* body as a set of abstract, dialectical principles: in other words, it is not just about 'masses and a supposed relation between these masses . . . [but] relations, defined in terms of social situations, and relations between these relations'.
> (Evans-Pritchard, 1940, p. 236, cited in Macdonald, 2001, p. 65)

The fact that systems theory in public relations has tended to focus on organisations as actors, rather than on people as members of cultures, may go some way towards explaining the severely functionalist view that has dominated the field, which remains short of the reflexivity that developed in anthropology in the 1970s as postcolonial perspectives came to the fore.

Anthropology evolved rapidly in the latter part of the twentieth century, to take account of postcolonial critiques, and also to define as legitimate research sites cultural contexts that are mini- or subcultures of the culture inhabited by the aspiring anthropologist; for example, childhood (James, 2001), health and medicine (Bloor, 2001), education (Gordon et al., 2001), science and technology studies (Hess, 2001), deviance (Henslin, 2001, pp. 3–34; Hobbs, 2001, pp. 204–219) and more specific studies into, for example, Hell's Angels, the police (Van Maanen, 2001, pp. 234–251) or football hooligans (Giulianotti, 2001, pp. 85–105).

Ethnographic Practice

Anthropologists regard ethnography as a distinctive feature and the main research method of anthropology, exemplified by immersion in the studied culture, participant observation and the collection of data through a variety of methods including field notes and informal interviews. However, ethnographic practices arose not solely within social and cultural anthropology but also within sociology, where the influence of the Chicago School is often cited, although according to Bryman this should be modified given the amount of non-ethnographic quantitative research that emerged from this source (Bryman, 2001, pp. xiii–xiv). Bryman argued that the influence of symbolic interactionism to ethnography's emergence and establishment, has perhaps not been sufficiently acknowledged (Bryman, 2001, pp. xiv).

Ethnography is an unusual concept in public relations, not least because its approach runs counter to the drums of the dominant paradigm in the field. Ethnography entails a high degree of reflexivity not present in most public relations research. According to Tedlock:

> Ethnography involves an ongoing attempt to place specific encounters, events, and understandings into a fuller, more meaningful context. It is not simply the production of new information or research data, but rather the way in which such information or data are transformed into a written or visual form . . . it combines research design, fieldwork, and various methods of enquiry to produce historically, politically, and personally situated accounts, descriptions, interpretations, and representations of human lives. As an inscription practice, ethnography is a continuation of fieldwork rather than a transparent record of past experiences in the field. The ongoing nature of fieldwork connects important personal experiences with an area of knowledge; as a result, it is located between the interiority of autobiography and the exteriority of cultural analysis.
>
> (Tedlock, 2000, p. 455)

Such rich multilayered and reflexive interpretive work has been largely missing from public relations, although a forthcoming special issue of *Public Relations Review* (L'Etang, Hodges and Pieczka, forthcoming) has sought to stimulate this type of work in the field.

As Atkinson and colleagues pointed out, ethnography is located in, 'intellectual terrain [that] is normally contested . . . subject to . . . constraints and contradictions . . . a site of debate and contestation' (Atkinson et al., 2001, p. 1). Bryman likewise highlighted the fact of divergent perspectives, but also the aspects of convergence in the practice, in his summary definition:

> Ethnographers immerse themselves in a society to collect descriptive data via fieldwork concerning the culture of its members from the perspective of the meanings members of that society attach to their social world, and render the collected data intelligible and significant to fellow academics and other readers.
>
> (Bryman, 2001, p. 1)

Numerous definitions of ethnography encompass the practice of 'fieldwork' and 'textual products' (Atkinson et al., 2001, p. 2) and have defined parameters within which research techniques can be defined as ethnography, as follows:

A commitment to the first-hand experience and exploration of a particular social or cultural setting, on the basis of (though not exclusively by) participant observation. Observation and participation (according to circumstance and the analytic purpose at hand) remain the characteristic features of the ethnographic approach . . . fieldwork entails the use of other research methods . . . conversations and interviews are often indistinguishable from other forms of interaction and dialogue . . . In literate societies the ethnographer may well draw on textual materials as sources of information and insight into how actors and institutions represent themselves and others . . . the ethnographer . . . [may draw] . . . on a very diverse repertoire of research techniques—*analysing spoken discourse and narratives, collecting and interpreting visual materials (including photography, film and video)*, collecting oral history and life history materials and so on.

(Atkinson et al., 2001, p. 5, italics added)

The activities described could be usefully employed by a public relations practitioner as part of research into an organisation and its culture(s) and identities. Anthropological insight and ethnographic methods could have considerable benefits for public relations practice in understanding organisational contexts and the cultural practice of particular communities. In short, ethnography could be applied as a research tool by PR consultants just as it is in marketing or management.

Furthermore, public relations consultants can be regarded as a particular speech community, which possesses its own 'communicative repertoire, speech event, speech act, shared language attitudes etc.' (Keating, 2001, p. 288), and therefore an appropriate object of study in themselves. Ethnographies of work have analysed how people do their jobs, how and why they take decisions, and stresses and tensions experienced in a great variety of workplaces and in relation to the gamut of jobs, with high and low status in the wider culture. Such research has the potential to reveal unexpected dynamics and relationships to reveal realities that run counter to 'official' versions. For example, Smith pointed out that:

The study of the unacknowledged, the hidden, the insider knowledge, the unwritten but pervasive rules governing jobs . . . [there exist] 'understudied occupations' often considered unskilled and sometimes considered to be marginal or trivial . . . conversely, ethnographic researchers have taken the work of professionals and semi-professional and rendered them ordinary, accessible and routinized.

(Smith, 2001, p. 222)

The public relations occupation aspires to professional status (Pieczka and L'Etang, 2001) and the status of strategic management, and these aspirations form underpinning assumptions of much PR research. Yet there has been little direct observation of the extent of bureaucratic management and processes of industrialisation and exploitation in public relations, or even the nature of routines; for example, only Pieczka (2006b) has sought to interrogate the nature of public relations expertise.

Applying Anthropology to Workplace Practices

The application of anthropology to business has been controversial within anthropology, not least because such applied anthropology was tainted with colonialism and ideology, certainly within Europe, whose colonial administrators sought anthropological information and commissioned ethnographic research in order to better understand the inhabitants of colonial territories. UK Government funding supported the Colonial Social Science Research Council (CSSRC) from 1944 to 1962, 'an organization which advocated a practical research agenda for anthropology in the colonies' (Baba, 2006, p. 84). However, when Israel Sieff, co-founder of Marks & Spencer, led a group of British industrialists to request British anthropologists to engage with issues of employee relations and productivity:

> The industrialists were rebuffed . . . with the reply that anthropology was an exploratory discipline and thus could not be used for anything so concrete as recommendations for businesses.
>
> (Baba, 2006, p. 84)

It was therefore American anthropology that led the way in industrial contexts and organisational culture through its involvement in the Hawthorne studies in the late 1920s, following which a number of American anthropologists developed a strong interest in modern institutions, especially corporations and industrial relationships (Baba, 2006, p. 88). Shifts in social science towards quantitative work and the popularity of contingency theory led to a decline in industrial anthropology; and political and ideological critiques of the 1960s and 1970s resulted in its fragmentation into Marxist-inspired critiques, ethnographies of work and the professions, and studies of industrialization in non-Western contexts (Baba, 2006, p. 91–92). Anthropology has informed and inspired organisational behaviour and management, ethnographic design of products and services, and the disciplines of consumer behaviour and marketing (Baba, 2006, p. 98) and is relevant to a consideration of public relations in relation to those contexts, as an agent, a service, a participant and a consumer within organisational cultures, as well as in its contribution in various societal contexts: local, national and international.

Anthropology and the ethnographic methods not only contributed 'the native's point of view' to organisational culture, but offered qualitative data that were unusual in managerial and psychological fields (Baba, 2006, pp. 99, 101). Within public relations the instrumental approach to 'corporate culture' is prevalent, reflecting its intrinsic bias towards management agendas, ideologies and discourses. This approach sees culture as a management tool or possession that may be contrasted with the interpretivist approach, which sees organisational culture as emerging from all practices, values, assumption, behaviours, struggles, dreams, successes, failures, emotions and relationships (L'Etang, 2008, p. 193). Along with that, the managerial instrumentalism of the PR field has tended towards quantitative rather than interpretive research. Since top business schools in the US are teaching future business leaders and managers the philosophies and skills of ethnography (Baba, 2006, p. 111) it would seem prudent for PR scholars and educators to incorporate such perspectives and research skills in their teaching. The current state of play is that, generally, ethnography does not tend to be mentioned in books and articles on applied public relations research for practice.

Marketing's engagement with ethnography, which began in the 1980s (Mariampolski, 2006, p. 5), has been instrumental in application, even though it challenges the positivist assumptions that dominated the field for many years. In particular, ethnography offered insights that could contribute to new product development, brand innovation and consumer behaviour. Overall, marketing ethnography focuses on issues that impact brand and business development 'whose purposes are confined to advancing client-driven interests rather than those of a disciplinary, societal, or industry focus' (Mariampolski, 2006, p. 51). From Mariampolski's perspective:

> Ethnographic research brings marketers, designers, and planners as close to the consumer as possible in order to solve important business problems . . . Ethnography is effectively used in marketing when little is known about a targeted market or when fresh insights are desired about a segment or consumer-related behavior . . . Multinational and cross-cultural studies are well-suited to ethnographic approaches.
>
> (Mariampolski, 2006, p. 3).

Marketing anthropology has also appropriated territory that public relations practitioners and academics might see as under their jurisdiction: those of corporate culture and corporate social responsibility.

> Corporate cultures exert an important influence on both the internal and external experience of the organization. They influence such weighty matters as employee satisfaction and retention, worker productivity, operations and governance, successful adaptation of technology, relationships with customers and suppliers, the level of customer satisfaction, relationships-to-the-community-at-large, and corporate social responsibility . . .

> In major organizations, corporate cultures have an impact on a variety of
> issues that are essential to the profitability and success of the enterprise.
> (Mariampolski, 2006, p. 30).

In short, anthropology and ethnography have given the marketing discipline the opportunity to encroach on the 'soft skills' that are often thought
of as intrinsic to the public relations 'seat of the pants' approach to practice.
Interpretive approaches can provide scholars and practitioners with alternative
worldviews and access to new intellectual and discourse communities.

Media anthropology is of central interest, given the proportion of time
that practitioners spend engaging with journalists. The linguistic turn in PR
(Motion and Leitch, Weaver et al, 2006) implies a greater focus on PR as source
for the construction of social realities in relation to the media. Anthropologists
have become interested in the media because:

> The media are cultural systems of the social construction of reality. This
> construction is made under distinct circumstances, with the tools of sym-
> bolic reasoning rather than argumentative reasoning. The anthropological
> approach asserts that these images are accepted precisely because they have
> the status of symbolic constructions and, having that status, they function
> and signify the same way that mythical and ritual systems belonging to
> nonmodern societies do.
> (Coman and Rothenbuhler, 2005, p. 9).

Media anthropology developed in the early 1990s as 'an alternative to social-
psychological effects research' (Coman and Rothenbuhler, 2005, p. 9).
Compared with marketing, anthropology is more centrally grounded within
media studies, not least because of its close link with cultural studies, as Coman
and Rothenbuhler explained:

> Media anthropology grows out of the anthropology of modern societies,
> on the one hand, and the cultural turn in media studies, on the other.
> It turns its attention from 'exotic' to mundane and from 'indigenous' to
> manufactured culture but preserves the methodological and conceptual
> assets of earlier anthropological tradition. It prepares media studies for
> more complete engagement with the symbolic construction of reality and
> the fundamental importance of symbolic structures, myth, and ritual in
> everyday life.
> (Coman and Rothenbuhler, 2005, p. 1).

Media anthropology encompasses ritual (and its implications for power)
(Couldry, 2005, p. 59), celebrity and symbolic power/cultism (Lardellier, 2005;
Rothenbuhler, 2005), religious and spiritual forms (Thomas, 2005), myth

(Lule, 2005), story telling (Schudson, 2005), performance (Petersen, 2005), audiences (La Pastina, 2005) and events (Dayan, 2005; Rothenbuhler, 2005; Zelizer, 2005).

Osorio suggested that key anthropological concepts that have emerged as useful in analysing media include ritual, assimilation, acculturation and diffusion. The last three have a connection to persuasion, and are therefore of interest to public relations scholars.

Media studies offers a useful exemplar for public relations, in that it demonstrates a depth and breadth of research that presently does not exist in public relations. In particular the role that public relations plays in the social construction of reality, and, in this context, its relationship to traditional and digital media, and its role in culture more widely remain to be explored in any depth.

What Could Anthropology Do for PR?

Anthropology and the ethnographic tradition offer public relations alternative lines of enquiry. Anthropological cultural concepts can be used to interpret the role of public relations in a rather different way from the established dichotomy of manager/technician. Public relations practitioners can be seen as story-tellers and myth-makers, who help create and maintain organisational rituals employing symbols thought to create unifying meaning. Their role is instrumental, but the stuff of their work is necessarily cultural. Within organisation studies, management consultants have already been described as 'witch doctors'; in the anthropological context this is rather loose usage since the term has been used to encompass healers who use supernatural means or traditional healing, as Stevens pointed out:

> Useages of the label are inadequate because they confuse witchcraft, sorcery, magic, spirit invocation, shamanism . . . [and] a great deal of traditional practices have been variously designated . . . some referents or synonyms are medicine man (or woman), native doctor, diviner, prophet, shaman, healer, curer, spiritualist, herbalist, exorcist.
>
> (Stevens, 2005, p. 2317)

The term has fallen into disrepute because it 'combines implications of ignorance and backwardness' (Stevens, 2006, p. 2318). Nevertheless, the term is used outside anthropology and in organisational literature, so it may be a useful, if rather hostile metaphor.

A deeper understanding of these terms, and their role in cultures may help us to understand the antipathy and fear of 'spin doctors'. It may also provide further insight into the work and role of the public relations consultant. For example, 'Traditional healers typically draw on a wide stock of spiritual, mystical, material and psychological methods, and may combine several in a specific treatment'.

(Stevens, 2006, p. 2317)

Within organisations, public relations practitioners must be able to read and understand cultural traits, norms and taboos. A more nuanced understanding could be advanced by analysing organisational cultural folkways (customs that contribute to order and stability including social conventions and manners); mores (morally inspired conventions to which society requires members to conform); laws (political regulation); and belief systems (including scientific, philosophical, religious and supernatural) (Murty and Vyas, 2006, p. 634).

Anthropological ideas could liberate the public relations field, change research agendas and revolutionise the politics of the discipline and its modernist tendencies. Action anthropology and ethnography can open up areas of action research and build collaborative platforms among and between the many micro cultures with which public relations engages. An anthropological focus on organisational and societal contexts could productively reshape the discipline and the practice, but more importantly can provide much deeper understandings of public relations cultures and public relations in culture than are currently available.

Bibliography

Alanazi, A. (1996). Public relations in the Middle East: The case of Saudi Arabia. In Culbertson, H. and Chen, N. (Eds.) *International public relations: A comparative analysis*. Mahwah, NJ: Lawrence Erlbaum, pp. 239–256.

Atkinson, P., Coffey, A., Delamont, S., Lofland, J. and Lofland, L. (Eds.) (2001). *Handbook of ethnography*. London: Sage.

Baba, M. (2006). Anthropology and business. In Birx, H. (Ed.), *Encylopedia of anthropology*. London: Sage, pp. 83–117.

Birx, H. (2005). Introduction. In Birx, H. (Ed.), *Encylopedia of anthropology*. London: Sage, pp. xvii–li.

Bloor, M. (2001). The ethnography of health and medicine. In Atkinson, P., Coffey, A., Delamont, S., Lofland, J. and Lofland, L. (Eds.), *Handbook of ethnography*. London: Sage, pp. 177–187.

Braun, S. (2007). The effects of the political environment on public relations in Bulgaria. *Journal of public relations research*, 19(3), 199–228.

Bryman, A. (2001). Introduction: A review of ethnography. In Bryman, A. (Ed.) *Ethnography, Vols I–IV*. London: Sage, pp. ix–xxxix.

Chen, N. (1996). Public relations in China: The introduction and development of an occupational field. In Culbertson, H. and Chen, N. (Eds.) *International public relations: A comparative analysis*. Mahwah, NJ: Lawrence Erlbaum, pp. 121–154.

Coman, M. and Rothenbuhler, E. (2005). The promise of media anthropology. In Rothenbuhler, E. and Coman, M. (Eds.), *Media anthropology*. London: Sage, pp. 1–12.

Coombs, T., Holladay, S., Hasenaur, G. and Signitzer, B. (1994). A comparative analysis of international public relations: Identification and interpretation of similarities and differences between professionalization in Austria, Norway, and the United States. *Journal of public relations research*, 6(1), 23–39.

Cooper-Chen, A. (1996). Public relations in Japan: beginning again for the first time. In Culbertson, H. and Chen, N. (Eds.) *International public relations: A comparative analysis*. Mahwah, NJ: Lawrence Erlbaum, pp. 223–239.

Couldry, N. (2005). Media rituals: Beyond functionalism. In Rothenbuhler, E. and Coman, M. (Eds.), *Media anthropology*. London: Sage, pp. 59–69.

Culbertson, H. and Chen, N. (Eds.) (1996). *International public relations: A comparative analysis*. Mahwah, NJ: Lawrence Erlbaum.

Curtin, P. and Gaither, K. (2005). Privileging identity, difference, and power: The circuit of culture as a basis for public relations theory. *Journal of public relations research*, 17(2), 91–115.

Curtin, P. and Gaither, K. (2007). *International public relations: Negotiating culture, identity and power*. London: Sage.

Dayan, D. (2005). The Pope at reunion: Hagiography, casting and imagination. In Rothenbuhler, E. and Coman, M. (Eds.), *Media anthropology*. London: Sage, pp. 165–177.

Denzin, N. and Lincoln, Y. (Eds.) (2000). *Handbook of qualitative research* (second edition). Thousand Oaks: Sage.

Ekechai, D. and Komolslevin, R. (1996). Public relations in Thailand: Its function and practitioners' roles. In Culbertson, H. and Chen, N. (Eds.) *International public relations: A comparative analysis*. Mahwah, NJ: Lawrence Erlbaum, pp. 155–170.

Giulianotti, R. (2001). Participant observation and research into football hooliganism: reflections on the problems of entrée and everyday risks. In Bryman, A. (Ed.), *Ethnography, Vol. II*. London: Sage, pp. 70–84.

Gonzalez, H. and Akel, D. (1996). Elections and Earth matters: Public relations in Costa Rica. In Culbertson, H. and Chen, N. (Eds.) *International public relations: A comparative analysis*. Mahwah, NJ: Lawrence Erlbaum, pp. 273–298.

Gordon, T., Holland, J. and Lehlma, E. (2001). Ethnographic research in educational settings. In Atkinson, P., Coffey, A., Delamont, S., Lofland, J. and Lofland, L. (Eds.), *Handbook of ethnography*. London: Sage, pp. 188–203.

Henslin, J. (2001). Studying deviance in four setting: Research experiences with cabbies, suicides, drug users and abortionees. In Bryman, A. (Ed.), *Ethnography, Vol. II*. London: Sage, pp. 3–34.

Hess, D. (2001). Ethnography and the development of science and technology studies. In Atkinson, P., Coffey, A., Delamont, S., Lofland, J. and Lofland, L. (Eds.), *Handbook of ethnography*. London: Sage, pp. 234–245.

Hobbs, D. (2001). Ethnography and the study of deviance. In Atkinson, P., Coffey, A., Delamont, S., Lofland, J. and Lofland, L. (Eds.), *Handbook of ethnography*. London: Sage, pp. 204–219.

Hodges, C. (2005). 'Relaciones humanas': The potential for PR practitioners as cultural intermediaries in Mexico City. Unpublished PhD thesis, University of Bournemouth, Bournemouth, UK.

Hodges, C. (2006). 'PRP culture': A framework for exploring public relations practitioners as cultural intermediaries. *Journal of communication management*, 10(1), 80–93.

Hofstede, G. (1980). *Culture's consequences*. Beverly Hills, CA: Sage.

Horsle, P. (2004). Norway. In van Ruler, B. and Verčič, D. (Eds.) *Public relations and communications management in Europe: A nation-by-nation introduction to public relations theory and practice*. Berlin: Mouton de Gruyter, pp. 261–276.

James, A. (2001). Ethnography in the study of children and childhood. In Atkinson, P., Coffey, A., Delamont, S., Lofland, J. and Lofland, L. (Eds.), *Handbook of ethnography*. London: Sage, pp. 246–257.

Kanso, A. (1996). Standardization versus localization: public relations implications of advertising practices in Finland. In Culbertson, H. and Chen, N. (Eds.) *International public relations: A comparative analysis*. Mahwah, NJ: Lawrence Erlbaum, pp. 299–316.

Keating, E. (2001). The ethnography of communication. In Atkinson, P., Coffey, A., Delamont, S., Lofland, J. and Lofland, L. (Eds.), *Handbook of ethnography*. London: Sage, pp. 285–301.

Kim, W. (1996). Positive and normative models of public relations and their relationship to job satisfaction among Korean public relations practitioners. Unpublished Master's thesis, University of Florida, Gainsville, USA.

Kim, Y. (2009). Professionalism and diversification: The evolution of public relations in South Korea. In Sriramesh, K. and Verčič, D. (Eds.) *The global public relations handbook: theory, research and practice*. London: Routledge, pp. 140–154.

Koper, E. (2004). United Kingdom. In van Ruler, B. and Verčič, D. (Eds.) *Public relations and communications management in Europe: A nation-by-nation introduction to public relations theory and practice*. Berlin: Mouton de Gruyter, pp. 467–484.

La Pastina, A. (2005). Audience ethnographies: A media engagement approach. In Rothenbuhler, E. and Coman, M. (Eds.), *Media anthropology*. London: Sage, pp. 139–148.

Lardellier, P. (2005). Ritual media: Historical perspectives and social functions. In Rothenbuhler, E. and Coman, M. (Eds.), *Media anthropology*. London: Sage, pp. 70–78.

Lehtonen, J. (2004). Finland. In van Ruler, B. and Verčič, D. (Eds.) *Public relations and communications management in Europe: A nation-by-nation introduction to public relations theory and practice*. Berlin: Mouton de Gruyter, pp. 107–120.

L'Etang, J. (2008). *Public relations: Concepts, practice and critique*. London: Sage.

L'Etang, J. (2010). "Making it real": Anthropological reflections on public relations, diplomacy and rhetoric. In Heath, R. (Ed.) *The Sage handbook of public relations*. Los Angeles: Sage, pp. 145–162.

L'Etang, J. (2011). Imagining public relations anthropology. In Edwards, L. and Hodges, C. (Eds.) *Public relations, society and culture*. London: Routledge, pp. 15–32.

L'Etang, J. (forthcoming 2012). Public relations, culture and anthropology: Towards an ethnographic research agenda. *Journal of public relations research*, 24(2).

Lule, J. (2005). News as myth: Daily news and eternal stories. In Rothenbuhler, E. and Coman, M. (Eds.), *Media anthropology*. London: Sage, pp. 101–110.

Macdonald, S. (2001). British social anthropology. In Atkinson, P., Coffey, A., Delamont, S., Lofland, J. and Lofland, L. (Eds.), *Handbook of ethnography*. London: Sage, pp. 60–79.

Mariampolski, H. (2006). *Ethnography for marketers: A guide to consumer immersion*. London: Sage.

Mortensen, M. (1996). Public relations: An alternative to reality? In Culbertson, H. and Chen, N. (Eds.) *International public relations: A comparative analysis*. Mahwah, NJ: Lawrence Erlbaum, pp. 317–340.

Motion, J. and Leitch, S. (1996). A discursive perspective from New Zealand: Another world view. *Public relations review*, 22, 297–309.

Murty, K. and Vyas, A. (2006). Cultural traits. In Birx, H. (Ed.), *Encylopedia of anthropology*. London: Sage, pp. 633–635.

Petersen, M. (2005). Performing media: Toward an ethnography of intertextuality. In Rothenbuhler, E. and Coman, M. (Eds.), *Media anthropology*. London: Sage, pp. 129–138.

Pieczka, M. (1997). Understanding in public relations. *Australian Journal of Communication*, 24(2), 65–80.

Pieczka, M. (2002). Public relations expertise deconstructed, *Media, Culture and Society*, 24, 301–323.

Pieczka, M. (2006a). Public relations expertise in practice. In L'Etang, J. and Pieczka, M. (Eds.), *Public relations: Critical debates and contemporary practice*. Mahwah, NJ: Lawrence Erlbaum Associates, pp. 279–302.

Pieczka, M. (2006b). 'Chemistry' and the public relations industry: An exploration of the concept of jurisdiction and issues arising. In L'Etang, J. and Pieczka, M. (Eds.), *Public relations: Critical debates and contemporary practice*. Mahwah, NJ: Lawrence Erlbaum Associates, pp. 303–330.

Pieczka, M. and L'Etang, J. (2001). Public relations and the question of professionalism. In Heath, R. (Ed.) *Handbook of public relations*. Thousand Oaks, Sage: pp. 223–237.

Rhee, Y. (2002). Global public relations: A cross-cultural study of the excellence theory in South Korea. *Journal of public relations research*, 14(3), 159–184.

Ritzer, G. (2000). *The McDonaldization of society*. Thousand Oaks, CA: Pine Forge Press.

Ritzer, G. (2002). *McDonaldization: The reader*. Thousand Oaks, CA: Pine Forge Press.

Rothenbuhler, E. (2005). The church of the cult of the individual. In Rothenbuhler, E. and Coman, M. (Eds.), *Media anthropology*. London: Sage, pp. 91–100.

van Ruler, B. (2004). The Netherlands. In van Ruler, B. and Verčič, D. (Eds.) *Public relations and communications management in Europe: A nation-by-nation introduction to public relations theory and practice*. Berlin: Mouton de Gruyter, pp. 277–290.

van Ruler, B. and Verčič, D. (Eds.) (2004). *Public relations and communications management in Europe: A nation-by-nation introduction to public relations theory and practice*. Berlin: Mouton de Gruyter.

Schudson, M. (2005). News as stories. In Rothenbuhler, E. and Coman, M. (Eds.), *Media anthropology*. London: Sage, pp. 121–128.

Smith, V. (2001). Ethnographies of work and the work of ethnographers. In Atkinson, P., Coffey, A., Delamont, S., Lofland, J. and Lofland, L. (Eds.), *Handbook of ethnography*. London: Sage, pp. 220–233.

Sriramesh, K. (2009a). Introduction. In Sriramesh, K. and Verčič, D. (Eds.), *The global public relations handbook: Theory, research, and practice*. London: Routledge, pp. xxxiii–xi.

Sriramesh, K. (2009b). The relationship between culture and public relations. In Sriramesh, K. and Verčič, D. (Eds.), *The global public relations handbook: Theory, research, and practice*. London: Routledge, pp. 47–61.

Sriramesh, K. and Verčič, D. (Eds.). (2009). *The global public relations handbook: Theory, research, and practice*. London: Routledge.

Sriramesh, K. and White, J. (1992). Societal culture and public relations. In Grunig, J. (Ed.) *Excellence in public relations and communication management*. Hillsdale, NJ: Lawrence Erlbaum, pp. 597–617.

Stevens, P. (2005). Witch doctor. In Birx, H. (Ed.) *Encyclopedia of anthropology*. Thousand Oaks: Sage, pp. 2317–2318.

Tedlock, B. (2000). Ethnography and ethnographic representation. In Denzin, N. and Lincoln, Y. (Eds.), *Handbook of qualitative research*. London: Sage, pp. 455–487.

Terry, V. (2005). Postcard from the Steppes: A snapshot of public relations and culture in Kazakhstan. *Public relations review*, 31, 31–36.

Thomas, G. (2005). The emergence of religious forms in television. In Rothenbuhler, E. and Coman, M. (Eds.), *Media anthropology*. London: Sage, pp. 79–90.

Tilson, D. and Alozie, E. (Eds.) (2004). *Towards the common good: Perspectives in international public relations*. Boston, MA: Pearson.

Van Maanen, J. (2001). The informant game: Selected aspects of ethnographic research in police organizations. In Bryman, A. (Ed.), *Ethnography, Vol. II*. London: Sage, pp. 234–251.

VanSlyke Turk, J. (1996). Romania: From publicate past to public relations future. In Culbertson, H. and Chen, N. (Eds.) *International public relations: A comparative analysis*. Mahwah, NJ: Lawrence Erlbaum, pp. 341–348.

Verčič, D., Grunig, L. and Grunig, J. (1996). Global and specific principles of public relations: Evidence from Slovenia. In Culbertson, H. and Chen, N. (Eds.) *International public relations: A comparative analysis*. Mahwah, NJ: Lawrence Erlbaum, pp. 31–66.

Vidich, A. and Lyman, S. (2000). Qualitative methods: Their history in sociology and anthropology. In Denzin, N. and Lincoln, Y. (Eds.) *Handbook of qualitative research* (2nd edn.). Thousand Oaks, CA: Sage, pp. 37–84.

Vujinovic, M. and Kruckeberg, D. (2010). The local, national and global challenges of public relations: A call for an anthropological approach to practicing public relations. In Heath, R. (Ed.) *The Sage handbook of public relations*. London: Sage.

Watson, M. (2005). *Anthropology and public relations: Annotated bibliography of recent and significant research of import to practitioners*. Published for the Institute for Public Relations, USA.

Weaver, K., Motion, J. and Roper, J. (2006). From propaganda to discourse (and back again): Truth, power, the public interest and public relations. In L'Etang, J. and Pieczka, M. (Eds.) *Public relations: Critical debates and contemporary practice*. Mahwah, NJ: Lawrence Erlbaum, pp. 7–22.

Wernick, A. (1991). *Promotional culture: advertising ideology and symbolic expression*. London: Sage.

White, J., L'Etang, J. and Moss, D. (2009). The United Kingdom: Advances in practice in a restless kingdom. In Sriramesh, K. and Verčič, D. (Eds.) *The global public relations handbook: Theory, research and practice*. London: Routledge, pp. 381–406.

Zelizer, B. (2005). Finding aids to the past: Bearing personal witness to traumatic public events. In Rothenbuhler, E. and Coman, M. (Eds.), *Media anthropology*. London: Sage, pp. 199–209.

14

CORPORATE PUBLIC RELATIONS AS A PROFESSIONAL CULTURE

Between Management and Journalism

Dejan Verčič and Jon White

Societal and corporate cultures have been recognized as important antecedents to public relations practice, and are affected by the practice (Banks, 1995; Macmanus, 2000; Sriramesh et al., 1992; Sriramesh and White, 1992). In this chapter we consider corporate public relations culture as an antecedent and as a consequence of public relations practice and its relation to the top management of contemporary organizations, primarily businesses. Is the professional culture of corporate public relations practitioners harmonized with corporate top management culture? We believe that it is not. Business and public relations cultures are different because of different traditions, because of different educational routes to both professions that attract different types of personality, and because of different types of remuneration (see, for example, early discussions of this in Mason, 1974, and Slatter, 1976). These differences have important consequences for the values that members of these two professions hold and therefore the different cultures they build. This cultural divide, however, is both positive and negative and in the final part of this chapter we will elaborate that.

Origins of Public Relations in Economics and Management

Public relations practice is, it is claimed, part of management, a management function. Professional associations (IABC, IPRA, PRSA, CIPR, the Global Alliance of Public Relations and Communication Management, etc.) and academics now argue that public relations is concerned with management of relationships and communication (van Ruler and Verčič, 2002, 2005; van Ruler et al., 2004; Verčič et al., 2001). Verčič and Grunig (2000) demonstrated that economics and strategic management are concerned with public relations problems and that "it is precisely via social science theories, such as public relations theory, that economic and managerial theories can gain practical relevance for everyday applications, a relevance that they often miss" (p. 9). Botan and Hazleton (2006) happily reported that, in 2003, in the US the mean annual wage for public relations managers was $74,750 and for purchasing managers $73,479 (according to data published by the U.S. Bureau of Labor Statistics). However, it would be wrong to conclude that public relations practitioners are full members of the managerial profession and that they share the same values as their top management colleagues. We argue that for several reasons public relations practitioners and general/strategic managers come from different traditions. The roles attract different types of people, and involve differences in education and remuneration. These differences lead on to different values and different cultures. We see this difference in culture as both productive and frustrating.

Origins of Public Relations in Journalism and Communication

Management studies are historically linked to the use of scientific methods in studying human affairs, for example, sociology in the study of bureaucratic organizations, scientific observation in attempts to study and manage work, and psychology in the study of human relations at work. The core idea underlying scientific management is that we can use the same methods for studying humans and their interrelationships as we do for studying nature (van Ruler and Verčič, 2005; Verčič and Grunig, 2000).

One of the founders of public relations, Edward Bernays, claimed the same for public relations, yet history took another turn. Public relations became linked to communication studies and is most commonly studied within colleges of journalism and communication. Compared with general/strategic management, which is seen as "hard" and linked to studies of military strategy and calculus, public relations is seen as "soft" and linked to studies of writing and "being good."

These different identities of the professions and of its academic formations attract different types of students (with public relations studies becoming nearly exclusively female) and producing different types of graduates. That public relations is not an equal member of the core management family of disciplines is seen in the fact that public relations managers are not trained within MBA studies as other "core" managers are. The reason for that is a very simple one: MBA schools are rated, among other things, by the initial salaries that graduates get when they move from the world of schooling to the world of work. Starting salaries in public relations are simply too low for MBA schools; if included, they would pull the average salary of graduates on a focal school downward and that would be reflected in the rating of the school.

Location of public relations studies within schools of communication and journalism has important consequences for formation of young professionals. They simply speak a different language from the one developed in core general/strategic management studies, and they miss fundamental tools to locate their work in general/strategic management frameworks, such as the frameworks provided by project and program management. This is the reason why public relations professionals regularly report "Linking business strategy and communication" as one of their most important issues today and for the future (see Zerfass et al., 2010).

Business Education and Public Relations

White and Verčič (2001) looked at how managers are educated in relation to public relations topics such as corporate citizenship, reputation, and building legitimacy and trust. They examined 100 MBA programs and found out that future managers are not educated to appreciate social environment problems they will encounter in their future jobs. They speculated that "there is a strong indication of one possible reason why managers do not appreciate the contribution public relations could bring to their work" (p. 199): they simply do not understand it. As public relations students are myopic about business realities of their work, so are managers myopic in relation to the social realities they face. McCracken (2009) argues for a new management role and a function: that of a Chief Culture Officer. We believe that this function is already occupied by corporate communication.

Business and Management Culture, and Public Relations

Hofstede (2010) describes levels of mental programming, in which culture provides one level of programming. Culture is a feature of, and emerges from, group life. Professional groups develop their own cultures, as do organizations. Culture is often described as "the way we do things around here," involving patterns of behavior that are based on values, beliefs, traditions, and practices. Hofstede's own studies were of differences in management practices, as these could be traced back to differences in national culture, whereby managers differ in their exercise of authority, their willingness to initiate and to innovate, and their attitudes towards rules.

Business and management cultures are based on priorities for business performance, and for monitoring and controlling performance to achieve business objectives. Authority is exercised and power used as means to ends relating to business performance.

Only recently have public relations practitioners come to see their practice as one that is to be assessed in terms of its contribution to business and organizational performance (Zerfass, 2010). Before, objectives of the practice were expressed in terms such as "doing good and gaining recognition," as a matter of developing mutual understanding between organizations and publics, or in terms of reputation management. The then Institute of Public Relations in the United Kingdom tried in the mid 1990s to recast the practice as one concerned with reputation management, whereby reputation is managed in attempts to influence behavior.

What has been missing in discussions of the role of public relations has been a focus on the achievement of *precise* business and organization objectives. Again using an example from the UK's Public Relations Consultants Association (PRCA), it is now recognized that evaluation of public relations activities must tie public relations activities to their contribution to the achievement of business and organizational objectives.

By reasons of their professional preparation, most practitioners do not have this focus in mind in their approach to practice. Practitioners still enter the practice in a number of ways, from prior careers in other areas, such as journalism, or from education programs that may focus on communication as the main task of practice. It is exceptional among groups of practitioners early in their careers to find many with specific business or management backgrounds.

Public relations practice still centers on communication, and related concerns for creativity in developing messages, or skillful use of media. As this chapter is being written, there is an obsession in the practice, reflected in the content of professional conferences, with the impact and use of social media. Public relations practitioners tend to find the details of business management—such as allocation and management of resources, and needs to calculate likely profitability of activities—of much less interest (White, 2001).

At the risk of oversimplifying cultural differences between the two groups, managers value performance, the achievement of results, and the exercise of managerial power and authority in the service of organizational and personal objectives. Public relations practitioners value social analyses pointing to the need for clever and creative use of communication to reach audiences and to influence behavior.

These differences are not irreconcilable, but have some consequences to be drawn out and recognized. First, managers as a group would benefit from expanding their consideration of performance to include the social impacts of performance, and from testing the social acceptability of hoped-for results. This would lead to improvements to management decision making and to courses of action that would, in the longer term, lead to more successful outcomes.

Managers will need more preparation for the social dimensions of their roles, and for the communication skills needed to be effective in modern management.

Public relations practitioners, it has been said by many commentators on the practice, need to become more comfortable with the language, preoccupations, and approaches of their colleagues in other areas of management

(Gregory and White, 2008). This has important implications for the preparation of public relations practitioners, and for the location of programs of public relations education in colleges and universities to ensure close links between education for practice, and education in business and management.

Conclusions

Public relations has been traditionally linked to journalism and it is in transition toward becoming more obviously a part of management. This transition has both positive and potentially negative consequences. By becoming a part of management, public relations should be drawing on a general management body of knowledge. For the individual practitioner, closer familiarity with this body of knowledge will lead to increased confidence and greater ability to work closely with managers at the most senior levels. Greater knowledge, confidence, and contribution will come to be reflected in budgets and salaries. However, while public relations draws closer to the management profession, it will also need to guard the unique perspective that it brings to the decision-making table. Public relations is specialized in bringing society ("publics") to the attention of organizations and their leaders. It is valuable as long as it can be detached enough from other specialized management functions so that it can sense, feel, and interpret that society ("publics"). From this perspective, public relations culture will never blend completely with general/strategic corporate management culture. Differences that enrich general management vision are needed today more than ever.

References

Banks, S. P. (1995). *Multicultural public relations: A social-interpretative approach*. Thousand Oaks, CA: Sage.

Botan, C. and Hazleton, V. (2006). Public relations in a new age. In Botan, C. and Hazleton, V. (Eds.), *Public relations theory II*. Mahwah, NJ: Lawrence Erlbaum Associates, pp. 1–18.

Gregory, A. and White, J. (2008). Introducing the Chartered Institute of Public Relations work on research and evaluation. In van Ruler, B., Tkalac Verčič, A., and Verčič, D. (Eds.), *Public relations metrics: Research and evaluation*. New York: Routledge, pp. 307–317.

Hofstede, G. (2010). *Culture and organizations: Software of the mind*. New York: McGraw Hill.

McCracken, G. (2009). *Chief culture officer: How to create a living, breathing corporation*. New York: Basic Books.

Macmanus, T. (2000). Public relations: The cultural dimension. In Moss, D., Verčič, D., and Warnaby, G. (Eds.), *Perspectives on public relations research*. London: Routledge, pp. 159–178.

Mason, R. S. (1974). What's a public relations director for, anyway. *Harvard Business Review*, September–October, 120–126.

van Ruler, B. and Verčič, D. (2005). Reflective communication management, future ways for public relations research. In Kalbfleisch, P. (ed.), *Communication yearbook 29*. Mahwah, NJ: Lawrence Erlbaum Associates, pp. 239–273.

van Ruler, B. and Verčič, D. (2002). *The Bled manifesto on public relations*. Ljubljana: Pristop.

van Ruler, B., Verčič, D., Bütschi, G., and Flodin, B. (2004). A first look for parameters of public relations in Europe. *Journal of Public Relations Research*, 16, 35–63.

Slatter, S. P. (1976). Strategic planning for public relations. *Long Range Planning*, 13, 57–60.

Sriramesh, K. and White, J. (1992). Societal culture and public relations. In Grunig, J. E. (Ed.), *Excellence in public relations and communication management*. Hillsdale, NJ: Lawrence Erlbaum Associates, pp. 597–614.

Sriramesh K., Grunig, J. E., and Buffington, J. (1992). Corporate culture and public relations. In Grunig, J. E. (Ed.), *Excellence in public relations and communication management*. Hillsdale, NJ: Lawrence Erlbaum Associates, pp. 577–595.

Verčič, D. and Grunig, J. E. (2000). The origins of public relations theory in economics and strategic management. In: Moss, D., Verčič, D., and Warnaby, G. (Eds.), *Perspectives on public relations research*. London: Routledge, pp. 9–58.

Verčič, D., van Ruler, B., Bütschi, G., and Flodin, B. (2001). On the definition of public relations: A European view. *Public Relations Review*, 27, 373–387.

White J. (2001). Fee setting in public relations consultancies: A study of consultancy and client views of current practice and recommendations to contribute to the development of best practice. A report prepared for the PRCA, London.

White, J. and Verčič, D. (2001). An examination of possible obstacles to management acceptance of public relations' contribution to decision making, planning and organization functioning. *Journal of Communication Management*, 6, 194–200.

Zerfass, A. (2010). *Assuring rationality and transparency in corporate communication: The role of communication controlling from a management point of view*. Paper presented at the 13th International Public Relations Research Conference, Miami, FL.

Zerfass, A., Tench, R., Verhoeven, P., Verčič, D., and Moreno, A. (2010). *European Communication Monitor 2010: Status quo and challenges for communication management in Europe—Results of an empirical survey in 46 countries*. Brussels: EACD, EUPRERA.

15

PUBLIC RELATIONS FIRMS AND THEIR THREE OCCUPATIONAL CULTURES

Dejan Verčič

Public relations practitioners work in public relations firms, in-house in companies or other organizations, or as freelancers (self-employed practitioners). This chapter focuses on people working in public relations firms and their cultures. There are three types of public relations firms. Every public relations firm incorporates more characteristics of one type than the others. Each type nurtures a different culture of public relations and influences the different ways that the practitioners experience public relations work, as well as the different ways in which clients and everybody else perceive the public relations practice.

The first type of public relations firm is the public relations agency. They sell the experience of their staff: mostly the journalistic and editorial competencies of ex-journalists and ex-editors in the publicity or media relations market. Their culture is a publicist, journalistic culture, largely influenced by the previous socialization of their personnel in media organizations.

The second type of public relations firm is the public relations service. They sell efficiency in the production and distribution of communication media. Although they sell functionally similar services to the public relations agencies, their approach is detached from the journalist media ethos. Unlike agencies, they sell not experience but value for money. Their employees are predominantly young women who have just graduated or are still at school. Their culture is a business culture and predominantly commercial (buy cheap and sell expensive).

The third type of public relations firm is the public relations consultancy. They sell expertise built on research and education and they have a broader sense of their responsibilities, not only to clients and owners but also to their internal associates and to society at large—at least in an idealized universe (I am not naive here and I am fully aware of management consultancy's darker sides as reported by Craig, 2005, and Kihn, 2005). They employ well-educated and aspiring staff with clear expectations about their career path towards the top of the consultancy sector. They have a professional culture.

We can illustrate the differences between the three types of public relations firm using the 7-S framework developed by the McKinsey Company, a global management consulting firm, and popularized by Peters and Waterman (1982). The framework has seven components, each starting with the letter S: strategy, structure, systems, skills, staff, style, and shared culture (Table 15.1).

Public relations agencies have opportunistic strategies: they follow crises to help corporate 'victims' define their public positions or search for opportunities to place their stories in the mass media. Their structures are simple and informal, suiting the personal styles of their (ex-)journalist founders. The systems are loose, as ex-journalists manage by necessity. The basic skills that the agencies nurture are writing and editing, combined with networking that, on the one hand, facilitates the publication of stories in the media and, on the other, helps gain new business. The staff is composed of a core of ex-journalists and ex-editors surrounded by supporting staff. The style is informal, which suits media people. Shared values include an appreciation of craftsmanship and developing good stories, which could be considered art in themselves. (Many of the terms used in this section are based on the writings of Maister, 2003, 2004; Mills and Friesen, 2001; Mintzberg, 1989; Quinn, Anderson, and Finkelstein, 2001; Sennett, 2006.)

Public relations services use advertising value equivalent (AVE) as their strategy (which reflects the fact that many of them are owned by advertising or media communication conglomerates): media produced and distributed by

TABLE 15.1 Three Types of Public Relations Firms in the 7-S Framework

	Agency	*Service*	*Consultancy*
Strategy	Opportunism	Advertising Value Equivalent	Develop, deploy, grow
Structure	Simple, informal	MP3	Operating adhocracy
Systems	Loose	Contingent	Leverage
Skills	Writing, editing, networking	Flexibility, specialization	Conceptual, analytical, consulting
Staff	Ex-journalists and ex-editors	Young women and managers	Hyper-selected graduates
Style	Creative	Organization and control	Empathic and visionary
Shared values	Craftsmanship	Efficiency, profitability	Perfection

Source: Created by author using elements of the McKinsey 7-S framework (Peters and Waterman, 1982).

public relations services are cheaper than publicity generated by advertising, which has to pay for media space (more on that below). Their structure can be described as like an MP3: highly flexible and easy to be reproduced, but with a limited number of operations in whatever order. Systems are therefore contingent, yet extant and accountable. Skills that are valued in the staff, which is predominantly young and female (and thus relatively less costly), include both flexibility and specialization. The style is organization and control, enabling the creation of shared values of efficiency and profitability.

Public relations consultancies have strategies for developing ideas and people, deploying them in dealing with problems and forwarding their careers and the firm as a whole. The structure is an operational adhocracy, in which different projects are led by the knowledgeable people who best suit the clients. The systems are based on leverage, which allows consultancies to have the correct mix of more and less expert people (who are also more and less expensive) working on projects, thus also making business sense in terms of cost rationality. The skills needed in such an environment are conceptual, analytical, and consulting. The staff is carefully selected to form an elite and has studied public relations, business, or related subjects at the graduate level. The leadership style is emphatic about nurturing talent and cultivating innovation. Shared values are about perfection, doing the best possible thing at the right time and place.

Table 15.1 is not a classification scheme that exclusively and comprehensively allows us to place empirical firms into these three categories. It is a typology in that it identifies the ideal forms of public relations firms with the underlying assumption that empirical public relations firms perform better if they are close to their paradigms and, inversely, that their performance suffers if they exhibit more characteristics of one type, yet try to behave like another type. For example, it is dangerous for agencies to behave like services or consultancies, for services to behave like agencies or consultancies, and for consultancies to behave like agencies or firms. This chapter simply outlines a theoretical framework for analyzing public relations firms in the typology research tradition, which is common in management (Doty and Glick, 1994) and has already been introduced into public relations research (van Ruler, 2004a).

"Culture Eats Strategy for Breakfast"

In the *Encyclopedia of Public Relations*, Hinrichsen wrote the entry entitled "Public relations agency" and her description begins: "A public relations agency, or firm, is a company hired by another organization to provide certain services. Some 3,000 or more public relations counselling firms operate in the United States" (Hinrichsen, 2005: 685). It is important to observe that the *Encyclopedia* entry is for "Public relations agency" alone (not for firms or consultancies). The same author uses the same term in the *Handbook of Public Relations*, edited by the same editor for the same publisher. (In *Lesly's Handbook of Public Relations and Communications* [Lesly, 1998], one can only read about "public relations counsels"—which also stands for public relations agencies and services.) Two paragraphs below the initial explanation of the public relations agency, Hinrichsen writes:

> Some companies prefer to use the term *firm* to denote their emphasis on counselling and strategic planning and to differentiate themselves from advertising agencies. Public relations is a management team concept that the term *agent* or *agency* doesn't imply. Many, though, use the terms interchangeably.
>
> (Hinrichsen, 2005: 685)

As we presented in Table 15.1 above, the distinctions between agencies, services, and consultancies are more than just about symbolic labels: they differ in the functions they perform for clients, the people they employ, and how they work. For that reason, I advocate terminological precision instead of creative indeterminism. The saying that "Culture eats strategy for breakfast" is often attributed to the management guru Peter Drucker, and this sentence perfectly summarizes why it is important to distinguish between the different types of public relations firms and their corresponding cultures. Agencies and services cannot develop consulting talent, and good consulting work can never be cheap.

From a cultural point of view, words matter. If people use a new term to differentiate from an earlier one, that makes sense to them and it is a cultural practice *par excellence*: "Culture is defined and bounded by the subjective experience of communities of persons who share an understanding that some important aspects of their lives differentiates them from other groups" (Banks, 1995: 21). It is *"systems of meaning that group members acquire through experiential apprenticeship"* (Banks, 1995: 10, italics in original), or, as Hofstede (1984: 23) put it, it is a "collective programming of the mind that distinguishes the members of one human group from another." Cultures are values and practices that hold people together (Sennett, 2006). They can refer to social cultures or organizations as cultural entities (organizations "have" cultures or even "are" cultures, hence study of organizational culture; MacManus, 2000).

This chapter proposes to distinguish between agencies, services, and consultancies as three different types of public relations firms. They are all service enterprises, but they are different in who they are, what they sell, and how they do it. Agencies primarily sell experience, services sell efficiency, and consultancies sell expertise. Agencies have publicity cultures, services have business cultures, and consultancies have professional cultures. These cultures are not mutually exclusive and can coexist in the same firm—though, if they do, one always dominates the other two. If public relations firms develop strategies that are contrary to their culture, their strategies will fail—unless there is a profound exercise in change management involved that transforms the very culture of the firm.

Public Relations Agencies: Publicity Culture

The public relations industry was conceived by ex-journalists. Whether the first public relations business entity was the Publicity Bureau founded in 1900 by George Michaelis (Cutlip, 1994) or the office named Parker & Lee after its owners Ivy Lee and George Parker (Hiebert, 2005) in 1904 is an interesting question in itself, but both entities were offspring of journalism and at least one of them can claim to be the first public relations agency (although the term "public relations" itself was first used in its present meaning 20 years later by Edward Bernays, so it is possible to claim that he is the founding father of modern public relations; Tye, 1998). About 100 years after Michaelis and Parker & Lee started their businesses, Hinrichsen (2001: 451) began her look inside a contemporary public relations agency with the following image:

> In rows of cubicles, smartly dressed young people talk to journalists on the phone, tap at their computer keyboards or pore over spreadsheets. Occasionally, one hears running feet in the hallway, especially if it is time for the express mail pickup.

The majority of public relations work performed in agencies today is still related to the media and the generation of publicity. Journalists and editors still exit their profession to capitalize on their experience in public relations as media relations and crisis communication specialists (e.g., Ansell, 2010). Bentele and Wehmeier (2009) give estimates for Germany that around a third of the current public relations practitioners entered this occupational field from journalism (see also Bentele and Junghänel, 2004; Ruler 2004b, 2009, for the Netherlands).

The culture in public relations agencies is built around values that are shared with editorial people in the media on the market. Good writing and visuals, attracting the attention of audiences, spinning stories for better ratings—all these can be said to belong to both public relations agencies and market journalism. The core people in public relations agencies, often their founders, were first inculturated and socialized in mass media organizations before moving into public relations, bringing the values of their original employment with them.

Public Relations Services: Business Culture

After World War II, public relations developed into a serious business sector that, by the end of the twentieth century, had overtaken many traditional industries in terms of human and financial indicators. The largest public relations company in terms of turnover, Burson–Marsteller, was created in 1953 (Harold Burson studied journalism, but served during World War II in the U.S. Army's psychological warfare operations [PSYOPS], an experience similar to that of Dan Edelman, the founder of the largest independent public relations company today; Morley, 2009). In 1985, it became the first in the industry to reach US$100 million in revenues. In 1992, it was the first to reach $200 million. By 2000, it was employing over 1,600 people in a network spanning 34 countries with 24 offices in the Asia/Pacific area, 35 in Europe, the Middle East, and Africa, 19 in North America, and 10 in Latin America (sic) (Rudgard, 2003). The U.S. Council of Public Relations Firms estimates that around 20,000 public relations practitioners work for public relations firms in the United States and more than 40,000 worldwide (Hinrichsen, 2005). At the same time, 5,000 U.S. companies and 2,000 trade associations have public relations departments and some of them employ as many as 800 people. Surveys of the industry in Europe show that between a fifth and a quarter of all practitioners work for firms or operate as freelancers (being the largest group after corporate practitioners, followed by the government/political and non-profit/association sectors; see Zerfass et al., 2009, 2010). For the US, some estimate that they form a relative majority with over 40 per cent of all practitioners (*PRWeek*, cited in Wilcox et al., 2011: 28). Veronis Schuler Stevenson's *Communications Industry Forecast, 2009–2013* estimates the value of the U.S. public relations market at €4 billion (reported in ICCO, 2010).

This growth of public relations into a business (Hinrichsen, 2001) was slow for its first 100 years or so. Then, in the mid 1970s, large advertising agencies and marketing conglomerates began buying into the public relations market and, by the late 1980s, only one out of the top 10 public relations agencies was left independent (Edelman). With this takeover came a greater need to differentiate them from advertising agencies and, for that reason, in the 1980s many public relations agencies changed their titles to public relations firms (Broom, 2008). The simultaneous opening up of media markets with the corresponding fragmentation of media audiences has been moving marketing communication from advertising towards public relations-generated publicity in editorial areas of the media (Tench and Yeomans, 2006). This is widely popularized by marketing and management bestsellers (Ries and Ries, 2002; Lawson, 2006) and marketing academics (Kotler, 2003). Public relations-generated editorials are often promoted as "free publicity" or "free advertising," thus giving the impression of good value for money. A marketing communication textbook defines publicity in this context as the "non-personal stimulation of the demand for a product, service, place, idea, person, or organization through the unpaid placement of significant news regarding the product in the print or broadcast medium" (Boone et al., 2010: 521). Demand for publicity in marketing communication is steadily growing and globalizing, as the International Communications Consultancy Organisation observes in its *World Report* for 2010 (ICCO, 2010).

The American Association of National Advertisers has even found public relations-generated publicity to be the most effective of all the marketing communication techniques (Cooper, n.d.). By the 1990s, advertising companies that were larger siblings of public relations agencies had bought all but one of the top 10 public relations firms. Public relations as a market service became an addendum to the large advertising and marketing services conglomerates that dominate the global market: according to its website (http://www.wpp.com/wpp/companies/) on 25 November 2010, WPP Group Plc, the largest marketing communication conglomerate in the world, owned 464 public relations offices around the world, including the brands Burson–Marsteller, Carl Byor & Associates, Chime Communications, Cohn & Wolfe, Hill & Knowlton, and Ogilvy Public Relations; Omnicom Group owned Fleishman–Hillard, Ketchum, and Porter Novelli; while the Interpublic Group owned Weber Shandwick—all large and respected multinational public relations firms. In 2009, two of the largest advertising festivals included public relations among their competition categories: the Cannes Lions Festival (http://www.canneslions.com/)—which described itself in 2010 as the "international festival of creativity"—and the Golden Drum (http://www.goldendrum.com/)—self-described as the "advertising festival and media meeting."

This amalgamation of public relations into the advertising world brought an easy way to demonstrate value for money, called advertising value equivalent (AVE)—which is a calculation of the financial worth of media space "gained" as an editorial through media relations if it had been purchased for advertisements. Although public relations associations oppose the use of AVE as a measure of the value of public relations (Global Alliance et al., 2010), its simplicity keeps its alive. It is easily understood by people used to advertising.

Public relations services firms are not only involved in the generation of publicity. Some are full-service agencies, offering everything from media relations to lobbying, corporate, consumer, community, internal, and financial communication. Many are specialized in event management or interactive media. Some are no more than temporary employment agencies used to outsource technical work in the area from corporations to cheaper and more flexible establishments. Nevertheless, whatever they do, they are using the cost of their service to compete, first against advertising agencies and then among themselves.

In the arms of advertising and marketing conglomerates, public relations firms have developed into public relations services. Their focus is value for money and their cultures are business cultures. Many of them operate as communication factories with a specialized but flexible workforce, young and mostly female, organized and supervised by professional managers who are responsible for the efficiency and profitability of the business.

Public Relations Consultancies: Professional Cultures

Management consultancies in general sell ideas to management. They are about innovation and thought leadership in management (Laud, 2004). When Edward Bernays invented the term *public relations counsel* in the 1920s, it was to apply the notion of engineering to the management of public relationships between organizations and the various stakeholders on which they depend for their existence (Bernays, 1923, 1928a,b, 1955, 1965, 1986). To Bernays, public relations was a sort of applied social psychology.

There were many counsels who, like Bernays, saw public relations as being founded on social sciences, but it was not until 1980s that research and academic teaching in public relations developed (Howard, 2010). Drawing from other social sciences was simply not enough to ground a separate profession:

> Biology, chemistry and physics do not make up medical science, much less a physician. In the same way, psychology, sociology, communication and political science do not make up public relations science, much less a competent practitioner and even less so a competent public relations organization.
>
> (van Ruler et al., 2008: 4)

Observing that "[a]bstract knowledge has been considered a defining feature of the professions by all schools of thought in the sociology of professions," in the middle of the 2000s Pieczka still notes "the fragmentary and poorly developed body of abstract knowledge in public relations and its weak institutional basis in academia" (Pieczka, 2006: 279–280): "If we cannot assume that public relations practice is based on the application of a body of abstract knowledge, then what is it based on?"

One impetus for the growth of public relations as a form of communication management throughout the twentieth century can be said to be linked to the growth of the intangibles in the economy (Verčič, 2002). Public relations firms saw an opportunity to develop and sell "reputation management" (Fombrun and Meyer, 2004). The multinational public relations firm Shandwick (later Weber Shandwick) was trying to establish itself as the leader in this exercise. A similar impetus was the conceptualization of "intellectual capital," composed of human, structural, and customer capital (Stewart, 1997).

A new type of multinational public relations firm is represented by Financial Dynamics, which described itself on its website on 25 November 2010 as "the world's leading strategic communication firm" (http://www.fd.com). It employed 700 people in 25 countries, but, unlike the majority of large public relations multinationals, it was not owned by an advertising or a marketing conglomerate. It was owned by FTI Consulting, which had a very different human profile:

> Within our ranks, we have forensic accountants; former chief executives and political leaders; Nobel laureates; former SEC professionals; top-ranking economists; certified turnaround professionals; interim management professionals; corporate investigation specialists; banking and securities professionals; certified public accountants; chartered financial analysts; and corporate, financial and crisis communications specialists.
>   (http://www.fticonsulting.com/about-fti/who-we-are.aspx)

In such an environment, it is much easier to behave like a normal management consultancy, which Maister (2004: 18) characterized by saying that: "People do not join consulting for *jobs*, but for *careers*. They have strong expectations of progressing through the organization."

Public relations consultancies respond to corporate, government, and nongovernmental organization needs at the top level. Today's organizations can employ staff to do all kinds of public relations work. If that is so, it is only natural that those public relations services that are not feasible for them to do in-house will be bought on the market (Forman, 2002) because they can be bought cheaper or because their internal growth would be too expensive to defend. Cheaper services are provided by public relations service firms and those that are too expensive for internal growth by consultancies.

Public relations consultancies have professional cultures of striving for perfection in delivering advice to clients, and in quality of work carried out to implement the solutions set out in the advice offered. To work at this level, consultancies must be able to call, first of all, on strong conceptual competence that allows the understanding of the client's situations and the basis for clear solutions. Only based on that can analytical work commence, which can guide professional work. However, the general environment of public relations is only just beginning to support that type of work by providing graduates in public relations and scientific research in the field (van Ruler et al., 2008).

The future of public relations firms depends on their capability to transform themselves into management consultancies by the better selection of their entrants, by training them in consultancy and negotiation skills, and by unifying their approach to setting fees, which is currently undermining normal profitability through overservicing (White and Myers, 2001).

The Eclecticism of Public Relations Cultures

The three types of public relations firms—agencies, services, and consultancies—with three different cultures—journalistic, business, and professional—are idealized classifications. As such, they do not exist in their pure forms in the real world. We can construct them in our heads as an abstraction and we can empirically test them as theories. In front of us, we always meet public relations companies that combine traits belonging to all three types, usually with one simply more prevalent than the other two.

Our differentiation of cultural types in public relations also enables us to form propositions on their layering. Two such propositions can be deduced from public relations literature:

1 *Historical proposition on public relations industry cultures:* The three public relations cultures—media, business, and professional—are consecutive in the dominance they can claim among public relations firms. Publicity culture was dominant in the form of public relations agencies in the first half of the twentieth century, business culture began taking over the dominance in the form of public relations firms in the second half of the twentieth century, and professional culture is claiming dominance in the form of public relations consultancies in the new millennium. Not that consultancies dominate in numbers; empirically they are in minority, but the majority of firms would like to be (like) them, or even claim, without any basis, that they are.

However, history is far from purity and linearity. Although the dominant forms—agency, service, or consultancy—may have been following each other in dominance, there is a real conflict over words, power, and money on the ground.

2 *The hierarchical proposition on public relations industry cultures:* All three public relations cultures—media, business, and professional—coexist in public relations consultancies but they are related to differences in positions within them. Publicity culture exists at the lower levels among the public relations technicians, business cultures in the middle level among the public relations middle-level managers, and professional culture at the top. This would be consistent with how efficiency, experience, and expertise are sold in management consultancies in general (Maister, 2003).

As already quoted above, Hinrichsen (2001: 451) begins her look inside an agency with the following image:

In rows of cubicles, smartly dressed young people talk to journalists on the phone, tap at their computer keyboards or pore over spreadsheets. Occasionally, one hears running feet in the hallway, especially if it is time for the express mail pickup.

But she continues: "Meanwhile, behind closed doors, the senior counsellors advise clients on a crisis, a pending merger or a major shareholder announcement. This is a public relations firm."

However, it is important to note that management (Hofstede, 1984) and public relations are fundamentally North American concepts (Verčič and Grunig, 2000). It has been documented that, in Europe, what is referred to here as public relations exists under different names and comes from different sources, if not from the Old Greek sophists in the fifth century BC, then at least from the Ages of Reason and Enlightenment in the seventeenth and eighteenth centuries (van Ruler and Verčič, 2004a; cf. van Ruler and Verčič, 2004b; Sriramesh and Verčič, 2009). Even as the term *public relations* is culturally loaded with its origins in U.S. English (van Ruler and Verčič, 2002; van Ruler et al., 2001a,b, 2004). This has direct effects on the progress of the professionalization of public relations outside the US and, again, more studies are needed to get a clearer picture. Societal (public) legitimization is crucial for any economic or political enterprise to succeed (Verčič, 2008) and public relations firms are no exception. Although London established itself as an important center for headquarters of public relations firms, the sector is largely dominated by U.S. companies. Fifty percent or more of public relations revenue is generated by the top 10 firms and public relations firms owned by Omnicom (U.S. based), Interpublic (U.S. based) and WPP (UK based), each earning about US$1 billion in annual fees (Morley, 2009). It is impossible to overestimate the influence of the U.S. public relations firms. They are globally American, in the same way as Coca-Cola or Disney.

Conclusions

Public relations firms exhibit multiple cultures. They are varied and they are further differentiated each in itself. It is possible to explore the different subcultures of people working in the same public relations firm, just as it is possible to observe the major types of public relations firms that operate in the national, regional, and global markets. There are public relations agencies that sell experience in publicity making, often employing former prominent journalist and editors. There are public relations services that efficiently produce and distribute traditional and new media for corporate, government, and nonprofit clients. And there are public relations consultancies selling expertise in an emerging discipline of public relations, communication management, or strategic communication. Public relations agencies have a publicist culture, whereas public relations services have a business culture, and public relations consultancies have a professional culture. These are the three paradigms of public relations firms.

References

Ansell, J. (2010). *When the headline is you: An insider's guide to handling the media.* San Francisco, CA: Jossey-Bass.

Banks, S. P. (1995). *Multicultural public relations: A social-interpretative approach.* Thousand Oaks, CA: Sage.

Bentele, G. and Junghänel, I. (2004). Germany. In van Ruler, B. and Verčič, D. (Eds.), *Public relations and communication management in Europe: A nation-by-nation introduction to public relations industry theory and practice.* Berlin: Mouton de Gruyter, pp. 261–275.

Bentele, G. and Wehmeier, S. (2009). From literary bureaus to a modern profession: The development and current structure of public relations in Germany. In Sriramesh, K. and Verčič, D. (Eds.), *The global public relations handbook: Theory, research, and practice. Expanded and revised edition.* New York: Routledge, pp. 407–429.

Bernays, E. L. (1923). *Crystallizing public opinion.* New York: Boni and Liveright.

Bernays, E. L. (1928a). Manipulating public opinion: The why and the how. *American Journal of Sociology*, 33, 968–971.

Bernays, E. L. (1928b). *Propaganda.* New York: Horace Liveright.

Bernays, E. L. (Ed.) (1955). *The engineering of consent.* Norman, OK: University of Oklahoma Press.

Bernays, E. L. (1965). *Biography of an idea: Memoirs of public relations counsel.* New York: Simon and Schuster.

Bernays, E. L. (1986). *The later years: Public relations insights, 1956–1986.* Rhinebeck, NY: H & M Publishers.

Broom, G. M. (2008). *Cutlip and Center's effective public relations* (10th edn.). Upper Saddle River, NJ: Prentice-Hall.

Boone, L. E., Kurtz, D. E., MacKenzie, H. F., and Snow, K. (2010). *Contemporary marketing* (2nd Canadian edn.). Toronto: Nelson Education.

Cooper, A. (n.d.). Ten reasons marketers are moving money to PR. A speech published by on the website of the Council of Public Relations Firms. Retrieved from http://www.prfirms.org/_data/n_0001/resources/live/Cooper%20Top%2010.pdf.

Craig, D. (2005). *Rip-off! The scandalous inside story of the management consulting money machine.* London: Original Book Company.

Cutlip, S. M. (1994). *The unseen power: Public relations, a history.* Hillsdale, NJ: Lawrence Erlbaum Associates.

Doty, D. H. and Glick, W. H. (1994). Typologies as a unique form of theory building: Toward improved understanding and modelling. *Academy of Management Review*, 19, 230–251.

Fombrun, C. J. and Meyer, S. D. (2004). Reputation consulting. In Fombrun, C. J. and Nevins, M. D. (Eds.), *The advice business: Essential tools and models for management consulting.* Upper Saddle River, NJ: Pearson, pp. 345–359.

Forman, J. (2002). *Corporate communication: At the center of the global organisation.* A research report. Sponsored by the Council of Public Relations Firms. Retrieved from http://www.prfirms.org/index.cfm?fuseaction=Page.viewPage&pageId=613 &parentID=474.

Global Alliance, ICCO, IPR, PRSA, and AMEC US. (2010). *Barcelona declaration of measurement principles*. Barcelona, Spain: Global Alliance, ICCO, IPR, PRSA, and AMEC US. Retrieved from http://www.amecorg.com/newsletter/BarcelonaPrinciplesforPRMeasurementslides.pdf.

Hiebert, E. (2005). Lee, Ivy. In Heath, R. L. (Ed.), *Encyclopedia of public relations, Vol. 1*. Thousand Oaks, CA: Sage, pp. 482–486.

Hinrichsen, C. L. (2001). Best practices in the public relations agency business. In Heath, R. L. (Ed.), *Handbook of public relations*. Thousand Oaks, CA: Sage, pp. 451–459.

Hinrichsen, C. L. (2005). Public relations agency. In Heath, R. L. (Ed.), *Encyclopedia of public relations, Vol. 2*. Thousand Oaks, CA: Sage, pp. 685–687.

Hofstede, G. (1984). *Culture's consequences: International difference in work related values*. London: Sage.

Howard, J. (2010). The evolution of UK PR consultancies 1985–2010. In Watson, T. (Ed.), *The proceedings of the first international history of public relations conference*. Bournemouth, UK: Bournemouth University, pp. 156–187. Retrieved from http://media.bournemouth.ac.uk/downloads/IHPRC-2010-Proceedings.pdf.

ICCO. (2010). *ICCO world report, 2010*. n.p.: ICCO. Retrieved from http://www.prfirms.org/_data/n_0001/resources/live/ICCO%20World%20Report%202010.pdf.

Kihn, M. (2005). *House of lies: How management consultants steal your watch and then tell you the time*. New York: Warner Business Books.

Kotler, P. (2003). *Marketing insights from A to Z: 80 concepts every manager needs to know*. Hoboken, NJ: John Wiley & Sons.

Laud, R. L. (2004). Innovation: The growth engine of consulting. In Fombrun, C. J. and Nevins M. D. (Eds.), *The advice business: Essential tools and models for management consulting*. Upper Saddle River, NJ: Pearson, pp. 42–55.

Lawson, R. (2006). *The PR buzz factor: How using public relations can boost your business*. London: Kogan Page.

Lesly, P. (1998). The place and function of the public relations counsel. In Lesly, P. (Ed.), *Lesly's handbook of public relations and communications* (5th edn.). Lincolnwood (Chicago), IL: NTC Business Books, pp. 697–715.

MacManus, T. (2000). Public relations: The cultural dimension. In Moss, D., Verčič, D., and Warnaby, G. (Eds.), *Perspectives on public relations research*. London: Routledge, pp. 159–178.

Maister, D. (2003). *Managing the professional service firm*. London: Simon & Schuster.

Maister, D. H. (2004). The anatomy of a consulting firm. In Fombrun, C. J. and Nevins M. D. (Eds.), *The advice business: Essential tools and models for management consulting*. Upper Saddle River, NJ: Pearson, pp. 17–31.

Mills, D. Q. and Friesen, G. B. (2001). Empowerment. In Crainer, S. and Dearlove, D. (Eds.), *Financial Times handbook of management* (2nd edn.). London: Pearson Education, pp. 325–342.

Mintzberg, H. (1989). *Mintzberg on management: Inside our strange world of organizations*. New York: Free Press.

Morley, M. (2009). How to manage your global reputation: The public relations agency. In Sriramesh, K. and Verčič, D. (Eds.), *The global public relations handbook: Theory, research, and practice. Expanded and revised edition*. New York: Routledge, pp. 861–869.

Peters, T. J., and Waterman, R. H., Jr. (1982). *In the search of excellence: Lessons from America's best-run companies*. London: Harper & Row.

Pieczka, M. (2006). Public relations expertise in practice. In L'Etang, J. and Pieczka, M. (Eds.), *Public relations: Critical debates and contemporary practice*. Mahwah, NJ: Lawrence Erlbaum Associates, pp. 279–301.

Quinn, J. B., Anderson, P., and Finkelstein, S. (2001). Leveraging intellect. In Crainer, S. and Dearlove, D. (Eds.), *Financial Times handbook of management* (2nd edn.). London: Pearson Education, pp. 587–594.

Ries, A. and Ries, L. (2002). *The fall of advertising & the rise of PR*. New York: HarperCollins.

Rudgard, A. (2003). Serving public relations globally: The agency perspective. In Sriramesh, K. and Verčič, D. (Eds.), *The global public relations handbook: Theory, research, and practice. Expanded and revised edition*. New York: Routledge, pp. 459–477.

van Ruler, B. (2004a). The communication grid: Introduction of a model of basic communication strategies in public relations practice. *Public Relations Review*, 30, 123–143.

van Ruler, B. (2004b). The Netherlands. In van Ruler, B. and Verčič, D. (Eds.), *Public relations and communication management in Europe: A nation-by-nation introduction to public relations theory and practice*. Berlin: Mouton de Gruyter, pp. 261–275.

van Ruler, B. (2009). Public relations in the polder: The case of the Netherlands. In Sriramesh, K. and Verčič, D. (Eds.), *The global public relations handbook: Theory, research, and practice. Expanded and Revised Edition*. New York: Routledge, pp. 449–470.

van Ruler, B. and Verčič, D. (2002). *The Bled manifesto*. Ljubljana: Pristop Communications.

van Ruler, B. and Verčič, D. (2004a). Overview of public relations and communication management in Europe. In van Ruler, B. and Verčič, D. (Eds.), *Public relations and communication management in Europe: A nation-by-nation introduction to public relations theory and practice*. Berlin: Mouton de Gruyter, pp. 1–11.

van Ruler, B. and Verčič, D. (Eds.). (2004b). *Public relations and communication management in Europe: A nation-by-nation introduction to public relations theory and practice*. Berlin: Mouton de Gruyter.

van Ruler, B., Verčič, D., Bütschi, G., and Flodin, B. (2001a). On definition of public relations: a European view. *Public Relations Review*, 27, 373–387.

van Ruler, B., Verčič, D., Flodin, B., and Bütschi, G. (2001b). Public relations in Europe: A kaleidoscopic picture. *Journal of Communication Management*, 6, 166–175.

van Ruler, B., Verčič, D., Bütschi, G., and Flodin, B. (2004). A first look for parameters of public relations in Europe. *Journal of Public Relations Research*, 16, 35–63.

van Ruler, B., Tkalac Verčič, A., and Verčič, D. (2008). Public relations metrics: Measurement and evaluation—An overview. In van Ruler, B., Tkalac Verčič, A. and Verčič, D. (Eds.), *Public relations metrics: Research and evaluation*. New York: Routledge, pp. 1–18.

Sennett, R. (2006). *The culture of the new capitalism*. New Haven, CT: Yale University Press.

Sriramesh, K. and Verčič, D. (Eds.). (2009). *The global public relations handbook: Theory, research, and practice. Expanded and revised edition*. New York: Routledge.

Stewart, T. A. (1997). *Intellectual capital: The new wealth of organizations*. London: Nicholas Brealey Publishing.

Tench, R. and Yeomans, L. (2006). *Exploring public relations*. Harlow, UK: FT Prentice Hall.

Tye, L. (1998). *The father of spin: Edward L. Bernays & the birth of public relations*. New York: Crown Publishers.

Verčič, D. (2008). Public relations and power: How hard is soft power? In Zerfass, A., van Ruler, B., and Sriramesh, K. (Eds.), *Public relations research: European and international perspectives and innovations.* Wiesbaden, Germany: VS Verlag für Sozialwissenschaften, pp. 271–279.

Verčič, D. (2002). Thorsten Veblen, business and communication: Is organizational communication censored? In Eskelinen, S., Saranen, T. and Tuhkio, T. (Eds.), *Spanning the boundaries of communication.* Jyväskylä, Finland: University of Jyväskylä, pp. 121–132.

Verčič, D. and Grunig, J. E. (2000). The origins of public relations theory in economics and strategic management. In Moss, D., Verčič, D., and Warnaby, G. (Eds.), *Perspectives on public relations research.* London: Routledge, pp. 9–58.

White, J. and Myers, A. (2001). Fee setting in public relations consultancies: A study of consultancy and client views of current practice and recommendations to contribute to the development of best practice. An unpublished report prepared for the Public Relations Consultants Association. London: PRCA.

Wilcox, D. L., Cameron, G. T., Reber, B. H., and Shin, J.-H. (2011). *THINK public relations.* Boston, MA: Allyn & Bacon.

Zerfass, A., Moreno, A., Tench, R., Verčič, D., and Verhoeven, P. (2009). *European communication monitor 2009: Trends in communication management and public relations—Results of a survey in 34 countries.* Brussels: EACD, EUPRERA.

Zerfass, A., Tench, R., Verhoeven, P., Verčič, D., and Moreno, A. (2010). *European communication monitor 2010: Status quo and challenges for communication management in Europe—Results of an empirical survey in 46 countries.* Brussels: EACD, EUPRERA.

CONTRIBUTORS

Editors

Krishnamurthy Sriramesh (PhD, University of Maryland at College Park, 1992) is Professor of Public Relations at the College of Business of Massey University in Wellington, New Zealand. He has taught at 10 universities on four continents. He has won several teaching and research awards including top-three papers at international conferences and the prestigious Pathfinder Award from the Institute for Public Relations (USA) for "original scholarly research contributing to the public relations body of knowledge." He has co-edited *The Handbook of Global Public Relations: Theory, Research, and Practice*, which won the PRIDE award presented by the National Communication Association (USA). He also has co-edited *Public Relations Research: European and International Perspectives* and edited *Public Relations in Asia: An Anthology*. Between these books, he has contributed to chronicling, for the first time in the field, information about public relations in about 50 countries and regions of the world. He also has presented over 80 research papers, seminars, and talks in over 30 countries. In addition to authoring over 30 book chapters, he has published over 30 research articles in refereed journals. He serves as the Associate Editor of the *Journal of Communication Management* and is a member of the editorial board of several journals such as the *Journal of Communication, Journal of Public Relations Research*, *Public Relations Review*, *Management Communication Quarterly*, and the *Digital Review of Asia-Pacific*.

Dejan Verčič (PhD, London School of Economics, 2000) is Professor at the University of Ljubljana and Visiting Professor at the University of Lugano (Switzerland). He is founder of the communication consultancy Pristop in Ljubljana, Slovenia. His most recent book is *The Global Public Relations*

Handbook: Theory, Research, and Practice (with K. Sriramesh, enlarged edition 2009, Routledge). He has published in *Communication Yearbook, International Journal of Strategic Communication, Journal of Communication Management, Journal of Political Marketing, Journal of Public Relations Research*, and *Public Relations Review*. In 2000 and 2010 he received special awards from the Public Relations Society of Slovenia and in 2001 he was awarded the Alan Campbell-Johnson Medal for outstanding service to international public relations by the UK Chartered Institute of Public Relations (of which he is a Fellow). Professor Verčič served, inter alia, as the Chairman of the Research Committee of the IABC Research Foundation and as the President of the European Public Relations Education and Research Association (EUPRERA). Since 1994, he has organized an annual international public relations research symposium, BledCom. He is President of the Ethics Committee of the Public Relations Society of Slovenia and a member of the European Communication Monitor (ECM) research team.

Contributors

Matthew R. Allen, MA, APR, is a graduate of the San Diego State School of Journalism and Media Studies, and is currently serving as a Public Affairs Officer in the United States Navy. Over the past 16 years of his career, Matthew has served aboard multiple naval vessels, all of which have spent time operating in the Middle East in support of coalition operations in Iraq and Afghanistan. In addition to these regional deployments, he has held public affairs assignments in military headquarters staffs in Manama, Bahrain, and other locations throughout the Middle East. This has prompted a research focus aimed at quantifying and qualifying the traits which inhibit or improve cross-cultural communication. The discussion in this text provides only a glimpse of these challenges by using a case study of the unique relationship between members of the Arab media and U.S. public affairs officers.

Günter Bentele, Dr. phil., is Full Professor of Public Relations at the University of Leipzig since 1994 and holds the first chair of Public Relations (Öffentlichkeitsarbeit/PR) in the German-speaking countries. He studied German literature, linguistics, communication, and media studies, and earned his PhD in 1982 and his Habilitation-degree (a German second doctoral degree) in 1989 at the Free University in Berlin. From 1974 to 1989 he worked as Assistant and Assistant Professor at the Free University, Berlin, and from 1989 to 1994 he was Associate Professor of Communication and Journalism Studies at the University of Bamberg. He is author, co-author, editor, and co-editor of about 40 books, and has written more than 180 scientific articles in the fields of public relations, communication theory, journalism, and semiotics.

Aleš Debeljak graduated in comparative literature from the University of Ljubljana and received his PhD from the Maxwell School of Citizenship and Public Affairs, Syracuse University, New York. Debeljak has published 13 books on cultural criticism and eight books of poems in his native Slovenian. He has won several awards, including the Slovenian National Book Award, and was named Ambassador of Science of the Republic of Slovenia. A member of the editorial board of the international magazines *Sarajevo Notebooks* and *Verse*, a contributing editor of *Cultural Sociology* and www.fastcapitalism.com, Dr. Debeljak is a Recurring Visiting Professor at College d'Europe, Natolin-Warsaw, teaches cultural studies at the University of Ljubljana, Slovenia, and is a member of European Council on Foreign Relations.

David M. Dozier (PhD, Communication Research, Stanford University, 1978) is a public relations researcher and educator. He is author or co-author of over 50 books, articles, and papers related to practitioner roles, use of research in the practice, and strategic management of public relations. He was a co-investigator of the influential Excellence Study (James E. Grunig, principal investigator). He is recipient of the Institute for Public Relations' Pathfinder Award, the PRSA Foundation Jackson, Jackson & Wagner Behavioral Science Award, and PRSA's Educator of the Year Award. He is a Professor in the School of Journalism & Media Studies, San Diego State University, where he heads the public relations program and the military public affairs officer program.

Mohan J. Dutta is Professor of Communication and Associate Dean for Research and Graduate Education in the College of Liberal Arts at Purdue University. Professor Dutta teaches, conducts research, and engages in activist projects in the areas of postcolonial politics of social change, postcolonial public relations theory, public relations and resistance, poverty and hunger, and culture-centered approaches to health communication. His work on public affairs and policy making emphasizes the creation of culture-centered entry points that foreground the decision-making capacity of local communities at the margins of contemporary neoliberal economies. Most recently, his research on healthcare inequalities has been funded by the Agency for HealthCare Research and Quality (AHRQ), and seeks to create discursive entry points to decision making in underserved communities. With an emphasis on healthcare disparities and health care reform, Professor Dutta conducts fieldwork in several marginalized sectors of the globe including the US, India, Singapore, Bangladesh, and Nepal.

Lee Edwards is Lecturer in Communications (Public Relations) at the Institute of Communications Studies, University of Leeds. She has taught on professional, postgraduate, and undergraduate courses in communications in both business and media contexts. Prior to joining the academic world in 2004, she was a practitioner specializing in technology PR and worked with some of the largest global technology brands during her professional career, including Microsoft, Dell, and Siemens. Her PhD focused on the operation of power in and through public relations and she is particularly interested in PR's professional project, diversity within the PR profession, postcolonial and critical race theories as applied to PR, and the relationship between PR and the media. With Caroline E. M. Hodges, she is co-editor of *Public Relations, Society and Culture: Theoretical and Empirical Explorations* (Routledge, 2011) and has published on her areas of interest in a range of journals and books.

Kingsley Eyita was born in Akwa Ibom State, Nigeria, and is of Niger Delta extraction. He has a BSc (Hon) in Mass Communication and a Masters in Mass Communication, with a specialist focus on public relations and advertising, from the University of Lagos. Following his studies he joined Dornier-Nigerian Navy as Manager of Communication and Resources. Kingsley left Dornier-Nigerian Navy in 1994 to establish his private corporate communications agency: Kee Kommunications Nigeria Limited, which is a member of the Public Relations Association of Nigeria (PRICAN). Kingsley is also a member of the Nigerian Institute of Public Relations (NIPR). Kee Kommunications has served a good number of organizations in the public and private sectors. In his quest to deepen the knowledge of public relations in Nigeria, in 2006, Kingsley established the Public Relations and Communication Resource Centre in Abuja, Nigeria, which offers public relations training. Presently, Kingsley is studying for his PhD at the University of Pretoria in South Africa. His thesis is on corporate social responsibility, using the oil and gas multinationals in Nigeria and other stakeholders as a case study. Kingsley has presented papers in numerous workshops, especially those organised by the NIPR. He has also undertaken many publications to strengthen and promote the field of Marketing Communications.

Jarrod Haar, PhD, is Associate Professor in the Department of Strategy & Human Resources Management, Waikato Management School, and he is of Maori descent, with tribal affiliations being Ngati Maniapoto and Ngati Mahuta. His research focuses predominately on work–family issues and their influence on employees and organizational outcomes. He is the principal researcher in a Major New Zealand Marsden grant-supported project exploring the role of cultural support amongst indigenous employees (contract number UOW806). This study examines the role that cultural support can play upon indigenous employees. His work has appeared in academic outlets such as the *International Journal of Human Resource Management, Stress and Work*, and *Small Group Research*.

Robert L. Heath is Professor Emeritus at the University of Houston. He is the author of several books on public relations approaches, crisis communication, and strategic management, and has contributed hundreds of chapters, articles, and conference papers on issues management, public relations, crisis communication, risk communication, corporate social responsibility, environmental communication, emergency management, rhetorical criticism, and communication theory. He has lectured nationally and internationally in academic settings and for companies, governmental agencies, professional associations, and non-governmental organizations. He has conducted company and community research, held research positions with public relations firms, and developed company and community response plans.

Marco V. Herrera B. is the founder and CEO of Grupo Public, a Mexican firm specializing in public relations and communications. He is a consultant for matters pertaining to communications, public affairs, and crisis management for multinational companies and international organizations in Latin America. Herrera is a member of the World Research Committee for the Public Relations Institute, and a member of the committee that drew up the Global Alliance Stockholm Accords. He has been the President of the Mexican Association of Public Relations Professionals (PRORP), and Vice-President of the Confederation of Marketing Communications of Mexico (CICOM). He studied diploma courses in Political Analysis and in Public Policy at the Center for Research and Teaching Economics (CIDE), and a diploma course in Political Communications and Electoral Marketing at The Graduate School of Political Management, George Washington University. Herrera writes an editorial in the newspaper *El Financiero* and collaborates with various media channels as a political and communications analyst.

Yi-Hui Christine Huang is Professor of the School of Journalism and Communication at The Chinese University of Hong Kong. She received her PhD in mass communication from the University of Maryland, USA. Dr. Huang's research interests include public relations management, crisis communication, conflict and negotiation, and cross-cultural communications and relationships. Her research awards include the Best Article Award in Public Relations Scholarship awarded by the National Communication Association, USA, the Distinguished Research Award given by the National Science Council, ROC, and Top Paper Award given by the International Communication Association. She has served on the editorial board for journals such as the *Journal of Communication*, *Communication Theory*, and *Public Relations Review*.

Nnadozie Izidor was born in Akabuka, the oil-rich region of Rivers State, in Nigeria. In 1998, he gained admission to study for a degree in Petroleum

Engineering at the Rivers State University of Science and Technology, Nigeria. Two years later, his course preference changed, and he left the university for Igbinedion University, Okada, in Nigeria, where he graduated with a BSc (Hon) in Political Science & Public Administration. While at Igbinedion University, he did a placement with the Ministry of Social Development, Benin, in Nigeria, where he gained some experience in the Nigerian public sector. After graduation, he taught social studies and government in a secondary school at Onueke, Ebonyi State, in Nigeria, before travelling to the UK in 2007 for a Masters degree in business management and professional development. After his MSc he got a marketing assistance job with Klarius UK Ltd. In 2009, he left the job and returned to the University of Central Lancashire, in Preston, UK, to pursue his PhD. His PhD research has been focused on the instruments of stakeholder engagement between the oil MNCs in Nigeria and their host communities. Nnadozie Izidor is an Associate Member of the Institute of Strategic Management, Nigeria (2006), and also a member of the British Academy of Management (2010). Diversification in knowledge and experience has been his driving force. His research interests lie in business, politics, and society.

Julia Jahansoozi was born in Iran and grew up in the UK and Canada. She is the Director of the MSc in Public Communications Management at Stirling Media Research Institute, University of Stirling. She has worked in public relations practice in both Canada and the UK in both consultancy and in-house roles within the private and non-profit sectors. Julia received both her PhD and MSc in Public Relations from the University of Stirling and completed her BSc in Psychology and Political Science at the University of Victoria, Canada. In 2009 she was awarded the Günter-Thiele-Award for Excellent Doctoral & Postdoctoral Theses. Her areas of research include organization–public relationships and international public relations. She sits on the editorial board of *Journal of Communication Management* and is the book review editor for the new journal *Public Relations Inquiry*.

Shirley Leitch is Deputy Vice Chancellor Academic at Swinburne University of Technology in Melbourne, Australia. She has previously served as Dean of Commerce at the University of Wollongong and Pro Vice Chancellor of Public Affairs at the University of Waikato in New Zealand, where she held a personal chair in corporate communication. Professor Leitch has held posts at the University of Auckland (her alma mater), Massey University, and Victoria University of Wellington and is an A-ranked scholar under the New Zealand PBRF research assessment system. She has undertaken a number of senior advisory roles for government and industry. Over the past two decades, her research work has focused on public communication, particularly in relation to controversial science and technology. She is currently an international researcher on the NZ$1.6 million Foundation for Research, Science and Technology project *Building our Productivity: Understanding Sustainable Collective Productivity in NZ Firm* as well as an active member of the Technology, Economy and Society Program within Swinburne's Tier 1 Research Centre, the Institute for Social Research.

Jacquie L'Etang has pursued critical themes relating to public relations since the late 1980s and early 1990s, when she published articles on PR, corporate social responsibility (CSR), and business ethics, subsequently collaborating with Magda Pieczka on *Critical Perspectives in Public Relations* (1996) and a follow-up volume, *Public Relations: Critical Debates and Contemporary Practice* (2006). She is author of *Public Relations in Britain: A History of Professional Practice* (2004), the textbook *Public Relations: Concepts, Practice and Critique* (2008), and more than 50 chapters and articles on a range of themes including rhetoric, diplomacy and public diplomacy, history, propaganda, ethics, CSR, and anthropology. In 2007 she was awarded a prize for contribution to the literature by the University of Girona. She is founding editor (with Jordi Xifra and Tim Coombs) of *Public Relations Inquiry* (launches 2012). Jacquie teaches public relations and public communication at the University of Stirling, Scotland, and is a Visiting Professor at the University of Ulster.

Judy Motion is Professor of Communication in the Journalism and Media Research Centre at the University of New South Wales, Australia. Professor Motion's research agenda has been to develop an understanding of the socio-cultural and political impacts of organizational and societal change drawing upon discourse theories. She led a five-year research program investigating socially and culturally sustainable biotechnology and is currently an international researcher on a New Zealand project investigating sustainable productivity. Her research has been published in numerous journals including *Public Relations Review*, *Journal of Public Relations Research*, *Discourse Studies*, *Public Understanding of Science*, *Organization Studies*, *European Journal of Marketing*, *Journal of Communication Management*, *Media Culture and Society*, and *Management Communication Quarterly*.

María Antonieta Rebeil Corella is Director of the Research Center for Applied Communication (CICA) and Academic Director of the Doctorate Program in Applied Communication for the School of Communications at the Universidad Anahuac México Norte. She has emerged as both a consultant and a researcher in the field of social communication for over 30 years. Dr. Rebeil has participated in the writing of several chapters of books, among which are the Mexican Case in *The Global Public Relations Handbook: Theory, Research and Practice*. She has edited and co-edited several books, among which are *Ethics and Cultural Identity: The Influence of Media Content* (2010), *Ethics, Violence and Television* (2008), *Strategic Communication in Organizations* (2006, 2nd edn. 2008), the *XIII, XIV, and XV Yearbooks CONEICC Communication Research* (2006, 2007, and 2008), and *The Power of Communication in Organizations* (1997, 2nd edn. 2000). She was the Research Coordinator for the National Council for Teaching and Research in Communication Sciences (CONEICC), and has been included as a named member of Mexico's National Research System (SNI) at Level II. Also, she is evaluator for the National Accrediting Council of Communication (CONAC). Dr. Rebeil studied Communication at ITESO University and gained a Masters degree in Education at Stanford University and a PhD in Social Sciences at Universidad Iberoamericana.

Jens Seiffert, MA, studied communication and media science, and political science at the University of Leipzig, and Charles University in Prague, Czech Republic. He is Research Assistant to the Chair of Public Relations at the Department of Communication Management and Public Relations, University of Leipzig, writing his PhD thesis on "Public Trust: Examination of a Communicative, Social Mechanism." Beyond public trust, his fields of research are general PR theory, culture and PR, strategy and management, and PR history. Jens Seiffert is a past fellow of the Frederick Ebert Foundation and holder of a scholarship from the foundation for the promotion of PR science at the University of Leipzig.

Bey-Ling Sha (PhD, University of Maryland at College Park, 1999) is Associate Professor of Public Relations in the School of Journalism & Media Studies at San Diego State University. Her research areas include cultural identity, activism, and gender. Dr. Sha's scholarly work has been published in the *Journal of Public Relations Research*, *Public Relations Review*, *Public Relations Journal*, *Journalism & Mass Communication Quarterly*, and *Journal of Promotion Management*, as well as in various book chapters. She has won research honors from every major communication and public relations association in the US. Previously, Dr. Sha worked as Public Affairs Officer for the U.S. Census Bureau, where she helped oversee the execution and evaluation of the promotional campaign for the 2000 census, which won a 2001 Silver Anvil Award of Excellence from the PRSA. Her other professional awards include the 2007 Professional of the Year from the San Diego chapter of PRSA, the 2010 Outstanding Advocacy Award from the National PTA® and the 2005 President's Award from the International Listening Association. For her teaching, Dr. Sha won the 2007 Outstanding Faculty Award from San Diego State University and the 2004 Outstanding Faculty Award from the University of Maryland, College Park. She is accredited in public relations by the Universal Accreditation Board (UAB), which oversees the world's largest certification program in public relations.

Ting-Ling Sha (PhD, University of Houston, 2010) is Principal in an urban elementary school near Houston, Texas. Her research areas include self-regulated learning, motivation, students' engagement, ethnic identity, and academic achievement. Her research has been presented at the American Educational Research Association Annual Conference, American Psychological Association Annual Convention, Southwest Educational Research Association Annual Meeting, and the Frontiers in Education Annual Conference. In 2007 and 2008, Dr. Sha won the Dean's Graduate Paper Award from the College of Education, University of Houston. Her research has been published in the *Journal of Engineering Education*. Dr. Sha won the Asian Educator Award from the Houston Chinese Community Center in 2009. She serves on the executive board of directors for the Houston Chinese Community Center.

Natalie T. J. Tindall (PhD, University of Maryland, 2007) is Assistant Professor in the Department of Communication at Georgia State University. She earned an MA in Mass Communication at the University of South Florida and joined the Georgia State University Communication Faculty after a tenure-track appointment at the University of Oklahoma. Dr. Tindall has undertaken research in areas including identity, diversity, and power in the public relations function; identity and health messages; fundraising and philanthropy; organizational culture and stereotypes within historically Black fraternities and sororities; and the intersection of public relations and marketing with minority health. Her research has been published in the *Public Relations Review*, *Howard Journal of Communications*, *PRism*, and the *Journal of Public Relations Research*.

Jon White works independently and internationally as a consultant in management, organization development, and public affairs, maintaining links with a number of academic institutions involved in teaching and research into aspects of public relations and corporate communication practice. He is an Honorary Professor in Cardiff University's Department of Journalism, Media and Cultural Studies and also contributes to teaching and research programs at Henley Business School, the University of Central Lancashire, and universities in Switzerland and Germany. He is currently working on communication-related training programs with the Foreign and Commonwealth Office in the UK, the European Commission and Parliament in Brussels and Luxembourg, and European agencies elsewhere in Europe. Private sector clients have included Shell, Siemens, British Airways, and National Express. He has a doctorate from the London School of Economics and Political Science, where he has also led seminars on corporate communication, and he is the author of two books, a number of book chapters, and articles on topics related to management, organizational development, social research, public relations, and corporate communication management.

AUTHOR INDEX

SUBJECT INDEX